★ ★ ★

GOD
SAVE
THE SOUTH

And a Treasure Chest of Forbidden Information

LitPrime Solutions
21250 Hawthorne Blvd
Suite 500, Torrance, CA 90503
www.litprime.com
Phone: 1 (209) 788-3500

© 2021 John Thomas Nall. All rights reserved.

No part of this book may be reproduced, stored in a retrieval system, or transmitted by any means without the written permission of the author.

Published by LitPrime Solutions   03/06/2021

ISBN: 978-1-953397-60-7(sc)
ISBN: 978-1-953397-59-1(hc)
ISBN: 978-1-953397-61-4(e)

Library of Congress Control Number: 2020925531

Any people depicted in stock imagery provided by iStock are models, and such images are being used for illustrative purposes only.

Certain stock imagery © iStock.

Because of the dynamic nature of the Internet, any web addresses or links contained in this book may have changed since publication and may no longer be valid. The views expressed in this work are solely those of the author and do not necessarily reflect the views of the publisher, and the publisher hereby disclaims any responsibility for them.

CONTENTS

An Introduction To John T. Nall vii
Acknowledgments ix
My Dedication To xi

CHAPTER ONE

An Ordinance 1
I am The South 2
The Legend of the Gray 4
The Battle of Stone Mountain in Georgia 5
A Letter to Dixie 6
A Nation Under Occupation 8
The Confederate States Of America 14
Do We Need to Secede Again? 16
The Proclamation of Independence 17
The Confederate States Congressional Declaration Of War & Its Maritime Seizure Policy 19
Confederate States Of America 21
Our Southern Culture 23
More Than Eatin' Grits: The Differences in North and South 25
Sustaining Grace 27
The Ten Commandments 28
Mount Rushmore 30
The Declaration of Independence 31

CHAPTER TWO

A Review of The Declaration of Independence of The United States of America. 39
Lee's New School History Of The United States 41
Liberty 43
The Litmus Test for American Conservatism 52
By The President Of The United States 55
Recognition of the Confederacy by Foreign Powers 58
Battle Hymn of the Republic. 60
The Crumbling of an Empire 63
The Mythical American Civil War 64
Barrancas: The First Shots Fired in the Rebellion. 67
Three-Fifths Compromise 73
The Straw that Broke the Camels Back 77
The Guilded Cage. 79
Diverse Confederacy 83
What Was Role of Black Southern in Civil War? 84
Amos Rucker-Black Confederate 86
Confederate National Crest. 88
The President and the Constitution 89

CHAPTER THREE

A Prayer of Declaration of Rights. 93
The Great National Seal of the Confederate States of America 94
The Third National Flag of the Confederate States of America. 99
Do You Sing Praises for Lincoln? 100
Jefferson Davis: Our Greatest Hero 102
The Constitution of the Confederate States of America 111
Address From The Congress to the People of the Confederate States Of America 127
The Institution of American Slavery 142
Is the Confederacy Really Evil? 145
The Legality of Secession. 147

Questions About the Conflict 153
Intresting Historical Facts You May Not Know! 161

CHAPTER FOUR

Chronology Of Secession From the Union 169
Ordainance of Secession 13 Confederate States of America 171
Confederate States of America 184
A Short History of the 49th Regiment of the North Carolina Troops 208
The Confederacy Is Liberated 211
You're A Confederate … But Don't Know it? 214
A Message From the President of the Confederate Society of America 216
The Confederation vs Federal Autocracy 219
The Communist Revolution of 1861 against the United States And Against The Confederate States of
America 223
The Lincoln Putsch: America's Bolshevik Assisisted **Revolution** 224
Lincoln's Socialist Legions 226
Ever Wonder Where the **Lincolnites** Get Their Arguments? Look No Further Than Karl Marx 229
Communist Support For The Union And For **"Reconstruction"** 233
Lincoln's War: Conflict? 235
Abraham Lincoln's Civil War Against New York /Part One/ 258
Abraham Lincoln's Civil War Against New York /Part Two/ 268
The Jacobin Yankees 275
Federal **POW** Propaganda 278

CHAPTER FIVE

Our American Holocaust 287
Democracy Versus **Republic**: Definition One 295
An Important Distinction: Democracy Verses Republic Definition Two 299
A Principle of the Traditional American Philosophy 306
Sic Semper Tyrannis 311
What You Didn't Know About Isreal 313

The Bible Speaks Of The Confederate 315
God Verses Science ... 317
The Mayflower Compact. ... 321
Seven Verses Of The Bible ... 322
A Brief History Of The **League of the South Governor Zebulon B. Vance** Chapter of Rowan County *North Carolina* CSA ... 325
Our Chapter's Main Goals. ... 327
Outstanding Chapter Award ... 328
A Northern View Of The **Council Of Conservative Citizens** ... 329
Blood And Water. ... 332
The Mission Statement of the British National Party ... 335
A **Christian** Confederate Soldier's Prayer. ... 337
The Hated White Race ... 338
Remember The **"Alamo"** ... 340
My Dearest Yankees, ... 342
An Introduction Into The **Confederate's Prayer** ... 345
A **Confederate Soldier's Prayer** ... 346
Why Should "**God Bless America?**" ... 347
America's Path Of Self Destruction ... 350
A Prayer For The **South** ... 356
Your Important Collection Of Quotations And Statements ... 357
When Grandma Goes To Court ... 446
Free Advertisements. ... 447
Confederate States of America ... 449
So, You Want to Secede? ... 451
Official Confedeerate States of America Government Website ... 452
Lee's New School **History** of the **United States** ... 453
For Christ and Country ... 455
A Conversation About Race. ... 456
Websites And Mailing Addresses ... 457
Truthful Reading For You're Library ... 459
My Book Project ... 461
My Closing Statements ... 463

AN INTRODUCTION TO JOHN T. NALL

John Thomas Nall is registered as an Independent voter and he considers himself as a Conservative Libertarian. He is presently a member of the (Confederate Society of America) and a life member with the (Council of Conservative Citizens). He is a life member with (Gun Owners of America) a life member with the (National Rifle Association) and a life member with the (Motorcycle Riders Club of America).

He has been a Southern Activist from the time he was of the age of eighteen. He is also the author of his first published book (For Christ & Country). He has also received the Honor Roll Awards with the National Rifle Association.

1. Institute for Legislative Action-1995 Honor Roll.
2. NRA Legion of Honor-1st of October of 1996.
3. NRA ILA Defender of the Second Amendment Award in 1998.
4. Millennium Honor Roll—the 22nd of November of 2000.

"Your children's children will live under Communism. You Americans are so gullible. NO, you won't accept Communism outright; but we'll keep feeding you small doses of Socialism until you finally wake up and find that you already have Communism. We won't have to fight you; WE'LL SO WEAKEN YOUR ECONOMY, until you fall like overripe fruit into our hands."

By: Nikita Khrushchev-Soviet Union-1959

ACKNOWLEDGMENTS

All Glory to our Father in Heaven for His mercy and grace! His support in our everyday life and most importantly, His son (Jesus Christ). I would like to thank my sister, Cynthia Anita Myers, for her support and the rest of my family and friends. Also, I could not forget my Southern (Confederate American people) and my extended kindred family. And last but not the least, I would like to thank AuthorHouse and LitPrime for publishing my book projects.

FOR CHRIST AND COUNTRY!
By: John Thomas Nall

★ ★ ★
MY DEDICATION TO

I would like to dedicate this book project to my two nephews (Robert Michael Smith) & (Mark Alexander Smith). May they always remember that by having God as their Co-Pilot. They will never be alone and unprotected. Life is filled with choices, and the choices they will make will change the world in which they live. They may not change this world indirectly. But they can change the lives of those they have touched within this world. And by doing this, the world can be a better place for their children's future.

CHAPTER ONE

AN ORDINANCE

An Ordinance to dissolve the union between the State of North Carolina and the Other States United with her under the Compact of Government Entitled he Constitution of the United States

We the People of the State of North Carolina, in convention assembled, do declare, and ordain, and it is hereby declared and ordained, That the ordinance adopted by the State of North Carolina in the Convention of 1789, whereby the Constitution of the United States was ratified and adopted, and also Acts and parts of Acts of the General Assembly, approving and adopting amendments to the said constitution, are hereby repealed, rescinded, and abrogated.

We do further declare and ordain that the union now subsisting between the State of North Carolina and the other States, under the title of "The United States of America," is hereby dissolved, and that the State of North Carolina is in full possession and exercise of all those Rights of Sovereignty which belong and appertain to a Free and Independent State.

I AM THE SOUTH

Heroic dead in Chickamauga, in Shiloh's fields, on the bloody hills of Manassas, and the mountains of Kennesaw. I am the South. I am the Mississippi, the cotton fields of Alabama, and the piney woods of the Carolinas. I am the coalfields of Virginia and Kentucky, the Florida coast, and the Louisiana bayou. I am Richmond, the capital of the Confederacy. I am the forests, fields, mountains, and rivers. I am the quiet villages and the cities that never sleep. I am the heritage that's been forgotten. I was born on April 12, 1861, in the harbor of Charleston, South Carolina, and the Constitution of the Confederate States of America is my birth certificate. According to its best interest, the bloodlines of the South run through my veins, for I offer a freedom that each state should regulate its own affairs. I am many things and many people. I am the South. I am millions of living souls and ghosts of thousands who died for me. I am the farmer-made-soldier who did not turn his back during Pickett's Charge.

I am the Rebel Yell that was heard across many of my rolling fields protecting our homeland. I am Robert E. Lee and Thomas J. "Stonewall" Jackson. I stood at Fort Sumter and fired the shot heard through our young nation. I am Longstreet, Hood, and Patrick R. Cleburne. I am Generals Johnston and Beauregard and President Jefferson Davis.

I remember how we fought in Gettysburg, Cold Harbor, Vicksburg, and Atlanta. When duty called, I answered and stayed until it was over. I left my dying memory of a way of life that is being still. You see me in the twilight and hear me in "Dixie" as the past continues to fade each year.

Yes, I am the South, and these are the things I represent. I was conceived by force, and God willing, I'll spend the rest of my days remembering my birth. May I always possess the integrity, courage, and the strength to keep my heritage alive, to remain a loyal Southerner, and to stand tall and proud to the rest of the world.

★ GOD SAVE THE SOUTH ★

Do not forget who we are, what we are, and where we came from. This is my goal, my hope, and my prayer.

—Written by ninety-five-year-old Louise Weeks of Hampton, Georgia, two weeks before her death.
—"God Save the South" is compliment of the former Governor Zebulon B. Vance chapter of the League of the South of Rowan County, NC, CSA.

✯ ✯ ✯

THE LEGEND OF THE GRAY

On May 10, 1911, there was a Confederate veterans meeting in Little Rock, Arkansas, to mark the fiftieth year since the War of Southern Independence started. It was the largest gathering of Confederate veterans since the war. The atmosphere was jubilant, to say the least. The town was overflowing with people to the point that tent cities surrounded the town.

Streets were covered in Confederate flags, and Southern pride filled the air. When the festivities were over, the aged Southern veterans gathered at the train depot. As they exchanged their parting goodbyes, the feeling was that this could be the last gathering of the Confederates in gray as so many were aged.

About that time, a very elderly Southern Negro woman, who was in attendance, heard them talking. She slowly walked over to the group of white veterans and began to speak. "You white folks got it all wrong!" she said.

"What wrong?" asked one old Southern soldier.
"This ain't the last Great Gathering of the Gray!" she said. "Far beyond your lifetime and mine, there will be another Great Gathering of the Gray—so great that when it happens, it will change history for all time. They will come from the four winds, and this, sir, will be the Great Gathering of the Gray."

This legend lay forgotten by most of our folks until the summer of 1992.
—Compliments of the former Governor Zebulon B. Vance chapter of the League of the South (PO Box 208, Rockwell, NC, CSA, 28138-0208). This mailing address was in Rockwell, while the meetings were held in Salisbury, N.C.

It is the opinion of this author that the statement that "they will come from the four winds" may be in reverence to the Rapture of Christian Confederate soldiers and the returning of Jesus Christ.

★ ★ ★

THE BATTLE OF STONE MOUNTAIN IN GEORGIA

It is little known that Sherman, when arriving at the front to see what was holding up his march to the sea, found a Confederate on top of Stone Mountain. He was waving signal flags and hurling curses at the enemy below. Sherman immediately ordered his adjutant to send his best man up that mountain to "throw that Reb off of it." Up went Sergeant McGurk, an eight-foot, two Irishman. After a slight lull in the signaling, a loud thump was heard at the base of the mountain. There lay McGurky, never to move an inch more to the sea.

Sherman then ordered the best ten men in the regiment to clear that "no-good, murdering, signaling, and shouting Reb off of my mountain." Up went ten Yankees armed with swords, bayonets, revolvers, and rifles. Again the signaling and shouting paused. A few minutes later, another ten blue-clothed Yankees bounced one by one down the mountain. Never again would they taste the salt of the ocean.

Well, Sherman was really steamed! He then sent 150 handpicked soldiers up the mountain. This time, they took a howitzer with them in addition to every small arm available. The signaling hardly paused before the figures of 149 troopers caromed down from the mountain. The 150th soldier limped back down the mountain, blooded, weak, and near to his last breath.

Sherman rushed over to him, dismounted, and put his ear to the soldier's mouth to catch his words. The soldier's words were, "Go around the mountain, General. It's a trap. There are two of them up there!"
—A seldom told story about the Battle of Stone Mountain in Georgia, as found in the July 1865 issue of Reader's Digest.

★ ★ ★

A LETTER TO DIXIE

My people—sons and daughters of our beloved Confederacy—let me share with you what you may not know or have forgotten!

Our founding fathers of Northern and of Southern birth rose up against the empire of Great Britain long ago. And the principles of liberty were born to a new nation. The United States of America was founded by the people during the colonial War of Independence. And the understanding of what our liberties were had been written down in our Declaration of Independence and the federal Constitution of the Republic. We, the people, by the leadership of our founding fathers and the blessing and guidance of our Heavenly Father, gave birth to true freedom that this world has never known before.

But man is caught in the middle of the war between good and evil, and this world is the grand prize. Everything that is good by man can also become bad and twisted by evil hearts. Nothing is forever except the kingdom of God. And a time had come to when our Southern ancestors felt that those ideas which were sacred, and noble were soon to be lost. The Republic and principles of liberty that had been won in battle and handed down to the following generations were in danger. We acted upon those rights. We withdrew from the United States and restored that very same republic form of government and liberties that were rightfully ours.

Thus, a new nation had been born:the Confederate States of America. And we and our future generations are constitutionally known as Confederate Americans. It is true that the war had broken out because of this. Now that once and the great nation of liberty was now going to condemn and deny those very same rights of liberty to our new nation. We fought and defended those very same rights that were given to us by the spilled blood of previous generations.

★ GOD SAVE THE SOUTH ★

We were overwhelmed and occupied by those we were once members with by our free will. Now, as part of the American empire, we are still trying to maintain our identity and from becoming extinct as a people and as a race.

According to the principles of the Declaration of Independence of the United States of America and the historical fact of the ratification of the Confederate States' Constitution, including establishing our first president, a second republic was born within this North American continent. A victory or defeat in defending our nation does not change this reality. It only determines whether or not we remain as free people able to govern ourselves. But now, our nation is bound by force to be part in this socialistic, centralized American empire. And our children are being reconditioned to become good citizens (slaves) to this empire. They are also being reconditioned for the coming new world order.

We can only hope that someday like all empires, it will crumble, and we will be ready to take back those true liberties that once were our ancestors and live our lives as a free people, as Confederate Americans! Or if we must, we shall wait until the time that Jesus Christ makes this world His footstool, and we shall make our case to Him. Because He is true! So, take heart, my people, for all is not lost, and the truth shall be known, and justice shall prevail.

By: John Thomas Nall

A NATION UNDER OCCUPATION

Part of the claims of the Confederacy Movement is that the Confederacy is a nation under occupation by the United States government; in reality, it is more than a simple belief and is actually a legitimate fact. Not only is it a fact that the C.S.A. is a nation under occupation, but it is also true that the current state governments in Virginia, North Carolina, South Carolina, Georgia, Alabama, Florida, Mississippi, Arkansas, and Texas were illegally put in place.

C.S. General Robert E. Lee surrendered his military forces at Appomattox on April 7th of 1865; however, this was only a surrender of Lee's army and not the government of the Confederate States of America. Most of the C.S.A. government officials either fled to Europe or Canada; however, President Jefferson Davis was captured and held for two years by the union.

Never during the entire time of Davis' imprisonment did he surrender the government to the union. Never at any point in time did any member of the government sign a treaty with the union, nor did they ever surrender the government of the CSA. The union did in fact go to the State Houses of Virginia, North Carolina, South Carolina, Georgia, Alabama, Florida, Mississippi, Arkansas, Louisiana, and Texas and at gunpoint ordered the elected government out of the office and instated a puppet government loyal to the union.

[From the Reconstruction Act of 39th Congress:]

From Section One:

… said rebel States shall be divided into military districts and made subject to the military authority of the United States, as hereinafter prescribed, and for that purpose Virginia shall constitute the First District; North Carolina and South Carolina the Second District; Georgia, Alabama, and Florida. The Third District; Mississippi and Arkansas the Fourth District; and Louisiana and Texas the Fifth District.

From Section Two:

That it shall be the duty of the President to assign to the command of each said districts an officer of the army, not below the rank of Brigadier-General, and to detail a sufficient military force to enable such officer to perform his duty and force his authority within the district to which he is assigned.

(The South remained under military occupation for 12 years, to ensure that the puppet government that was instated would remain in force. The military did not allow any of the rightful government to participate, nor did they allow any Confederate to vote or participate in their own government. Furthermore, the union forced the Confederate States to create a new constitution, not of the will of the people, but constructed of the will of the union).

[From Section five of the Reconstruction Act of 39th Congress:]

"That when the people of anyone said rebel States shall have formed a constitution of government in conformity with the Constitution of the United States in all respects, framed by a convention delegates elected by male citizens of said State twenty one years old and upward, of whatever race, color, or previous condition, who have been resident in said States for one year previous to the day of such election, except such as may be disfranchised for participation in the rebellion, or for felony at common law …"

(Not only did the scallywags, carpetbaggers, and union military get to dictate what was in the Constitution, it had to pass the approval of the [US] Congress. When does a State Constitution EVER have to be approved by the Federal government, especially one controlled by the South-Hating Radical Republicans under Thaddeus Stevens)?

[From Section five of the Reconstruction Act of 39th Congress:]

"… and when such constitution shall have been submitted to Congress for examination and approval, and Congress shall have approved the same, and when said State, by a vote of its legislatures elected under said constitution, shall have adopted the amendment to the Constitution of the United States, proposed by the Thirty-Ninth Congress, and known as article fourteen, and when said article shall have become a part of the Constitution of the United

States, said State shall be declared entitled to representation in Congress, and Senators and Representatives shall be admitted therefrom on their taking the oaths prescribed by law, and then thereafter the preceding sections of this act shall be inoperative in said State: Provided, that no person excluded from the privilege of holding office by said proposed amendment to the United States shall be eligible as a member of the convention to frame a constitution for any of said rebel States, nor shall any such person vote for members of such convention."

(Not only did Congress need to approve the Constitutions, but the States had to be forced to approve the illegal 14th Amendment to the US Constitution before the puppet government was even allowed representation in the Federal government. Adding insult to injury, aside from disallowing most anyone who actually represented the South from participating in elections, government office, or the construction of a Constitution, the union forced those who did participate in swearing an Oath that they would not only abide by everything the US government wanted, they would "encourage others to do so as well).

[From the Supplementary Reconstruction Act of the 40th Congress:] From Section one: (An Oath)

"… I am twenty-one years old: that I have not been disfranchised for participation in any rebellion or Civil War against the United States, nor for felony committed against the laws of any State or of the United States; that I have never been a member of any legislature, nor held any executive or judicial office in any State and afterwards engaged in insurrection or rebellion against the United States, or given aid or comfort to the enemies thereof: that I have never taken an Oath as a member of Congress of the of the United States, or as an officer of the United States, or as a member of any States Legislature, or as an executive or judicial officer of any State, to support the Constitution of the United States, and engaged in insurrection or rebellion against the United States or given aid or comfort to the enemies thereof; that I will faithfully support the Constitution and obey the laws of the United States, and will, to the best of my ability, encourage others so to do, so help me God."

(The Confederates were NOT in insurrection against the United States, nor were they in rebellion. The Confederacy was enacting their own rights allowed by Natural Law, the intentions of the founding fathers, the Ninth and tenth Amendments to the US Constitution, and their own State Constitutions to alter, abolish, or reform their government as the people deem necessary).

The Confederacy has (and had) NO desire to overthrow the United States, they wish to be separate from them, free to continue the Constitutional Republic as established by the likes of Thomas Jefferson, George Washington, and George Mason. On the other, the union did not see it that way, as they then went on to allow the military to dictate the time, place, and manner of holding elections ... an enumerated power is given EXCLUSIVELY to the Congress. It is UNCONSTITUTIONAL, by virtue of the US, Confederate and States Constitutions, to allow the military to set the time, place, and manner of elections were invalid).

[From Section two of the Supplementary Reconstruction Act of the 40th Congress:]

"... that after the completion of the registration hereby provided for any State, at such time and places therein as the commanding general shall appoint and direct, of which at least thirty days public notice shall be given, an election shall be held of delegates to a convention for the purpose of establishing a constitution and civil government for such State loyal to the Union ..."

(Not only did the military set the time, place, and manner of elections ... they were the registrars, overseers, and qualifiers of the returns). Each of these functions goes against the Constitution of not only the United States, but the Confederate States, including the individual States.

[From Section Four of the Supplementary Reconstruction Act of the 40th Congress]

"... That the Commanding General of each district shall appoint as many boards of registration as may be necessary, consisting of three loyal officers or persons, to make and complete the registration, superintend the election, and make return to him of the votes, lists of voters, and of the persons elected as delegates

By a plurality of the votes cast at said election; and upon receiving said returns he shall open the same, ascertain the persons elected as delegates according to the returns of the officers who conducted said election, and make proclamation thereof ...

... said convention, when organized, shall proceed to frame a constitution and civil government according to the provisions of this act and the act to which is it supplementary; and when the same shall have been so framed, said constitution shall be submitted by the convention for ratification to the persons registered under the provisions of this act at an election to be conducted by the officers or persons or to be appointed by the commanding General ..."

(The Southern States were not given representation by the puppet government in Congress until they abided by the whim of the union).

[From Section Five of the Supplementary Reconstruction Act of the 40th Congress]

"... If the Congress shall be satisfied that such constitution meets the approval of a majority of the qualified electors in the State, and if the said constitution shall be declared by Congress to be in conformity with the provisions of the act to which this is supplementary, and the other provisions of said act shall have been complied with, and the said constitution shall be approved by Congress, the States shall be declared entitled to representation, and Senators and Representatives shall be admitted therefrom as therein provided."

(The Union took it upon itself to declare ILLEGAL the rightfully elected governments of the various Southern States, and their rightfully instituted Constitutions to be null and void). The union declared that the South would remain under the authority of the US Congress. NO STATE shall EVER be under the authority of Congress ... The House and Senate shall represent the people and the States respectively.)

From the Supplementary Reconstruction Act of July 19th 1867: From Section One]

"... the government then existing in the rebel States of Virginia, North Carolina, South Carolina, Georgia, Mississippi, Alabama, Louisiana, Florida, Texas, and Arkansas, were not legal States governments; and thereafter said governments, if continued, were to be subject in all respects to the military commanders of the respective districts, and to the paramount authority of Congress."

(The Congress illegally gave the Union military the power to remove anyone from office (elected or otherwise) that they so desired, to be replaced by whomever they chose. Therefore, the puppet States governments were, and are at the mercy of the manipulations of the union).

[Section Two of the Supplementary Reconstruction Act of July 19th, 1867:]

"That the commander of any district named in said act shall have power, subject to the disapproval of the General of the Army of the United States, and to have effect till disapproved, whenever in the opinion of such commander the proper administration of said act shall require it, to suspend or remove from office, or from the performance of official powers, any officer or person holding or exercising, or professing to exercise, any civil or military office or duty in such district under any power, election, appointment, or authority derived from, or granted by, or claimed under, any so-called State or the government thereof, or any municipal or other division thereof; and upon such suspension or removal such commander, subject to the disapproval of the General as aforesaid, shall have power to provide from time to time for the performance of the said duties of such or person so suspended or removed, by the detail of some competent officer or soldier of the army, or by the appointment of some other person to perform the same, and to fill vacancies occasioned by death, resignation, or otherwise."

(After 12 years of coercion, conditioning, and military occupation, the States were allowed to participate in the Federal Union under the helm of the puppet governments instated by the same. To this day, the South has to follow different rules, and is held under tighter restrictions than the rest of the States in the union. It is time for us to wake up and educate the masses. We ARE a NATION under occupation, and the Federal Union has been naming the tune to which we dance too, and we are most certainly are dancing with the devil.) By: Curtis Patronella

If you are interested in buying Southern Products and may want to study more on the subject of Confederate American or Southern History, visit the website of [www.dixieoutfitters.com], on the internet.

Authors Comment: The condition that our Confederacy is going through with the Federal Empire, is in a lot of ways similar to what the nation of Israel went through with the Roman Empire. It will be much like what the world will suffer under the New World Order & the anti-Christ.

THE CONFEDERATE STATES OF AMERICA

When, during human events, it becomes necessary for one people to dissolve the political bands which have connected them with another, and to assume among the powers of the earth, the separate and equal station to which the laws of nature and of nature's God entitle them, [a decent respect to the opinions of mankind requires that they should declare the causes which impel them to the separation.] First paragraph of the Declaration of Independence.

(Therefore, being that each Southern State, did write a [Declaration of Causes of Secession] or [Articles of Secession,] does fall in line with the requirements by the Declaration of Independence and is also supported by the 9th and 10th Amendments of the Constitution of the United States of America. This shows that there was [No American Civil War,] to ever take place between the Confederacy and the union. Nor is it written that No States that secedes from the union is required to receive an approval from any other State Members in the union. Nor does a succeeding State from the union is required permission from the United States government to withdraw its membership. It can only mean that the Confederate States is, in fact, a true and separate nation that is now part of the Federal American Empire of the United States of America).

It would fall under the same reasoning, that if the Federals rejected the reasons of secession by the Southern States under the violation of the Constitution over slavery and the heavy burden of taxes, that secession under any reason would be unjustifiable! Another word! If the Federal government were to pass unnatural or unmoral laws, no state could secede. If the Federals were to violate or trample upon the Constitution, no State can secede. If the Federal government were to become tyrannical and oppressive, no State could withdraw its membership.

If the government fails in providing the safety and the security of the nation, protecting the borders and so forth, no State can withdraw. If the United States continual to guide the States into the New World Order, no States can reject them. And if the Federal government can regulate to us as to what kind of freedom and how much we will be allowed to have over the Constitution? Then this can only mean that we are [slaves] and we are not truly free, according to our founding fathers.

Secession was meant to be a safety net for the State governments to protect their people or Citizens. It is a natural course of action during any kind of danger. In truth, it is and always will be an act of self-preservation for any people or of Individual Rights.

DO WE NEED TO SECEDE AGAIN?

The question as to whether the Southern States should secede is mote. We are already seceded and are now an occupied nation. We are not made less occupied by the passing of time, nor by being granted the semblance of self-government. Occupied nations do not secede from occupation; they are 'liberated.' Thirteen Southern States lawfully and constitutionally seceded, as was their inalienable right, given of Almighty God in creation. [That any people shall determine for themselves, what manor of society, government and nation shall be theirs. The Confederate States of America, a separate, distinct and independent nation, was arrogantly, illegally and unconstitutionally invaded, conquered, occupied, subjugated, and culturally cleansed. In violation of the laws of Almighty God and man.

A testimony is given under force, the threat of force or duress, is not acceptable in a court of law. In like manner, the Articles of Secession remain in effect, having been withdrawn as a result of force. Only free, sovereign and independent State government holds the authority to rescind the Confederate States Constitution and withdraw the Articles of Secession. No Southern States Government since 1865 has met those qualifications. Therefore, both remain valid and effective!

The word ladies and gentlemen are "Liberation" since we are already seceded. The historic truths supporting such a viewpoint should be self-evident to all concerned. One has therefore the option of accepting or denying the self-evident. The skeptics are free to deliver the documents whereby the Confederate States Constitution was rescinded as the instrument of surrender, signed by President Jefferson Davis.

Contrary to the doubters and the doom and gloomier, in due course of time, the "Liberation" of the Confederate States of America, will come to pass, lawfully y, peacefully and honorably. God save the South!

By: Charles Goodson
From the Southern Party

THE PROCLAMATION OF INDEPENDENCE

We the people of the Sovereign States and territories constituting and entitled the Confederate States of America, hereby proclaim before Almighty God and all who may read these presents that as our forefathers lawfully, peacefully, and constitutionally seceded from that voluntary Union of States entitled The United States of America and formed a new nation, according to their reserved political rights.

And the Inalienable Rights endowed them by their Creator, so the aforementioned States and territories were, are and remain now sovereign political entities within a voluntary national confederation, conjointly constituting one independent nation amongst the nations of this world and styled 'The Confederate States of America.'

We further declare that these inalienable truths are, and in no way can be, negated or compromised by the historic fact that the nation so founded was once aggressively arrogantly and illegally invaded, overrun, occupied and subjugated by a superior external force, and thus subjected to war crimes and other crimes against humanity and brutally denied rights of life, liberty and due process of law, nor by the fact that our citizenry (when no longer able to defend their homes or persons and denied, by that brute force the basic human right to self-determination and choice of manner of government) were compelled as states and territories, to retract their articles of secession and rejoin, against their manifest will, their former and repudiated union.

We hereby declare that all such pretend acts, having been performed without the mandate of the consent of the governed, and outside the duly ratified Confederate States Constitution, were, are, and forever shall be null and void, and so the dates of secession of the several States and territories (each acting in its sovereign capacity) continue in unbroken validity from the said dates, as shall the dates of secession of any such further States of the American Union as may, at any time, choose to resume their sovereign status among the nations of the world.

By: Charles Goodson, of the Southern Party And we declare before God Almighty, and call the peoples of the world to witness, our belief that, as men are created equal under Him, so are nations sovereign and equal in His sight, and as no man have the rights to oppress another, so no nation may oppress another nation, enter their lands by force or force their political will or culture upon another people. By means direct or indirect.

Upon these just and unbreakable grounds, we confidently pray the grace and divine providence of Almighty God, which our cause may be vindicated and our right to self-determination again openly acknowledged before Him.

Deo Vindice!

THE CONFEDERATE STATES CONGRESSIONAL DECLARATION OF WAR & ITS MARITIME SEIZURE POLICY

Since the political position of the United States government was to put down a group of rebellious States and would not recognize their sovereignty as a so-called new nation, it had never formally declared the existence of a State of war between the two sections. The Confederate Legislature, now embodied in Richmond, Virginia, however, did. And approved on the (6th of May of 1861), the honorable Howell Cobb, of Georgia, President of the [Confederate States Congress approved an act recognizing the State of War which then existed].

With this, the President of the Confederate States was granted congressional approval to make use of all land and naval forces to wage war against its former government. Any United States vessel that found itself harbored within the borders of the new Confederacy prior to April the 5th of 1861, were entitled thirty days from the publication of the act to set sail for a friendlier port without molestation.

To ensure the seagoing vessels provided no threat to the existing government and citizens of the Southern States, President Davis was given authorization to revoke or annul any such letters of marque granted to the commander and crew of the ships. A suitable description of the ship along with weight, force, names and addresses of each owner as well as the intended number of crew members, were to be filed with the State Department.

These maritime vessels were required to give bond to the present government of $5.000 dollars, the amount doubling for larger ships that sailed with crews of 150 sailors or more. The Captain and crew capturing any such vessel enemy to the Confederate government were thus allowed a portion of the worth of any prize which would fall into their hands after engagement. The monetary value was distributed between its commanding officer and sailors making up the ship's company.

The crew of the captured vessel would be immediately turned into the port authority and delivered over to the port's district marshal for safekeeping. Each prisoner captured from a vessel hostile to the government had a bounty of $20.00 dollars which was paid courtesy of the Confederate States Treasury Department.

Every private vessel was required to keep a thorough and non-fraudulent log on all transactions of captured prizes. Any failure in not turning in their log over for inspection upon arriving in port would cause them to lose their letter of marquee and become susceptible to the laws governing piracy and suffer what the justice system would award. The President, having accepted the act, laid out specific instructions to the ship's masters to maintain respect towards those vessels claiming neutrality in the Great War that was now joined. Vessels claiming neutral status were to remain exempt apart from finding contraband of war aboard.

All weapons and shipbuilding materials were considered liable to seizure. The line was drawn in the sand, and all were hastily preparing to get out of harm's way. The Confederate States had formally declared their State of War, and hell was following in its wake.

By: Daniel Moran 2003

Mr. Moran is a feature writer on the US-Civilwar.com writer's staff. He may be contacted with your questions, ideas and requests at: dmoran@us-civilwar.net

CONFEDERATE STATES OF AMERICA

LETTER OF PRESIDENT DAVIS TO PRESIDENT LINCOLN ON THE 27TH OF FEBRUARY OF 1861

Montgomery, February 27th, 1861.

The President of the United States: Being animated by an earnest desire to unite and bind together the respective countries by friendly ties, I have appointed M.J. Crawford, one of our most settled and trustworthy citizens, as special commissioner of the Confederate States of America to the government of the United States; I have now the honor to introduce him to you, and ask for him a reception and treatment corresponding to his station and to the purpose for which he is sent. Those purpose he will more particularly explain to you. Hoping that through his agency. &c. [sic]

JEFF'N DAVIS

For the purpose of establishing friendly relations between the Confederate States and the United States, and reposing special trust, &c, Martin T. Crawford, John Forsyth, and A.B. Roman are appointed special commissioners of the Confederate States to the United States. I have invested them with full and all manner of power and authority for and in the name of the Confederate States and to confer with any person or persons duly authorized by the government of the United States being furnished with like powers and authority and with them to agree, treat, consult, and negotiate of and concerning all matters and subject interesting to both nations, and to conclude and sign a treaty, convention or conventions, touching the premises, transmitting the same to the President of the Confederate States for his final ratification by and with the consent of the Congress of the Confederate States.

Given under my hand at the city of Montgomery this 27th day of February, A.D. 1861, and of the Independence of the Confederate States the eighty-fifth.

JEFF'N DAVIS
ROBERT TOOMBS, Secretary of States.

A Resolution for the Appointment of Commissioners to the government of the United States; February 25th, 1861-Message to Congress February, 1861. Source; Richardson, James D.

A Compilation of the Messages and Papers of the Confederacy, including the Diplomatic Correspondence 1861-1865-Nashville: United States Publishing Company, 1905-The Avalon Project at Yale Law School.

OUR SOUTHERN CULTURE

Unlike the war of multiculturalism, Southern Culture of Confederate Americans or Southerners is a blend of the best qualities of different races and nationalities that came together in living in harmony. Where they may differ in race or as of former nationalities, they have in common in character as neighbors for the same values and principles of society. With Christianity as a foundation for family, and society they also had a strong devotion to the understanding and defense toward the liberty of the Republic that had define their Constitutional Rights. While the Confederacy is not without fault, or sin. They have proven themselves to be right in most cases in history.

And regardless of any strife now and then between the races and views. One thing has always been true, to defend the family and home and State. Anything else that may have been a thorn in the side of the South is ignored in order to deal with a major threat that will affect them all. The Federal Union has not ever been in a position to judge and sentence the Confederate people. Because as it is written in the Holy Bible, no one is without sin.

The North had issues just as everyone else in the world do. I remember a statement made from the Star Trek T.V. show. A Borg that was part human and part machine had made a statement to the crew of the (Enterprise), "You will all be assimilated, and resistance is futile." And that is what assimilation has done to our Confederate people. Reconstruction of the minds and hearts of many people is in truth assimilation and extermination of a society, people, and race.

The war of the "Socialist 'Liberals' Democrats" toward all Southern forms of institutions has been to break the heart and soul of the Confederate Americans. And let's not forget the Republicans either! They all are assimilating us all for the New World Order. Communism has worked harder against the occupied Confederacy than anyone else in the New American Union (Empire). And this war is still going on. Public schools and colleges, television and diversity classes. They have taken positions in areas of law and authority. And even used the U.S. President to force military troops in enforcing social engineering of integration in the schools. This was in violation of the majority of the people and in violation of the constitution in itself.

While the freedom of association should never be denied to anyone. The use of military against the judgment and will of the people is, in fact, a crime. The violation of State Rights and enslavement into a centralizing block of a Union was hard enough upon a free South. But, now with the sterilization of the history that is written about Southern history and the multiculturalism, including the continuation of reconstruction by this new Union Block marches on without accountability and restrains. God have mercy on us all!

By: John Thomas Nall

MORE THAN EATIN' GRITS: THE DIFFERENCES IN NORTH AND SOUTH

In my experience in the North, I have found that there are many more differences in North and South than people really realize. I'm not talking about eating different foods or speaking with different accents, but outlooks on life in general. Now if you were to ask your average Yankee what outlooks were different you'd probably get something like "Southerners are more racist, and behind the times." This is the mentality beat into their heads by the liberal Southern hating media.

All Southerners know that we aren't any more racist than anywhere else, nor are we behind the times, unless holding on to culture and traditions constitutes being behind the times. The fact is Southerners just try to keep what they hold dear. We like our culture and our way of life and really don't appreciate being told that it's backwards or wrong by outsiders.

Though, the Yankees have been doing that since before the USA even existed. We even had a bloody war to hammer the point home. I can really understand why the Southern States attempted to separate into their own nation, given the vast political differences between the two. The North has, since the formation of this country, favored a strong government. The South on the other believed, and still do, that the real power belongs to the states and the people at the local level. We don't like outsiders telling us what we can and cannot do and Southerners have shown that again and again. First in the War for American Independence, then when Texas fought a bloody war for its independence from Mexico, and again in the War for Southern Independence. Three wars just to show that we controlled our own destiny.

Unfortunately, the North felt that they could do a better job governing Southerners than Southerners could, and so they invaded, laid waste, conquered, and occupied a country who wanted nothing more than their God given right to govern themselves as they see fit. That isn't how the North viewed it then, and it isn't how the North views it now.

That is shown when the strong central government commands the States instead of the other way around. Until I came to the North, I couldn't figure out what had gone wrong with the government. Everyone I knew thought the central government was too big, but yet it seemed we could do nothing about it at the ballot box. When I began to discuss with the Yankees, I came to realize the reason as to why? They think that a government should regulate almost everything, and it should also make accommodations for the self-claim and less fortunate and minorities. In the South, we believe that a man is to make it on his own. We are a proud people. Proud of our culture, our families, and the North has done its best to cast us in a bad light, we're proud of our heritage and history.

To be a Southerner is more of a cultural identity than to be a Northern. The reason is, in my opinion, that the Yankees are culture chasers. They discuss the beauties and wonders of so many different cultures without really having one of their own. When you want to go out to eat in New York, you have to decide by which nationality you're in the mood for.

That rarely happens in the South. When we eat, we just eat food, not by nationality. Though many different cultures are wonderful, I just believe that a person needs one of their own. Many of our Southern people would agree with that, and that is why we are opposed to the multiculturalists' views, and not because we are bigots. No matter what other people may tell you, if you experience the North, you'll find that the White and Black Southerners have a lot more in common than the White Southerners with the White Northerners, or Black Southerners with Black Northerners. As far as religion goes we all know why the South is considered to be the Bible belt. I have met so many atheists and the new age religionists in the North that I've become truly shocked! I have always taken for granted that everybody believes in God. In the North you cannot assume anything.

Needless to say, the North and the South are two separate and different peoples. We speak differently, eat differently, think differently, and live differently. Governments should govern a certain people based on their beliefs and lifestyles, not because they share some common boundaries or freed themselves from an empire at the same time. It is time for our Southern people to come to realize just how alien our neighbors to the North really are, and decide if we really want them to control our lives and the lives of our children, or if we want to control our own lives.

Never forget what the North has done to our people and what they are still doing to us to this very day. The war might be over, but we are not the same nation and it may never will be. FOR THE CAUSE!

By: An unknown Author.

★ ★ ★
SUSTAINING GRACE

Grace releases within us supernatural strength to keep going in the midst of pain and suffering.

Grace ignites within us determination to keep going no matter what.
Grace echoes in our spirit that God is with us to be our friend and supporter.
Grace keeps pointing us to God's goal of teaching us.
Grace reminds us that our Father enables us to become stronger in faith and a deeper intimacy with Him.
Grace assures us that God is in control and sets limits on what we can bear.

Grace awakens our faith with conviction that God will turn our tough times for something good.

By: Charles F. Stanley

THE TEN COMMANDMENTS

As reported by Moses who claimed to have received them from God about 1490 B.C. This served as the civil Constitution of a Nation of Israel from which statutes and judgments ensued. These laws were theocratic but formed the basis of Western Law predating Roman Legal influence and are accepted by Christian, Jewish, and Islamic Religions as fundamental civil laws. The Confederacy also embraces these civil laws and holds that they may be on display in any public building of the Confederate States of America and various C.S.A. States are likewise admonished to allow public displays at their courthouses according to the preference of their citizens.

EXODUS 20:1-17 KING JAMES VERSION

1. I am the Lord thy God, which have brought thee out of the land of Egypt, out of the house of bondage.

2. Thou shalt have no other gods before me.

   Thou shalt not male unto thee any graven image, or any likeness of anything that is in heaven above, or that is in the earth beneath, or that is in the water under the earth:

   Thou shalt not bow down thyself to them, nor serve them: for I the Lord God am a jealous God, visiting the iniquity of the fathers upon the children unto the third and fourth generation of them that hate me.

   And showing mercy unto thousands of them that love me and keep my commandments.

3. Thou shalt not take the name of the Lord thy God in vain: for the Lord will not hold him guiltless that taketh his name in vain.

4. Remember the Sabbath Day, to keep it holy.
    Six days shalt thou labor, and do all thy work:

    But the seventh day is the Sabbath of the Lord thy God: in it thou shalt not do any work, thou, nor thy son, nor thy daughter, thy manservant, nor maidservant, nor thy cattle, nor thy stranger that is within thy gates:

    For in six days the Lord made heaven and earth, the sea, and all that in them is, and rested the seventh day: Wherefore the Lord blessed the Sabbath Day and hallowed it.

5. Honor thy father and thy mother: that thy days may be long upon the land which the Lord thy God giveth thee.

6. Thou shalt not kill (murder).

7. Thou shalt not commit adultery (In spirit or flesh).

8. Thou shall not steal.

9. Thou shalt not bear false witness against thy neighbor (lying).

10. Thou shalt not covet thy neighbor's house; thou shalt not covet thy neighbor's wife, nor his manservant, nor his maidservant, nor his ox, nor his ass, nor anything that is thy neighbors (long for or won't).

★ ★ ★

MOUNT RUSHMORE

I have looked upon the faces of two nations,
A nation of now and of once before,
A fracture within the reflection in its former self,
From a Republic of Liberty into a Centralized Democracy,
And yet what am I told to believe?
That history is not what it seems?
Could the truth have been withheld from me?
Because the reflection in the mirror is the reverse of one's own self,
And the opposite of one's own truth,
Can all of the facts represent the same image of a nation that is no more?
I ponder upon this question in order to seek this very truth,

By: John Thomas Nall

THE DECLARATION OF INDEPENDENCE

When during human events, it becomes necessary for one people to dissolve the political bands which have connected them to another, and to assume among the powers of the earth, the separate and equal station to which the laws of nature and of nature's God entitle them, a decent respect to the opinions of mankind requires that they should declare the causes which impel them to the separation.

We hold these truths to be self-evident, that all men are created equal, that they are endowed by their creator with certain unalienable Rights that among these are life, Liberty, and the pursuit of happiness. That to secure these Rights, Governments are instituted among Men, deriving their just powers from the Consent of the Governed. That whenever any form of Government becomes destructive of these ends, it is the Right of the People to alter or to abolish it, and to institute new Government, laying its foundation on such principles, and organizing its Powers in such forms, as to them shall seem most likely to effect their Safety and Happiness.

Prudence, indeed, will dictate that Governments long established should not be changed for light and transient Causes; accordingly all experience have shewn, that Mankind are more disposed to suffer, while evils are sufferable, than to right themselves by abolishing the forms to which they are accustomed. But when a long train of abuses and usurpations, pursuing invariably the same Object evinces a design to reduce them under absolute Despotism, it is their right, it is their duty, to throw off such Government, and to provide new Guards for their future security. Such has been the patient sufferance of these Colonies; and such is now the necessity which constrains them to alter their former Systems of Government.

The history of the present King of Great Britain is a history of repeated injuries and usurpations, all having in direct Object the establishment of an absolute Tyranny of over these States. To prove this, let facts be submitted to a candid world. He has refused his Assent to Laws, the most wholesome and necessary for the public good. He has forbidden his Governors to pass Laws of immediate and pressing importance, unless suspended in their till his Assent should be obtained; and when so suspended, he has utterly neglected to attend them. He has refused to pass other Laws for the accommodation of large districts of people, unless those people would relinquish the right of Representation in the Legislature, a right of inestimable to them and formidable to tyrants only.

He has called together legislative bodies at places unusual, uncomfortable, and distant from the depository of their public Records for the sole purpose of fatiguing them into compliance with his measures. He has dissolved Representative Houses repeatedly, for opposing with manly firmness his invasions on the rights of the people. He has refused for a long time, after such dissolutions, to cause others to be elected; whereby the Legislative powers, incapable of Annihilation, have returned to the People at large for their exercise; the State remaining in the meantime exposed to all the dangers of invasion from without, and convulsions within.

He has endeavored to prevent the population of these States; for that purpose, obstructing the Laws for Naturalization of Foreigners; refusing to pass others to encourage their migrations hither, and raising the conditions of new Appropriations of Lands. He has obstructed the Administration of Justice, by refusing his Assent to Laws for establishing Judiciary powers. He has made Judges dependent on his Will alone, for the tenure of their offices, and the amount and payment of their salaries. He has erected a multitude of New Offices and sent hither swarms of Officers to harass our people and eat out their substance.

He has kept among us, in times of peace, Standing Armies without the Consent of our legislatures. He has affected to render the Military independent of and superior to the civil power. He has combined with others to subject us to a jurisdiction foreign to our constitution, and unacknowledged by our laws, giving his Assent to their Acts of pretended Legislation:

For Quartering large bodies of armed troops among us: For protecting them, by a mock Trial, from punishment for any Murders which they should commit on the Inhabitants of these States: For cutting off our Trade with all parts of the world: For imposing Taxes on us without our Consent: For depriving us in many cases of the benefits of Trial by Jury:

For transporting us beyond Seas to be tried for pretended offences: For abolishing the free System of English Laws in a neighboring Province, establishing therein an Arbitrary government, and enlarging its Boundaries so as to render it at once an example and fit instrument for introducing the same absolute rule into these Colonies: For taking away our Charters, abolishing our most valuable Laws, and altering fundamentally the Forms of our

Governments: For suspending our own Legislatures, and declaring themselves invested with power to legislate for us in all cases whatsoever.

He has abdicated Government here, by declaring us out of his Protection and waging War against us. He has plundered our seas, ravaged our Coasts, burnt our towns, and destroyed the Lives of our people. He is at this time transporting Large Armies of foreign Mercenaries to complete the works of death, desolation, and tyranny, already begun with circumstances of Cruelty and perfidy scarcely paralleled in the most barbarous ages, and totally unworthy the Head of a civilized nation. He has constrained our fellow Citizens taken Captive on the high Seas to bear Arms against their Country, to become the executioners of their friends and Brethren, or to fall themselves by their Hands.

He has excited domestic insurrections amongst us and has endeavored to bring on the inhabitants of our frontiers, the merciless Indian Savages, whose known rule of warfare is an undistinguished destruction of all ages, sexes, and conditions. In every stage of these Oppressions, we have petitioned for Redress in the most humble terms: Our repeated Petitions have been answered only by repeated injury. A Prince, whose character is thus marked by every act which may define a Tyrant, is unfit to be the ruler of a free people.

Nor have We been wanting in attentions to our British brethren. We have warned them from time to time of attempts by their legislature to extend an unwarrantable jurisdiction over us. We have reminded them of the circumstances of our emigration and settlement here. We have appealed to their native justice and magnanimity, and we have conjured them by the ties of our common kindred to disavow these usurpations, which would inevitably interrupt our connections and correspondence. They too have been deaf to the voice of justice and of consanguinity. We must, therefore, acquiesce in the necessity, which denounces our separation, and hold them, as we hold the rest of mankind, Enemies in War, in Peace Friends. We, therefore, the Representatives of the UNITED STATES OF AMERICA, in General Congress, Assembled, appealing to the Supreme Judge of the world for the rectitude of our intentions, do, in the Name, and by Authority of the good People of these Colonies, solemnly publish and declare, That these United Colonies are, and of Right ought to be FREE AND INDEPENDENT STATES; that they are Absolved from all Allegiance to the British Crown, and that all political connection between them and the State of Great Britain, is ought to be totally dissolved; and that as Free and Independent States, they have full Power to levy War, conclude Peace, contract Alliance, establish Commerce, and to do all other Acts and Things which Independent States may of right do.

And for the support of this declaration, with a firm reliance on the protection of divine Providence, we mutually pledge to each other our Lives, our Fortunes, and our sacred Honor.

★ JOHN THOMAS NALL ★

The men who signed the Declaration of Independence were all members of the Continental Congress. Most of them were lawyers, farmers or planters, and businessmen. They had all worked in politics in their home colonies. The 56 signers were American born, except for eight men born in the British Isles. The oldest signer was the widely respected Benjamin Franklin, then 70 years old. The youngest were two South Carolinians, Thomas Lynch and Edward Rutledge, both 26.

Some of the signers are known to history for their actions during and after the Revolution. Two of these men- John Adams and Thomas Jefferson-later were Presidents. The occupations listed here are those they had when the Declaration was written.

John Adams, Massachusetts, lawyer, age 40 (1735-1826).
Samuel Adams, Massachusetts, politician, age 53 (1722-1803).
Josiah Bartlett, New Hampshire, physician, age 46 (1729-1795).
Carter Braxton, Virginia, planter, age 39 (1736-1797).
Charles Carroll of Carrollton, Maryland, planter, age 38 (1737-1832).
Samuel Chase, Maryland, lawyer, age 35 (1741-1811).
Abraham Clark, New Jersey, farmer, lawyer, age 40 (1726-1794).
George Clymer, Pennsylvania, merchant, age 37 (1739-1813).
William Ellery, Rhode Island, lawyer, age 48 (1727-1820).
William Floyd, New York, farmer, age 41 (1734-1821).
Benjamin Franklin, Pennsylvania, writer, scientist, statesman, age 70 (1706-1790).
Elbridge Gerry, Massachusetts, shipping merchant, age 31 (1744-1814).
Button Gwinnett, Georgia, planter, age about 41 (c. 1735-1777).
Lyman Hall, Georgia, physician, age 52 (1724-1790).
John Hancock, Massachusetts, shipping merchant, age 39 (1737-1793).
Benjamin Harrison, Virginia, planter, age about 50 (c. 1726-1791).
John Hart, New Jersey, farmer, age about 65 (c. 1711-1779).
Joseph Hewes, North Carolina, businessman, age 46 (1730-1779).
Thomas Heyward, South Carolina, planter, lawyer, age 29 (1746-1809).
William Hooper, North Carolina, lawyer, age 34 (1742-1790).
Stephen Hopkins, Rhode Island, farmer, public official, publisher, age 69 (1707-1785).
Francis Hopkinson, New Jersey, lawyer, musician, writer, age 38 (1737-1791).
Samuel Huntington, Connecticut, lawyer, age 45 (1731-1796).

★ GOD SAVE THE SOUTH ★

Thomas Jefferson, Virginia, lawyer, planter, writer, age 33 (1743-1826).
Richard Henry Lee, Virginia, planter, age 44 (1732-1794).
Francis Lightfoot Lee, Virginia, planter, age 41 (1734-1797).
Francis Lewis, New York, businessman, age 63 (1713-1802).
Philip Livingston, New York, merchant, age 60 (1716-1778).
Thomas Lynch, South Carolina, planter, age 26 (1749-1779).
Thomas McKean, Delaware, lawyer, age 42 (1734-1817).
Benjamin Rush, Pennsylvania, physician, age 30 (1745-1813).
Edward Rutledge, South Carolina, lawyer, age 26 (1749-1800).
Roger Sherman, Connecticut, merchant, judge, age Arthur Middleton, South Carolina, planter, age 34 (1742-1787).
Lewis Morris, New York, landowner, age 50 (1726-1798).
Robert Morris, Pennsylvania, merchant, financier, age 42 (1734-1806).
John Morton, Pennsylvania, surveyor, farmer, age about 52 (c. 1724-1777).
Thomas Nelson, Virginia, planter, merchant, age 41 (1738-1789).
William Paca, Maryland, lawyer, age 37 (1740-1799).
Robert Treat Paine, Massachusetts, lawyer, age 45 (1731-1814).
John Penn, North Carolina, lawyer, age 36 (1740-1788).
George Read, Delaware, lawyer, age 42 (1733-1798).
Caesar Rodney, Delaware, landowner, legislator, age 48 (1728-1784).
George Ross, Delaware, lawyer, age 46 (1730-1779).55 (1721-1793).
James Smith, Pennsylvania, lawyer, age about 57 (c. 1719-1806).
Richard Stockton, New Jersey, lawyer, age 46 (1730-1781).
Thomas Stone, Maryland, lawyer, planter, age 33 (1743-1787).
George Taylor, Pennsylvania, ironmaster, age 60 (1716-1781).
Matthew Thornton, New Hampshire, physician, age about 62 (c. 1714-1803).
George Walton, Georgia, lawyer, age 35 (1741-1804).
William Whipple, New Hampshire, merchant, age 46 (1730-1785).
William Williams, Connecticut, businessman, official, age 45 (1731-1811).
James Wilson, Pennsylvania, lawyer, political writer, age 33 (1742-1798).
George Witherspoon, New Jersey, clergyman, educator, age 53 (1723-1794).
Oliver Wolcott, Connecticut, lawyer, judge, age 49 (1726-1797).
George Wythe, Virginia, lawyer, age 50 (1726-1806).
Webster's New World Dictionary of American Language with Student Hand Book 1974.

CHAPTER TWO

A REVIEW OF THE DECLARATION OF INDEPENDENCE OF THE UNITED STATES OF AMERICA

The Declaration of Independence of the United States falls under different classifications. (An Article of Secession), (A Letter of Divorcement), (A Letter of Grievance), & (A Document of the Principles of Liberty). It was this very understanding of this document that led to the Secession of Texas from Mexico. It was also the understanding of this document that brought forth the Southern States divorcement with the United States and formed a New Nation. It is also this document that led to the writing of (The Declaration of Southern Independence) by: John P. George, Jr. of Crawfordville, Georgia C.S.A., that was published in my first book project, (FOR CHRIST AND COUNTRY). The understanding of liberty and the principle of it as a Constitutional Foundation with a Moral Christian guidelines has never belonged to just one nation.

And the goal of true liberty and freedom is when others are willing to take those ideas and believes and apply it for themselves, people, and nation. And to deny this very Sacred Right, is to declare that only those that can themselves upon others, shall determine as to who shall be free and what kind of freedom, they will be claimed for them. And most of the time political gain and not principles will determine as to why another nation will recognized the right of liberty for a new nation. The very understanding of all this is not to force your will upon others, but to allow the people the free will to think for themselves and to allow them to protect and to preserve their identity and values that God has bless them with. Even now, any other American Nation with their flags or not consider to be American.

Only if you're an empire can you be an American, and only the flag of that empire is an American flag. The very thought of the ideas of our founding fathers has become foolish to the leaders of this American Empire and the dreamers of the coming of the New World Order. When our God the father is denied His place in our society and home, then what shall fall upon our nation as a whole?

And how long will that shiny symbol of liberty and hope for the future starts to become tarnish? The Principles of Liberty does define the Rights of a Free People. And some people or nations may not always view or understand this concept. So, they would deny those rights to anyone else that longs for it. Its connection to Christianity and society of a people and as a nation does give it strength and endurance against oppression and tyranny. It helps them to know that being that they were created in the same image of their Creator, that they must if all ells fail, stand up and fight or die if need be to remain truly free!

Not free from morality (Biblical teachings) and natural laws (continuation of our people, race, and identity in our culture and caretakers of this world). Not free from responsibility and the results by their actions. But, to live the true dream of freedom! Because to remain free is the very determination to fight for freedom and if need be to die for it. If you were to look very closely at the Declaration of Independence, you will see that the Southern States did follow the Declaration of Independence to the letter of the law and established the (Article of Secession for each State. And that they did ratified the Constitution of the Confederate States. And they established a President which made the Confederate States a certified nation. Just like the United States had done before. And under the ninth and tenth Amendment to the U.S. Constitution, the Southern States did act within their own sovereign rights.

BY: John Thomas Nall

LEE'S NEW SCHOOL HISTORY OF THE UNITED STATES

12. The Right of Secession. —The Southern States had no desire for war and no purpose of trespassing on the rights and liberties of the other States; but they felt it their duty to vindicate their own, and they determined to reclaim the powers they had yielded to the Federal Government in ratifying the Constitution. The right to withdraw from the Union had been reserved by some of the States when they ratified the Constitution. This right had been universally acknowledged in the early days of the Republic, and New England on more than one occasion thought of exercising it. Page: 253.

13. The Secession of Seven Southern States. —South Carolina was the first to take the momentous step. Her convention met, as soon as the election of Mr. Lincoln was certain, and passed, on December 20, 1860, an "Ordinance of Secession," which separated the State from the Union and took back all powers which, in 1788, she had entrusted to the Federal Government. By February 1861, Mississippi, Alabama, Georgia, Louisiana, and Texas had seceded. These States felt that Mr. Lincoln had been elected on a platform opposed to Southern interests, their rights would be ignored. Page: 253.

16. Mr. Buchanan's Views. —Before secession was an accomplished fact, the Thirty-sixth Congress met. In his annual message, Mr. Buchanan spoke of the alarming condition of affairs. He thought that no State had the right to leave the Union; but that, if she did, the Federal Government had no power to force her to remain in it, and he urged Congress to make concessions which would reconcile the hostile sections. Page: 255.

21. The Forts in the South. —The forts within the seceded States had been built on ground granted by them to the United States. When they withdrew from the Union they naturally thought this property should revert to

them. Accordingly, they took possession of all of it except the defenses at Charleston and a few other forts, and made overtures to obtain these, without strife, from the Federal Government. Page: 257.

22. Fort Sumter.—South Carolina had been promised President Buchanan that, if the forts were not molested, he would make no attempt to reinforce the garrison in Charleston harbor. Repeated assurances were given at Washington that "the military status at Charleston would be maintained." Yet, Major Anderson, commanding at Fort Moultrie, removed the garrison into the stronger defenses of Fort Sumter, and proceeded to dismantle and, as far as possible, to destroy the works at Fort Moultrie. The Star of the West with troops and arms concealed abroad was secretly sent in strengthen the garrison. When she arrived off Charleston harbor, her mission had become known, and she was fired upon and driven back by land batteries. Page: 257.

1907 Edition Richmond, Virginia

LIBERTY

This very word has been confused by rewritten history and political parties in pursuing for more greed and power. And it comes to the point that what is true liberty of today is not true liberty that was established on this American Continent. So, to begin with, we must understand what the word (Sovereignty) really means? So, let us take a good look at the different meanings of the word!

Sovereignty-adj, 1. Above or superior to all others; chief; greatest; supreme. 2. Supreme in power, rank, or authority. 3. of holding the position of ruler; royal; reigning. 4. Independent of all others [a sovereign State]. 5. Excellent; outstanding. 6. Very effectual, as a cure or remedy.

N, 1. A person who possesses sovereign authority of power; specific, a monarch or ruler. 2. A British gold coin valued as 20 shillings or one-pound sterling, no longer minted for circulation.

Webster's New World Dictionary Third College Edition Copyright 1991, 1988 by Simon & Schuster Inc.

Self-will, to associate or withdraw, to choose or to reject, to act in self-preservation, freewill.

Now if you wanted to know as to what better definition this word [Sovereignty] would be? I would say it is the Declaration of Independence. And the Declaration of Southern Independence. These Birth Certificates would be another I would like to extend my definitions to this word: class of clarifications of what freewill means. And don't forget the individual States constitutions also.

In fact, if the American Empire were to be honest with you. They do not really recognize the State's to be sovereign. The federal government of the United States has overthrown the States of the Union, by declaring themselves as master over the Constitution of the United States. This is in violation against the original Republic that had been established by the founding fathers.

Out of fear and hatred propaganda toward the Southern States, the Union States had voluntary surrender their sovereignty to the federal unknowingly by helping their federal government into enslaving the Confederacy. The State members of the Union had believed that by invading and enslaving the Confederacy, this would prevent the Union from being destroyed.

This kind of thinking is not only a contradiction to the understanding of the Declaration of Independence! It is also a contradiction to the free and Sovereign States that had ratified the Constitution of the United States and had established the federal government. If the federal government of the United States had from the very beginning been a central government, without a federal constitution, without the States constitutions, than we could discuss that maybe succession would have been destructive toward another different version of the Union.

With a much simpler and deeper understanding. And you can find that the U.S. Republic was just as safe with 28 States as it would have been with the 13 original States. Make no mistake about it! The federal government according to the Union Constitution is not the head of the body of the Republic. Where does it say in the U.S. Constitution that the federal government is sovereign over the States and may rule over them as the head of the body? Being that the Constitution limits the amount of power to the federal government would make the federal government to be the body and not the head and fulfilled the will of all of the member States in the voluntary Union.

The Constitutional Republic of these voluntary State members is far different from any other form of governments throughout the whole world. In other countries and nations, you will find; Monarchy, Democracy, National Socialism or Fascism, Socialism or Communism, including the old Republic of the Roman Empire, and so forth. But the Constitutional Republic of the United States and of the Confederate States is indeed unique within our world. The Constitutional States or Countries, that joined together freely to ratify a federal constitution for a federal government of the Republic while still maintaining the sovereignty of each of the States. To surrender a small portion of power from each State for the federal government in order to fulfill its duties in the interest and security of all member States.

The experimental Republic that was established by our founder's had not failed in its true function. But was hijack and replaced with two nations of the Republics and built as a Centralized Empire on top of them, by enslaving the Confederacy and the original Union of the Republic, not this present [Union of Democracy] together and becoming a shadow government of its former self. Now, for the experiment of the Republic to work, it must complete its full cycle.

Succession is the final phase that completes the will of the people (States), in the Declaration of Independence. Liberty is an experiment that must be allowed to evolve according to the ideology of freedom that our ancestors had established.

The one lesson that I have learned from history is that it is nearly impossible to secure the safety and fulfilled the overwhelming needs of the State members. It is best to keep the membership of the States limited in a Constitutional Republic. In this way, regulated amount of State memberships in the Union & Confederacy would be far easier to care for the needs and concerns including the safety of each State member.

Now, some Yankee's do not understand as to why the Southern people continual to have what they call, (Civil War Reenactments)? They somehow believe that we are living in the past! For the unreconstructed Confederate American, the answer is very simple. The Colonel Soldier who fought for Independence and the Confederate Soldier who fought to maintain it had fought for that very understanding of freedom. The Confederate Soldier is the extension of the Colonel Soldier. They are two side of the same coin! One fought for Independence and handed it down to the future generations that fought to maintain it. To us that has not been brainwashed by propaganda in Union government public school history books, they or more or less the one in the same. The Yankee Soldier had chosen to follow the path of the Red Coats (British Soldier).

With a clear understanding, of the original Declaration of Independence, the Confederate States of America fought to remain a free nation! They did not fight to become free as some would come to believe, because the Southern States we're acting on the freedom that had been handed down to every State in the Union from the war of Great Britain.

If the United States government was correct in saying that the Southern States had acted in disobedience, then the United States government must make a public apology to the nation of Great Britain and disband all powers of the government of the United States and all states of the Union, including the occupied Confederacy, and must pledge allegiance to the Crown and Parliament of Great Britain.

We should also understand that nothing has ever been mention in neither the U.S. Constitution nor the Declaration of Independence that says that any State that had ratified the Constitution of the United States or joined the Union here after must remain in the Union forever. This would be an act of treason against liberty in itself! Yet, under the bayonet and occupation, the States of the Confederacy was forced to add in their States Constitution that they can never leave the Union again!

You see, the citizens of the American Empire have been conditioned to think and to believe that without the federal government, a nation cannot exist! However, this is not true when it comes to a Constitutional Republic. It was the States that created the federal constitution and of the federal government. It is the States that are in truth who are the nation as compact members in the Union or Confederacy. As it is written in the Declaration of Independence, it is the people that have the authority to make changed or to abolish it. So, even without the federal government, the nation still remains, regardless if it may be the United States of America or the Confederate States of America.

When the thirteen colonies or States had withdrawn from the Union Empire of Great Britain, it was in the manner and principle that the Southern States acted upon. If secession hadn't been the act of the people, than the Declaration of Independence as (the Official Birth Certificate of Liberty) would have never given birth to the understanding of natural liberty of mankind.

And did you know that the Declaration of Independence does give a justification for a Civil War, under the right circumstances? If you we are to look at the document more closely, you'll see the rights of the people in maintaining their own government. But, this wouldn't just imply only to the federal government, but to all forms of government. Because this document is stating of the rights of the people in general. And no specific form of government was ever mentioned in the Declaration of Independence.

According to the Radical Republican Historical History, the United States had a Civil War with the rebellion Southern States that tried to destroy the Union because of secession. But the problem with this myth is this!

1. The Southern States legally left the Union.
2. The Southern States had no desire to invade or to overthrow the federal government of the United States.
3. The Southern States has never constitutionally left the Confederacy and rejoined the Union under their own free will.

4. The Confederate States government had sent delegates to Washington D.C. to speak to the United States President, Abraham Lincoln, for peaceful terms for both nations. But, Lincoln would not recognize them nor their nation and refused to discuss the matter.
5. The federal government of the Confederate States had dispersed during the movement to a haven in Texas during the unconstitutional war and invasion by the United States of America.
6. Which means the Confederate States nation still exists after all of this time. The compact between the Countries or States is the very essence that makes a nation and not any federal government.
7. The United States President; Abraham Lincoln, violated the peaceful transaction of the forts to the Confederacy that belongs to the individual States. He refused to complete the agreement that was made by the former President; Buchanan that held office before him and tried to reinforce them with troops. This was an act of aggression.
8. The Confederate States government nor the President has ever surrender under any terms, sign a peace treaty, or sign any documents in stating that the Confederacy (Southern States) was in error during action that they had taken.
9. Because of the violation in agreement by the United States in returning the military forts back to the States. And trying to send reinforcements of U.S. troops that were sent to retake and to control these forts.

The Amendments & (Bill of Rights) was created to remind the Federal government of the authority and power of the States Members. But, this was done away with under Lincoln and the Radical Republican Party. It was believed by the Federalist, that the Federal government had created the States, and not the other way around.

But it was the States in the Union had caused the Congress of the Confederate States to make a Declaration of War them. If the Southern States were still in the Union, then they would not be able to make a Declaration of War against their own federal government. Now only Congress can declare war, not the President, nor the States themselves. Remember, the Constitution of the Confederate States of America is virtually the same as the United States of America. It was just more up to date during that time.

The United States of America, Constitutional Republic or Centralized Democracy (Empire) as of yet had an actual (Civil War). But that could change! Now many of the Constitutional Member States of the Union and some of the occupied Constitutional Member States of the Confederacy are working toward passing a bill that declares their State Sovereignty under the 10th Amendment of the U.S. Constitution. And some of them may have the sovereignty bill pass and some will not. And this State Sovereignty movement Resolution began back in 1995 and is still in progress as of 2009.

The first Constitutional President of the Confederate States of America; Jefferson Davis had this statement: *"The principles for which we contend is bound to reassert itself though it may be at another time and in another form."* Ladies and Gentlemen, I believe that this statement just came to past. With the Socialist Liberal Democrats in the government of the United States and of the office of Presidency and Vice-Presidency of 2009. We can safely say that the Union States including the occupied C.S.A. are being pushed to the point of no return.

If the member States of the Union had wanted to declare their sovereign Rights under the 10th Amendment, then they should have done it during the illegal invasion by their own U.S. President, Abraham Lincoln. And once they had done so, they should have refused to bear arms and remain neutral, instead of invading the Confederacy and destroying the Constitutional Republic that had been found upon by our Founding Fathers of Liberty.

Please keep this in mind, every State in the Union, has the right to declare their Sovereign Rights under the 10th, and to declare these rights, they will be required to back it up in one form or another. They will have to be willing to reject anything that the Federals try to force upon them that would be unconstitutional.

For there are only three things that a States Member can do.

1. Reject anything that the federal government tries to force upon them.
2. And if that does not work, then succeed from the compact or membership with the other States.
3. Or work together with the other Constitutional State Members in restoring the federal government of the Union, or Confederacy.

The States will try to restore their federal government through the proper channels of the law. But if the federal government has become so corrupt that the States cannot regain control and power over their own government, then according to the Declaration of Independence, they have the right to take it back by force. And this is what we can truly declare to be a Civil War. If two political parties went to war to control the same government, then this also would be a Civil War. Now at any time if the federal government should collapse for any reason, the Member States can restore it with something better, if that is really possible?

All three steps that are above are defended under the Declaration of Independence. But, don't think that a tyrannical government is going to roll over and play dead? Far from that! And do not forget that the United States government had indeed surrender most of their powers into the hands of the United Nations. Please understand this, my friends! The United Nations does not recognize the Constitutional Republic of the United States nor the Confederate States of America. Nor do they recognize the States Constitutions. And trust me when I say that they will not recognize the United States succeeding from the United Nations. So, the Constitutional Member States in the Union not only have to worry about going to war with their own government, but with the United Nations as well. The United Nations is working toward in creating a New World Order, with possibly a Socialist Foundation. And they will not surrender their powers to anyone.

This Now World Order will trigger the coming of anti-Christ and next the true Christ Jesus. It's going to happen; it's just the question of when? The Confederate Nation does have limited access to the U.S. Constitution under the authority of the United States government. And as citizens of the Empire or, (American Citizens), we are all in truth, slaves! I say this because the Sovereignty of the States and our Federal Constitution of the Confederate States was taken from us. But, because of the mental reconstruction, or brainwashing, most people are ignorant and naive to realize it.

We have even had some honorable reconstructed Confederate American politicians who have tried to work toward in restoring the Federal Constitution of the United States back under the Republic of our founders. But, what they don't understand is that as an American Citizen, in a Democracy of the United States, they are in truth not Constitutional Citizens of the Republic of the United States. Only true Citizens of the Union have the right to restore the Constitutional Republic of the Union. If you have ever seen the movie (Star War), where the Federation of Planets was transformed into an Empire? Then you might get the picture! And I'm just using the movie flick as an example believes that everything is the same since the beginning and nothing has ever changed.

Some of the occupied Southern States has declared their Sovereignty under the 10th Amendment of the U.S. Constitution thus far and this is very honorable and patriotic thing to do! But, it is also null and void! Because all of the Southern States are without sovereignty and being that these Confederate States rights had been violated under the understanding of the Declaration of Independence and that her State Constitutions had been violated, she is still a servant (slave) to what is left of the American Empire.

Regardless what nation may enslave the Confederacy, she is still a nation! Not by winning the war or battles in her land (War Between the States). But by the standards that had been established in writings by our founders of our American liberties. The fate of the United States is far from being a nation anymore. She is dying a slow death! She has gone from a Constitutional Republic to a Socialized Centralized Democracy. Now she has prostituted herself to other nations and is being absorbed by them.

But, even as part of the American Empire, the Southern States can legally and constitutionally declare their State Sovereignty under [Article VI. Paragraph 6.] Constitution of the Confederate States of America Provisional Government. But, as a Centralized Democracy, the United States government will not recognize any of the proclamations of Sovereignty from any State, regardless they are Union or Confederate, and had not since 1861.

Consider this as an example:

Think of the Constitutional Republic as a wheel! The spokes would be the Constitutional States. And the hub in the center of the wheel would be the Federal Constitution. The bike which is the federal government would be resting on top of the hub of both wheels. The weight if the bike is pushing down on both hubs of both wheels. It is also pushing down on the bottom of the spokes underneath and pulling the spokes that are on top. When the spokes are working together to maintain the balance of the weight of the bike through the hub that is holding. Now, imagine the front and rear brakes of the bike being the Declaration of Independence. If the bike should run out of control or is required to maintain control the speed of the bike, then the Declaration of Independence would be in place to help in providing extra support for the wheels.

The Constitutional Republic is designed to help in maintaining balance and power and to provide safety and security for the States, not the federal government. The Constitutional Republic also strives to care for the needs of all of the States, which is a difficult thing to do! But, if some of the States should decide to ride shotgun over the other States or if some party tries to create an empire by enslaving all the rights or powers that belongs to the States through the federal government. Then the voice of the people (each State), can act accordingly to the Declaration of Independence that would defend their best interest accordingly.

The only obligation that the States have to one another is through the Federal Constitution. It was by the ratifying the Federal Constitution that all of the States had the desire and accepted the compact, (Union) & (Confederacy) in the first place.

None of the States, at no time had ever surrendered their own State Constitution or sovereignty when they had joined neither the Union nor the Confederacy. The Federal Constitution of both nations are covering the basic rights that belongs to all each State, and by making it clear that the federal government has a clear understanding through the Federal Constitution. As to what they are.

★ GOD SAVE THE SOUTH ★

And just to make it very clear to anyone with a brain, slavery was (never the reason) the Confederate States fought so bravely and gallantly to defend her borders and to remain as a free people. No more than the Colonies or States that had slaves and fought the same to become free! It is time that the citizens of this American Empire to overcome their ignorance of true American History and the continual brainwashing propaganda, and submission that we have come to accept since the 1860's. It is time for all of us to wake up form this dreadful coma!

By: John Thomas Nall

THE LITMUS TEST FOR AMERICAN CONSERVATISM

Abraham Lincoln is thought by many as not only the greatest American Statesman, but as a great conservative. He was neither. Understanding this is a necessary condition for any genuinely American conservatism. When Lincoln took office, the American polity was regarded as a compact between sovereign States which had created a central government as their agent, hedging it in by a doctrine of enumerated powers.

Since the compact between the States was voluntary, secession was considered an option by public leaders in every section of the Union during the antebellum period. Given this tradition—deeply rooted in the Declaration of Independence—a great Statesman in 1860 would have negotiated a settlement with the Americans killed by Hitler and Tojo. By the end of the war, nearly one half of the White male population of military age was either dead or mutilated. No country in World War II suffered such casualties of that magnitude. Not only would Lincoln not receive the Confederate Commissioners, but he also refused, for three crucial months, to call Congress. Alone, he illegally raised money, illegally raised troops, and started the war.

To crush the Northern opposition, he suspended the (writ of habeas corpus) for the duration of the war and rounded up some 20,000 political prisoners. (Mussolini arrested some 12,000 but convicted only 1,624.) When the chief justice of the Supreme Court declared the suspension blatantly unconstitutional and ordered the prisoners released, Lincoln ordered his arrest. disaffected States, even if it meant the withdrawal of some from the Union.

But, Lincoln had even refused to accept the Confederate Commissioners, much less negotiate with them. Most of the Union could have been kept together, Virginia, North Carolina, Tennessee, and Arkansas voted to remain in the Union even after "State" (West Virginia) and the Confederacy was formed; they reversed themselves only when Lincoln decided on WAR of COERCION. A great Statesman does not seduce his people into needless war; he keeps them out of it.

When the Soviet Union dissolved by peaceful secession, it was 70 years old—the same age as the United States when it dissolved in 1860. Did Gorbachev fail as a Statesman because he negotiated a peaceful dissolution of the U.S.S.R? Likewise, if all the States west of the Mississippi were to secede tomorrow, would we praise, as a great Statesman, a president who refused to negotiate and launched total war against the civilian population merely to preserve the Union?

The number of Southerners who died because of Lincoln's invasion was greater than the total of all

This American Caesar shut down over 300 newspapers, arrested editors, and smashed presses. He broke up State Legislatures: arrested Democratic candidates who urged an armistice; and used the military to elect Republicans (including himself in 1864, by a margin of around 38,000 popular votes). He illegally created an imported a large army of foreign mercenaries. B.H. Liddell Hart traces the origin of modern total war to Lincoln's decision to direct war against the civilian population.

Sherman acknowledged that, by the rules of war taught at West Point, he was guilty of war crimes punishable by death. But who was to enforce those rules? These actions are justified by (Nationalist Historians) as the energetic and extraordinary efforts of a great helmsman rising to the painful duty of preserving an indivisible Union.

But, Lincoln had inherited no such Union from the Framers. Rather, like Bismarck, he created one with a policy of bold and iron. What we call the "Civil War" was in fact America's French Revolution, and Lincoln was the first Jacobin President. He claimed legitimacy for his actions with a "conservative" rhetoric, rooted in a historically false theory of the Constitution which held that the States had never been sovereign.

The Union crated the states, he said, not the States created the Union. In time, this corrupt and corrupting doctrine would suck nearly every reserved power of the States into the central government. Lincoln seared into the American mind an ideological style of politics which, through a sort of alchemy, transmuted a federative "Union of states" into a French revolutionary "Nation" launched on an unending global mission of achieving equality.

Lincoln's corrupt constitutionalism and his ideological style of politics have, over time, led to the hollowing out of traditional American society and the obscene concentration of power in the central government that the

Constitution was explicitly designed to prevent. A genuinely American conservatism, then, must adopt the project of preserving and restoring the decentralized federative polity of the Framers rooted in State and local sovereignty. The central government has no constitutional authority to do most of what it does today.

The first question posed by authentic conservative politics is not whether a policy is good or bad, but what agency (the States or the central government—if either) has the authority to enact it. This is the principle of subsidiarity: that as much possible should be done by the smallest political unit. The Democratic and Republican parties are Lincolnian parties. Neither honestly questions the limits of the federal authority to do this or that. In 1861, the central government broke free from Jefferson called "the chains of the Constitution," and we have, consequently, inherited a fractured historical memory.

There are now two Americanisms: Pre-Lincolnian and post-Lincolnian. The latter is Jacobinism by other means. Only the former can lay claim to being primordial conservatism.

By: David W. Livingston

He is a professor of philosophy at Emory University and the author of (Philosophical Melancholy and Delirium) University of Chicago Press Copyright 2003, www.ChroniclesMagazine.org-

BY THE PRESIDENT OF THE UNITED STATES

A proclamation for the military invasion of the Confederacy—April 15, 1861

Declaration of War Against the Combination of States, specifically South Carolina, Georgia, Alabama, Florida, Mississippi, Louisiana, and Texas

Whereas the laws of the United States have been for some time past, and now opposed, and the execution thereof obstructed, in the States of South Carolina, Georgia, Alabama, Florida, Mississippi, Louisiana and Texas, by <u>combinations</u> too powerful to be suppressed by the ordinary course of judicial proceedings, or by the powers vested in the Marshals by law,

Now therefore, I, Abraham Lincoln, President of the United States, in virtue of the power in me vested by the Constitution, and the laws, have thought fit to call forth, and hereby do call forth, the militia of the several States of the Union, to the aggregate number of seventy-five thousand, <u>in order to suppress said combinations, and to cause the laws to be duly executed.</u> The details, for this object, will be immediately communicated to the State authorities through the War Department.

★ ★ ★

★ JOHN THOMAS NALL ★

ANNOTATION AND ANALYSIS OF LINCOLN'S DECLARATION OF WAR AGAINST THE CONFEDERATE COMBINATION-April 15, 1861

After analyzing the speaking characteristics of [Abraham Lincoln] in regards to his ability to twist and fabricate according to his perceived need, meanings, while on paper appearing to have not so directly stated, and applying this along with the politics espoused, especially in his Inauguration Speech of March 4, 1861, the following (-) text and italicized additions have been inserted to give the actual meaning and intentions of this proclamation of April 15, 1861.

Whereas the laws of the United States have been for some time past, and now are opposed, and execution thereof obstructed, (by Secession) the States of South Carolina, Georgia, Alabama, Florida, Mississippi, Louisiana and Texas, by combinations (called the Confederate States of America) too powerful to be suppressed by ordinary course of (Federal) judicial proceedings, or by the powers vested in the (Federal) Marshals by law,

Now therefore, I, Abraham Lincoln, President of the United States, in virtue of the power (I am assuming by my own invention of the meanings intended) in me vested by the Constitution, and the (tax) laws,* have thought fit to call forth, and herby call forth, the militia of the several States of the Union, to the aggregate number of seventy-five thousand, (in order to invade the territory of said combination with an overwhelming military force) in order to suppress said combinations (by force), and to cause the laws (of the Union) to be duly executed. The details, for this object (of armed military aggression and conquest against that combination, the Confederate States of America), will be (ordered) <u>immediately communicated</u> to the State authorities <u>through the War Department.</u> **

*Article I. Section 8 of the Constitution states: "The Congress shall have Power to lay and collect Taxes, Duties, Imposts and Excises, to pay the Debts and provide for the common Defenses and General Welfare of the United States; **but all Duties, Imposts and excises shall be uniform throughout the United States ..."** This Constitutional provision has been blatantly violated by the Northern Union at the expense of the South with tax laws the Northern controlled congress voted exclusively against the South. **The violation of this Constitutional prohibition voided the contract of the Union that even necessary for the secession of the Southern States.**

**In his inaugural speech of April 29, 1861, President Jefferson Davis stated: "The declaration of war made against this Confederacy by Abraham Lincoln, the President of the United States, in proclamation issued on the 15th day of the present month rendered it necessary, in my judgment, that you [the Congress of the

Confederate States of America] should convene at the earliest practicable moment to devise the measures necessary for the defense of the country." …

"This is the lamentable and fundamental error [that the Federal Government was Sovereign over the subservient States] on which rests the policy that culminated in his declaration of war against these Confederate States." … "Scarcely had the President of the United States received intelligence of the failure of the scheme which he had devised for the reinforcement of Fort Sumter, when he issued the Declaration of War against this Confederacy which has prompted me to convoke you" … "The President of the United States called for an army of 75,000 men, whose first service was to capture our forts. It was a plain declaration of war which I was not at liberty to disregard of my knowledge that under the Constitution of the United States the President was usurping a power granted exclusively to the Congress."—*[www.confederatestatesofamerica.org/] Dec 15 of 2007.*

Update: The CSAGov.org web site that was that's in the Advertisement Section has been updated to [www.CSAGovernment.org] Thank you; author

RECOGNITION OF THE CONFEDERACY BY FOREIGN POWERS

It provides, nevertheless, for the emergency of the population of a territory, which has already been occupied by the invader, spontaneously taking up arms to resist the invading forces, without having had time to comply with the above requirements; they, too, are to be treated as belligerents "if they respect the laws and customs of war." In naval An historical fact, yet one not generally known that (Great Britain) recognized the belligerency of the (Confederate States) on May 13, 1861; (France) did likewise on June 30, 1861; (Spain) on June 17, 1861; and (Portugal) on July 29, 1861. The (Czar of Russia), on July 30, 1861 refused to assume a position of neutrality as between North and South and made no recognition of Southern belligerency.

Taken from Conklin's "Vest-Pocket Argument Settler", originally copyrighted 1898.

BELLIGERENCY

From 1911 Encyclopedia Belligerency,

The state of carrying on war (Lat. Bellum, war, and gerere, to wage) in accordance with the laws of nations. Insurgents are not such excluded from recognition as belligerents, and, even where not recognized as belligerents by the governments against which they have rebelled, they may be so recognized by a neutral State, as in the case of the (American Civil War), when the Southern States were recognized as belligerents by Great Britain, though regarded as rebels by the Northern States. The recognition by a neutral state of belligerency does not, however, imply recognition of independent political existence. The regulations annexed to The Hague Convention relating the laws and customs of war (29th of July), contain a section entitled "Belligerents" which is divided into three chapters, dealing respectively with (i.)

The Qualifications of Belligerents; (ii.) Prisoners of War, (ii.) The sick and Wounded. To entitle troops to the special privileges attaching to belligerency, chapter i. Provides that all regular, militia or volunteer forces shall alike be commanded by persons responsible for the acts of their men, that all such shall carry distinctive emblems, recognizable at a distance, that arms shall be carried openly, and operations conducted in accordance with the usages of war observed among civilized mankind.

War, privateering having been finally abolished as among the parties to it by the declaration of Paris, a privateer is not entitled, as between such parties, the rights of belligerency.

As between States, one of whom is not a party to the Declaration; the right to grant letters of morgue would remain intact for both parties, and the privateer, as between them, would be a belligerent; as regards neutrals, the situation would be complicated.

★ ★ ★
BATTLE HYMN OF THE REPUBLIC

*An Honest Examination of the Motives behind the Composition of
a Most Effective Example of Humanistic Propaganda*

There are many beautiful, inspiring, spiritual hymns and songs of the Christian church that were born out of adversity, during times of revival or God's rich dealings with His servants. These songs and hymns we must deeply revere and appreciate for their rich meaning and spiritual value. However, there are some songs that have been adopted into Christian hymnody that do not belong there because of their history, and/or doctrine. One such song that has crept into the Christian church and its worship, unnoticed, is the song entitled, "The Battle Hymn of the Republic." This song should not be considered a hymn of our Faith, because of it sinister origin, the attitude and actions that it promoted and the liberal philosophy of it's authored, Mrs. Julia Ward Howe.

Can be briefly summed up as the fatherhood of God and the brotherhood of all men.

By her own statements, it is very clear as to what her opinion was concerning Jesus Christ. "Not until the Civil War did I officially join the Unitarian Church and accept the fact that Christ was merely a great teacher with First, concerning Mrs. Howe, she is commonly known as a writer and social reformer, and not a Bible-believing Christian. After her marriage to Dr. Samuel Gridley Howe in 1843, they moved to Boston and became associated with the famous Unitarian "Church of the Disciples," pastured by the well-known Unitarian transcendentalist, James Freeman Clark. Mrs. Howe and her husband became deeply involved in the anti-slavery movement of the 1840's and 50's and edited one of its papers, the "Boston Commonwealth." In her zeal and desire for social reform at any cost, Mrs. Howe came to revere the basest of men such as John Brown, the Kansas murderer and terrorist.

After the infamous murdering rampage at Harper's Ferry when John Brown was condemned to die, Mrs. Howe believed that "John Brown's death" will be holy and glorious. John Brown will glorify the gallows like Jesus glorified the cross. As a Unitarian, her religious views were not based on the fundamental Theo Centric (God-centered) doctrines of the Scriptures, but upon the 19th century liberal anthropocentric (man-centered) beliefs of the higher critics, poetic mystics, and the advocates of transcendental meditation. These beliefs no higher claim to preeminence in wisdom, goodness and power than many other men." "Having rejected the exclusive doctrine that made Christianity and special forms of the only way of spiritual redemption, I now accept the belief that not only Christians but all human beings, no matter what their religion, are capable of redemption." These are the same fallacies and heresies which are espoused by the religious and academic liberal establishment yet today.

On the writing of the words of the song "The Battle Hymn of the Republic," with the blessings of U.S. President Lincoln, she wrote words to a popular tune of the day that could be used as a rallying cry of the North in support of their invasion of the Christian South.

The message of this song shrouded in religious terms was intended to convince the people of the North that they were involved in a "Holy War" for a righteous cause. Simply stated, it was used as typical war propaganda by the Lincoln administration for brainwashing the citizens of the North in their invasion and destruction of the South. Ever since Mrs. Howe wrote the words to this song in December 1861, many sincere well-meaning Christians have unknowingly sung with religious seal and fervor without understanding its original intent and meaning. Along with other prominent Unitarians, as Mrs. Howe viewed the Union troops of the "Army of the Potomac." She was then inspired to write the words that are known and sung today.

She portrayed the Union Army as the "coming of the glory of the Lord" going to "trample out the vintage where the grapes of wrath are stored," She plainly states that "I have seen Him (God) in the watch fires of a hundred circling (Union) camps." To her, Lincoln's 75,000 volunteers were the "Army of God" going forth to slaughter the evil resisters of social reform and progressive centralized government. The "burnished rows of steel" that she mentioned referred to the polished Union cannons that rained down death and destruction upon not only the Confederate soldier, but upon Southern Cities and countryside.

Currently in American history, "The South" was quite different in many ways from the North. The South was more an agrarian while the North was more industrialized. The South more rural while the North more urban; the South advocated the traditional interpretation of the Constitutional principles of our American Founders for States Rights, and local government control as opposed to the Northern Republican party view of centralized government powers; the people of the South were more traditional in maintaining their culture, whereas the North was rapidly losing the cultural traditions through the influx of more liberal ideas of equalitarianism; the educational institutions of the South were more conservative in thought and practice as opposed to the Northern concepts of universalism, humanism, deism and rationalism that had crept into its once great academic institutions such as Harvard and Yale; at this critical time in our history the South was definitely more adamant in its stalwart defense of traditional (Calvinistic Christianity) that dated back to the early reformers while the religious establishments of the North were accepting and promoting the fallacious anti-Bible concepts of the more modernistic approach to such truths as the authenticity and inerrancy of the Scriptures.

In summation, the South held to and practiced a more Biblical form of Christianity while the North was straying from its roots of Puritanism and Biblical foundations. During the "War Between the States" of 1861-1865, it was only in the army of the Confederate States of America that God had blessed with a real spiritual revival among the officers and common soldiers where it was estimated by contemporary Chaplains and pastors that approximately 100,000 men were genuinely converted to Christ, which became the origin of the Southern "Bible Belt."

This is a thrilling story within itself that needs to be told to all Southern parishioners, but it seems to be a kept secret known only to a few. This information is given in hopes of informing our Christian worship is not worthy of our acceptance. Let us heed the admonition of the Apostle Paul given in 1 Corinthians 14:15, to sing not only with spirit, but with the understanding also.

By: Charles A. Jennings.

★ ★ ★
THE CRUMBLING OF AN EMPIRE

We are seeing a process which began with the fall of the Old Republic of Sovereign States, now come to Fruition. The war for Southern Independence was not a "Union" victory in the classical sense. The term "Union" is definitive of a voluntary uniting as was the case with the Old Republic. The Confederacy and the Old Republic both effectively lost the war. What emerged was an empire, a Consolidation of Socialist states. In effect a Republic and a Confederacy entered "The War and an empire emerged. The armed might which brought them victory, also brought them the 'arrogance of power.' The empires past, Sodom and Gomorrah, Babylon, and Rome for example, would feel quite at home under these conditions. The process is not unknown in history, only our modern technology and nomenclature is different.

None of us know the details of how this will play out; we can only imagine in general terms. Those who may have wondered at how the crumbling of such a powerful world class empire begins; wonder no more. We of the Southern tradition, believing in, and having a deep historical heritage, of honor, honesty, integrity, duty and faith. Who measure our politicians in terms of principles and Statesmanship? We cannot completely comprehend the mindset of 'those people.' Who would rip and tear at the very foundation of an empire their own forefathers must surely have believe in, having given their life's blood?

I have long believed the Yankee Empire will fall, and that, by their own hand. And yes, they are that foolish! This process we are seeing unfold in Florida, bears that out. There should be no doubt, while this situation, in and of itself, may not bring down the empire. It most certainly exemplifies the process and the course, in which it will follow. We are witnesses to the beginnings of the end of the last 'World Class Superpower.' This modern Babylonian Empire is not invincible, nor immortal. It will fall! The Cause of the South will be vindicated! God save the South!

By: Mr. Thomas E. Guinn

⋆ ⋆ ⋆

THE MYTHICAL AMERICAN CIVIL WAR

In your U.S. government public school history books, you will find that their version of this Civil War took place between the Northern and the Southern sections of the United States of America. That the South had committed treason for leaving the Union and was fighting for slavery. And! That they were responsible for tearing the nation apart, meaning the United States. All these accusations are all faults and lies! I would like to take a moment to explain as to my reasons of why? But, before I do, I have a question for you! Before the government (public) schools came on the scene, how were the children thought? Did George Washington go to a public school? Did Jefferson Davis go to a public school? And what is the purpose for government public schools? Answer: to make the citizens (subjects) loyal to the federal government & for social reform into a socialist society! Just something for to think about!

1. **A Civil War:** A Civil War is when two factions are fighting to take control over the powers of that same government. For a Civil War to come into being, the circumstances must be different. If the South had remained in the Union and decided to make war on the North to control the Federal government, then a Civil War would be afoot. Or, if one section decided not to go through the voting phase and took it by force, then you would have a Civil War. If the Republican and the Democratic Parties went to war for the control over the government of the United States, then you have a Civil War.

    But, since the Southern States had withdrawn their membership from the Union and Ratified a new Federal Constitution for their new provisional government. Then a Civil War never took place against the United States government. The Confederate States government did not nor was able to invade and make war just to overthrow the Union government. To do such a foolish act would defeat the purpose of leaving the Union in the first place. The Southern States only repeated the same actions and principles of secession, as did the Colonies that left Great Britain, as they felt it to be justified.

The Confederate States fought a defensive war and only invaded the United States out of desperation. The Confederate Americans knew that they could never win the war in a total victory. But, if they could push the United States to a point that they would prefer a peace treaty with the Confederacy, then true victory could be claimed by the Confederacy. It has always been the desire of the Confederate people to be at peace with the Union. But the defense of family, home, country, and liberty cannot be ignored in one's own duty.

2. **Fighting for Slavery:** Slavery for the slave States was once protected under the U.S. Constitution. What most people have never understood is that to the South, (principle always overrides circumstances). To believe in slavery or not, was not the main issue! If slavery could not be protected under the Constitution, then how could anything else in the Constitution could be protected? When the South left the Union, all slaves from those States were no longer protected, and should if any slave were to flee to one of the Union States, they would be forever free. Just as some of the European Nations have done, the Confederate States had already taken the first small steps to terminate the Southern slave institution, without causing the collapse of the economy. Only a slave from the United States could be sold in these Confederate of States. And any slave that fought for the defenses for the South had earned the right to be free. Some masters had freed their servants before or during the war. Agriculture slavery would have ended in the normal manner and time within the Confederate Nation. However, Industrial slavery is still an issue throughout the United States & our occupied Confederate Nation. Over worked and under paid, safety issues and heavy taxes from our pay checks and the value of the Yankee currency dropping, are always denying the people the right to prosperity. (Freeing the Slaves: Only Congress of the United States and not their President can free the slaves within their nation's borders, by voting to cancel the protection of slavery in their Federal Constitution. The same goes for the Confederate States Congress. The President cannot free any slaves in another nation no more than he can legally free the slaves in his own nation.

3. **Treason:** A division of views did take place in the United States and the Confederate States. And you had spies on both sides. You also had those who committed Treason against their own nation. The biggest division was as to who or what you should be loyal too? To the ideas of the Republic and the values of those who had founded it? Or, should it be to an all-powerful government that requires unconditional loyalty and submission? While others may not know and understand the transformation that has taken place in their own government, believing it to remain as it had been founded and still rising in its defense! Loyalties do die hard! And some had believed that a central government could right all what they believed to be wrong in this sinful world. And the question should come to your mind as how is it that a spy or

double spy could give or sell information to any buyer and it would be treason? But politicians can violate the Constitution which prevents them from riding shotgun over the people and it's not considered to be treason? Does not portraying the trust of the people qualifies as an act of treason? If your own military we are used by your government to violate your rights, would that not be consider as an act of treason?

4. When politicians decide the definition of liberty and tells you what our rights will be, is that not treason? Think about it!

By: John Thomas Nall

BARRANCAS: THE FIRST SHOTS FIRED IN THE REBELLION

The firing on Fort Sumter in Charleston's harbor traditionally marks the opening of the Rebellion. But before this assault on April 14, 1861, there was another battle—the first shots of the Civil War—hundreds of miles down the south of Florida. On Jan. 8, 1861, United States Army guards repelled a group of men intending to take Fort Barrancas in Pensacola Harbor. Historians say that this event could be considered the first shots fired on Union forces in the Civil War. [1]

Fort Barrancas, located on a barrier island, was one of four fortified areas that marked the Southern defenses. Fort Barrancas has been a site for harbor fortifications since 1763, when the British built a fort. The Spanish captured Pensacola from the British in 1781and constructed their own fortification on the site, calling it San Carlos de Barranca. The Spanish word Barranca means bluff, which fairly describes the location of the fort [2]

The United States began construction fortifications at Pensacola in the 1820s, when Pensacola Bay was chosen as the site for a Navy Yard. Along with Fort Barrancas, which defended the Navy Yard, there were Fort Pickens and Fort McRee, both located on islands at the entrance to the bay, (Fort McRee has been completely destroyed by the shifting sands of the barrier island it was located on.) The Advance Redoubt, near Fort Barrancas, was an infantry fort, designed to stop overland movement of the enemy troops toward the Navy Yard.

Fort Pickens was the largest installation that fortified the Pensacola Harbor. Constructed between 1829-1834. Pickens was located at the western tip of Santa Rosa Island, just offshore of the mainland. Construction was supervised by Colonel William H. Chase of the Corps of Army Engineer. Using slave labor, the fort used over 22 million bricks and was designed to be impregnable. Ironically, Chase was later appointed by the State of Florida to command its troops and seize for the South the very fort he had built [3]

That the defensive positions were of critical importance was realized by the Union and the Confederacy. On Jan. 5, Senator Yulee wrote from Washington to Joseph Finegan at Tallahassee, "The immediately important thing to be done is the occupation of the forts and arsenals in Florida." Union soldiers in Florida occupied the Apalachicola arsenal at Chattahoochee, containing a small number of arms, 5,000 pounds of powder and about 75,000 cartridges; Fort Barrancas, with 44 cannons and ammunition; Barrancas barracks, where there was a field battery; equipped with 201cannons with ammunition; Fort McRee, 125 seacoast and garrison cannons; Fort Taylor in Key West, with 60 cannons; Key West barracks, 4 cannons; Fort Marion, with 6 field batteries and some small arms; and Fort Jefferson on the Tortugas.

Sen. Yulee pointed out, "The naval station and forts at Pensacola were in consequence." There was then on the mainland one company of Federal artillery, commanded by John H. Winder, later to be promoted to general in the Confederate service. On account of Winder's absence Lieutenant Adam J. Slemmer was in charge. [4]

At the time of the Secession, Fort Pickens had not been occupied since the Mexican War. Lt. Slemmer, responsible for the U.S. forces at Fort Barrancas, decided that in spite of the dilapidated condition, Pickens was more defensible than any of the other posts in the area. His decision was accelerated around midnight of Jan.8 when his troops repelled a group of men intending to take the fort. In consolidating his position, Lt. Slemmer destroyed over 20,000 pounds of powder at Fort McRee, spike the guns at Barrancas, and evacuated his 80troops to Fort Pickens. Because of his tactical thinking. Fort Pickens remained in Union hands throughout the Civil War. [5]

A native Pennsylvanian, Adam J. Slemmer was graduated from West Point in 185 as brevet second Lieutenant 1st Artillery. He was promoted to first lieutenant in 1854. Lt. Slemmer oversaw the small artillery garrison quartered at Fort Barrancas when the Secession crises occurred. With an under-manned garrison far from Washington, Lt. Slemmer considered his situation at Fort Barrancas to be untenable. The naval establishment, consisting of a minimal sea force and the Navy Yard, was under Commodore James Armstrong. Both Slemmer and Armstrong had been told that an attempt to seize the military works would be made as soon as the Florida politicians should declare the State's secession—and secession was imminent. Federal posts in Florida and Alabama had already been seized, and hostile troops were gathering at Pensacola.

On Jan. 10, to the greater security of Fort Pickens, then unoccupied. That was the date in which the Florida Convention passed the Ordinance of Secession. On the same mourning, about 500 insurgents of Florida, Alabama and Mississippi appeared at the gate of the Navy Yard and demanded its surrender. Commodore Armstrong was powerless, for three-fourths of the 60 officers under his command were disloyal. Lt. Slemmer decided to concentrate his forces to defend only one fort, and moved his four score troops

Commander Ebenezer Farrand was among the insurgents who demanded the surrender, and flag-Officer Renshaw immediately ordered the National Standard to be pulled down. The post, with ordnance stores valued at $156,000, passed into the hands of the authorities of Florida. The insurgents took possession of Forts Barrancas and McRee.

Two days later, on Jan 12, Florida and Alabama troops took the mainland bases and demanded that Lt. Slemmer surrender Fort Pickens. That night, a deputation went to the fort, consisting of Captain Randolph, Major Marks and Lieutenant Rutledge. They demanded the peaceful surrender of Pickens to the governors of Alabama and Florida, but Slemmer declined to recognize the authority of those officials. Lt. Slemmer held his position until an informal agreement, or "truce," was established between President Buchanan's Administration and Florida. (The terms were that Southern troops would not attack Pickens so long as Union troops remained abroad nearby ships and did not reinforce the fort).

The two vessels in the harbor, "the supply and Wyandotte," steamed out under truce, but remained in the possession of the United States officers. The 80 men under Slemmer at Fort Pickens remained defiant. The following night, a small party of armed men from the mainland reconnoitered on the island and a (few shots were fired from the fort). On Jan. 15, Col. W. H. Chase, a U.S. Army officer of Massachusetts who had worked on building the forts and was thoroughly familiar with Pensacola Bay's defenses, visited Fort Pickens in company with Capt. Farrand. Chase oversaw all insurgents in that region and Farrand had been second of command at the Navy Yard. Chase obtained an interview with Slemmer and tried to persuade him to "avoid bloodshed" by quietly surrendering the fort. Col. Chase said in conclusion, "Consider this well, and take care that you will so act as to have no fearful recollections of a tragedy that might have avoided; but rather to make the present moment one of the most glorious, because Christian-like, of your life." Slemmer, it can be said, did make that a "glorious moment of his life" by refusing to give up the fort.

(Nothing remained to the State forces except to make an assault. But the Florida Senators in Washington and other Representatives, including Senator Jefferson Davis, telegraphed advising that no blood should be shed. [6] On Jan. 18, another demand was made for the surrender of the fort, and this too was refused. A siege of that stronghold was begun).

In the meantime, the government in Washington was sending reinforcements to Forts Taylor and Jefferson. On Jan. 21, Capt. Israel Vogdes, with a company of artillerymen, was ordered to sail on the sloop-of-war "Brooklyn and Fort Pickens." On being informed of the overt act and violating the truce, Senator Mallory telegraphed to a Mr. Slidell that it would doubtless provoke an attack upon the fort by the force of 1,700 men assembled under Col. Chase. (Slidell urged that President Buchanan be informed that Fort Pickens would not be molested if reinforcements were not sent). Capt. Vogdes was then instructed not to land his men unless hostilities begun. Lt. Slemmer, deprived of the promised aid of naval establishment, was now left to his own resources. The fort was one of the strongest on the Gulf Coast. There were 54 guns in position and provisions for five months, but the garrison consisted of only 81 officers of men.

The situation remained tense, with Capt. Vogdes' men on shipboard off Santa Rosa Island, and the Alabama and Florida volunteers on shore engaged in strengthening their defenses. On Feb. 11, Lt. Slemmer protested the erection of battery that he observed volunteers working at. Col. Chase promptly answered that the erection of batteries was not aiming at an attack on Fort Pickens, yet he would give orders for its discontinuance. [7]

*Several days after the inauguration of Abraham Lincoln, Capt. Vogdes was ordered by General Winfield Scott to land his company, "reinforce Fort Pickens, and hold the same until further orders." With that order, the condition of existing peace was broken. * Capt. Vogdes requested the cooperation of Capt. Adams who commanded the fleet to help him make a landing. Adams refused, saying his instructions forbade such action so long as there was no aggressive movement on the part of the Confederate forces. In the meantime, General Braxton took command at Pensacola on Mar. 11and ordered the resumption of work on the batteries. He informed the Federal Commander that this action was justified "as a means of defense, and especially so under the threats of the new Administration." The number of insurgents at Pensacola increased rapidly, and the Lincoln Administration resolved to send relief to Fort Pickens. A small squadron was dispatched from New York for this purpose. Navy Lieutenant J.L. Worden was sent overland to Pensacola with orders to Capt. Adams, in command of the vessels off Fort Pickens, to throw reinforcements into that work immediately.

Lt. Worden reached Pensacola on Apr. 10. On his overland trip, Worden had observed the war fever and preparations. Fearing arrest, he acquainted himself with the contents of the dispatches and then tore them up. He frankly told Gen. Bragg that he was sent by his government with orders to Capt. Adams, and that they were not written, but, oral. Bragg gave the lieutenant a pass for his destination. Fortunately, Worden's message was delivered in the neck of time for Bragg was on the point of attacking the fort. (The Reinforcements were thrown in and the plan was foiled). Worden returned to Pensacola and was permitted to take the train cars for Montgomery, Alabama. (At that moment, Bragg was informed by a spy that Fort Pickens had been reinforced).

Mortified by his stupid blunder in letting Worden pass to and from the squadron, he telegraphed the Confederate government as Montgomery that Worden had practiced "falsehood and deception" in gaining access to the squadron and recommended his arrest. Lt. Worden was seized on Apr. 15, put in jail, treated with scorn by the Confederates, and kept a prisoner until the following November when he was exchanged. Lt. Worden, whose timely delivery of orders to Capt. Adams foiled Gen. Bragg's attack, had become the first prisoner-of-was held by the insurgents. Worden later distinguished himself in command of the Monitor at Hampton Roads.

A few days after the reinforcement of Fort Pickens, two vessels appeared bearing several hundred troops and ample supplies under Col. Harvey Brown. After four months defending Fort Pickens in the face of enemy guns, Lt Slemmer and his band of troops were worn by fatigue. They were relieved and sent to Fort Hamilton, New York, to rest. The grateful population of New York honored them. The President gave Slemmer the commission of Major, and afterward of Brigadier; and the New York Chamber of Commerce struck a series of bronze medals as presents to the Commander and men of the brave little garrison. [8]

Reinforcements continued to be sent to Fort Pickens and the number of insurgents intended to assail it also increased, until, in May, they numbered over 7,000. But events of very little importance occurred in that vicinity during the ensuing summer. As a result of Slemmer's actions, Pensacola remained a major Union stronghold throughout the war.

By: Walter Giersbach

Timeline of Early 1861 (6)

Jan. 6—State troops seize the Arsenal at Apalachicola.
Jan. 7—State troops seize Fort Marion at St. Augustine.
Jan. 8—Li. Slemmer's troops repel insurgents from Fort Barrancas.
Jan. 10—Florida passes it Ordinance of Secession; Lt. Adam Slemmer transfers Union troops from Barrancas Barracks to Fort Pickens.

Jan. 12—State troops seize the Pensacola Navy Yard, Fort Barrancas, Fort McRee, and Barrancas Barracks. Confederate officials demand the surrender of Fort Pickens.
Jan. 14—U.S. forces garrison Fort Taylor.
Jan. 18—Confederate officials again demand the surrender of Fort Pickens.
Jan. 18—Union troops garrison Fort Jefferson in the Dry Tortugas.

Footnotes and Bibliography

Tulane University, http://tulane.edu/-later/Pickens.html
From the personal research of Andy Bennett,
Tulane University
http:///www.civilwarhome.com/Florida2.htm
Tulane University
E History, http://www.ehistory.com/uscw/library/periodicals/ahotcw/section05/130.cfm
http://www.civilwarhome.com/Florida2.htm
E History, http://www.ehistory.com/uscw/features/battles/statea/florida/0001.cfm

About the Author:

Walter Giersbach has an abiding interest in the Civil War and New England history. Two great-grandfathers served, respectively, in 1864-66 with the 7th Regt. Vermont Volunteers and in 1861 with Connecticut's 2nd Artillery. Four sets of maternal ancestors were also caught up in King Philip's War of 1675-76. Walt's career was in corporate communications before returning to creative writing. He has had several short stories and articles published and is working on a novel. He lives in Cambridge, Mass, and can be reached at w.giersbach@att.net

Published online: 01/30/2005
http://www.militaryhistoryonline.com/civilwar/misc/barrancas.asx

THREE-FIFTHS COMPROMISE

The **Three-Fifths Compromise** was a compromise between Southern and Northern States reached during the Philadelphia Convention of 1787 in which three-fifths of the population of slaves would be counted for enumeration purposes regarding both the distribution of taxes and the apportionment of the members of the United States House of Representatives. It was proposed by delegates James Wilson and Roger Sherman.

Delegates opposed to slavery generally wished to count only the free inhabitants of each State. Delegates supportive of slavery, on the other hand, generally wanted to count slaves at their actual numbers. Since slaves could not vote, slaveholders would thus have the benefit of increased representation in the House and the Electoral College; was only a secondary issue. The final compromise of counting slaves as only three-fifths of the actual numbers reduced the power of the slave relative to the original proposals, but is still generally credited with giving the pro-slavery forces disproportionate political power in U.S. government from the establishment of the Constitution until the Civil War. For example, in the period prior to 1850, Southerners held the Presidency for 50 of 62 years, and 18 of the 31 Supreme Court Justices were Southerners despite the North having nearly twice the population by 1850.

The three-fifths compromise if found in Article 1, Section 2, and Paragraph3 of the United States Constitution:

"Representatives and direct Taxes shall be apportioned among the several States which may be included within this Union, according to their respective Numbers, which shall be determined by adding to the whole Number of free Persons, including those bound to Service for a Term of Years, and excluding Indians not tax, **three fifths of all Persons.**"

The three-fifths ratio was not a new concept. It originated with 1783 amendment proposed to the Articles of Confederation. The amendment was to have changed the basis for determining the wealth of each State, and hence it tax obligations, from real estate populations as a measure of produce wealth. The proposal by the committee of the Congress had suggested that taxes "shall all be supplied by the several Colonies in proportion to the number of inhabitants of every age, sex, and quality, except Indians not paying taxes." [1] [2] The South immediately objected to this formula since it would include slaves, who were viewed primarily as property, in calculating the amount of taxes to be paid. As Thomas Jefferson wrote in his notes on the debates, "The Southern States would be taxed 'according to their numbers and their wealth conjunctly, while the Northern would be taxed on numbers only." [3]

were opposed). The proposed ratio was, however, a ready solution to the impasse After proposed compromises of ½ by Benjamin Harrison of Virginia and ¾ by several New Englanders failed to gain sufficient support. Congress finally settled on the three-fifths ratio proposed by James Madison. [4] But this amendment ultimately failed, falling two States short of the unanimous approval required for amending the Articles of Confederation (only) New Hampshire and New York that during the Constitutional Convention. In that situation, the alignment of the contending forces was the reverse of what had obtained under the Articles of Confederation. In amending the Articles, the North wanted slaves to count for more than the South did, because the objective was to determine taxes paid by the States to the Federal Government. In the Constitution Convention, the more important issue was representation in Congress, so the South wanted slaves to count for more than the North did.

Effects

The three-fifths ratio or "Federal Ratio" had a major on the pre-Civil War political affairs due to the disproportionate representation of slaveholding States. For example, in 1793 slave States would have been apportioned 33 seats in the House of Representatives had the seats been assigned based on the free (i.e., voting) population; instead, they were apportioned 47. In 1812, slaveholding States had instead 76 instead of the 54 they would have had; in 1833, 98 instead of 73. As a result, Southerners dominated the Presidency, the Speaker of the House, and the Supreme Court in the period prior to the Civil War. [3]

Historian Garry Wills has postulated that without the additional 'slave' votes, Jefferson would have lost the presidential election of 1800. Also," ... slavery would have been excluded from Missouri ... Jackson's Indian removal policy would have failed ... the Wilmot Proviso would have banned slavery in territories won from Mexico ... the Kansas-Nebraska bill would have failed ..." [6] However, other historians have criticized Will's analysis as simplistic. [7] For example, while the three-fifths compromise could be seen to favor Southern States (which generally had a larger slave populations), the Connecticut Compromise tended to favor the Northern States (which were generally smaller). Support for the new Constitution rested on the balance of these sectional interest. [8]

Following the Civil War and abolition of slavery by the Thirteenth Amendment to the United States Constitution (1865), the three-fifths clause was rendered moot. Section 2 of the Fourteenth Amendment to the United States Constitution (1868) later superseded Article 1, Section 2, and Clause 3. It specifically States that Representatives shall be apportioned … counting the whole number of persons of each State, excluding Indians not taxes …"

Notes

1. Wills pg. 51
2. Hannis Taylor (1911). The Origin and Growth of the American Constitution: An Historical Treatise. Houghton Mifflin Company, 131.
3. Wills pg. 51-52
4. Wills pg. 53
5. Wills pg. 5
6. Wills pg. 5
7. A SLAVE TO THE SYSTEM?-Thomas Jefferson and Slavery. Hoover Institution (January 19, 2004). Retrieved on 2008-02-20.
8. Banning, Lance (August 31, 2004). Three-Fifths Historian. The Claremont Institute. Retrieved on 2008-01-21.

Reference

Wills, Gary. "Negro President": Jefferson and the Slave Power. Houghton, 2003. ISBN 0-618-3439-9

Further Reading

Hanes Walton Jr. & Robert C. Smith. American Politics and the African American Quest for Freedom. Pearson Longman, 2006 (3rd Edition). ISBN0-321-29237-5

Henry Wiencek. "An Imperfect God: George Washington, his slaves, and the creation of America." Farrar, Straus, and Giroux, 2003. Wikipedia, the free (liberal) encyclopedia

Authors View:

1. The European population in the Southern States was much smaller in the South than the North.
2. The population growth of slavery in the South was maintained by the Northern slave trade.
3. Despite all of the Southern States that voted against Abraham Lincoln, he still became President.
4. The North feared the expansion of slavery into the Western territories because the South would gain a balance of power in the government. Some may have feared that the South would dominate the voting booths. While others believe in the institution of slavery to be wrong and should be forbidden.

★ ★ ★
THE STRAW THAT BROKE THE CAMELS BACK

There have been other issues that had created much strife between the Northern and of the Southern States in the Union. But as to why the Southern States had such fear of the election of Lincoln was a very simple one. For one reason was that they knew he was a Radical Centralist of the Republican Party. The other reason was for the fact that, he supported a much higher tax. This is the very main subject that caused the American Colonies to secede from England and lead to the Colonel War for Independence of 1776. However, while the Colonies fought for Independence, the Southern States fought to maintain and preserve it!

The North was constantly trying to raise taxes on the Southerners through tariffs of all imported goods in order to protect the inefficient big business in the North. These big businesses could not compete with the manufactured goods from England and France with whom the South traded cotton with. The Southern States did not have factories and was required to import most of the finished goods that they produce. The coming age of the Industrial Revolution had allowed England and France to out produce and ship more products across the Atlantic that were cheaper than the products from manufacturers of the Northern States. When Lincoln was elected as the U.S. President, he and the United States Congress immediately passed the (Morrill Tariff bill.)

This was the highest tax increase, in the history of the United States up to that time. This had more than double the import tax rate from 20% to 47%. This import tax had served to bankrupt many Southerners. And though the States of the South represented only about 30% of the population of the United States! The South paid 80% of the tariffs collected. That would be 80% from 100%. Oppressive taxes, and the denial of the Rights of the States to govern themselves, another words, State Rights. This and the Federal Government had pushed the Southern States into legally in withdrawing from the Union. Since the Southerners had escaped the tax by withdrawing from the Union, the only way the North could collect this oppressive tax was to invade the Confederate States of America and to force that nation at gun point back into the Union.

It was to collect this import tax to satisfy his Northern Industrialist supporters. This was one of the main reasons for invading the South, by Mr. Abraham Lincoln. Slavery was not an issue for the war. The Lincoln's War cost the lives of 600,000 Americans. The Republic of a Free and Sovereign States had been envisioned by the United States founders, had been destroyed by the victory of the Northern States. It was a rich man's war to be sure with! The average and low-income citizens of the United States gain nothing honorable from that war, in the end; much less in saving the Union that was founded by our founders. So, the tool of propaganda was used to gain support of the Yankee population with statements like, (If the States were to leave, the Union would crumble) or (the North is fighting to free the slaves.) Eventually, people started to realize the real actions of Mr. Lincoln. Then came his enforcement of the draft, and the imprisoned of his own people without trail, just because they had denounced his unconstitutional goals of invasion and conquest. Eventually it came to the point that the Yankee people were confused as to what the war was all about? And just like today! It's politics as usual!

By: John Thomas Nall

"Let us rise to the call of freedom-loving blood that is in us and send our answer to the tyranny that clanks its chains upon the South. In the name of the greatest people that have ever trod this earth. I draw the line in the dust and toss the gauntlet before the feet of tyranny." The honorable Alabama Governor George Wallace (1963) during the (Civil Rights)—Communist Party USA & Federal interference in the Southern States) at the time of the Vietnam War.

✦ ✦ ✦
THE GUILDED CAGE

Birds make wonderful pets for millions of people. The cheery, happy songs they sing in the morning reach a special spot deep in our very soul. Birds love freedom and the very act of flying. These amazing creatures are meant to always be free just as the Creator made them. The animal world is filled with everything imaginable which swims, runs, crawls, creeps and flies from A to Z. This reminds us of where we are on this planet in the grand plan of things. Millions of creatures everywhere make a fantastic myriad of sounds seemingly just for our listening pleasure, as they go about their daily routines. They rarely get sick. Nor are they depressed or divorced. Creatures are, for the most part, quite tolerant of other species around them unless they are on the menu. Witness the waterholes and lakes in Africa, where often prey and predator must come to drink while keeping one eye on each another.

This still is a beautiful planet in so many ways, despite the atmosphere of fear, greed, and hatred. All of us must take time every single day to appreciate that. Go touch another human being, a tree, a bush, or a flower, or even a weed. There is a magic here, invisibly embodied in the advanced engineering of every living thing, even in a weed.

Yet there is something dark and ominous that has made our big marble especially threatening to us as humans in recent years. It is an intangible fear, an invisible but definite application of increasing fear of the unknown. For millions of non-human creatures living everywhere all around our planet, not even one of them comprehends the psychological fear that we do in the "civilized" world. Nor has the bushman's fear level increased one miniscule amount that lives in Australia, South America, Africa or many other remote on our planet. He knows nothing of the fear assigned to yellow, orange, or red by the controllers.

Early in the last century there was Pavlov who learned how to train dogs. It was an early form of mind control. They stood on a grid of wires in a cage, and when a bell rang the dog also received an electric shock. This painful affliction made them foam at the mouth. He later discovered no shock was required for this reaction-simply ringing the bell would achieve the same affect. It was in that era that serious control of human beings began.

We have all heard of the man who coming from a war zone, hits the dirt when he hears a passing car back-fire thinking it is a mortar round. It is an extreme form of conditioning, which is the result of a repeating traumatic experience. Not unlike April 15th for most Americans. Do we as a part of the civilized societies, have an increased and conditioned fear not unlike Pavlov's dogs? Fear is only a state of mind, an intangible. Yet if left unchecked it can cripple anyone. We should be living each day to have joy, not fear.

History repeatedly demonstrates that governments use fear to control people. In the dark ages, it was an axe on the neck. Later other instruments of death were invented and used, to instill fear to the very core of the populace. Punishment is not about punishing someone for a crime, because the reality is that no punishment can undo any crime no matter how serious or minor. It is more about making example out of them to deter others.

A resent documentary-like movie came out that showed a highly trusted, fanatically patriotic U.S. federal agent sold secrets to the Soviets. He did more damage to the government than any other spy before him. In the end, the man could have easily been executed for what he did. At least two deep cover U.S. agents in the former USSR were shot because of this information. Yet this man was given a life sentence at a Colorado "Super-Max" prison, where he spends 23 out of 24 hours a day in solitary.

Does this punishment undo anything he has done? Will it bring back the dead? No. Punishing this man accomplishes nothing, except to make his remaining life miserable. He was punished this way to be an EXAMPLE to other U.S. agents everywhere. Simply executing him would have created a fleeting memory. With his life sentence in solitary, being highly publicized, government agents everywhere will never forget his punishment is still on-going. Imprisonment functions more as a deterrent to others who might consider doing a crime to society. And this man's punishment also instills fear in the populace, in a clever and indirect way. What about the "Super-Max" prison? It's an institution intended for the most dangerous, violent people and has a purposely bad reputation. A non-violent person sent to one of these places sends a clear message.

Not really about Prisons-the very name conjures up steel doors without doorknobs, bad odors from the cells, forced sex and unsavory people who have wronged society. A truly brutal, physical place unfit even for human beings. These places are called "correctional institutions," But, the rate of return for inmates is incredibly high. Much like being in the army, men and women can become acclimated to prison life. And no longer fear it. If they learn something there (or were truly changed in a positive way by the experience) they would never return. Statistics prove these places don't correct anything, but just make people worse. There are a few institutions that have attempted to change this.

We have bushmen, birds, and animals and all creeping, swimming, walking creatures upon the face of the earth. And there are the prisons. The bottom line is that these institutions of lower learning are, built for those who interfere with the working society in one way or another. It is someone harming someone else. Living on Earth, you just cannot pull the cord on the bus to get off at the next stop then things get unpleasant. Life is a giant version of living in a deep-sea underwater habitat without a scuba suit-you cannot go outside and live and likewise you can't escape the Earth. Even orbiting astronauts have sooner or later.

There are the animals and bushmen, and there is us. We are raised from infancy to "fit in." (Pre-school starts the process of socialization. Then on to public school, saying the pledge allegiance to the flag every day. You believed every word the teachers taught you because you've been previously taught to trust them.) You must go to college, get a good job, get married and you too, can become an upstanding member of society. And above all, never break any rules. You can even be President one day if you want too. These are the principles to living a happy life, or so we are taught by our well-meaning teachers and parents. Usually, they have no idea what they are doing.

But wait-where is the gilded cage? You are standing in it! Can you see the bars? They are separating those that lead the masses, from the masses. The invisible bars of the gilded cage have only as much strength as you give them, yet the ends of these bars held by invisible concrete you make. This invisible concrete is formed solely from the precepts and perceptions you have because of your life-long learning and training process. When you were very young you weren't inside the cage you built. But your parents and peers already in a cage have unwittingly helped you mix up and pour those invisible concrete foundations.

Is there paint for this, for this concrete and bars, that when applied will help increase its strength? It's called fear. In places like the UK, the government has turned fear into a science and methodology, using it to increase government grip on their populace daily. Supposedly this is all about protecting them from terror. Yet that's not the purpose. When a terror attack took place in their subways, the world was told that more than a dozen cameras weren't working that day. The fact alone speaks volumes.

Millions of people all over the world have witnessed the construction in the UK of a new cage built inside the bigger, gilded cage. The British people inside their inner cage cannot see what has happened to them, because they are too busy mixing their own individual batches of concrete to hold their own sets of bars. People in China and North Korea finished mixing their concrete a very long time ago.

Millions of people outside the UK today are pointing, laughing and proclaim, "that madness won't ever happen in MY country!" Oh, how wrong they are. That invisible concrete is everywhere and will only begin to crumble when people everywhere began to wake up and realize the construction is taking place. The cage begins as a virtual construct, like a brick wall inside a video game. But, all of us must recognize the cage itself is based on fabricated fear and spread the word to others. Take time to touch someone else each day even if you live alone, or touch a plant, flower or a tree every morning. Be not afraid to marvel at all you see and feel. This is just one of the steps in making the invisible concrete to blow away, and with it the bars will fall. Governments never want the people to overcome their fears. Cages are not built overnight, but just by one bar at a time. And who is exempt from residence in the big and beautiful cage? The simple bushman is because he never learned how to mix concrete.

By: Ted Twietmeyer
February 21st 2007
(www.rense.com)
(www.data4science.net)

Authors note: The purpose of a cage is not so much in keeping something out, as much as it is to keep something in! Cages come in many forms, spiritually, mentally, and physically. You can create your own cage, or you enemies can create one for you.

DIVERSE CONFEDERACY

The myths exist that the Confederate Army was a sea of lily-White Protestant faces with and occasional Black "body servant." The truth is something far different. The Confederate Army had more than 10,000 Native American soldiers from more than two-dozen tribes, including Cherokee Brigadier General Stand Watie. There were more than 5,000 Hispanic Confederates and some, like Col. Ambrosio Ganzales and Loretta Velazquez, even came from Cuba. Nearly 3,500 Jewish Confederates lent their service and were among the last to die for the South.

Foreigners from many countries served as Officers and enlisted men, including Filipino solders out of New Orleans. The 19th Louisiana infantry was known as "Lee's Foreign Legion" and there was all-Polish cavalry united. According to the federal census reports in 1860, four million Blacks lived in the Southern States at the outbreak of the war and 261,988 were free men.

The great majority of these Blacks remained in the South during the war and supported the Confederacy by growing food and making war supplies. Black Southerners slave and free, were servants, clerks, hospital orderlies, wagon drivers, and engineer labor forces, but were also Chaplains, scouts, foragers, combat soldiers and feared sharpshooters.

Records have been deliberately altered and facts suppressed by the Federal government but estimates of Black Confederates on the battlefield range from 10,000-50,000. They served willingly and they died in Union P.O.W camps rather than take the Union Oath of Loyalty. Together with Southerners descended from waves of Irish, Scottish, and German immigrants, the Confederate Army stood as a group of men whose only qualification was, "Will you fight?"

(www.dixieoutfitters.com)

✦ ✦ ✦

WHAT WAS ROLE OF BLACK SOUTHERN IN CIVIL WAR?

Atlanta (AP)—like other members of the Sons of Confederate Veterans, Emerson Emory says he wants to preserve his Southern heritage. His mission, however, is especially challenging—and controversial. The 74-year-old Dallas psychiatrist is Black, and his insistence that many Black Southerners not only supported the Confederacy but fought for it in the Civil War often draws reactions ranging from skepticism to outrage.

"Most of the reaction was among friends in the Black Race-they couldn't understand," Emory said, "I think it's one of those things that they don't want to hear anything about." While recognition of the role Black soldiers played for the Union, dramatized in the movie "Glory," has grown in the past decade, there remains little recognition-or even acknowledgment-of Black Confederates. There is sharp debate about their numbers, if any, and why they would have supported the South.

Summer in his request to pay tribute to Black Confederates at ceremonies in Washington that honored nearly (200,000 Black soldiers) who fought in the Civil War. The African American Civil War Foundation's historian wrote that the memorial was dedicated to the troops who fought to end slavery and expressed Emory, a World War II veteran, was turned down last doubt that Black men served the Confederate Army.

Civil rights leaders also criticized the teachers of a class last fall at Randolph Community College in North Carolina. The teachers-Sons of Confederate Veterans members like Emory-contended that some slaves were loyal to the South. Charles Kelly Barrow, a Zebulon, Ga., high school teacher who is White, has spent years researching Blacks in the Confederacy. Besides many disbelieving Blacks, he said, there are also Whites who don't want to admit that Blacks fought for the South. "They're in opposition either way. Certain people have always tried to divide White and Black Southerners," Barrow's 1995 book, "Forgotten Confederates," as an anthology that draws upon wartime newspaper accounts, later accounts of Civil War reunions, essays, obituaries and pension records to offer evidence of Blacks serving the Confederacy.

Some Southern heritage buffs estimate their numbers at anywhere from 38,000 to 90,000men, mainly serving as laborers, Teamsters, Musicians and Cooks. As early as 1863, Confederate Maj. Gen Patrick Cleburne urged that Blacks be enlisted as soldiers. There was opposition from Confederates who questioned whether men serving as soldiers cold be returned to slavery after the war and who would work the region's farms if slaves were taken away.

[In March 1865, the Confederate Congress authorized Black soldiers, but there's little indication that any-Black Confederate unites went to war. However, there are accounts that, from the wars beginning, Blacks in gray sometimes were armed in battle.]

-Nation-The Salisbury Post, Sunday, February 21, 1999-3A-North Carolina**********

✦ ✦ ✦

AMOS RUCKER-BLACK CONFEDERATE

According to our papers, this person and last year's subject, Bill Yopp, do not officially exist. Since the WBTS officially believed that the South had fought for slavery and not freedom, slaves and free blacks fighting for the Confederacy do not officially exist, yet some 5000 have been identified in Texas and Arkansas alone. Herewith another forgotten Confederate, Amos Rucker:

Amos Rucker was born in Elbert County, Georgia, a slave of Col. Sandy Rucker, of the 33rd Georgia Infantry. Amos went to war with his young master, a body servant at first showing prowess in the procurement of needed supplies when no one else could. There was always a chicken cooking on Col. Rucker's campfire no matter how scant the provisions were.

Amos was not to remain a body servant, however, as he would soon find himself in the thick of battle. He was found to be a brave soldier when he picked up the weapon of a dead member of his unit and charged the enemy line. He exhibited such bravery that he was to perform as a combat soldier for the remainder of the war.

He was attached to the staff of General Patrick Cleburne and became the servant of General Cleburne's first cousin, D.C.J. Cleburne. It was the duty of Amos to call the roll after each battle and he committed to memory the entire company.

But Amos was not merely a roll-caller. Before the surrender he received a severe wound to his left breast and a leg wound left him permanently crippled. After the war Amos joined the W.H.T Walker Camp, UCV, of Atlanta. On the second Monday of each month he would always be found at the meetings at 102 Forsyth Street an Atlanta and was always proud to sow his excellent memory by reciting name of every member of his old Company from A to Z. It is said that he would solemnly add "here" or "dead" after each name.

★ GOD SAVE THE SOUTH ★

Amos always said that "My folks gave me everything I want." It is true. The members of the Camp provided well for Amos even helping him acquire a house on the West Side of Atlanta. His attorney for the real estate transaction and later for the settlement of his care of his dear wife Martha, was one John M. Slaton, a member of the John B. Gordon Camp, SCV, and later Governor of Georgia. Old Amos was such a fixture at meetings that he never missed one until just before his death when he sent a message to the members: "Give my love to the boys."

His death brought universal sorrow to Atlanta. His body lay in state while hundreds of Atlantans representing many of the best families of the city, silently paid their respects. The members of Camp Walker paid all funeral expenses and bought a plot for him and his wife at Southview Cemetery, the famous black cemetery.

Funeral services were conducted by Confederate General and UCV Commander-in-Chief Clement A. Evans of Atlanta. His pallbearers were Governor Allen D. Candler, General A.J. West, Mayor William Lowndes Calhoun, Ex-Postmaster Amos Fox, and Camp Walker Commander F.A. Hilburn, J. Sid Holland, and R.S. Osbourne, Confederate veterans all. An article in the Confederate Veteran in 1909 related the sadness: "Very tenderly they carried the old veteran to his grave, clothed in his uniform of gray and wrapped in a Confederate flag, a grave made beautiful by flowers from comrades and friends, among which a large design from the Daughters of the Confederacy was conspicuous in its red and white."

The Rev. Dr. T.P. Cleveland led the prayer and several of Amos 'favorite songs were sung.' Just before the casket was lowered into the grave, Capt. Tip Harrison recited the poem, "When Rucker Called the Roll." The newspapers noted that Amos "had a firm and abiding faith in the integrity and righteous dealing of the Southern White friends.

To him the Confederate Veterans was the highest type of American manhood, and for him he was ready to give service unto death at almost any time. Although he has gone, he will not be soon forgotten, for he was friend of every son of a Confederate Veterans as well as the Confederates themselves." This article is taken from a speech given by CSV Spokesman P. Charles Lunsford several years ago, which information was gratefully given to your editor.

★ ★ ★
CONFEDERATE NATIONAL CREST

The confederate national crest is a dedication to all of the confederate Americans of the past, future, and of the present, regardless of race or sex. it is a reminder to our people of the fact that we are confederate Americans. the words "deo volente" are Latin for "if god is willing"; and psalm 91 is a scripture that every Christian confederate American should come to embrace in their hearts. The confederate national crest is not the creation of the confederate states' government or of its member states. May we always be humble and put the will of god first, trusting him to protect us.

Amen

By: John Thomas Nall

THE PRESIDENT AND THE CONSTITUTION

The former U.S. President Abraham Lincoln had stated in his Emancipation of Proclamation, that all the slaves that are in the Confederacy which was not under his control are now free. And that the slaves under Union control are not free. So, let us take a closer look at this! If the Confederate States were, indeed, not a nation, and could not ever leave the Union, than that would mean that the Southern States would still be under the law of the Constitution of the United States! And it would also mean that the President could not violate his country's Constitution and end slavery in the South! But this would also mean that the President could not end slavery in the North either!

Now! The President cannot end slavery in the South without the occupation of his Nations military, nor could he not end the institution of slavery within his own borders. Only Congress can withdraw such a law and be able to establish another way to maintain the economy. The Lincoln's speech had been nothing more than a propaganda tool, a [Ghost Letter]. Why? Because he had no legal authority to be put into effect. It was a weapon of deception, a sociological warfare. In order to cause an uprising, the Southern slaves in hope it would start a race riot. And even though Lincoln was a tyrant! He was a very intelligent one. He also wanted to stop other nations that we're giving aid to the Confederacy by denouncing slavery.

Adolf Hitler, during World War II used a similar method against France. And his army had walked right in without firing a shot. His Nazi Air Force had flooded the French skies with flyers of Nostradamas predictions of France, in surrendering to Germany. And that is exactly just what they did!

By: John Thomas Nall

CHAPTER THREE

★ JOHN THOMAS NALL ★

WANTED

DEAD OR ALIVE!
W. T. SHERMAN

FOR

WAR CRIMES

AGAINST THE SOUTHERN PEOPLE

★ ★ ★

A PRAYER OF DECLARATION OF RIGHTS

Be as it's written that I _____, am a child of Christ. That I am an heir with Christ. That I have become of royalty, through the blood of Christ. That all of the blessings that are written in your Holy Book belong to your children in Christ. I also proclaim these rights belonging to me! And for every time that you would close a door in my life, that you shall also open another door for me, and that you will guide me through it.

That you have taken care of all my needs and concerns. That you have fulfilled them all according to your words. I hold you to your Holy Words that are written within these pages of your Holy Bible. That I shall also receive all your blessings that are in stored for me, and so, I have put within your hands, all of my hopes and dreams, including the destiny and purpose of my life into your hands. I proclaim all your Holy Words to be true. In the name of my Lord Jesus Christ, Amen. By: John Thomas Nall 29th /Nov/05

★ ★ ★
THE GREAT NATIONAL SEAL OF THE CONFEDERATE STATES OF AMERICA

Deo Vindice
"God Will Vindicate"

One of its The Great Seal of the Confederacy was engraved in 1864, by the late Joseph S. Wyon, of London, England, predecessor of Messrs J. S. and A.B. Wyon, chief engravers of Her Majesty's Seals, and reached the Confederate States Capitol of Richmond Virginia, not long before the evacuation of the city, April 3rd, 1863. It was of silver, and in diameter measured nearly four inches. At the evacuation it was overlook by the Confederate authorities, and subsequently fell into the passion of the late genial and accomplished Colonel John T. Pickett, of Washington, D. C., who, after having several electrotype copies in copper, silver and gold plating made from it, presented the original to Colonel William E. Earle, of Washington, D.C. This last gentleman on December 27th, 1888 formally presented it to the State of South Carolina. The announcement of the gift elicited from the Picayune, in its issue of January 6th, 1889, the interesting report Representatives, held with Hon. Thomas J. Semmes, of New Orleans, which follows:

Mr. Semmes said it always afforded him pleasure to converse on the events of the war, particularly the transactions of the Confederate Senate. He was attorney-general of Louisiana in 1861. When it becomes necessary to elect to the Confederate Senate, organized under the New Constitution, Mr. Semmes and General Edward T. Sparrow were chosen senators from this State. In drawing for terms he drew that for four years, while General Sparrow drew that for six years. This was at Richmond, Va., February, 1862.

In speaking of his services in the Senate, Mr. Semmes said he was appointed a member of the finance committee in conjunction with Hon. R.M.T. Hunter, of Virginia, and Hon. Robert Barnwell, of South Carolina and a member of the judiciary committee, of which Hon. B.H. Hill was chairman. He was also chairman of joint committee on the Flag and Seal of the Confederate States. He drafted under the direction of Hon. R.M.T. Hunter, the (tax) in kind bill, which practically supported the Confederacy during the last two years of the war.

As a member of the finance committee, he advocated the sealing and calling in of the outstanding Confederate currency, on the ground that the purchasing power of the new currency to be issued in exchange would be greater than the total amount of the outstanding currency in its then depreciated condition. He made a report from the judiciary committee adverse to martial law.

Upon being questioned as to the seal he had questioned as to the seal he has designed, Mr. Semmes said it was a device representing an equestrian portrait of Washington after the statue which surmounts his monument in the Capital square at Richmond surrounded with a wreath, composed of the principal agricultural products of the Confederacy, and having around its margin the words; Confederate States of America, 22nd February 1862, with the motto; "Deo Vindice."

In the latter part of April-1864, quite an interesting debate was held on the adoption of the motto. The House resolutions fixing the motto; as "Deo Duce Vincemus," being considered, Mr. Semmes moved to substitute "Deo Vindice majores aemulamur." The motto had been suggested by Professor Alexander Dimitry. Mr. Semmes thought "Deo Vindice" sufficient and preferred it. He was finally triumphant.

In this connection it is appropriate and interesting to reproduce the speech made by Mr. Semmes on that occasion. It was fallows; Mr. President—"I am instructed by the Committee to move to strike out the words "duce Vincemus" in the motto and insert in lieu thereof the words "Vindice majores aemulamur", under the guidance and protection of God we endeavor to equal even excel our ancestors." "Before discussing the proposed change in the motto, I will submit to the Senate a few remarks as to the device on the Seal."

The Committee has been greatly exercised on this subject, and it has been extremely difficult to come to any satisfactory conclusion. This is a difficulty, however, incident to the subject, and all to the subject, and all that we have to do is to avoid what Visconti calls 'an absurdity in bronze.

"The equestrian statue of Washington has been selected in deference to the current popular sentiment. The equestrian figure impressed on our Seal will be regarded by those skilled in glyptic as to a certain extent indicative of our origin. It is a most remarkable fact that an equestrian figure constituted the Seal of Great Britain from the time of Edward the Confessor down to the reign of George III, except during the short interval of the protectorate of Cromwell, when the trial of the King was substituted for the man on horseback. Even Cromwell retained the equestrian on the Seal of Scotland, but he characteristically mounted himself on the horse. In the reign of William and Mary the Seal bore the impress of the King and Queen both mounted on horseback.

Washington has been selected as the emblem for our shield, as a type of our ancestors, in his character of "princeps majorum," In addition to this; the equestrian figure is consecrated in the hearts of our people by the local circumstance that on the gloomy and stormy 22nd February 1862, our permanent government was set in motion by inauguration of President Davis under the shadow of the Statue of Washington. "The Committee is dissatisfied with the motto on the Seal proposed by the House Resolution. The motto proposed is as follows; "Deo Duce Vincemus"—(Under the leadership of God we will conquer.)

The word "duce" is too pagan in its signification, and is degrading to God, because it reduces him to the leader of an army; for scarcely does the word "duce" escape the lips before the imagination suggests "exercitus," an army for a leader to command. It degrades the Christian God to the level of pagan gods, goddesses and heroes, as manifest from the following quotation; "Nil desperandum Tenero duce." This word duce is particularly objectionable because of its connection with the word "Vincemus"—(we will conquer.) This connection makes God the leader of a physical army, by means of which we will conquer, or must conquer.

If God be our leader, we must conquer, or He would not be the God of Abraham, and Isaac, and Jacob, nor the God of the Christians. This very doubt implied in the word "Vincemus" so qualifies the omnipotence of the God to be our leader, that it imparts a degrading signification to the word; "duce" in its relations to the attributes of the Deity. The word; "Vincemus" is equally objectionable because it implies that war is to be our normal state; besides, it is in the future tense—"we will conquer." The future is always uncertain, and therefore it implies doubt. What becomes of our motto when we shall have conquered? The future becomes an accomplished fact, and our motto thus loses its significance.

In addition to this there are only two languages in which th words will and shall are to be found—the English and the German—and they are used to qualify a positive condition of the mind and render it uncertain; they are repugnant to repose, quit, absolute and positive existence. As to the motto proposed by us, we conquer with the House in accepting the word; "Deo"—God. We do so in conformity to the expressed wishes of the framers of our Constitution, and the sentiments of the people and of the army. The preamble of the Provisional Constitution declares that "We, the deputies of the sovereign and independent States of South Carolina, etc., invoking the favor and guidance of Almighty God, do ordain, etc."

In this respect both our Constitutions have deviated in the emphatic manner from the spirit that presided over the construction of the Constitution of the United States, which is silent about the Deity. Having discarded the word "duce," the committee endeavored to select in lieu of it a word more in consonance with the attributes of the Deity, and therefore more imposing and significant. They think success has crowned in the selection of the word "Vindex," which signifies an assenter, a defender, Protector, deliverer, liberator, a mediator and a ruler or guardian. "Vindex" also means an avenger or punisher.

No word appeared more grand, more expressive, or significant than this. Under God as the asserter of our rights, the defender of our liberties, our protector against danger, our mediator, our ruler, and guardian, and as the avenger of our wrongs and punisher of our crimes, we endeavor to equal or even excel our ancestors. What word can be suggested of more power, and so replete with sentiments and thoughts consonant with our idea of the omnipotence and justice of God?

(At this point the committee hesitated whether it was necessary to add anything further to the motto; "Deo Vindice." These words alone were sufficient and impressive, and, in the spirit of the lapidary style of composition, were elliptical and left much to the play of the imagination. Reflection, however, induced us to add the words; "majores aemulamur," because without them there would be nothing in the motto referring to the equestrian figure of Washington. It was thought better to insert something elucidative or adaptive of the idea to be conveyed by that figure. Having determined on this point, the committee submitted to the judgment of the Senate the words; "majores aemulamur," as best adapted to express the ideas of (our ancestors.) "Patres" was first suggested, but abandoned because "majores" signifies ancestors absolutely, and is also more suggestive than "Patres."

The latter is a term applied to our immediate progenitors who may be alive, whereas (majores) conveys the idea of a more remote generation that has died. That being disposed of the question as to the proper signification of the word; "aemulamur," Honorable emulation is the primary signification of the word, in its secondary sense it is true it includes the idea of improper rivalry, or jealousy. But it is used in its primary and honorable sense by the most approved authors.

The secondary and improper sense of the aemulari is excluded in the proposed motto by the relation it bears to "Deo Vindice." This relation excludes the idea of envy or jealousy because God, as the asserter of what is right, justifies the emulation, and as a punisher of what is wrong checks excess in case the emulation runs into improper envy or jealousy. In adopting the equestrian figure of Washington, the committee desires distinctly to disavow any recognition of the embodiment of the idea of the (cavalier.) We have no admiration for the character of the cavalier of 1640 any more than for his opponent, the Puritan. We turn with disgust from the violent and licentious cavalier, and we abhor the acerb, morose, and fanatic Puritan, of whom Oliver Cromwell was the type.

In speaking of Cromwell and his character, Guizot says that (he possessed the faculty of lying at need with an inexhaustible and unhesitating hardihood which struck even his enemies with surprise and embarrassment.) This characteristic seems to have been transmitted to the descendants of the pilgrims who settled in Massachusetts Bay to enjoy the liberty of persecution. If the cavalier is to carry us back to days earlier than the American Revolution, I prefer to be transported in imagination to the field of Runnymede, when the barons extorted Magna Charta from the unwilling John.

But I discard all reference to the cavalier of old, because it implies a division of society into two orders, an idea inconsistent with (Confederate Institutions.) Mr. Semmes moved to amend by substituting "Vindice" for "Duce" and it was agreed to. In taking his leave, the reporter was informed by Mr. Semmes that he did not know the seal was in existence and was glad to learn that it had been presented the State of South Carolina, the first State which seceded from the Union.Source: Southern Historical Society Papers. Vol. XVI. Richmond Virginia. January-December 1888. (Authors Comment: Unfortunately, the Confederate States government had dispersed before using the Seal on any government documents due to the invasion & occupation by the United States of America.

THE THIRD NATIONAL FLAG OF THE CONFEDERATE STATES OF AMERICA

The Third and final National Flag of our (Constitutional Nation of the Republic,) was created by an Act of the Congress of the Confederate States (Second Congress, Session II,) and approved by the C.S. President on the 4th day of March of 1865, four years to the day after the first raising of our First National Flag (The Stars and Bars) in Montgomery, Alabama.

The Flag Act of 1861 of the flag in the following language: The Congress of the Confederate States of America, do enact that the flag of the Confederate States shall be as follows. [The width two-thirds of its length, with the union 'now used as the battle flag' to be in width-fifths of the flag, and so proportioned as to leave the length of the field on the side of the union twice the width of the field below, to have the ground red and a broad blue saltier thereon, bordered with white and emblazoned with mullets or five pointed stars, corresponding in number to that of the Confederate States : the field to be white, except the outer half from the union to be red bar extending the width of the flag.]

Authors Comments: The Third National Flag of the Confederate States of America is still the Constitutional & Legal National Flag of the Confederacy. Despite the known fact that the occupied Confederacy is part of the American (U.S.) Empire.

∗ ∗ ∗
DO YOU SING PRAISES FOR LINCOLN?

To my fellow Southern Compatriots, do you praise Abe Lincoln? Do you express shame for the secession of the Southern States? Do you brag about the gallant and noble cause of the Yankee invaders? Of course not! Then why do so many repeat the (Yankee lie) about Kentucky? On most (Southern) websites and many (Southern books,) the (Yankee lie) is repeated. Most of them, if they say anything at all about Kentucky and, secession, say that (Kentucky never officially seceded) … that simply is not true!

Kentucky had declared itself a neutral State; however, if neutrality was broken, the State would pledge to become part of the Confederacy. When Lincoln requested 75.000 men to serve in the Union army, Kentucky Governor Beriah Magoffin, a Southerner sympathizer, refused to comply and stated that Kentucky would … Furnish no troops for the wicked purpose of subduing her sister Southern States.

As a matter of fact, the people of western Kentucky (along with Western Tennessee) were very impatient about secession. Representatives from the counties in the Jackson purchase region of Western Kentucky and Tennessee met in my hometown of Mayfield, Kentucky to discuss the creation of a new (State of Jackson,) to be formed from portions of Tennessee and Kentucky. This plan was scrapped after Tennessee had seceded.

The people of Kentucky had to go to more trouble to secede than any other State in Dixie! The Legislature of Kentucky turned coward and went on their promise to the people, they voted against secession. The people were outraged at their turncoats (Representatives,) wouldn't let it stand.

The Kentuckians decided that since their legislature violated their solemn promise to seceded, they were left no option but to follow the course of their (Colonial Forefathers,) when they seceded from England. They held a convention of the people, Kentucky presiding over this convention was Henry C. Burnett, a U.S. Congressman from the Western District.

Mr. Burnett with a total of one hundred & sixteen Representatives from 68 of the 110 counties in the State (that's nearly 2/3 of the remaining 42 counties were represented by letters or (proxies) expressing a desire to secede) unanimously voted for secession, when you add in the (proxy) votes from the letters of the other 42 counties ... That's 100 %! They went on to elect George W. Johnson as the provisional Confederate Governor, and to establish Mr. Bowling Green as the State Capital. Governor Johnson was killed in the battle of Shiloh, and Richard Hawes became his replacement.

Henry C. Burnett went on to become one of Kentucky's Representatives to the Confederates States Congress. These were not self-appointed no bodies; they were Representatives, leaders from the various counties and communities from across the State. That is a far cry from the: (official myth), that Kentucky was split on the issue. Of course, there were certain individuals that opposed secession, as there were in every Southern State. But, the (Lion's share) of Kentucky firmly favored and supported the Confederacy, and her noble cause.

The (official myth) says that most of Kentucky leaned toward the (Union) ... an absolute lie! The (official myth) says Kentucky didn't (officially secede) ... another lie! Now friends, if Kentucky's secession wasn't (official), then neither was the Declaration of Independence, for you see, that wasn't passed through the normal channels of the (established government) either. Besides, according to the worshippers of Lincoln, none of the States legitimately seceded ... Which any serious student of history knows is a lie! The (official history), since the time of (Dis-honest-Abe,) has been a series of (official lies) ... just as it remains today. With the (Politically Correct) headlines, this will become tomorrow's (history.)

Please, do not act as a mouthpiece for the (Yankee lie.) Correct any misrepresentation that you might have published anywhere. The truth has always been an enemy of the Empire and an ally of Dixie! Let's put it out there and quit aiding the enemy, by repeating their lies and advancing their cause. **God Bless Dixie!**

By; Joe Gresham—July-2004.

All rights reserved. Permission to redistribute or republish in its full and complete form, is granted provided credit is given, and email and website address are included.

Joe Gresham
(*Dixiecrat@hotmail.com*)
Chairman of the Southern Independence Party of Kentucky
(*www.kentuckysip.homestead.com*)

* * *

JEFFERSON DAVIS: OUR GREATEST HERO

During and after the war for Southern Independence, Jefferson Davis was accused of a variety of villainies. Not all his accusers were Yankees, but Northerners made the most extensive and lasting attacks upon Davis. In one of these insults-a letters embossed with an American eagle crushing (Secession) and holding proudly in its beak, a U.S. banner announcing (Death to Traitors)—a New Yorker wrote, "Jeff Davis, you rebel traitor here is the beauty of America. One of the greatest treasures that ever waved over your sinful head.

Now, I will not you to look at this motto and think of me for-say death to Secession [sic] and death to all traitors to their country and these are my sentiments exactly. Yours not with respect for I can never respect a traitor to his country, a cursed traitor." The same view of Davis as being among the arch traitors in our annuals was expressed just as emphatically years later by Theodore Roosevelt and Harvard Professor Albert T. Perkins.

Davis became, and remained to Northerners, the quintessential wrongdoer. Later generations of liberal progressives would consider him an American Hitler. Immediately after the War for Southern Independence, Yankee authorities put Davis in jail and left him there for (two years without a trail.) While they tried to implicate him in the assassination of Lincoln, alleged cruelty to Federal prisoners, and treason itself. Though never brought to trial or convicted of any crime, Davis received abundant abuse in the Yankee press and on the podium. During and after the war, the New York Times depicted him as a murderer, a cruel slave-owner whose servants ran away, a liar, a boaster, a fanatic, a confessed failure, a hater, a political adventurer, a supporter of outcast and outlaws, a drunkard, an atrocious misrepresented, an assassin, an incendiary, a criminal who was gratified by the assignation of Lincoln, a henpecked husband, a man so shameless that he would try to escape capture by disguising himself as a woman, a supporter of murder plots, an insubordinate soldier, an unwholesome sleeper, and a mean-spirited malingerer.

★ GOD SAVE THE SOUTH ★

Anti-Davis sentiment was more than mere newspaper talk. Following the war, the citizens of Sacramento, California was true to their vigilante tradition, hang Davis in effigy. A few months later the Kansas Senate passed a resolution to hang him in person. More than ten years after the war ended, widespread opposition prevented him from speaking anywhere in the North. In 1876 a Yankee newspaper editor answered the question, should Davis be given amnesty, with a resounding (NO), and in 1880 a man cheered for Jefferson Davis in Madison, Indiana, was shot!

"Malice and slander have exhausted their power against you," a Southerner tried to assure the continually criticized the Confederate States President. At the end of the Nineteenth Century an observer noted: "I believe there never was a time when a whole people were more willing to punish one man than the people of the North to punish Mr. Davis, for alleged crimes." Twenty years after Davis's death, handbills accusing him in Lincoln's assassination still circulated, and the New York Times published an editorial, denouncing plans for a Southerner to donate for use on the new battleship Mississippi a silver service with the likeness of Jefferson Davis etched on each piece.

More than a hundred years had passed before the Congress of the United States officially forgave Davis, for being the President of the Confederacy. No other Confederate leader had to wait so long for either official or unofficial exoneration. By the early 1900s, Robert E. Lee, the greatest Yankee killer of all time, had become a national hero, absolved of his sins, and soon considered so harmless that the government allowed his picture to be hung on the walls of Southern (public schools) alongside those of Washington and Lincoln.

When I was young, several Southern schools were named in honor of Jefferson Davis, but since then most, if not all of those have been forced to change their names to dishonor the Confederate States President. Such efforts to disgrace him bothered even Southerners who were never his (friend.) "I never believed he was a very great man, or even the best President the Confederate States might have had," wrote, John S. Wise. "But he was our President." Whatever shortcomings he may have had, he was a brave, conscientious and loyal son of the South. He did his best, to the utmost of his ability, for the Southern Cause. He without being a whit worse than the rest of us was made to suffer for us as was no other man in the Confederacy. And through it all he never, to the day of his death, failed to maintain the honor and the dignity of the trust confided to his keeping.

It distresses me to this day," admitted Wise, "Whenever I hear anybody speak disparagingly of this man, who was unquestionably devoted to the (Cause) for which he lived and died, and who was infinitely greater than his traducers." Davis knew how much he was maligned. He rejected an invitation to visit the North in 1875, explaining 'the tide of unreasoning prejudice against me, in your section, was too strong to be resisted." "Demagogues, who know better, have found it easier to inflame and keep alive the passion of the war by personifying the idea [that] I instigated and precipitated it."

Yankee's had even stronger reasons for damning Davis. He was, after all, a wholehearted supporter of those symbols of Southern wickedness that the Union military might had discredited-Slavery, States Rights, and Secession. Davis had defended slavery, described the federal government as having 'no inherent power, all of it possesses by the States,' and he was emphatic on the legitimacy and necessity of secession.

"The temper of the Black Republicans is not to give us our rights in the Union, or allow us to go peaceably out of it," he declared in January of 1861. "If we had no other cause, this would be enough to justify secession, at whatever hazard." A few days later he reported to his old friend, President Franklin Pierce: "Mississippi, not as a matter of choice but of necessity, has resolved to enter on the trail of secession. Those who have driven her to this alternative to threaten her of the right to require that her government shall rest on the consent of the governed."

The invidious comparisons made between Davis and Lincoln during and after the war, by foreigners further embittered Northerners. For example, William Howard Russell's, published diary contained this unflattering contrast; "[Davis] is certainly a very different looking man from Mr. Lincoln. He is a gentleman." Or consider the remarks of Percy Greg whose (Tribute to Confederate Heroes) appeared in 1882. He praised Davis as having; "more moral and intellectual powers than any twenty Federal Statesmen's. And a man vastly superior in every way to the (rail-splitter) … whose term, had he died in his bed four or five years later, would have been remembered only as marking the nadir of American political decline; the culmination of vulgarity. Lincoln's uncleanness of language and thought", insisted Greg "would hardly have been tolerated in a Southern bar."

Perhaps even the contrast between the (gentlemanly) advocated by Davis and the comprehensive destruction practiced by such terrorizes of civilians as Sherman and Sheridan embarrassed some Yankees. Davis believed that war should be consisting solely of combat between organized armies. He abhorred the killing of civilians and the destruction of private property during hostilities. Years after the war, when General Grant was dying of cancer, Davis wrote; "I have felt a human sympathy with him in suffering, the more so because I think him so much better than the pillaging, house-burning, women persecuting Sherman and Sheridan." Judah P. Benjamin recalled that [when it was urged upon Jefferson Davis, not only by friends but by members of his Cabinet, that it was his duty to the people and to the army to repress outrages by retaliation, he was immovable in his resistance to such counsels, insisting that it was repugnant to every sentiment of justice and humanity that the innocent should be made victims for the crimes of such monsters."

Davis proudly proclaimed after the war; "I am happy to remember that when our army invaded the enemy's country, their property was safe." What made Davis so distinct and so utterly intolerable to most Yankees was his refusal to admit any guilt or apologize for his actions and the cause he led. He told the veterans of the Army of Tennessee who came to Mississippi to honor him in 1878: "Your organization was appropriate to preserve the memories and cherished brotherhoods of your soldier life, and cannot be objectionable to any, unless it be to one who holds your services to have been in an unworthy cause and your conduct such as called for repentance and forgiveness."

Davis reminded these old soldiers that they must maintain pride in their cause as well as in their soldierly conduct. "The veterans who shoulders his crutch to show how fields were won must not be ashamed of the battle in which he was wounded," "To higher natures success is not the only test of merit; and you, my friends, though you were finally unsuccessful, have the least possible cause to regret the flag under which you marched or the way you upheld it." Given this opportunity to explain his views to an understanding audience, Davis unburdened himself. "Every evil which has befallen our institutions is directly traceable to the perversion of compact of the Union and the usurpation by the Federal Government of undefeated powers." He contented.

"The events are too recent to require recapitulation, and the ruin they have wrought, the depravity they developed, require no other than the material and moral wreck which the country presents." Davis still believed in secession; "My faith in that right as an inherent attribute of State (Sovereignty), was adopted early in life, was confirmed by study and observation of later years, and had passed, unchanged and unshaken, through the severe ordeal to which it has been subjected." He could express such views, he told his listeners, because he had no "desire for a political future."

His only desire was to establish (the supremacy) of the truths on which the Union was founded." As for himself, he asserted, "I shall die, as I have lived, firm in the (States' Rights faith)." Throughout his remaining years, Davis reiterated these views in speeches, letters, and interviews. He told an appreciative audience of Southerners in 1882; "Our cause was so sacred, that had I known all that has come to pass, had I known all that was to be inflicted upon me, all that my country was to suffer, all that our posterity was to endure, I would do it all over again. [Then a great applause came from the audience.] A year earlier, Davis has written to a fellow Southerner; "Nothing fills me with deeper sadness than to see a Southern man apologizing for the defense we made of our inheritance & denying the great truths on which all our institutions were founded.

To be crushed by superior force, to be robbed & insulted, were great misfortunes, but these could be borne while there remained manhood to assert the truth, and a proud consciousness in the rectitude of our course. When I find myself reviled by Southern papers as one renewing (dead issues,) the pain is not caused by the attack upon myself, but by its desecration of the memories of our fathers and their sacred honor. To deny the justice of their cause, to apologize for its defense, and denounce it as a dead issue, is to take the last of their stakes, that for which they were willing to surrender the other.

A reporter who interviewed Mr. Davis a few years before he died discovered that the Confederate States President's heart [was] as warm as ever for the land he has loved so well and that Davis (did not desert during the war and has not deserted since.)

His steadfastness, his refusal to desert his cause, made Davis particularly obnoxious to his enemies. He was so unlike those Southerners who after the war disassociated themselves from their past as quickly as did certain Germans after World War II, and thus gained American forgiveness and patronage. Davis was just the opposite of his fellow Mississippian Confederate General James L. Alcorn, who announced shortly after the war; "You were right Yankee! We are and never have been out of the Union; secession was a nullity. We will now take the oath to support the Constitution and the laws of the United States." As proof of his sincerity, Alcorn became a Republican governor of Mississippi in 1869 and a Republican member of the U.S. Senate in 1871.

He also recouped his wartime financial loses and increased his property holdings. Good Yankees approved of such (enlightened) new Southerners as Alcorn, who were (eager to keep step with the North in the onward march of the Solid Nation), as one man expressed it; "They disapproved of Jefferson Davis and their newspapers castigated him as (unrepentant) and the greatest enemy of the South."

Davis still carries such encumbrances. Was he alive today, even the most skilled public relations firm would have difficulty packaging him for the market? He was too honest and too politically incorrect to be elected to public office, or even to have any future in higher education, that last refuge of scoundrels. Scarcely any university professor would want Davis as a colleague. He probably would be as unsuccessful today in business as he was after the war. I even doubt that he could have found employment as a radio talk-show host. He was too dignified and too proud to truckle.

Yankees would have liked nothing better than to recast Jefferson Davis as a repentant sinner asking for forgiveness, but he refused to accommodate them. Instead, he assumed the burden of the lost cause, becoming the symbolic defender of not just the Confederacy and the proud Southern tradition, but of its people, their culture, and what Yankees judge to be their unforgivable past.

Jefferson Davis is, and should be, our greatest hero! Like no other, he withstood criticism and denigration without kowtowing or wavering. Asking for no pardon, he refused to denounce his people or his cause. His image ought to be everywhere to remind us that for more than a hundred years he has symbolized our courage, our pride, and our unity. In 1882, a year after the publication of his two-volumes defense of himself and of the Confederate cause, Davis advocated what Yankees considered totally unforgivable-a history of the South, written by and for Southerners. "I would have our children's children to know not only that our cause was just," he told the members of the Southern Historical Society, "but to have them know that the men who sustained it were worthy of the cause for which they fought."

Davis, full of hope and passion, outlined in this remarkable address, just what he believed ought to be how it should be used. "It is our duty to keep the memory of our heroes green," he announced. "We want our side of the war so fully and exactly stated, that the men who come after us may compare and do [us] justice." Davis did not call for objectivity. "I will frankly acknowledge that I would distrust the men who served the Confederate cause and was capable of giving a disinterested account of it. [Again, with a second applause.] "I would not give two pence for a man whose heart was so cold that he could be quite impartial," admitted Davis.

"You may ask the schoolboy in the lowest form, who commanded at the Pass of Thermopylae. He can tell you, but my friends there are few in this audience who, if I ask them, could you tell me who commanded at Sabine Pass. And yet," said Davis, "that battle of Sabine Pass was more remarkable that the battle of Thermopylae, and when it has orators and poets to celebrate it, will be so esteemed by mankind.

His appeal for orators and poets to preserve the deeds of heroic Southerners reveals that Davis understood the South's heritage. Southerners, like their Celtic ancestors, were oral and aural people who perpetuated much of their past in stories and songs. Davis compared the Confederacy's military heroes with their Scottish forebears: "May it come not come to pass that in some hour of need, future generations, aware of the grandeur and virtues of these men will in a moment of disaster cry out the ancient Scot.

"O FOR AN HOUR OF WALLSCE WIGHT, OR WELL TRAINED BRUCE TO LEAD THE FIGHT, AND CRY ST. ANDREW AND OUR RIGHT."

History, Davis believed, must inspire those who learn it. "Let the rising generation learn what their fathers did," he implored, "and let them learn the still better lesson to emulate not only the deeds, but the motives which prompted them. May God grant that sons ever greater than their fathers may rise whenever their country needs them to defense her cause." [Applause.] The kind of history that Davis advocated was unacceptable to Yankees. First, it was incompatible with the so-called scientific history taught in German seminars and in the later nineteenth century being popularized in the United States by Yankee professors. As adapted for Americans, this history stressed the evolution of New England institutions and how they contributed to the greatness of the United States.

There was no place in such history for either the bard or the poet upon whom Davis relied to celebrate Southern values and heroes. Second, a history of the South that revered Southerners and their values rather than Northerners and their values would undermine all that the war had decided. To the victor went the power to write the history that justified the victory. It was that simple! British history is really history imposed upon the non-English peoples of the British Isles by their English conquerors! The same may be said of the history of the United States. What passes for standard American history is Yankee history written by New Englanders or their puppets to glorify Yankee ideals and heroes.

Students. Something should be done to enlighten them. In the twentieth century, Yankees gained increasing control over the historical journals, the university presses, the commercial publishing houses, and the production and distribution of professional historians; consequently, the Yankee version of the American past become the history most often taught in the colleges and in the public schools.

It is precisely this condition that Mississippian Dunbar Rowland first complained about eighty years ago. "It seems to be admitted on all sides that the people of the South are neglecting the teaching of Southern History in all our institutions," he informed the governor. That we are neglecting this important field of instruction is made evident by the astonishing amount of ignorance of Southern and State history among the rising generation of college

Part of the problem has been that the professors who taught the South's adopted the [New South] doctrine of national unity as readily as Southern Businessmen. North Carolina educator (Robert Bingham) announced in 1884 that "the blessing that ever befell us was a failure to establish a [Southern] nationalism." Bingham boasted that 'the past of the South is irrevocable, and we do not wish to recall it. The past of the South is irreparable, and we do not wish to repair it." Yet, this teaching of Yankee ideas and biases in Southern public schools, which Francis Butler Simkins labeled, "the education that does not educate," often has been offset "by the survival of overwhelming traditions." Robert Warren testified that his sympathetic view of Confederate history was obtained not from schoolroom, but rather "from the air around me."

If today the South's air is still full of Confederate history, the bookshelves are not. Yankees now control the writing, publishing, and marketing of most books on the South's history and culture. Yankee professors and Southerners who think like Yankees have taken over most Southern colleges and universities. Southerners who believe in the traditions that Jefferson Davis appreciated are finding themselves unemployable, denied careers in higher education by national forces that systematically discriminate against them. Only Yankees and Scalawags who truckle to the enemies of Southern history and culture get important jobs where they could train college teachers. Most Southerners are relegated to academic Siberia where they receive low pay, scant research opportunities, and rarely see gifted students.

Something not yet fully understood, but that could destroy our culture, has occurred during the more than forty years that I have been a college professor. Discrimination against Southerners has always existed, but today in education it is rampant, trying to find jobs for young Southerners is difficult in a market that favors political correctness and disdains Southerner. No university, not even one in the South, wants to hire a native son, especially one who appreciates Southern traditions. Not only has Jefferson Davis remained unforgiving by his enemies; so, have the Southerners who came after him. We are being reduced to the status once imposed on our Celtic relatives-the Scots, the Welsh, and the Irish-by their English neighbors. God help us!

By: Dr. Grady McWhiney

Dr. McWhiney holds an endowed chair in Southern history at Texas Christian University, Fort Worth, and is the author of a number of books, including (Attack & Die) and (Cracker Culture: Celtic Ways in the old South.) This address was given in conjunction with the national meeting in Nashville at the Jefferson Davis birthday celebration in Centennial Park, on the third day of June of 1995.

★ JOHN THOMAS NALL ★

GOD SAVE THE SOUTH

WRITTEN AND COMPOSED BY EARNEST HALPHIN

THE CONSTITUTION OF THE CONFEDERATE STATES OF AMERICA

We, the people of the Confederate States of America, each State acting in its sovereign and independent character, to form a permanent federal government, establishing justice, ensure domestic tranquility, and secure the blessings of liberty to ourselves and our posterity-involving the favor and guidance of Almighty God-do ordain and establish this Constitution for the Confederate States of America.

ARTICLE I
Section 1.

All legislative Powers herein delegated shall be vested in a Congress of the Confederate States, which shall consist of Senate and House of Representatives.

Section 2.

1. The House of Representatives shall be composed of members chosen every second year by the people of the several States: and the electors in each State shall be citizens of the Confederate States and have the qualifications requisite for electors of the most numerous branches of the States Legislature: but no person of foreign birth, not a citizen of the Confederate States, shall be allowed to vote for any officer, civil or political, State or Federal.
2. No Person shall be a Representative who shall not have attained the age of twenty five years, and be a citizen of the Confederate States, and who shall not, when elected, be an inhabitant of that State in which he shall be chosen.

3. Representatives and direct taxes shall be apportioned among the several States which may be included within this Confederacy, according to their respective numbers, which shall be determined by adding to the whole number of free persons, including those bound to service for a term of years, and excluding Indians not taxed, three fifths of all slaves. The actual enumeration shall be made within three years after the first meeting of the Congress of the Confederate States, and within every subsequent term of ten years, in such manner as they shall by law direct. The number of Representatives shall not exceed one for every fifty thousand: but each State shall have at least one Representative: and until such enumeration shall be made, the State of South Carolina shall be entitled to choose six: the State of Georgia ten: the State of Alabama nine: the State of Florida two: the State of Mississippi seven: the States of Louisiana six: and the State of Texas six.
4. When vacancies happen in the representation from any State, the Executive authority thereof shall issue writs of election to fill such vacancies.
5. The House of Representatives shall choose their Speaker and other officers: and shall have the sole power of impeachment: except that any judicial or other federal officer resident and acting solely within the limits of any State, may be impeached by a vote of two-thirds of both branches of the Legislature thereof.

Section 3.

1. The Senate of the Confederate States shall be composed of two Senators from each State, chosen for six years by the Legislature thereof, at the regular session next immediately preceding the commencement of the term of service: and each Senator shall have one vote.
2. Immediately after they shall be assembled in consequence of the first election, they shall be divided as equally as may be into three classes. The seats of the Senators of the first class shall be vacated at the expiration of the second year, of the second class at the expiration of the fourth year, and of the third class at the expiration of the sixth year, so that one third may be chosen every second year: and if vacancies happen by resignation, or otherwise, during the recess of the Legislature of any State, the Executive thereof may make temporary appointments until the next meeting of the Legislature, which shall then fill such vacancies.
3. No person shall be a Senator who shall not have attained to the age of thirty years, and be a citizen of the Confederate States: and who shall not, when elected, be an inhabitant of the State for which he shall be chosen.
4. The Vice-president of the Confederate States shall be President of the Senate but shall have no vote, unless they be equally divided.

5. The Senate shall choose their other officers, and also a President pro tempore in the absence of the Vice-president, or when he shall exercise the office of the President of the Confederate States.
6. The Senate shall have the sole power to try all impeachments. When sitting for that purpose, they shall be on oath or affirmation. When the President of the Confederate States is tried, the Chief-justice shall preside; and no person shall be convicted without the concurrence of two-thirds of the members present.
7. Judgment in cases of impeachment shall not extend further than to removal from office, and disqualification to hold and enjoy any office of honor, trust or profit under the Confederate States: but the Party convicted shall, nevertheless, be liable and subject to indictment, trial, judgment, and punishment, according to law.

Section 4.

1. The times, places and manner of holding elections for Senators and Representatives, shall be prescribed in each State by the Legislature thereof, subject to the provisions of this Constitution: but the Congress may, at any time, by law, make or alter such regulations, except as to the times and places of choosing Senators.
2. The Congress shall assemble at least once in every year, and such meeting shall be on the first Monday in December, unless they shall, by law, appoint a different day.

Section 5.

1. Each House shall be the judge of the elections, returns, and qualifications of its own members, and a majority of each shall constitute a quorum to do business: but a smaller number may adjourn from day to day, and may be authorized to compel the attendance of absent members, in such manner and under such penalties as each House may provide.
2. Each House may determine the rule of its proceedings, punish its members for disorderly behavior, and with the concurrence of two-thirds of the whole number, expel a member.
3. Each House shall keep a journal of its proceedings, and from time to time to time, publish the same, excepting such parts as may in its judgment require secrecy, and the yeas and nays of the members of either House, on any question shall, at the desire of one-fifth of those present, be entered on the journal.
4. Neither House, during the session of Congress, shall, without the consent of the other, adjourn for more than three days, nor to any other place than that in which the two Houses shall be sitting.

Section 6.

1. The Senators and Representatives shall receive a compensation for their services, to be ascertained by law, and paid out of the Treasury of the Confederate States. They shall, in all cases except treason and breach of peace, be privileged from arrest during their attendance at the session of their respective Houses, and in going to and returning from the same; and for any speck or debate in either House, they shall not be questioned in any other place.
2. No Senator or Representative shall, during the time for which he was elected, be appointed to any civil office under the authority of the Confederate States, which shall have been created, or the emoluments whereof shall have been increased during such time: and no person holding any office under the Confederate States shall be a member of either House during his continuance in office. But Congress may, by law, grant to the principal officer in each of the Executive Departments a seat upon the floor of either House, with the privilege of discussing any measure appertaining to his department.

Section 7.

1. All bills for raising revenue shall originate in the House of Representatives; but the Senate may propose or concur with amendments as on other bills.
2. Every bill which shall have passed both Houses, shall, before it becomes a law, be presented to the President of the Confederate States: if he approves, he shall sign it: but if not, he shall return it with his objections to that House in which it shall have originated, who shall enter the objections at large on their journal, and proceed to reconsider it. If, after such reconsideration, two-thirds of that House shall agree to pass the bill, it shall be sent, together with the objections, to the other House, by which it shall likewise be reconsidered, and approved by two-thirds of that House, it shall become a law. But in all such cases, the votes of both Houses shall be determined by yeas and nays, and names of the persons voting for and against the bill shall be entered on the journal of each House, respectively. If any bill shall not be returned by the President within ten days (Sunday excepted) after it shall have been presented to him, the same shall be a law, in like manner as if he had signed it, unless the Congress by their Adjournment prevent its return, in which case it shall not be a law. The President may approve any appropriation and disapprove any other appropriation in the same bill. In such case he shall, in signing the bill, designate the appropriations disapproved: and shall return a copy of such appropriations, with his objections, to the House in which the bill shall have originated; and the same proceedings shall then be had as in case of other bills disapproved by the President.

3. Every order, resolution, or vote, to which the concurrence of both Houses may be necessary (except on questions of adjournment) shall be presented to the President of the Confederate States; and before the same shall take effect, shall be approved by him: or being disapproved by him, shall be repassed by two-thirds of both Houses, according to the rules and limitations prescribed in the case of a bill.

Section 8.

The Congress shall have power/

1. To lay and collect taxes, duties, imports and excises, for revenue to pay the debts, provide for the common defense, and carry on the Government of the Confederate States; but no bounties shall be granted from the Treasury; nor shall any duties or taxes on importations from foreign nations be laid to promote or foster any branch of industry: and duties, imposts, and excises shall be uniform throughout the Confederate States.
2. To borrow Money on the credit of the Confederate States.
3. To regulate commerce with foreign nations, and among the several States, and with the Indian tribes: but neither this, nor any other clause contained in the Constitution, shall be construed to delegate the power to Congress to appropriate money for any internal improvement intended to facilitate commerce: except for the purpose of furnishing lights, beacons, and buoys, and other aids to navigation upon the coasts, and the improvement of harbors, and the removing of obstructions in rivers navigation, in all which cases such duties shall be laid on the navigation facilitated thereby as may be necessary to pay the costs and expenses thereof.
4. To establish uniform laws of naturalization and uniform laws on the subject of bankruptcies throughout the Confederate States, but no law of Congress shall discharge any debt contracted before the passage of the same.
5. To coin money, regulate the value thereof, and of foreign coin, and fix the standard of weights and measures.
6. To provide for the punishment of counterfeiting the securities and current coin of the Confederate States.
7. To establish post-offices and post-routes: but the expenses of the Post-office Department, after the first day of March, in the year of our Lord eighteen hundred and sixty-three, shall be paid out of its own revenues.
8. To promote the progress of science and useful arts, by securing, for limited times, to authors and inventors, the exclusive right to their respective writings and discoveries.
9. To constitute tribunals inferior to the Supreme Court.
10. To define and punish piracies and felonies committed on the high seas, and offenses against the law of nations.

11. To declare war, grant letters of marquee and reprisal, and make rules concerning captures on land and water.
12. To raise and support armies, but no appropriation of money to that use shall be for a longer term than two years.
13. To provide and maintain a navy.
14. To make rules for the government and regulation of the land and naval forces.
15. To provide for calling forth the militia to execute the laws of the Confederate States, suppress insurrections and repel invasions.
16. To provide for organizing, arming, and disciplining the militia, and for governing such part of them as may be employed in the service of the Confederate States, reserving to the States respectively, the appointment of the officers, and the authority of training the militia according to the discipline prescribed by Congress.
17. To exercise legislation in all cases whatsoever, over such district (not exceeding ten miles square) as may, by secession of one or more States, and the acceptance of Congress, become the seat of Government of the Confederate States, and to exercise like authority over all places purchased by the consent of the legislature of the States in which the same shall be, for the erection of forts, magazines, arsenals, dockyards and other needful buildings, and
18. To make all laws which shall be necessary and proper for carrying into execution into the foregoing powers, and all other powers vested, by this constitution, in the Government of the Confederate States, or in any department or officer thereof.

Section 9.

1. The importation of Negroes of the African race, other than the slaveholding States or Territories of the United States of America, is hereby forbidden, and Congress is required to pass such laws as shall effectually prevent the same.
2. Congress shall also have power to prohibit the introduction of slaves from any State not a member of, or Territory not belonging to, this Confederacy.
3. The privilege of the writ of habeas corpus shall not be suspended, unless when, in cases of rebellion or invasion, the public safety may require it.
4. No bill of attainder, or ex post facto law, or law denying or impairing the right of property in Negro slaves, shall be passed.
5. No capitation or other direct tax shall be laid, unless in proportion to the census or enumeration herein before directed to be taken.

6. No tax or duty shall be laid on articles exported from any State, except by a vote of two-thirds of both Houses.
7. No preference shall be given, by any regulation of commerce or revenue, to the ports of one State over those of another.
8. No money shall be drawn from the Treasury, but consequence of appropriations made by law: and a regular statement and account of the receipts and expenditures of all public money shall be published from time to time.
9. Congress shall appropriate no money from the treasury except by a vote of two-thirds of both Houses, taken by yeas and nays, unless it be asked and estimated for by some one of the heads of departments, and submitted to Congress by the President: or for the purpose of paying its own expenses and contingencies; or for the payment of claims against the Confederate States, the justice of which shall have been judicially declared by a tribunal for the investigation of claims against the government, which it is hereby made the duty of Congress to establish.
10. All bills appropriating money shall specify in federal currency the exact amount of each appropriation, and the purposes for which it is made: and Congress shall grant no extra compensation to any public contractor, officer, agent, or servant, after such contract shall have been made or such service rendered.
11. No title of nobility shall be granted by the Confederate States: and no person holding any office or profit or trust under them, shall, without the consent of the Congress, accept of any present, emolument, office, or title, of any kind whatever, from any king. Prince or foreign state.
12. Congress shall make no law respecting establishment of religion, or prohibiting the free exercise thereof: or abridging the freedom of speech or of the press: or the right of the people peaceably to assemble and petition the government for redress of grievances.
13. A well-regulated militia being necessary to the security of a Free State, the right of the people to keep and bear arms shall not be infringed.
14. No soldier shall, in time of peace, be quartered in any house, without the consent of the owner: nor in time of war, but in a manner to be prescribed by law.
15. The right of the people to be secured in their persons, houses, papers, and effects, against unreasonable searches and seizures, shall not be violated: and no warrant shall issue but upon probable cause, supported by oath or affirmation, and particularly describing the place to be searched, and the person or things to be seized.
16. No person shall be held to answer for a capital or otherwise infamous crime, unless on a presentment or indictment of a grand jury, except in cases arising in the land or naval forces, or in the militia, when in actual service, in time of war, or public danger: nor shall any person be subject for the same offence

to be twice put in jeopardy of life or limb: nor be compelled in any criminal case to be a witness against himself: nor be deprived of life, liberty, or property, without due process of law: nor shall private property be taken for public use without just compensation.

17. In all criminal prosecutions the accused shall enjoy the right to a speedy and public trial by an impartial jury of the States and district wherein the crime shall have been committed, which district shall have been previously ascertained by law, and to be informed of the nature and cause of the accusation: to be confronted with the witness against him: to have compulsory process for obtaining witnesses in his favor: and to have the assistance of counsel for his defense.
18. In suits at common law, where the value in controversy shall exceed twenty dollars, the right of trial by jury shall be reserved: and no fact tried by a jury shall be otherwise re-examined in any court of the Confederacy than according to the rules of the common law.
19. Excessive bail shall not shall not required, nor excessive fines imposed, nor cruel and unusual punishments inflicted.
20. Every law, or resolution having the effect of law, shall relate to but one subject, and that shall be expressed in the title.

Section10.

1. No State shall enter into any treaty, alliance, or confederation: grant letters of marquee and reprisal: coin money: make anything but gold and silver coin a tender in payment of debts: pass any bill of attainder, ex post facto law, or law impairing the obligation of contracts, or grant any title of nobility.
2. No State shall, without the consent of the Congress, lay any imposts or duties on imports or exports, except what may be absolute necessary for executing its inspection laws: and the net produce of all duties and imports, laid by any State on imports or exports, shall be for the use of the Treasury of the Confederate States: and all such laws shall be subject to the revision and control of Congress.
3. No State shall, without the consent of Congress, lay any duty of tonnage, except on sea-going vessels, for the improvement of its rivers and harbors navigated by the said vessels: but such duties shall not conflict with any treaties of the Confederate States with foreign nations: and any surplus of revenue thus derived, shall after making such improvement, be paid into the common treasury: nor shall any State keep troops or ships of war in time of peace, enter into any agreement or compact with another State, or with a foreign power, or engage in war, unless actually invaded, or in such imminent danger as will not admit of delay. But when any river divides or flows through two or more States, they may enter into compacts with each other to improve the navigation thereof.

ARTICLE II

Section 1.

1. The Executive power shall be vested in a President of the Confederate States of America. He and the Vice-president shall hold their offices for the term of six years: but the President shall not be re-eligible. The President and Vice-President shall be elected as follows:
2. Each State shall appoint, in such manner as the Legislature thereof may direct several electors equal to the whole number of Senators and Representatives to which the State may be entitled in Congress: but no Senator or Representative, or person holding an office of trust or profit under the Confederate States, shall be appointed an elector.
3. The electors shall meet in their respective States and vote by ballot for President and Vice-president, one of whom, at least, shall not be an inhabitant of the same State with themselves: they shall name in their ballots the person voted for as President, and in distinct ballots the person voted for as Vice-president, and they shall make distinct list of all persons voted for as President, and of all persons voted for as Vice-president, and of the number of votes for each: which list they shall sign, and certify, and transmit, sealed, to the government of the Confederate States, directed to the President of the Senate. The President of the Senate shall, in the presence of the Senate and House of Representatives, open all the certificates, and the votes shall then be counted: the person having the greatest number of votes for President shall be the President, if such number be a majority of the whole number of electors appointed: and if no person have such majority then, from the persons having the highest numbers, not exceeding three, on the list of those voted for as President, the House of Representatives shall choose immediately, by ballot, the President. But, in choosing the President, the votes shall be taken by the States, the representation from each State having one vote: a quorum for this purpose shall consist of a member or members from two-thirds of the States, and majority of all the States shall be necessary to a choice. And if the House of Representatives shall not choose a President, whenever the right of choice shall devolve upon them, before the fourth day of March next following, then the Vice-president shall act as President, as in the case of the death or other constitutional disability of the President.
4. The person having the greatest number of votes as Vice-president shall be the Vice-president, if such number be a majority of the whole number of electors appointed: and if no person have a majority, then, from the two highest numbers on the list, the Senate shall choose the Vice-president: a quorum for the purpose shall consist of two-thirds of the whole number of Senators, and a majority of the whole number shall be necessary for a choice.

5. But no person constitutionally ineligible to the office of President shall be eligible to that of Vice-president of the Confederate States.
6. The Congress may determine the time of choosing the electors, and the day on which they shall give their votes: which day shall be the same throughout the Confederate States.
7. No person except a natural born citizen of the Confederate States, or a citizen thereof at the time of the adoption of this Constitution, or a citizen thereof born in the United States prior to the 20th December, 1860, shall be eligible to the office of President: neither shall any person be eligible to that office who shall not have attained the age of thirty-five years, and been fourteen years a resident within the limits of the Confederate States, as they may exist at the time of his election.
8. In case of the removal of the President from office, or of his death, resignation, or inability to discharge the powers and duties of the said office, the same shall devolve on the Vice-president: and the Congress may, by law, provide for a case of the removal, death, resignation or inability, both of the President and Vice-president, declaring what officer shall then act as President, and such officer shall act accordingly until the disability be removed, or a President shall be elected.
9. The President shall, at stated times, receive for his services, a compensation, which shall neither be increased nor diminished during the period for which he shall have been elected: and he shall not receive within that period any other emolument from the Confederate States, or any of them.
10. Before he enters on the execution of his office, he shall take the following oath or affirmation:
"I do solemnly swear (or affirm) that I will execute the office of President of the Confederate States, and will to the best of my ability, preserve, protect and defend the Confederate States, and will to the best of my ability, preserve, protect and defend the Constitution thereof."

Section 2.

1. The President shall be commander-in-chief of the army and navy of the Confederate States, and of the militia of the several States, when called into the actual service of the Confederate States: he may require the opinion, in writing, of the principal officer in each of the Executive Departments, upon any subject relating to the duties of their respective offices: and he shall have power to grant reprieves and pardons for offenses against the Confederate States, except in cases of impeachment.
2. He shall have power, by and with the advice and consent of the senate, to make treaties, provided two-thirds of the Senators present concur: and he shall nominate, and by and with the advice and consent of the Senate, shall appoint ambassadors, other public ministers and consuls, judges of the Supreme Court, and all other officers of the Confederate States, whose appointments are not herein otherwise provided for,

and which shall be established by law: but the Congress may by law vest the appointment of such inferior officers as they think proper, in the President alone, in the courts of law, or in the heads of departments.

3. The principal officer in each of the Executive Departments, and all persons connected with the diplomatic service, may be removed from office at the pleasure of the President. All other civil officers of the Executive Department may be removed at any time by the President, or other appointing power, when their services are unnecessary, or for dishonesty, incapacity, inefficiency, misconduct, or neglect of duty: and when so removed, the removal shall be reported to the Senate, together with the reasons, therefore.

4. The President shall have power to fill up all vacancies that may happen during the recess of the Senate, by granting commissions which shall expire at the end of their next session: but no person rejected by the Senate shall be reappointed to the same office during their ensuing recess.

Section 3.

The President shall, from time to time, give to the Congress information on the State of the Confederacy, and recommend to their consideration such measures as he shall judge necessary and expedient: he may, on extraordinary occasions, convene both Houses, or either of them: and in case of disagreement between them, with respect to the time of adjournment, he may adjourn them to such time as he shall think proper: he shall receive ambassadors and other public ministers: he shall take care that the laws be faithfully executed, and shall commission all the officers of the Confederate States.

Section 4.

The President, Vice-president, and all civil officers of the Confederate States, shall be removed from office on impeachment for, and conviction of, treason, bribery, or other high crimes and misdemeanors.

ARTICLE III

Section 1.

The judicial power of the Confederate States shall be vested in one Superior Court, and in such inferior courts as the Congress may from time to time ordain and establish. The judges, both supreme and inferior courts, shall hold their offices during good behavior, and shall, at stated times, receive for their services a compensation, which shall not be diminished during their continuance in office.

Section 2.

1. The judicial power shall extend to all cases arising under this Constitution, the laws of the Confederate States, and treaties made or which shall be made under their authority: to all cases affecting ambassadors, other public ministers and consuls: to all cases of admiralty and maritime jurisdiction: to controversies to which the Confederate States shall be a Party: to controversies between two or more States: between a State and citizens of another State, where the State is plaintiff: between citizens claiming lands under grants of different States, and between a State or the citizens thereof, and foreign States, citizens or subjects: but no State shall be sued by a citizen or subject of any foreign State.
2. In all cases affecting ambassadors, other public ministers and consuls, and those in which a State shall be party, the Supreme Court shall have original jurisdiction. In all the other cases before mentioned, the Supreme Court shall have appellate jurisdiction, both as to law and fact, with such exceptions and under such regulations as the Congress shall make.
3. The trial of all crimes, except in cases of impeachment, shall be by jury, and such trial shall be held in the State where the said crimes shall have been committed: but when not committed within any State, the trail shall be at such place or places as the Congress may by law have directed.

Section 3.

1. Treason against the Confederate States shall consist only in levying war against them, or in adhering to their enemies, giving them aid and comfort. No person shall be convicted of treason unless on the testimony of two witnesses to the same overt act, or on confession in open court.
2. The Congress shall have power to declare the punishment of treason, but no attainder of treason shall work corruption of blood, or forfeiture, except during the life of the person attainted.

ARTICLE IV

Section 1.

Full faith and credit shall be given in each State to the public acts, records, and judicial proceedings of every other State. And the Congress may, by general laws, prescribe the manner in which such acts, records, and proceedings shall be proved, and the effect thereof.

Section 2.

1. The citizen of each State shall be entitled to all privileges and immunities of citizens in the several States and shall have the right of transit and sojourn in any State of this Confederacy, with their slaves and other property; and the right of property in said slaves shall not be there impaired.
2. A person charged in any State with treason, felony, or other crime against the laws of such State, who shall flee from justice, and be found in another State, shall, on demand of the Executive authority of the State from which he fled, be delivered up to be removed to the State having jurisdiction of the crime.
3. No slave or other person held to service or labor in any State or Territory of the Confederate States, under the laws thereof, escaping or unlawfully carried into another, shall in consequence of any law or regulation therein, be discharged from such service or labor: but shall be delivered up on claim of the party to whom such slave belongs, or to whom such service or labor may be due.

Section 3.

1. Other States may be admitted into this Confederacy by a vote of two-thirds of the whole House of Representatives, and two-thirds of the Senate, the Senate voting by States; but no new State shall be formed or created within the jurisdiction of any other State: nor any State be formed by the junction of two or more States, or parts of States, without the consent of the Legislatures of the States concerned as well as of the Congress.
2. The Congress shall have power to dispose of and make all needful rules and regulations respecting the property belonging to the Confederate States, including the lands thereof.
3. The Confederate States may acquire new territory, and Congress shall have power to legislate and provide governments for the inhabitants of all territory belonging to the Confederate States, lying without the limits of the several States, and may permit them, at such times, and in such manner as it may by law

provide, to form States to be admitted into the Confederacy. In all such territory, the institution of negro slavery, as it now exists in the Confederate States, shall be recognized, and protected by Congress and by the territorial government: and the inhabitants of the several Confederate States and Territories shall have the right to take to such territory any slaves lawfully held by them in any of the States or Territories of the Confederate States.
4. The Confederate States shall guarantee to every State that now is or hereafter may become a member of this Confederacy, a Republican form of government, and shall protect each of them against invasion: and on application of the Legislature, (or of the Executive when the Legislature is not in session,) against domestic violence.

ARTICLE V

Section 1.

Upon the demand of any three States, legally assembled in their several Conventions, the Congress shall summon a Convention of all the States, to take into consideration such amendments to the Constitution as the said States shall concur in suggesting as the time when the said demand is made: and should any of the proposed amendments to the Constitution be agreed on by the said Convention-voting by the States-and the same be ratified by the Legislatures of two-thirds of the several States, or by Conventions in two-thirds thereof-as the one or the other mode of ratification may be proposed by the general Convention-they shall thenceforward form a part of this Constitution. But no State shall, without its consent be deprived of its equal representation in the Senate.

ARTICLE VI

Section 1.

1. The Government established by this Constitution is the successor of the Provisional Government of the Confederate States of America, and all the laws passed by the latter shall continue in force until the same be repealed or modified: and all the officers appointed by the same shall remain in office until their successors are appointed and qualified, or the offices abolished.
2. All debts contracted and engagements entered into before the adoption of this Constitution, shall be as valid against the Confederate States under this Constitution as under the Provisional Government.

3. This Constitution, and the laws of the Confederate States made in pursuance thereof, and all treaties made, or which shall be made, under the authority of the Confederate States, shall be the supreme law of the land, and the judges in every State shall be bound thereby, anything in the Constitution or laws of any State to the contrary notwithstanding.
4. The Senators and Representatives before mentioned, and the members of the several State Legislatures, and all executive and judicial officers, both Confederate States and of the several States, shall be bound, by oath or affirmation, to support this Constitution: but no religious test shall ever be required as a qualification to any office or public trust under the Confederate States.
5. The enumeration, in the Constitution, of certain rights, shall be construed to deny or disparage others retained by the people of the several States.
6. The powers not delegated to the Confederate States by the Constitution, nor prohibited by it to the States, are reserved to the States respectively, or to the people.

ARTICLE VII

Section 1.

1. The ratification of the Constitution of Five States shall be sufficient for the establishment of this Constitution between the States so ratifying the same.
When five States shall have ratified this Constitution in the manner before specified, the Congress, under the provisional Constitution, shall prescribe the time for holding the election of President and Vice-president, and for the meeting of the electoral college, and for counting the votes and inaugurating the President, They shall also prescribe the time for holding the first election of members of Congress under this Constitution, and the time for assembling the same. Until the assembling of such Congress, the Congress under the provisional Constitution shall continue to exercise the legislative powers granted them: not extending beyond the limited time by the Constitution of Provisional Government.
Adopted unanimously, March 11th, 1861

At Montgomery, Alabama

Author's notes: While the advancing of technology and industrialization, in time the Confederacy would have phased out slavery without crippling the economy. Machines would have replaced the slavery and the Confederate States constitution would have been updated as time marched on.

The Case of Texas v. White (74 U.S. 700). Chief Justice Chase in writing for the Court in its 1869 decision after the war.

"The Constitution, in all its provisions, looks to an indestructible Union, composed of indestructible States … Considered, therefore, as transactions under the Constitution, the Ordinance of Secession, adopted by the convention and ratified by most of the citizens of Texas, and all the acts of her Legislature intended to give effect to that Ordinance, were absolutely null. They were utterly without operation in law … Our conclusion, therefore, is that Texas continued to be a State, and a State of the Union, notwithstanding the transactions to which we have referred."

Author's Notes: According to the U.S. Supreme Court, the Declaration of Independence as an [Actual Right] would be illegal, Null and Void! Including the parts of the U.S. Constitution, like the ninth and tenth Amendments are also now illegal. And anything else that the Constitution may speak of in favor of the States would be illegal. Another word, the Supreme Court has rejected the Sovereignty of the States. It is clear, that the Supreme Court of the United States is corrupted and is a slave to the political leaders. The Supreme Court perceives the Constitution not through the eyes and values of our founders. But by a Centralized Socialist government. They are not faithful to the Constitution or to the people that had created the government.

ADDRESS FROM THE CONGRESS TO THE PEOPLE OF THE CONFEDERATE STATES OF AMERICA

A JOINT RESOLUTION IN RELATION TO THE WAR

Resolved by the Congress of the Confederate States, that the present is deemed a fitting occasion to remind the people of the Confederate States that they are engaged in a struggle for the preservation both of liberty and civilization; and that no sacrifice of life or fortune can be too costly which may be requisite to secure to themselves and their posterity the enjoyment of these inappreciable blessings; and to assure them that, in the judgment of the Congress, the resources of the country, if developed with energy, husbanded with care, and applied with fidelity, are more than sufficient to support the most protracted war which it can be necessary to wage for independence, and to exhort them, by every consideration which can influence freemen and patriots, to a magnanimous surrender of all personal and party feuds, to an indignant rebuke of every exhibition if factious temper, in whatever quarter, or upon whatever pretext it may made; to a generous support of all branches of Government, in the legitimate exercise of their constitutional powers, and to that harmonious unselfish and patriotic cooperation which can alone impart to our cause the irresistible strength which springs from united councils, fraternal feelings, and fervent devotion to the public will.

In closing the labors of the first Permanent Congress, your Representatives deem it a fit occasion to give some account of their stewardship; to review briefly what, under such embarrassments and adverse circumstances, has been accomplished; to invite attention to the prospect before us, and the duties incumbent on every citizen in this crisis; and to address such words of counsel and encouragement as the times demand.

Compelled, by a long series of oppressive and tyrannical acts, culminating at last in the selection of a President and Vice-President, by a party confessedly sectional and hostile to the South and her institutions, these States withdrew from the former Union and formed a New Confederate Alliance as an independent government, based on the proper relations of labor and capital.

This step was taken reluctantly, by constraint, and after the exhaustion of every measure that was likely to secure us from interference with our property, equality in the Union, or exemption from submission to an alien government. The Southern States claimed only the unrestricted enjoyment of the rights guaranteed by the Constitution.

Finding, by painful and protracted experience, that this was persistently denied, we determined to separate from those enemies who had manifested the inclination and ability to impoverish and destroy us. We fell back upon the right for which the Colonies maintained the war of the Revolution, and which our heroic forefathers asserted to be clear and inalienable.

The unanimity and zeal with which the separation was undertaking and perfected, finds no parallel in history. The people rose en masse to assert their liberties and protect their menaced rights. There never was before such universality of conviction among any people on any question involving so serious and so through a change of political and international relations.

This grew out of the clearness of the right so to act, and the certainty of the perils of further association with the North. The change was so wonderful, so rapid, so contrary to universal history, that many fails to see that all has been done in the logical sequence of principles, which are the highest testimony to the wisdom of our fathers, and the best illustration of the correctness of those principles. This government is a child of law instead of sedition, of right instead of violence, of deliberation instead of insurrection. Its early life was attended by anarchy, no rebellion, no suspension of authority, no social disorders, no lawless disturbances Sovereignty was not for one moment in abeyance.

The utmost conservation marked every proceeding and public act. The object was 'to do what was necessary and no more; and to do that with the utmost temperance and prudence." St. Just, in his report to the Convention of France, in 1793; *"A people have but one dangerous enemy, and that is government."*

We adopted no such absurdity. In nearly every instance the first steps were taken legally, in accordance with the will and prescribed direction of the constituted authorities of the seceding States. We were not remitted to brute force or natural law, or the instincts of reason. The charters of freedom were scrupulously preserved. As in the English revolution of 1666, and ours of 1776, there was no material alteration in the laws, beyond what was necessary to redress the abuses that provoked the struggle. No attempt was made to build on speculative principles.

The effort was confined within the narrowest limits of historical and Constitutional Right. The controversy turned on the records and monuments of the past. [We merely resisted innovation and tyranny and contended for our birthrights and covenanted principles of our race.] We have had our governors, general assemblies and courts, the same electors, the same corporations, the same rules for property, the same subordinations, the same order in the law and in the magistracy. [When the sovereign States met in council, they in truth and substance, and in a constitutional light, did not make but prevented a revolution.]

Commencing our new national life under such circumstances, we had a right to expect that we would be permitted, without molestation, to cultivate the arts of peace, and vindicate, on our chosen arena and with the selected type of social characteristics, our claims to civilization. It was thought, too, by many, that war would not restore to by an enlightened country, except on the direct necessity. That a people, professing to be animated by Christian sentiment, and who had regarded our peculiar institution as a blot and blur upon the fair escutcheon of their common Christianity, should make war upon the South for doing what they had a perfect right to do, and for relieving them of the incubus which they professed rested upon them by association, was deemed almost beyond belief by many of our wisest minds.

It was hoped, too, that the obvious interests of the two sections would restrain the wild frenzy of excitement and turn into peaceful channels the thoughts of those who had but recently been invested with power in the United States.

These reasonable anticipations were doomed to disappointment. The red glare of battle, kindled at Sumter, dissipated all hopes of peace, and the two governments were arrayed in hostility against each other. <u>We charge the responsibility of this war upon the United States.</u> <u>They are accountable for the blood and havoc and ruin it has caused. For such a war we were not prepared.</u>

The difference in military resources between our enemies and ourselves; the immense advantages in the possessed in the organized machinery of an established government; a powerful navy, the nucleus of an army, credit abroad, and illimitable facilities in mechanical and manufacturing power, placed them on "the vantage ground." In our infancy, we were without a seaman or soldier, without revenue, without gold or silver, without a recognized place in the family of nations, without external commerce, without foreign credit, with the prejudices of the world against us.

While we were without manufacturing facilities to supply our wants, our ports were blockaded; we had to grapple with a giant adversary, defend two thousand miles of seacoast and an inland frontier of equal extent. If we had succeeded in preventing any successes on the part of our enemy, it would have been a miracle. What we have accomplished, with a population so inferior in numbers and means so vastly disproportionate, has excited the astonishment and admiration of the world.

The war in which we are engaged was wickedly, and against all protests and the most earnest efforts to the contrary, forced upon us. South Carolina sent a commission to Washington to adjust all questions of dispute between her and the United States. One of the first acts of the Provisional Government was to accredit agents to visit Washington and use all honorable means to obtain a satisfactory settlement of all questions of disputes with that government. Both efforts failed. Commissioners were deceived and rejected, and clandestine but vigorous preparations were made for war.

In proportion to our perseverance and anxiety have been the obstinacy and arrogance in spurning offers of peace. It seems we can be indebted for nothing to the virtues of our enemy. We are obliged to his vices, which have endured to our strength. We owe as much to his insolence and blindness as to our precaution. The wager of battle having been tendered; it was accepted. The alacrity with which our people flew to arms is worthy of all praise. Their deeds of heroic daring, patient endurance, ready submission to discipline, and numerous victories, are with the fervent patriotism that prompted their early volunteering. Quite recently, score of regiments have reenlisted for the war, testifying their determination to fight until their liberties were achieved. Coupled with, and contributing greatly to this enthusiastic ardor, was the lofty courage, the indomitable resolve, the self-denying spirit of our noble women, who, by their labors of love, their patience of hope, their unflinching constancy uncomplaining submission to war, have shed an immortal luster upon their sex and country.

Our army is no hireling soldiery. It comes not from paupers, criminals, or immigrants. It was originally raised by the free, unconstrained, unpurchaseable assent of the men. All vocations and classes contributed to the swelling numbers. Abandoning luxuries and comforts to which they had been accustomed, they submitted cheerfully to the scanty fare and executive service of the camps. Their services above price, the only remuneration they have sought is the protection of their altars, firesides, and liberty.

In Norwegian wars, the actors were, every one of them, named and patronymic ally described as the King's friend and companion. The same wonderful individuality has been in this war. Our soldiers are not a consolidated mass, an unthinking machine, but an army of intelligent unites. To designate all who have distinguished themselves by special valor, would be to enumerate nearly all in the army. The generous rivalry between the troops from different States has prevented any special pre-eminence, and hereafter, for centuries to come, the gallant bearing and unconquerable devotion of Confederate soldiers will inspire the hearts and encourage the hopes and strengthen the faith of all who labor to obtain freedom.

For three years this cruel war has been waged against us, and its continuance has been seized upon as a pretext by some discontented persons to excite hostility to the government. Recent and public as have been the occurrences; it is strange that a misapprehension exists as to the conduct of the two governments about peace. Allusion has been made to the unsuccessful efforts, when separation took place, to procure an amicable adjustment of all matters in dispute. These attempts at negotiation do not comprise all that has been done.

In every form in which expression could be given to the sentiment, in public meetings, through the press, by legislative resolves, the desire of this people for peace, for the uninterrupted enjoyment of their rights and prosperity, has been made known. The President, more authoritatively, in several of his messages, while protesting the utter absence of all desire to all desire to interfere with the United States, or acquire any of their territory, has avowed that the advent of peace will be hailed with joy.

Our desire for it has never been concealed. "Our efforts to avoid the war, forced on us as it was by the lust of conquest and the insane passions of our foes, are known to mankind."

<u>The course of the Federal Government has proved that it did not desire peace and would not consent to it on any terms that we could possibly concede. In proof of this we refer to the repeated rejection of all terms of conciliation and compromise, to their recent contemptuous refusal to receive the Vice President, who was sent to negotiate for softening the asperities of war, and their scornful rejection of the offer of a neutral power to mediate between the contending parties. If cumulative evidence be needed, it can be found in the following resolution, recently adopted by the House of Representatives in Washington.</u>

"Resolved, that as our country and the very existence of the best government ever instituted by man are imperiled by the most causeless and wicked rebellion that the world has seen, and believing, as we do, that the only hope of saving this country and preserving this government is by the power of the sword, we are for the most vigorous prosecution of

the war until the Constitution and the laws shall be enforced and obeyed in all parts of the United States; and to that end we oppose any armistice, or intervention, or mediation, or proposition for peace, from any quarter, so long as there shall be found a rebel in arms against the government; and we ignore all party names, lines and issues, and recognize but two parties in this war-patriots and traitors."

The motive of such strange conduct is obvious. The Republican Party was founded to destroy slavery and the equality of the States, and Lincoln was selected as the instrument to accomplish this object. The Union was a barrier to the consummation of this policy because the Constitution, which was its bond, recognized and protected slavery and the sovereignty of the States. The Union must, therefore, be sacrificed, and ensure its destruction, war was determined on.

The mass of the Northern people was not privy to, and sympathized in no such design. They loved the Union and wished to preserve it. To rally the people to support of the war, its object was proclaimed to be "a restoration of the Union," as if that which implied voluntary assent, of which agreement was indispensable element and condition, could be preserved by coercion. It is absurd to pretend that a government, really desirous of restoring the Union, would adopt such measures as the confiscation of private property, the emancipation of slaves, systematic efforts to invite them to insurrection, forcible abduction from their homes, and compulsory enlistment in the army, the division of a sovereign State without its consent, and the proclamation that one tenth of the population of a State, and that tenth under military rule, should control the will of the remaining nine tenths.

The only relation between the two sections, under such policy, is that conqueror and conquered, superior and dependent. Rest assured, fellow citizens, that although restoration may still be used as a war cry by the Northern Government, it is only to delude and betray. Fanaticism has summoned to its aid cupidity and vengeance; and nothing short of your utter subjugation, the destruction of your State governments, the overthrow of your social and political fabric, your personal and public degration and ruin, will satisfy the demands of the North. Can there be a man so vile, so debased, so unworthy of liberty as to accept peace on such humiliating terms?

It would hardly be fair to assert that all Northern people participate in these designs. On the contrary, there exists a powerful political party which openly condemns them. The administration has, however, been able thus far, by its enormous patronage and its lavish expenditures to seduce, or by its legions of "Hessian" mercenaries to overawe the masses, to control the elections and to establish an arbitrary despotism. It cannot be possible that this state of things can continue. The people of the United States, accustomed to freedom, cannot consent to be ruined and enslaved in order to ruin and enslave us.

Moral, like physical, epidemics, have their allotted periods, and must, sooner or later, be exhausted and disappear. When reason returns, our enemies will probably reflect that a people like ours, who have exhibited such capabilities and extemporized such resources, can never be subdued; that a vast expanse of territory, with such a population, cannot be governed as an obedient colony. Victory would not be conquest. The inextinguishable quarrel would be transmitted "from bleeding sire to son" and the struggle would be renewed between generations yet unborn.

To impoverish us would be to dry up some of the springs of Northern prosperity to destroy Southern wealth is to reduce Northern profits, while the restoration of peace would necessarily reestablish some commercial intercourse. It may not be amiss, in this connection, to say at one time it was the wish and expectation of many at the South to form a treaty of amity and friendship with the Northern States, by which both peoples might derive the benefits of commercial intercourse and move on side by side in the arts of peace and civilization.

History has confirmed the lesson taught by Divine authority, that each nation, as well as everyone, should seek their happiness in the prosperity of others, and not in the injury or ruin of a neighbor. The general welfare of all is the highest dictate of moral duty and economic policy, while a heritage of triumphant wrong is the greatest curse that can befall a nation. Until some evidence is given of a change of policy on the part of the government, and some assurance is received that efforts at negotiation will not be spurned, the Congress are of opinion that any direct overtures for peace would compromise our self-respect, be fruitless of good, and interpreted by the enemy as an indication of weakness.

We can only repeat the desire of the people for peace, and our readiness to accept terms consistent with the honor and dignity and independence of the States, and compatible with the safety of our domestic institutions.

Not content with rejecting all proposals for a peaceful settlement of the controversy, a cruel war of invasion was commenced, which, in its progress, has been marked by a brutality and disregard of the rules of civilized warfare that stand out in unexampled barbarity in the history of modern wars. Accompanied by every act of cruelty and rapine, the conduct of the enemy has been destitute of that forbearance and magnanimity which civilization and Christianity have introduced to mitigate the asperities of war.

The atrocities are too incredible for narration. Instead of a regular war, our resistance of the unholy efforts to crush out our national existence is treated as a rebellion, and the settled international rules between belligerents are ignored. Instead of conducting the war as betwixt two military and political organizations, it is a war against the whole population. Houses are pillaged and burned; Churches are defaces; towns are ransacked; clothing of women and infants is stripped from their persons jewelry and mementoes of the dead are stolen; mills and implements of agriculture are destroyed; private salt works are broken up; the introduction of medicines is forbidden; means of subsistence are wantonly wasted to produce beggary; prisoners are returned with contagious diseases; the last morsel of food has been taken from families, who were not allowed to carry on a trade or branch of industry; a rigid and offensive "espionage" has introduced to ferret out "disloyalty"; persons have been forced to choose between starvation and helpless children and taking the oath of allegiance to a hated government; the cartel for exchange of prisoners has been suspended and our unfortunate soldiers subjected to the grossest indignities; the wounded at Gettysburg were deprived of their nurses and inhumanly left to perish on the field; helpless women have been exposed to the cruel outrages and to that dishonor which is infinitely worse than death; citizens have been murdered by the Butlers and McNeils and Milroys, who are favorite Generals of our enemies; refined and delicate ladies have been seized, bound with cords, imprisoned, guarded by Negroes, and held as hostages for the return of recaptured slaves; unoffending noncombatants have been banished or dragged from their quit homes, to be immured in filthy jails; preaching the gospel as been refused, except on condition of taking the oath of allegiance; parents have been forbidden to name their children in honor of "Rebel" chiefs; property has been confiscated; military governors have been appointed for States, satraps for provinces, and Haynaus for cities.

These cruelties and atrocities of the enemy have been exceeded by their malicious and bloodthirsty purposes and machinations about the slaves. Early in this war, President Lincoln averred his Constitutional inability and personal unwillingness to interfere with the domestic institutions of the States, and the relation between master and servant. Prudential considerations may have been veiled under conscientious scruples, for Seward, in confidential instruction to Mr. Adams, the minister to Great Britain, on 10th of March 1862, said.

"If the government of the United States should precipitately decree the immediate abolition of slavery, it would invigorate the declining insurrection in every part of the South."

Subsequent reverses and the reverses and the refractory, rebelliousness of the seceded States caused a change of policy, and Mr. Lincoln issued his celebrated proclamation, a mere "Brutum fulmem," liberating the slaves in the "insurrectionary districts." On the 24th of June 1776, one of the reasons assigned by Pennsylvania for her separation from the mother country was, that her sister colonies the "King had excited the negroes to revolt, and to imbrue their hands in the blood of their masters, in a manner unpracticed by civilized nations."

This probably had reference to the proclamation of Dunmore, the last royal Governor of Virginia in 1775, declaring freedom to all servants or Negroes, if they would join "for the reducing the colony to a proper sense of its duty."

The invitation to the slaves to rise against their masters, the suggested insurrection caused, says Bancroft, "a thrill of indignation to run through Virginia, effacing all differences of party, and rousing one strong, impassioned purpose to drive away the insolent power by which it had been put forth."

A contemporary analyst, adverting to the same proclamation, said "it was received with the greatest horror in all the colonies." The policy adopted by Dunmore, "says Lawrence in his notes on Wheaton, *"of arming the slaves against their masters, was not pursued during the war of the revolution; and when Negroes were taken by the English, they were not considered otherwise than as property and plunder." "Emancipation of slaves as a war measure has been severely condemned and denounced by the most eminent publicists in Europe and the United States. The United States, in their diplomatic relations, have maintained,"* says the Northern authority just quoted, *"that slaves were private property, and for them, as such, they have repeatedly received compensation from England."* Napoleon I was never induced to issue a proclamation for the emancipation of the Serfs in his war with Russia. He said,

"I could have armed against her a part of her population, by proclaiming the liberty of the Serfs. A great number of villages asked it of me, but I refused to avail myself of a measure which would have devoted to death thousands of families."

In the discussions growing out of the treaty of peace of 1814, and the proffered mediation of Russia, the principle was maintained by the United States that *"the emancipation of enemy's slaves is not among the acts of legitimate warfare."* In the instructions from John Quincy Adams, as Secretary of State, to Mr. Middleton, at St. Petersburg, October 18th, 1820, it is said; "The British have broadly asserted the right of emancipating slaves (private property) as a legitimate right of war. No such right is acknowledged as of law by writers who admit any limitation. The right of putting to death all prisoners in cold blood, and without special cause, might as well be pretended to be a law of war, or the right to use poisoned weapons, or to assassinate."

Disregarding the teachings of the approved writers on international law, and the practice and claims of his own government in its purer days, President Lincoln has sought to convert the South into a St. Domingo, by appealing to the cupidity, lust, and ferocity of the slave. Abraham Lincoln is but lineal descendant of Dunmore, and the important malice of each foiled by the fidelity of those who, buy meanness of the conspirators, would only, if successful, have been seduced into idleness, filth, vice, beggary, and death.

But, we tire of these indignities and enormities. They are too sickening for recital. History will hereafter pillory those who committed and encouraged such crimes in immortal infamy. General Robert E. Lee, in a recent battle order, stated to his invincible legions, that *"the cruel foe seeks to reduce our fathers and mothers, our wives and children, to abject slavery."* He does not paint too strongly the purposes of the enemy or the consequences of subjugation. What has done in certain districts is but the prologue of the bloody drama that will be enacted.

It is well that every man and woman should have some just conception of the horrors of conquest. The fate of Ireland at the period of its conquest, and of Poland, distinctly foreshadows what would await us. The guillotine, in its ceaseless work of blood would be revived for the execution of the "rebel leaders."

The heroes of our contest would be required to lay down their proud ensigns, on which are recorded the battle of their glory, to their arms, lower their heads in humiliation and dishonor, and pass under the yoke of abolition and tyranny. A hateful inquisition made atrocious by spies and informers; Star Chamber courts, enforcing their decisions by confiscations, imprisonments, banishments and death; a band of detectives, ferreting out secrets, lurking in every family, existing in every conveyance, the suppression of free speech; the deprivation of arms and franchises; and the ever-present sense of inferiority would make our condition abject and miserable beyond what freemen can imagine.

Subjugation involves everything that the torturing malice and devilish ingenuity of our foes can suggest-the destruction of our nationality, the equalization of Whites and Black, the obliteration of State lines, degradation to colonial vassalage, and the reduction many of our citizens to dreary, hopeless, remediless bondage. Hostile police would keep "order" in every town and city. Judged, like Busteed, would hold our courts, protected by Yankee soldiers. Churches would be filled by Yankee or Tory preachers. Every office would be bestowed on aliens.

Absenteeism would curse us with all its vices. Superadded to these, sinking us into a lower abyss of degradation, we would be made slaves of our slaves, hewers of wood and drawers of water for those upon whom God has stamped indelibly the marks of physical and intellectual inferiority. The past, or foreign countries, need not be sought into to furnish illustrations of the heritage of shame that subjugation would entail.

Baltimore, St, Louis, Nashville, Knoxville, New Orleans, Vicksburg, Huntsville, Newbern, Louisville and Fredericksburg, are the first fruits of the ignominy and poverty of Yankee domination. The sad story of the wrongs and indignities endured by those States which have been in the complete or partial possession of the enemy will give the best evidence of the consequences of subjugation. Missouri, a magnificent empire of agricultural and mineral wealth, is today a smoking ruin, and the theatre of the most revolting cruelties and barbarities.

The minions of tyranny consume her substance, plunder her citizens, and destroy her peace. The sacred rights of freemen are struck down, and the blood of her children, her maidens, and her old men, is made to flow, out of mere wantonness. No whispers of freedom go unpunished, and the very instincts of self-preservation are outlawed. The worship of God and the rites of scripture have been shamefully interrupted, and in many instances, the cultivation of the soil is prohibited to her own citizens. These facts are attested by many witnesses, and it is but a just tribute to that noble and chivalrous people that, amid barbarities almost unparalleled, they still maintain a proud and defiant spirit towards their enemies.

In Maryland, the judiciary, made subservient to executive absolutism, furnishes no security for individual rights or personal freedom; members of the legislature are arrested and imprisoned without process of law or assignment of cause, and the whole land groaned under the oppressions of a merciless tyranny. In Kentucky, the ballot box has been overthrown, free speech is suppressed, the most vexatious annoyances harass and embitter, and all the arts and appliances of an unscrupulous despotism are freely used to prevent the uprising of the noble patriots of "the dark and bloody ground."

Notes of gladness, assurances of a brighter and better day reach us, and the exiles may take courage and hope for the future. In Virginia, the model of all that illustrates human heroism and self-denying patriotism, although the tempest of desolation has swept over her fair domains, *no sign of repentances for her separation from the North can be found. Her old homesteads dismantled, her old homesteads dismantled, her ancestral relics destroyed, her people impoverished, her territory made the battleground for the rude shocks of contending hosts, and then, with hireling parasites, mockingly claiming jurisdiction and authority, the Old Dominion still stands with proud crest and defiant mien, ready to tramp beneath her heel usurper and tyrant, and to illustrate afresh her (sic simper tyrannis). The "proudest motto that ever blazed on a nation's shield or warrior's arms."*

To prevent such effects, our people are now prosecuting this struggle. It is no mere war of calculation, no contest for a particular kind of property, no barter of precious blood for filthy lucre. Everything involved in manhood, civilization, religion, law, property, country, home, is at stake. We fight not for plunder, spoils, pillage, and territorial conquest. The Government tempts by no prizes of "beauty or booty," to be drawn in the lottery of this war. We seek to preserve civil freedom, honor, equality, firesides, and blood is well shed when "shed for our family, for our friends, for our kind, for our country, for our God," Burke said; "A State, resolved to hazard its existence rather than abandon its object must have an infinite advantage over that which is resolved to yield, rather than carry its resistance beyond a certain point."

It is better to be conquered by any other nation than by the United States. It is better to be dependency of any other power than of that. By the condition of its existence and essential constitution, as now governed, it must be in perpetual hostility to us. As the Spanish invader burned his ships to make retreat impossible, so we cannot afford to take steps backward. Retreat is more dangerous than advance.

Behind us are inferiority and degradation, before us is everything enticing to a patriot. Our bitter and implacable foes are preparing vigorously for the coming campaign. Corresponding efforts should be made on our part. Without murmuring, our people should respond to the laws which the exigency demands. Everyone capable of bearing arms should relate to some effective military organization. The utmost energies of the whole population should be taxed to produce food and clothing, and a spirit of cheerfulness and trust in all wise and overruling Providence should be cultivated.

The history of the past three years has much to animate us to renewed effort, and a firmer and more assured hope. A whole people have given their hearts and bodies to repel the invader, and costly sacrifices have been made on the altar of our country. No similar instance is to be found of such spontaneous uprising and volunteering. Inspired by a holy patriotism, again and again have our brave soldiers, with the aid of heaven, baffled the efforts of our foes.

It is in no arrogant spirit that we refer to successes that have cost us so much blood and brought sorrow to so many hearts. We may find in all this an earnest of what, with determined and resolute exertion, we can do to avert subjugation and slavery-and we cannot fail to discern in our deliverance from so many and so great perils the interposition of that being who will not forsake us in the trials that are to come. Let us, looking upon the bodies of our loved and honored dead, catch inspiration from their example, and gather renewed confidence and honored dead, catch inspiration from their example, and gather renewed confidence and a firmer resolve to tread, with unfaltering trust, the path that leads to honor and peace, although it led through tears and suffering and blood.

We have no alternative but to do our duty. We combat for property, homes, the honor of our wives, the future of our children, the preservation of our fair land from pollution, and to avert a doom which we can read, both in the threats of our enemies and the acts of oppression, we have alluded to in this address. The situation is grave but furnishes no just excuse for despondency. Instead of harsh criticisms on the Government and our generals; instead of bewailing the failure to accomplish impossibilities, we should rather be grateful, humbly, and profoundly, to a benignant Providence, for the results that have rewarded our labors.

Remembering the disproportion in population, in military and naval resources, and the deficiency of skilled labor in the South, our accomplishments have surpassed those recorded of any people in the annals of the world. There is no just reason for hopelessness or fear. Since the outbreak of the war the South has lost the nominal possession of the Mississippi river and fragments of her territory.

But Federal occupancy is not conquest. The fires of patriotism still burn unquenchably in the breasts of those who are subject to foreign domination. We yet have in our uninterrupted control of territory, which, according to past progress, will require the enemy ten years to overrun. The enemy is not free from difficulties. With an enormous debt, the financial convulsion, long postponed, is surly coming. The short crops in the United States and abundant harvests in Europe will otherwise inevitable.

Many sagacious persons at the North discover in the usurpations of their Government the certain overthrow of their liberties. A large number revolt from the unjust war waged upon the South and would gladly bring it to an end. Others look with alarm upon the complete subversion of constitutional freedom by Abraham Lincoln, and feel, in their own persons, the bitterness of the slavery which three years of war have failed to inflict on the South, Brave and earnest men at the North have spoken out against the usurpations and cruelties daily practiced. The success of these men over the radical and despotic faction which now rules the North may open the way to peaceful negotiation and a cessation of this bloody and unnecessary war.

In conclusion, we exhort our fellow citizens to be of good cheer and spare no labor, nor sacrifices that may be necessary to enable us to win the campaign upon which we have just entered. We have passed through great trails of affliction but suffering and humiliation are the schoolmasters that lead nations to self-reliance and independence.

We beg that the supplies and resources of the country, which are ample, may be sold to the Government to support and equip its armies. Let all spirit of faction and past party differences be forgotten in the presence of our cruel foe. We should not despond. We should be self-denying. We should labor to extend to the utmost the productive resources of the country. We should economize. The families of soldiers should be cared for and liberally supplied. We entreat from all a generous and hearty cooperation with the Government in all branches of its administration, and with the agents, civil or military, in the performance of their duties.

Moral aid has the "power of the incommunicable," and, by united efforts, by an all comprehending and self-sacrificing patriotism, we can, with the blessing of God, avert the perils which environ us, and achieve for ourselves and children peace and freedom. Hitherto the Lord has interposed graciously to bring us victory, and His hand there is present power to prevent this great multitude which comes against us from casting us out of the possession which He has given us to inherit.

T.J. SEMMES,
J.L. ORR,
A.E. MAXWELL,
Committee on the part of the Senate.
J.W. CLAPP,
J.L.M. CYRRY,
JULIAN HARTRIDGE,
JOHN GOODE, JR.,
W.N.H. SMITH,
Committee of the House of Representatives.

Signed by Thomas S. Bocock, Speaker of the House of Representatives; Walter Preston, John McQueen, Charles W. Russell, W. Lander, A.H. Conrow, C.J. Munerlyn, Thomas S.Ashe, O.R. Singleton, J.L.Pugh, A.H. Arrington, Waller R. Staples, A.R. Boteler, Thomas J. Foster, W.R. Smith, Ro. J. Breckinridge, John M. Martin, Porter Ingram, A.H. Garland, E.S. Dargan, D. Funsten, Thomas D. McDowell, J.R. McLean, R.R. Bridgers, G.W. Jones, B.S. Gaither W. Ewing W.D. Holder, Dan. W. Lewis, Henry E. Read, A.T. Davidson, M.H. Macwillie, James Lyons, Casper W. Bell, R.B. Hilton, Charles J. Villere, J. W. Moore, Lucius J. Dupre, John D.C. Atkins, Israel Welsh, William G. Swan, F. Be Sexton, T.L. Burnett, George G. Vest, Wm. Porcher Miles, E, Barksdale, Charles F. Collier, P.W. Gray, W.W. Clark, William W. Boyce, Jon R. Chambliss, John J. McRae, John Perkins Jr., Robert Johnson, James Farrow, W.D. Simpson, Lucious J. Gartrell, M.D. Graham, John B. Baldwin, F.M. Bruce, Thomas B. Hanly, W.P. Kenan, C.M. Conrad, H.W. Bruce, David Clopton, W.B. Machen, D.C. DeJarnette. H.C. Chambers, Thomas Menees, S.A, Miller, James M. Baker, Roberts W. Barnswell, A. G. Brown, Henry C. Burnett, Allen T. Caperton, John B. Clark, Clement C. Clay, William T. Dortch, Landon C. Haynes, Gustavus A. Henry, Benjamin H. Hill, R.M.T. Hunter, Robert Jemison Jr., Herschel V. Johnson of Georgia: Robert W. Johnson of Arkansas: Waldo P. Johnson of Missouri: Augustus E. Maxwell, Charles B. Mitchel, W.S. Oldham, James L. Orr, James Phelan, Edwin G. Reade, T.J Semmes, William E. Simms, Edward Sparrow, and Louis T. Wigfall.

Source: Southern Historical Society Papers. Vol. I. Richmond, Virginia C.S.A. 1876. No.1

Author's Notes: It would be hard for most men to understand the final decisions of God. Even with the rightful justification of the Confederacy, God did allow the United States of America to enslave the Confederate States of America. Not because the South was in the wrong! And not because the Confederacy is not a true nation!

But it was required for the Confederate States to become part of a new empire to move forward in fulfilling the Scriptures of Revelations in the Holy Bible.

Without the War Between the States, World War I would not have taken place. The Confederate States had created the first iron ships. And when the Yankees stolen the information, they were able to modify and improve on the idea. The Union had improved on the rifle in battle. The Confederates created the first land mines. The Confederates were the first to use a submarine in battle. The Wright Brothers (Yankees) flew their airplane from Kitty Hawk, North Carolina. The trench war took place in the Confederacy. All of these ideas were used in World War I & II.

If the United States hadn't become a empire, the United Nations would have never been formed. The United Nations will lead us toward the New World Order and the anti-Christ. It was required for the Confederate States to lose their principles and the true understanding of freedom and liberty on the sacrificial alter of "Rights of Man," in order to lay the road map into the future. Everything in history will fit together like a puzzle to accomplish God's will. One Empire most be born to lay the foundation for another. Sodom and Gomorrah is transforming from two cities to a world wide scale version.

Strange as it may seem, one day I went to pay my car Insurance. I walked into the Insurance Agents office and notice a picture of Abraham Lincoln on his wall! A Southerner with a picture of an evil tyrant on his wall? I had no right to say anything because, it was his office and it is his picture! But, what if Adolf Hitler had won WWII? Most likely you would walk into a Car Insurance Office in Israel and find a photograph of Hitler! Why? Because, whoever wins the war, writes the history books.

It is called brainwashing! Lincoln and Martin Luther King Jr., who are in my view, are socialist, have become heroes in government schoolbooks. Socialist Engineering or Reform (Multi-Culturist) is being forced upon us today! Homosexuality, Miscegenation, Abortion, Fornication, Bastard Children. War against Christianity and elimination of the Caucasian people through race-mixing. Attack on our constitution & gun rights. All of these are leading up toward the coming One World Government. The Empire is being flooded with non-Europeans only! The only thing we can do is to, 1. Share the truth that is taking place right now, 2. Do not follow the ways of this world in controlling us, and 3. Share the gospel. 4. Live or die for Christ.

May God be with ya'll always!

THE INSTITUTION OF AMERICAN SLAVERY

The Northern Centralist & Socialist have for years used the subject of (Slavery as a Trojan horse, or an excuse) for invading and enslaving the Southern States who constitutionally left the Union. I do not support the institution of slavery, regardless if it is agriculture or Industrial. But when the citizens become dependent and submissive servants to the government that is when it truly becomes evil. I cannot at the same time condemn agriculture slavery as being evil or illegal.

According to the Holy Bible, slavery existed under the Mosaic Law and has no parallel. And that law did not originate but only regulated the already existing custom of slavery.

1. Exodus. 21:20, 21, 26, 27.
2. Leviticus. 25: 44-46.
3. Joshua. 9:6-27.

The worldly Institution of slavery would not be a sin or something that is evil. For if it were then, God would not allow His chosen people to practice such a thing. But, to violate these laws that God had put in place were to protect the servants or slaves, would then be a sin and become evil. Therefore, it would be far better not to allow slavery at all, to protect the would-be slave, and the would be master from such evil that may come about full circle. We also must remember that the Northern States and Socialist do not believe in the Holy Bible as a golden rule to define what is good or evil. And I am speaking of non-Christian Northerners only. Their views lean more toward the secular worldly views and emotions.

So long as the laws of slavery by the Creator were not violated, then slavery would not be morally wrong. And if it was the desire of the people not to own slave's, then that would be even better. However, one State does not have the right to force its ideas and will on another State. Each State governs themselves according to their own sovereign free will. We should remember that the United States Congress could have removed slavery from their Federal Constitution at any time, since most of the Southern Representatives were no longer members in the Union Congress to prevent it.

Yet, it took only two years after the War of Northern Aggression to pass it. Since that time the United States has not condemned nor invaded any other nation that practices slavery. Usually, politicians will preach moral justice or play situations to win the emotions of the people in order to deceive them and convince them into surrendering the people's right and freedom for false security in the government.

And when the politicians can influence the people through their emotions over the truth and reasonable thinking, does that not make the people themselves become somewhat like slaves? What is worse, to enslave the hearts and minds of the people, or just their physical bodies? Are in the end, is it not all the same? Politicians have used propaganda to make unnecessary wars, created false illusions of freedom, and patriotism as justification to all means for more power. Even promoting the false since of insecurity in return for more government control.

Tell me this! How do you eat an elephant? The answer is, "one bite at a time." And the people are is the "elephant." Despite all of this in being true, the truth is always ignored that in the end, slavery in the South was far better than in other slave nations and even far better than from native lands from which the slaves had come! You do not hear much about slavery in other countries around the world in today's news. Not even of Negros having slaves, or even having slaves of their own race.

Clearly the Socialist and the Radical Republicans uses this subject for repression against the Southern people. This subject is always being used like a cattle prod as a weapon, to enforce the self-guilt, and keep the Confederate Americans under submission. Neither one nation, nor race is without sin, nor have they not been guilty of some form of injustice in their own history. But, since the United States had so called won the military war against the Confederate States, then the United States is never wrong or without sin. And in her own mind, she can never be held accountable for all of her actions and WAR CRIMES against the Confederate nation and its people.

And the Confederacy will forever be condemned and marked to be [evil] in standing against socialist submission and reform. However, extermination against the Southern people was acceptable during that war. But in the eyes of God, truth prevails over might. Because truth, cannot be hidden or buried for long. And truth will not fade away! And yet, could it also be that to deny the truth and the truth of history is to be considered enslaving the people as well? Because you do not have to put chains upon the hands and feet of a people to enslave them! Just their minds and hearts. But, that's something for you to ponder upon!

By: John Thomas Nall.

IS THE CONFEDERACY REALLY EVIL?

Have you really given any thought to this question? I know that I have! But, we first must understand that anyone who opposes the Federal government is automatically classified to be evil and the bad guys. There are only three reasons that the former Union of the Republic went to war. One is that the Federalist wanted their unjust taxes that they were taking from the slave States. Two, is that the Federalist wanted to replace the Anti-Federalist Constitutional Republic with a Centralized Socialistic Democracy, transforming it into an (American Empire). Three, is that the Northern Citizens wanted to go to war because they were filled with fear that the Confederacy and its free trade could cause the Northern economy to collapse. And the Confederate American Citizens fought because they were invaded by a foreign nation without Constitutional just cause.

Two of the greatest enemies of Dixie and are still enemies to her people today, are the Federalist and the (Communist, Liberals, Progressives, or Socialists) which are all one of the same. Every time that the Southern people (Confederates) strive to come together, their enemies starts promoting their propaganda of hate and fear! Slavery, Racism, and any other names they can come up with. Their continuance in promoting their (Socialist Reform) are as the liberals likes to call it (Civil Rights Movement) is to enslave the people under a Socialistic America.

It is one thing to say that any person of (race or gender of a working class) who is having their Constitutional Rights violated, being treated as a second-class Citizen, or if any Human Rights have been violated against anyone for any reason, then the people has the right to stand on those issues and let their voice be heard! But, the Socialist has always claimed to be the defenders of the poor, the minorities or race, and the opposite sex, in order to push their Communist movement goals. Cloak & Dagger is how they play this evil goal of equality. The sin of slavery is not in itself a sin. But it could lead to sin! The Holy Bible and the United States Constitution had protected slavery. So, slavery could not be a sin! **But, to violate the guild lines in the Bible about slavery is a sin!** If a slave is mistreated or is forced into a lifetime of slavery (violating the seven years standard), than it becomes a sin.

And that sin falls to those that violated those requirements that God had established. It is far better to never own slave's, but times were different back then.

Some may argue that because some of the Southern States did leave the Old Union of the Republic, over slavery does not deserve the right to be a sovereign nation! Well, when the Colonies seceded from Great Britain, they had slaves, even in the Northern States. But, you would never hear a Northerner or a reconstructed Southerner admit to that! Great Britain and almost every nation on earth had slavery! Does this mean that nobody has a right to be a free nation? Absolutely not! In the South, slavery was an economical and Constitutional issue. To destroy slavery in that time would have caused the economy to collapse. And the Northern States refusing to return any of the runaway slaves, brought up questions as to the other Constitutional Rights that the Northern States agreed to keep when this (Union of the Republic was formed.) Other issues like, unfair taxes against the South for the benefit of the North also was causing bitter feelings. The North did not pay taxes that benefit toward the South, and the South did not benefit from the taxes that they were forced to pay to the North.

In the present Federalist Empire (America), the United States has a self-righteous view that they fought to destroy slavery by destroying the South. But, these are false feelings to avoid the real issues. Today, in America, we have abortions, Miscegenation's, infidelity, homosexual rights, adulteries, feminism lifestyles and other evil sins taking place in this Empire. The evil Liberals are attacking Christianity and Western culture including our laws of the land, which is based on the Holy Word of God, the Bible, including ignoring the common sense of Biology. They are even defending the Islam practice in the American Empire. And even though the United States had broken her covenant with the God of Israel, that our founding fathers had made, and destroying the Constitutional Republic of free sovereign States, and yet the South is still the scape goat for slavery that is past history and is no longer economically sound nor practical in our moderate industrial times! Will all of the nations on earth ever stop flying their nation's banners, symbols of so-called slavery? Will the United States ever stop flying their States and National Flags just because of past slavery? I doubt it! So, why should we Southerners (Confederates)?

By: John Thomas Nall

THE LEGALITY OF SECESSION

When they originally ratified the U.S. Constitution, at least three States-New York, Virginia, and Rhode Island- included clauses asserting the right to secede from the Union at a future time. Of the three States, the ratifications by New York and Virginia were considered necessary for the Union to have a chance to succeed. The debates within those two States received great attention. Both were large States, and their ratifications were uncertain for several months.

Virginia's ratification (with a vote of 89 to 79) came on June 25, 1788 and New York's (with a vote of 30 to 27) on July 26, 1788. Even though the ratifications by Virginia and New York occurred after the ratification of the Constitution by the necessary ninth stats, New Hampshire, on June 21, 1788, they were nevertheless still viewed as crucial. When the ratifications of Virginia and New York finally occurred, confidence was high that the New Nation would at least have a fighting chance to succeed.

Rhode Island's clause asserting its right to secede if often overlooked due to its being the last of the original thirteen States to ratify. Rhode Island's first attempt to ratify the Constitution, by referendum, had failed on March 4, 1788. The States finally ratified the Constitution (with a vote of 34 to 32), on May 29th 1790. This was nearly two years after the ratifications by New Hampshire, Virginia and New York, after the swearing in of George Washington as President, and after the House of Representatives had passed the Bill of Rights (September 25th 1789.)

Ten of the twelve Amendments passed by the House were ratified by the States and incorporated into the Constitution as "The Bill of Rights" on December 15th 1791. Some important facts should be pointed out:

First, the ratifications of the Constitution by New York, Virginia, and Rhode Island were not given conditionally upon those States being granted the right to secede by the other States.

Had that been the case, the ratifications would have been invalid. Ratifications of the Constitution had to be unconditional. Those who voted to ratify the Constitution in New York, Virginia, and Rhode simply put into writing a right they thought naturally belonged to their Respective States.

The States were voluntarily joining the Union, and most people believed the same principles toward self-governance that gave the States the right to withdraw from the Union. [*It is sometimes said that the way people think regarding that last point may be determined by whether they view as States joining the Union as making a contract or as joining a treaty. The right to unilaterally withdraw from treaties is generally accepted. The right to unilaterally withdraw from contracts is not generally accepted.*]

Second, the ratifications of Virginia, New York, and Rhode Island were unanimously accepted as valid. Those State's claims to the Right of Secession were understood and agreed to by other ratifiers, including George Washington who presided over the Constitutional Convention and served as a delegate from Virginia.

Third, many lawyers believe that the acceptance of these three ratifications (New York, Virginia, and Rhode Island) as valid guarantees all States the Right to Secede. This conclusion is based on the principle that whatever rights are held by some States must be held by all States. [Exceptional rights have been granted to some States to encourage them to join the Union. But those special rights were understood by all States already in the Union at the time the States granted special rights were accepted.]

Fourth, other States might have included clauses asserting their Right to Secede. However, they thought it unnecessary since the Constitution did not forbid secession and because it was believed that "States Rights" were preserved wherever the Constitution did not expressly transfer States powers to the federal government. (On December 15, 1791, this idea was incorporated into the Constitution as the Tenth Amendment which states, "The powers not delegated to the United States by the Constitution, nor prohibited by it to the States respectively, or to the people.) The belief of the Constitutions ratifiers was that the States were entering into a voluntary association and not giving up their sovereignty.

One of the Federalist Papers expressing the ideas that were persuasive in convincing States to join the Union is Federalist Paper #4. That publication, addressed to the "People of the State of New York, saying *"The powers delegated by the proposed Constitution to the federal government are few and defined. Those which are to remain in the States government are numerous and indefinite,"*

Fifth, several writings of the founders referred to the formation of the Union, under the Constitution as an experiment. Although many people clearly hoped the Union of States would long endure, very few people expressed great confidence that it would. More widespread were expectations that the States would withdraw from the Union if the arrangement were found to be unsatisfactory.

Sixth, for nearly seven decades, from the ratification of the Constitution to shortly before the Civil War, very few people questioned the right of the States to secede from the Union. Most people took the right to secede for granted, and secession had occasionally been considered by the States in the different regions of the country. After all, the country had formed largely through secession from British rule.

Secession has not incorrectly been called, "as American as apple pie."

Seventh, President Lincoln gave several arguments against the legality of secession. His first inaugural address contained four. A lot has been written about Lincoln's arguments; some people accept their validity, while other people reject them. As the likelihood of secession increased, most folks thought that secession might be a sad-or tragic, but not evil. But Lincoln's acquired greater appeal with the emotionalism produced by the attack on Fort Sumter on the April 12th-13th of 1861.

Eighth, some and perhaps even most, Americans believe that the issue of whether secession was legal was settled on the battlefield when the forces of the Union defeated the South. But, clearly the issue could not be settled that way! Americans accept it is improper and unjust to settle matters of legality through the use of force.

Ninth, one frequently repeated (maybe because Lincoln used it)-but very weak-argument involves comparing the reference to a "Perpetual Union" in Articles of Confederation to the reference of forming a "more perfect Union" in the Constitution. It is claimed that the "more perfect Union" under the Constitution would necessarily have to include the "perpetual" quality of the Union under the earlier Articles of Confederation. This argument makes little sense! It could just as well be argued that the Union under the Constitution is "more perfect" because it is not deemed necessarily perpetual but recognizes (by the absence of prohibition) the right of the States to secede. What makes this argument all the weaker is the fact that the Articles of Confederation refer to the "perpetual" nature of the Union no less than five times.

Considering such importance in the Articles of Confederation, it must be considered intentional that the Constitution has not even reference to the Union being "perpetual." Furthermore, the present Union is not "perpetual" in the sense that-as has happened in the past-new States can be formed from parts of existing States.

An agreement was reached at the time of the annexation of Texas that Texas may ultimately be carved into five separate States. The truth is that many points within the Articles of Confederation were abandoned in the new Constitution. During the Constitutional Convention, most people believed that the failures of the Articles of Confederation made a new Constitution imperative.

Tenth, when simple concepts of self-determination and self-governance of the peoples are discussed, people generally agree that the decisions-including the most basic decisions-regarding governance must be open to all generations of peoples, and not just the generations of peoples that lived decades or centuries ago.

Lincoln's "Democracy argument" offered that since the Constitution itself permits any kind of amendment (it prohibits only two kinds), the right to secede has been replaced by the right to [try to] amend the Constitution. But, suppose that in some generation, as happened during Lincoln's, the people in some State(s) are not satisfied with ultimately leaving crucial matters of governance up to the whims of others, many of whom are perceived as sharing sufficient common interests with themselves. Unlike Lincoln, those folks might find the right to [try to] amend the Constitution a totally inadequate placement for the right to secede. Shouldn't they be able to decide that question for themselves?

Eleventh, while Lincoln and much of his cabinet thought and gave lip-service to the idea that legal secession was impossible, and for that reason often refused to recognize the States as actually having "seceded" (done the impossible), they certainly acted toward those States as though real secessions had in fact occurred, both by taking Constitutional Rights away from these seceded States, and (Lincoln excepted, since he was dead) by making them go through a readmittance following the Civil War.

Twelfth, some scholars say that the Supreme Court's decision in 'Texas v. White' did settle the legality-of-secession question on the "con" side as firmly as many people have claimed. For one thing, the court did allow some possibility of legal secession by saying:

"The Union between Texas and the other States was as complete, as perpetual, and as indissoluble as the Union between the original States. There was no place for reconsideration, except through Revolution, or through consent of the States." (Emphasis mine.)

What was Texas v. White about? During the Civil War, the secessionist government of Texas had sold U.S. bonds after passing an ordinance repealing a requirement that the governor of Texas endorse the bonds before redeeming them. (The governor had refused to endorse secession and had been dismissed.) Following the war, Texas sued to recover bonds that had been transferred to George W. White and several others.

However, Texas' readmittance to the Union had been delayed by the States failure to satisfy Congress's demand that Texas ratify the Fourteenth Amendment. The issue of whether Texas was a State of the United States had bearing on whether the Supreme Court had jurisdiction in the case.

Since the legality of secession was not the main issue between Texas and the purchasers of the bonds, many people feel that the legality-of-secession issue was far from fully argued and adequately considered. The Supreme Court's decision in Texas v. White has remained very controversial.

Thirteenth, secession could occur in the U.S. by a Constitutional amendment. But an interesting point has been raised about how (rather than whether) mutually agreed-upon secession could be made legal through a Constitutional amendment (assuming unilateral secession is not already legal.) If the Constitutional amendment allowing for secession followed the same process as all the other amendments so far, which States would be allowed to vote on the question in the Two Houses? It has been argued that only the States not wishing to secede should be allowed to vote.

Otherwise, it could not be guaranteed that secession by Constitutional amendment would be mutually agreed-upon. Obviously, it could be considered mutually agreed-upon if the total votes among the States wishing to remain in the Union, was against the secession.

[On August the 20th 1998, Canada's Supreme Court ruled that province Quebec was the province considered) had no right to unilaterally secede, rather under Canadian law or under international law. However, the Court held that the desire of a province to secede obligated Canada's national government to negotiate with the province that desired to secede.

Such negotiations would be conducted according to standards that would be at the start neither guarantee secession nor rule out mutually agreed-upon secession. This seems to recognize in Canada a real possibility of mutually agreed-upon secession, i.e, of a secession having the approval of both the seceding province and the remaining portion of Canada.

Best Argument Against the Legality of Secession

Perhaps the best argument against the legality of secession is the one that rests upon secession being an "insurrection." Section VII of Article 1 of the Constitution gives Congress the power to call forth the militia to "suppress insurrections." However, many people would agree that secession is not an insurrection. They see secession as the withdrawal of recognition of an authority as lawful rather than the refusal to obey recognized lawful authority.

In addition, secession is not itself an aggressive action taken against the residue of States left within the Union. It is a point often overlooked, but some States that seceded during the Civil War are very proud of the fact that they did not declare war-or fight offensive war-against the Union, but only fought a defensive war in order to be able to govern themselves as they saw fit. Northerners should remember this if they wish to understand the thinking of many in the South.

By: George Desnoyers-October 13th 2005.

QUESTIONS ABOUT THE CONFLICT

- Did the South fought for or over the issue of slavery? Absolutely Not! The Confederate States fought because she had been invaded by a military force that was not of her own troops and was not given permission by any of the States Governments nor the C.S.A. Government to enter her own soil.

- Did the South leave the Union over the issue of slavery? Yes! Some of the Southern States did leave because of the problems that they were having over that subject. But, not all of the Southern States did leave for that reason. Some of them left, because they did not will not to spill the blood of their own people [kin], by joining the Union side. The rest left because of the oppression and because of the tyranny that was coming from the government of the United States.

- If Yes, then why? Some of the Southern States left the Union, not because they could not maintain that institution. For if that was the case than all they would have to do was to remain in the Union. Slavery was protected by the Constitution of the United States all the way up to two years after the War Between the States. Those States that left the Union did so for a few reasons. The population in the South was much smaller than in the North. To maintain a balance in the representation of the people's voice (voting power), in the Federal government, a slave was counted as a partial vote. Without the population of the slave vote of that time, the interest and concerns of those States would have fallen on deaf ears. If the Southern States had the same amount of the population as of in the North, then they would not need that extra partial vote. The second reason of understanding the Southern people is this! The government of the United States had failed in doing its duty by preventing slaves from being returned to the owners in the slaves States. They also had turned the other eye while the terrorism and murders by the Abolitionist group and leader John Brown. The murdering of slave owners and families, including the fact that they were trying to create a race war between the two races. So, if the Union Federal government would refuse to maintain this small part of the Constitution, then what guarantees would they do in protecting the rest of the people's rights in the Constitution? For that was the one the purpose in creating the Union government in the first place!

- ❖ What is the Union? Well, I can give you two examples! One would be the compact or agreement between the sovereign States that had joined together in an alliance that benefit the interest of all the parties involved. A Constitutional Republic, that was created by the States, known as members of the United [States] and Confederate [States]. The term of the United States means the States that are standing together in the benefit of the interest and concerns of all the members.

   The other would lean more toward the Federalist (Centralized) and Socialist or Communist forms. The Federalist believes that the Federal Constitution should be regulated by the Federal government instead of by the States. A (Centralized Democracy) government of power. They will determine as to how much freedom you should have and for how long. The Socialist or Communist goes far beyond that as to where the States or nothing more than provinces and has no limits or boundaries. All of them leans toward a solid mass of power where the will and the liberties of the people or null and void.

- ❖ Where would the C.S.A. be today if they had been allowed to secede? Every State that had sign the Constitution of the United States or became members in the Union afterwards, has never sign any document of surrendering their (Sovereign Rights.) It has always been understood by all members that if they join freely, they may also leave freely, should it come down to that. This was in agreement that all of the States understood when they had signed the Constitution of the United States. This was taught at West Point and it reflects upon the Rights of the States, and by the Declaration of Independence.

   The Southern States did secede, and that is already a fact. They had been out of the Union for four years and formed a nation of their own. And they defended her as such! If the Confederate States had not been forced back into the new Socialist Block Union, what would it be like now? It is always hard to say what the future would be like. But, all you can do is to look at the character and the principles or values of the people and try to give a positive outcome. The laws of the land would still be continually based on the Holy Bible and not being rewritten by secular ideas. The Confederacy would remain as a White majority and with other non-Whites would have the same rights as citizens. The United Nations would never be allowed in our borders. All Communist and National Socialists would be a threat to national security and be dealt with according to the law. Damn Yankees [illegal aliens] would not be allowed to live within our borders without citizenship. Slavery would have been phased out in time and the Confederate Constitution would have been updated through the years. She would not have been in WWI, but she would have been in WWII. She would not have been in all the other wars that that American Empire has been in.

The Socialist or Liberals if you like, always tries to portray itself as the champion, to convert any nation's government into a Communist one. The United States government (public schools) always portrays the Confederate States to be evil, to justify its unconstitutional invasion and war crimes during the war. They won the war; they write the books! Some people would like to paint a picture that the Confederacy would have evolved into apartheid or a National Socialist Nation like, Nazi Germany! But, this is a contradiction to the character of the people and the laws of the land which are founded on the Holy Bible. But, being that most Americans including Confederates are mostly ignorant and naive of real history, they believe whatever they are told! After all! If you cannot trust the government and you can't trust they Liberals (Socialist), who can you trust? The Jim Crow law would have never existed within the Confederate borders because the South has always been an integrated nation, just without the miscegenation and other sinful laws that the Liberals have been shoving down our thoughts since our enslavement. Now, don't get me wrong! My people are not without sin! And we are fall short from being perfect! But, if you were to look at our record since we have been part of the American Empire, it was the South that tried to restore the Constitutional Republic government back into the United States and failed. It was the South that stood against all Liberal (socialist reforms) or transformation. It was the South that stood against the New World Order, and socialist multi-culturist false utopia. Sadly, to say, with the continuous reconstruction upon the minds and hearts of my people, we are being destroyed, and yet, it is now being forced upon all the entire European race (or) in my opinion the lost ten tribes of Israel! Read the book: America and Britain in Prophecy By; David C. Pack. I would like to say one more thing on this subject! I do believe that the Confederate States Government would have prevented the United States plans in eliminating and actions of genocide against the Native America Indians after the war. In history, justice does not always prevail, and the good guys do not always win. But, everything in history does fit together like a puzzle. And had the C.S did win the war; it would have only prolonged the inevitable of the Anti-Christ, the New World Order and returning of Jesus Christ. According to the Holy Bible, the history of mankind is predestined in their outcome. And if Satan-Evil is free, changing history changes nothing in that concept in our own personal lives.

❖ Where would we be if the U.S.A had not allowed the C.S.A back into the Union and had kept her as a territory or possession with no voice in Congress or State matters? This is a very good question! First, we must understand that during the War Between the States, the United States stated that the Southern

States could not leave the Union and that it was a [War of Rebellion], which by the way sounds something like what Great Britain might say about the American Colonies!

After the war, they said that the Southern States was no longer in the Union and could be treated as a conquered territory. This means that it was perfectly justified for the Southern States to leave the Union! Then the nation of the Confederate States had to choose between two evils. [A.] Compromise the Sovereignty of the States Constitution and become subjects to the will of the Union Federal government. Or [B.] Continual to be treated as a conquered nation, meaning [possession.] And while the Confederate States government was forced to dispersed and never surrendered nor sign any peace treaty, the member States decided to choose the lesser of the two evils and become subjects to the Empire. It must be understood that the wording by the United States would not directly recognize the Confederate States as a Nation, but that in fact the Southern States was not recognized as being as sovereign States at all. That's why in politics, we have to read between the lines.

But, by putting the Confederate States in this saturation, United States Congress was stating that they truly did believe that the Southern States did leave the Union legally and lawfully! Because, they cannot force someone to rejoin the Union, if they had never left in the first place! And by violating the Constitutions of the States in the Confederacy, would be also making an indirect statement that the Declaration of Independence if invalid and wrong and that the American Colonies should never have left the First Union of (Great Britain) in the first place.

Know where in the declaration of Independence nor in the Constitution nor in any other documents you will find that the United States government had the right to interfere with any of the States from leaving the Union or to force them back in at gun point! Nor Will you find anything that gives them grounds to deny and recognized those States from coming together as a Nation. Imagine! If you were a member of a club, and you decided that the club which started off good at first was to be transformed into something that you felt uncomfortable with or felt threaten by. And since you believe that this club no longer stood for the things that you believed in, you decided to withdraw your membership. But the club says that once you are in, you're in for life! They beat you up and kill one of your friends or family members to make their point! Is this any different than joining the Mafia?

Even the Holy Bible will allow a divorce between a married couple under the right circumstances! Then, out of the kindest of their hearts, they say you must choose! What will it be? You can join us and knell to our will as a slave, or you can be treated lower than a conquered animal? What would you do if this had happened to you? Then later, they will tell you that this is FREEDOM! And from generation to generation, your decedents accept this concept to be the truth!

- Did the South have to win the war to become a Free Nation? I have heard some Southerners make the statement that the South was fighting for Independence, and with all due respect, this term is a contradiction to the Declaration of Independence and ignores that fact the South already had a government, President, Constitution that was ratified, currency, military, and peace treaties with the American Indian Tribes and so forth.

    In truth the South fought not for freedom, but to maintain that freedom that had been handed down to them from the victory during the (Colonial War of Independence) or (Revolutionary War of Independence) from Great Britain. When the Southern States did leave the Union, it was by the free will of the people of those States that had voiced it. When the Southern people stood up against the invasion to protect their homes and liberty, it was done by self-preservation and duty.

- When the United States had won the war, didn't that settle the issue about the Southern States? As far as the enslavement into the Union goes, Yes! Because that is an historical fact! But, that doesn't mean that they were in the right nor was it justified and legal. Nor does it disprove as to that the Southern States cannot be a nation. It is only by force by arms that they can make that statement. We must remember that the Southern States had stood side by side with the Northern States against the violations and the injustices by the King of Great Britain and has now became a subject to the former nation of the Constitutional Republic that they help in creating, [The United States of America.]

    In war, that which is right and that which is true is determined by the victor and not by true justice that is based on humanity and liberty. Another word's the good guys don't always win! What would happen if the Colonies had lost the war with Great Britain? It would mean that our understanding of liberty and freedom would have been re-written from the victor's point of view and the Colonies views of liberty would have been forever lost and forgotten in history.

- If the States could leave, wouldn't those States cause the Nation to collapse? Not under these circumstances, No. The United States has a membership of different sovereign States with a certain interest that brings them together. If some of the States were to leave the fellowship or membership, the other States would still maintain that national government for them all. The United States had started off with thirteen States and membership continual to grow all the way up to the 1860's when some of the Southern States withdrew their membership.

When the Colonies broke away from Great Britain's Empire, England did not collapse. Canada and Australia had also withdrawn its membership from Great Britain. Former Communist Russia did not collapse either! It only causes them to no longer to remain as a great Empire. Any time that more than one State was to leave the Union or Confederacy is basically saying that something is wrong with the federal government and it would be safer to withdraw from that membership. If the government starts to show favoritism for certain States over the other, or becomes corrupted and tyrannical, than for the safety and liberty of the people self-preservation has no option.

- ❖ But, without the federal government, the nation is no more! Not true! The federal government is only the extension of the hand of the member States. If the federal government were to collapse, that the States could reestablished that same form of government or replace it with something much better. Because it is the free membership of those States that are standing together to protect each other's interest that defines them as a country of a nation. Much like the body parts of a person.

The United States & Confederate States are unique compared to other nations of the world. In most cases other nations can only exist because it's the government that continues existence of those nations. To remove that center power, regardless if it's a monarchy or some other form of government, it could lead a nation into anarchy, Civil War, and so forth.

- ❖ But, what if the State of North Carolina, had decided to leave the Confederacy? According to the Declaration of Independence and the Southern Declaration of Independence: It is the right of the people, meaning the Citizens of each State to determine what is in their best interest. If the federal government becomes corrupt and cannot be corrected or if the federal government fails to protect and full fill its duties and obligations to all of the member States, or of if the government shows favoritism and can no longer maintain a balance of neutrality for all of the States, than any State has that individual right to withdraw their freedom of association as a member.

Secession in all reality would help to give the desire of that government to correct that problem to maintain that States membership or, to give the other States the desire to eliminate any corruption or tyranny within their own government. Naturally, if a State wants to leave over something that the other States may consider to be somewhat foolish? Then let them go! And should that State decides to rejoin later on, the member States can decide if it would be worth the trouble to allow that State back in! The member States can still maintain friendship with that former Member State. It is better to have a good friend, than an enemy!

- But didn't the U.S. President: Abraham Lincoln bring slavery to an end? Absolutely not! Abraham Lincoln had no authority beyond what the Constitution of the United States allowed him to have! Only the United States Congress has the right to modify the Constitution when it comes to making changes. The same implies with the Confederate States Congress and their Constitution.

  To allow the President that kind of power would put him in a position of becoming a tyrant. Slavery constitutionally ended in the United States two years after the war and even some Yankees still had their slaves up to that time. Slavery ended in the occupied Confederacy at gun point, instead of through the natural process, economically speaking. Any nation that would suddenly end slavery all at once at one time will cause the whole nation to collapse. It must be a slow transition in order to maintain the economy.

- Secession must be an act of treason! Not at all, in fact (Secession) is part of the mechanical device that helps in maintaining the Constitutional Republic in sustaining itself. Secession is like an overflow valve in the Radiator in your car when it is malfunctioning. To keep your radiator from bursting open, the extra water will go out of your overflow valve. Without secession, a true Constitutional Republic cannot maintain its true purpose and will cause that Constitutional Republic to die. Because it would deny the free-will of the citizens of the people in any of the States to embrace the Declaration of Independence for themselves. The Declaration of Independence and the Constitutional Republic are intertwined into one, in true liberty and sovereignty of the people in each of the States.

  You cannot deny them one without in some way compromising the rest! Secession is freedom from oppression! I personally don't believe that the States would have ratified the Constitution, if it was understood that secession was classified to be illegal and a treasonous act!

- But are we not free? First you should understand that freedom is a combination of things. The first step in freedom is to be spiritually free in Jesus Christ and applying the Holy Scriptures in your daily life. Second: is to know your true history that brought forth your freedom. Third is to understand and study the Declaration of Independence and your national and State Constitutions and the kind of government that had been founded, not what we have today!

The hard part about freedom is in understanding what it is not! It is not the soldiers fighting in foreign lands, because it is more of an empire objective than anything. It is not a symbol of a flag or any emblems, because they only represent that nation only! And that nation can change over the years and still have those same symbols. It is not pledging Allegiance to the flag, because the Pledge of Allegiance in reality is a self-form of brainwashing of loyalty toward that government and not toward the principles our liberty. When you give your pledge, it is unconditional and comes above anything and everyone ells, including God the Father! Give your allegiance only to our Father and Son in heaven. Your duty to your family and kindred people or race and nation is a natural born responsibility and obligation without contest. Also study how the Ten Commandments had laid the foundation and laws in our Western Civilization.

- Since the occupied Confederate Nation is now part of the United States, and the United States is a member in the United Nations, can the Confederacy ever leave? Most likely not! First we have to remember that the Confederate States is more [Constitutionally a separate Nation] than they are by force part of the new version of the American Empire. And that in truth the United States has not really ever had a real Civil War with the Southern States of the Confederacy.

Neither the government nor the President of the Confederate States has ever signed an unconditional surrender, or a peace treaty with the United States. It is true that even though the Confederate States did not voluntary join the United Nations and that she is a subject (slave) to the United States, the United Nations will not have recognized her at all as a nation. The United Nations with its transforming into a 'Socialistic World Government,' will in fact not recognized any of her members to be sovereign and independent nations anymore, including the Confederate States of America. These nations have prostituted themselves and their sovereignty for security and a false utopia society. They will suffer under the anti-Christ just as the whole world will suffer. Everybody should resist evil and fight for their rights. But, remember this, fighting for your rights does not carry any guarantees toward victory! But accepting the grace of God and the salvation through Jesus Christ does! We can only pray and asked Jesus Christ to recognize the Confederacy as a sovereign nation and to restore everything that was stolen and denied from her.

By: John Thomas Nall

✦ ✦ ✦
INTRESTING HISTORICAL FACTS YOU MAY NOT KNOW!

- ❖ H.K. Edgerton, is a Black Southern Heritage activist, and a former President of the N.A.A.C.P's Chapter in Ashville, North Carolina. At the age of 55, his most notable action was a march along with his brother from North Carolina to Texas. He also did the same march years later. But the national controlled media, ignored his historical act and devotion. Most American's knows nothing about his patriotism. Other Confederate Negros are following his footsteps and are being ignored by the national news.

- ❖ Only 6% of Southerners had owned slaves before the unconstitutional war against the Confederate States of America.

- ❖ Though the Southern States represented only about 30% of the U.S. population. They paid 80% of the tariffs collected.

- ❖ Oppressive taxes, denial of the States, to govern themselves, and an unrepresentative federal government had pushed the Southern States to legally withdraw from the Union and established a New Union of the Confederacy. It was not over slavery.

- ❖ Slavery was still legal in the U.S. Constitution even after the Southern States had withdrawn their membership from it.

- ❖ It was only required of the U.S. Congress to repeal the right to own slavery, after the Southern States were no longer Constitutional members in the Union. But at the time they had chosen not to do so.

- H.K. Edgerton, a Negro Christian Southerner, who walked to Texas from North Carolina in order to bring awareness of Southern Culture and history. On October the 13th of 2002 with a 2 P.M. prayer at the governor Zebulon B. Vance monument, he began his march. Wearing a Confederate States Infantry uniform and caring a different of variety of Confederate States Flags. He had walked 1,300 miles covering approximately seven Southern States. From Asheville, North Carolina to Austin, Texas C.S.A., a journey of about three months. He has also made this effort in order to support the Sons of Confederate Veterans Heritage Defense Fund, including the Southern Legal Resource Center. And even though Mr. Edgerton had made national history in Dixie Land. The Liberal [Politically Correct Socialist Media] had ignored him to make sure that his story would not break news throughout the United States. Only a few local News Stations has covered his story. He has also repeated the same march years later and as usual know one throughout the American Empire knows about it. He is continually making history and is being ignored by the national news of controlled information.

- 100.000 Negro Confederate Americans served and fought during the war of the invasion by the United States of America.

- In Charleston, South Carolina (1860), 125 free Negroes owned slaves. Six had owned ten or more. In North Carolina, 69 free Negroes owned slaves.

- 1860 Federal Censuses: 4 million Negroes were in the South and 261,988 were free and not slaves. 10,689 free Negroes lived in New Orleans. 3,000 of these owned slaves. Out of (28%), only (13%) of Caucasians owned slaves.

- In 1860, six Negroes in Louisiana owned 65 or more slaves. The Richards family owned 152 slaves. Antoine Dubuclet, another Negro slave magnate owned over 100 slaves. His Estate was valued at $264, 000 (in 1860 dollars), while the main wealth of Caucasian men was $3,978. Which brings up an interesting point? It just could be possibly that some runaway slaves might have been running from abusive Negro slave owners! But, I have no evidence to prove this theory.

- 620,000 needlessly lost their lives in the War to Prevent Southern Independence.

- The U.S.A. has pledged to defend Taiwan's right to exist as a free nation. Double standards are difficult to explain in the world of politics!

- Mr. Johnson was a member of the Communist Party USA, for ten years, during which he became one of the Parties highest-ranking Negro member. After he recurred to his Christian upbringing and left the Party. In writing his book titled, *"Color, Communism, and Common Sense."* From a brief selection is taken. The information revealed in his book is extremely damaging to the left, and to the whole (Civil Rights) movement. Archibald Roosevelt published the book in 1958. Mr. Johnson was killed shortly thereafter when he was struck by a hit and run car, while riding a bicycle.

- The American Continent had legalized slavery in 1654. That's 207 years before the Confederate States of America had ever existed.

- The Arab slave trade of African Negros lasted for 1400 years. The European transatlantic African Negros slave trade lasted for 300 years, and only 5% of the slaves were brought to the North American Continent. Yet, 95% were taken to South America and the Caribbean's. Today, the descendants of the African Negro slaves that were brought to North America have the highest standard of living of any Negros living anywhere in the world. In fact, they are astronomically better off than Negroes living in any nation in Africa today.

- [FREEDOM]: Dr. James Dobson teaches that faith and freedom are two sides of the same coin, saying that freedom without faith will degenerate into anarchy and chaos. And the only way to combat chaos is to LIMIT personal freedom through tougher, more intrusive laws, expanded police presence and bigger prisons. Dictators emerge from that circumstance.

- The Citizens of the United States or of the American Empire have been educated and conditioned to be loyal subjects through the government public schools. And most citizens have become so lazy and sorry that they have no desire to research other sources of information on any historical teachings which the Federal government was involved in. So, Americans have become naïve and ignorant and submissive to whatever they are told from the Federal Central government, television and entertainment. Authors Notes; Brain washing is another term we could call use.

- Federal Public Schools are also used to keep the Confederate Americans of different races divided and hostile toward each other, to prevent them from standing together as a Nation through the teachings of one-sided & half-truths Union history.

❖ Old Glory, the National flag of the United States, flew over legalized slavery for 90 years! (1776 to 1866.)

❖ Communism has murdered 100 million people and maybe more that has not been accounted for. Authors Notes; Yet Americans still are embracing (Liberalism-Socialism.)

❖ In 1783, the 'Treaty of Paris,' (England recognized the separate political and territorial sovereignty of each individual State): Article 1: "His Britannic Majesty acknowledges the said United States, viz., New Hampshire, Massachusetts Bay, Rhode Island and Providence Plantations, Connecticut, New York, New Jersey, Pennsylvania, Maryland, Virginia, North Carolina, South Carolina and Georgia, to be (free sovereign and independent States.) That he treats with them as such, and for himself, his heirs, and successors, relinquishes all claims to the government, property, and territorial rights of the same and every part thereof." Authors Note; this is proof that the States created the Federal government of the United States and not the other way around.

❖ [PART ONE] Francis Julius Bellamy (May 18th of 1855 to August 28th of 1931, a one-time Baptist minister and a prominent member of the Christian Socialist movement, wrote the original USA Pledge of Allegiance. First published in the September the 8th of the 1892 issue of (The Youth's Companion.) Bellamy then a committee chairman of the National Education Association, structured a public school programmed around a flag raising salute-his "Pledge of Allegiance." This Pledge has since come under several-sometimes-controversial-revisions.

Bellamy's original words were: (I pledge allegiance to my Flag and the Republic, for which it stands, one nation, indivisible, with liberty and justice for all). Bellamy considered adding the word "equality" to stand with "liberty" and justice," but feared it would be too controversial. In 1924, against Bellamy's wishes, the American Legion and Daughters of the American Revolution pressured the National Flag Conference to replace the words "my Flag" with "the Flag of the United States of America." In 1954, under pressure from the Knights of Columbus, Congress officially added the words "under God." … Source:deathdate:history. vinyard.net/pledgech4.htm;birthdate:

❖ The Church of Christ (The members of which are known as Christians) was established on Pentecost, AD 33. Islam's beginning date is AD 610, the date of Muhammad's revelation. Thus, Christianity was begun first, by just under 600 years. [Answers.com]—The oldest books of the New Testament were written about the year 80-100 AD after everyone involved in Christ's life or with firsthand experience off Christ had died, about 2000 years.—Emperor Constantine called the Council of Nicea in 325 AD, which is when the Bible was first put together: picking some ancient scrolls to include, and abandoning other ancient scroll's, almost arbitrarily. This was the beginning of the Catholic Church, Not St Peter.—(Christianity-33AD)—(Catholic-325AD)-(Islam610AD.) www.answerbag.com Authors Notes: This was the first Denominational Bible and Church.

- [PART TWO] The Pledge of Allegiance (1892) was the origin of the raised arm salute adopted later by the National Socialist German Workers Party (Nazis.) The Pledge was written by Francis Bellamy, cousin to Edward Bellamy (the author,) and both were self-proclaimed national socialist in the United States. The original Pledge began with a military salute the was then extended out toward the flag. In practice, the second gesture was performed palm down. The gesture was not an ancient Roman salute. All of these discoveries of the symbologist in Dr. Rex Curry (author of "Pledge of Allegiance Secrets.") The images of these salutes would be found in the movie "The Vanishing American" (1925 by George B. Seitz) based on the Zane Grey novel. The film covers the history of native American Indians, continuing through World War I history, as portrayed in this film, has been a succession of conquests of stronger races over the weaker ones. Life on a reservation is portrayed. The impact of WWI is shown (during that time, when the United States fought Germany, the United States used the stiff-armed salute.) For more information visit [www.RexCurry.net].

CHAPTER FOUR

CHRONOLOGY OF SECESSION FROM THE UNION

South Carolina * December 24th of 1860

Mississippi * January 9th of 1861

Florida * January 10th of 1861

Alabama * January 11th of 1861

Georgia * January 19th of 1861

Louisiana * January 26th of 1861

Texas * February 1st of 1861

{Formation of the Provisional Government of the Confederate States if America******* February 8th of 1861}

The Ratification of C.S.A. (Arizona Territory) on March 23rd of 1861

The United States President: Abraham Lincoln's unconstitutional declaration of War, against the Confederate States on April 15th of 1861

Because of the actions of the United States President, other Southern States withdrew their voluntary memberships.

Virginia * April 17th of 1861

Secession attempted by Maryland and was violated by U.S. Forces on April 17th of 1861.

Arkansas * May 6th of 1861

Tennessee * May 7th of 1861

North Carolina * May 21st of 1861

The Confederation of Chickasaw, Creek, Seminal & Choctaw Nations on July 1st of 1861

Cherokee Nation on August 21st of 1861

Missouri * October 31st of 1861

★ JOHN THOMAS NALL ★

Kentucky * November 20th of 1861

Quantrill's military attempt for the conquest of the State of Kansas on August 21st of 1861

Confederate American Cherokee Nation refused to surrender, yet had sign a Cease Fire Treaty with the United States in June 23rd of 1865

★ ★ ★

ORDAINANCE OF SECESSION 13 CONFEDERATE STATES OF AMERICA

SOUTH CAROLINA

AN ORDINANCE to dissolve the Union between the State of South Carolina and other States united with her under the compact entitled "The Constitution of the United States of America."

We, the people of the State of South Carolina, in convention assembled, do declare and ordain, and it is hereby declared and ordained, that the ordinance adopted by us in convention on the twenty-third day of May, in the year of our Lord one thousand seven hundred and eighty-eight, whereby the Constitution of the United States of America was ratified, and also all acts and parts of acts of the General Assembly of this State ratifying amendments of the said Constitution, are hereby repealed; and that the Union now subsisting between South Carolina and other States, under the name of the "United States of America," is hereby dissolved.

[Done at Charleston the twentieth day of December, in the year of our Lord, one thousand eight hundred and sixty.]

MISSISSIPPI

AN ORDINANCE to dissolve the Union between the State of Mississippi and other States united with her under the compact entitled "The Constitution of the United States of America."

The people of the State of Mississippi, in convention assembled, do ordain and declare, and it is hereby ordained and declared, as follows, to wit:

Section 1. That all the laws and ordinances by which the said State of Mississippi became a member of the Federal Union of the United States of America be, and the same are hereby repealed, and that all obligations on the part of the said State or the people thereof to observe the same be withdrawn, and that the said State doth hereby resume all the rights, functions, and powers which by any of said laws or ordinances were conveyed to the Government of the said United States, and is absolved from all the obligations, restraints, and duties incurred to the said Federal Union, and shall from henceforth be a free, sovereign, and independent State.

Sec. 2. That so much of the first section of the seventh article of the Constitution of this State as requires members of the Legislature and all officers, executive and judicial, to take an oath or affirmation to support the Constitution of the United States be, and the same is hereby, abrogated, and annulled.

Sec. 3. That all rights acquired and vested under the Constitution of the United States, or under any act of Congress passed, or treaty made, in pursuance thereof, or under any law of this State, and not incompatible with this ordinance shall remain in force and have the same effect as if this ordinance had been passed.

Sec. 4. That the people of the State of Mississippi hereby consent to form a federal Union with such as of the States as may have seceded or may secede from the Union of the United States of America, upon the basis of the present Constitution of the said United States, except such parts thereof as embrace other portions than such seceding States.

[*Thus ordained and declared in convention the 9th day of January, in the year of our Lord 1861.*]

FLORIDA

ORDINANCE OF SECESSION

We, the people of the State of Florida, in convention assembled, do solemnly ordain, publish, and declare. That the State of Florida hereby withdraws herself from the Confederacy of States existing under the name of the United States of America and from the existing Government of the said States; and that all political connection between her and the Government of said States ought to be, and the same is hereby, totally annulled, and said Union of States dissolved; and the State of Florida is hereby declared a sovereign independent nation; and that all ordinances heretofore adopted, in so far as they create or recognize said Union, are rescinded; and all laws or parts of laws I force in this State, in so far as they recognize or assent to said Union, be and they are hereby, repealed.

[Passed 10th Jan 1861.]

ALABAMA

AN ORDINANCE to dissolve the Union between the State of Alabama and the States united under the compact styled "The Constitution of the United States of America."

Whereas, the election of Abraham Lincoln and Hannibal Hamlin to the offices of President and vice-President of the United States of America, by a sectional party, avowedly hostile to the domestic institutions and to the peace and security of these people of the State of Alabama, preceded by many and dangerous infractions of the Constitution of the United States by many of the States and people of the Northern section is a political wrong of so insulting and menacing a character as to justify the people of the State of Alabama in the adoption of prompt and decided measures for their future peace and security, therefore:

Be it declared and ordained by the people of the State of Alabama, in Convention assembled. That the State of Alabama now withdraws and is hereby withdrawn from the Union known as "The United States of America." And henceforth ceases to be one of said United States, and is, and of right ought to be a Sovereign and Independent State.

Sec 2. Be it further declared and ordained by the people of the State of Alabama in Convention assembled, that all powers over the Treaty of said State, and over the people thereof heretofore delegated to the Government of the United States of America, be and they are hereby withdrawn from said Government, and are hereby resumed and vested in the people of the State of Alabama. And as it is the desire and purpose of the people of Alabama to meet the slaveholding States of the South, who may approve such purpose, in order to frame a provisional as well as permanent Government upon the principles of the Constitution of the United States.

Be it resolved by the people of Alabama in Convention assembled, that the people of the States of Delaware, Virginia, North Carolina, South Carolina, Florida, Georgia, Mississippi, Louisiana, Texas, Arkansas, Tennessee, Kentucky and Missouri, be and are hereby invited to meet the people of the State of Alabama, by their Delegates, in Convention, on the 4th day of February, A.D., 1861, at the city of Montgomery, in the State of Alabama, for the purpose of consulting with each other as to the most effectual mode of securing concerted and harmonious action in whatever measures may be deemed most desirable for our common peace and security.

And be it further resolved that the President of this Convention, be and is hereby instructed to transmit forthwith a copy of the foregoing Preamble, Ordinance, and Resolutions to the Governors of the several States named in said resolutions.

[Done by the people of the State of Alabama, in Convention assembled, at Montgomery, on this, the eleventh day of January, A.D. 1861.]

GEORGIA

We the people of the State of Georgia in Convention assembled do declare and ordain and it is hereby declared and declared and ordained that the ordinance adopted by the State of Georgia in convention on the 2nd day of January, in the year of our Lord seventeen hundred and eighty-eight, whereby the Constitution of the United States of America was assented to, ratified and adopted, and also all acts and parts of acts of the general assembly of this State, ratifying and adopting amendments to said Constitution, are hereby repealed, rescinded and abrogated.

We do further declare and ordain that the Union now existing between the State of Georgia and other States under the name of the United States of America is hereby dissolved, and that the State of Georgia is in full possession and exercise of all those rights of sovereignty which belong and appertain to a free and independent State.

[Passed on January 19th of 1861.]

LOUISIANA

AN ORDINANCE to dissolve the Union between the State of Louisiana and other States united with her under the compact entitled "The Constitution of the United States of America."

We, the people of the State of Louisiana, in convention assembled, do declare and ordain, and it is hereby declared and ordained. That the ordinance passed by us in convention on the 22nd day of November, in the year eighteen hundred and eleven, whereby the Constitution of the United States of America and the amendments of the said Constitution were adopted, and all laws and ordinances by which the State of Louisiana became a member of the Federal Union, be, and the same are hereby, repealed and abrogated; and that the Union now subsisting between Louisiana and other States under the name of "The United States of America" is hereby dissolved.

We do further declare and ordain, That the State of Louisiana hereby resumes all rights and powers heretofore delegated to the Government of the United States of America; that her citizens are absolved from all allegiance to said Government; citizens are absolved from all allegiance to said Government; and that she is in full possession and exercise of all those rights of sovereignty which appertain to a free and independent State.

WE do further declare and ordain, that all rights acquired and vested under the Constitution of the United States, or any act of Congress, or treaty, or under any law of this State, and not incompatible with this ordinance, shall remain in force and have the same effect as if this ordinance had not been passed.

[Adopted in convention at Baton Rouge this 26th day of January, 1861.]

TEXAS

AN ORDINANCE to dissolve the Union between the State of Texas and the other States united under the Compact styled ""the Constitution of the United States of America."

WHEREAS, The Federal Government has failed to accomplish the purposes of the compact of Union between the States, in giving protection either to the persons of our people upon an exposed frontier, or to the property of our citizens, and

WHEREAS, the action of the Northern States of the Union is violative of the compact between the States and the guarantees of the Constitution; and,

WHEREAS, The recent developments affairs make it evident that the power of the Federal Government is sought to be made a weapon with which to strike down the interests and property of the people of Texas, and her sister slave-holding States, instead of permitting it to be, as was intended, our shield against outrage and aggression; THEREFORE,

SECTION 1. We, the people of the State of Texas, by delegates in convention assembled, do declare and ordain that the ordinance adopted by our convention of delegates on the 4th day of July, A.D. 1845, and afterwards ratified by us, under which the Republic of Texas was admitted into the Union with other States, and became a party to the compact styled "The Constitution of the United States of America," be, and is hereby, repealed and annulled; that all the powers which, by the said compact, were delegated by Texas to the Federal Government are revoked and resumed; that Texas is of right absolved from all restraints and obligations incurred by said compact, and is a separate sovereign State, and that her citizens and people are absolved from all allegiance to the United States or the government thereof.

SEC2. This ordinance shall be submitted to the people of Texas for their ratification or rejection, by the qualified voters, on the 23rd day of February 1861, and unless rejected by most of the votes cast, shall take and be in force on and after the 2nd day of March, A.D. 1861.

PROVIDED. That the Representative District of Al Paso said election may be held on the 18th day of February 1861.

Done by the people of the State of Texas, in convention assembled, at Austin, this 1st day of February 1861.

[Ratified the 23rd Feb 1861 by a vote of 46,153 for & 14,747 against]

VIRGINIA

AN ORDINANCE to repeal the ratification of the Constitution of the United States of America by the State of Virginia and to resume all rights and powers granted under said Constitution.

The people of Virginia in their ratification of the Constitution of the United States of America, adopted by them in convention on the twenty-fifth day of June, in the year of our Lord, one thousand seven hundred and eighty-eight, having declared that the powers granted under said Constitution were derived from the people of the United States and might be resumed whensoever's the same should be perverted to their injury and oppression, and the Federal Government having perverted said powers not only to the injury of the people of Virginia, but to the oppression of the Southern slave-holding States:

Now, therefore, we the people of Virginia, do declare and ordain the ordinance adopted by the peoples of this State in convention on the twenty-fifth day of June, in the year of our Lord one thousand seven hundred and eighty-eight, whereby the Constitution if the United States of America was ratified, and all acts of the General Assembly of this State ratifying of this State and adopting amendments to said Constitution, are hereby repealed and abrogated; that the Union between the State of Virginia and the other States under the Constitution aforesaid is hereby dissolved, and that the State of Virginia is in the full possession and exercise of all the rights of sovereignty which belong and appertain to a free and independent State.

And they do further declare, that said Constitution of the United States of America is no longer binding on any of the citizens of this State.

This ordinance shall take effect and be an act of this day, when ratified by a majority of the voter of the people of this State cast at a poll to be taken thereon on the fourth Thursday in May next in pursuance of a schedule hereafter to be enacted.

Adopted by the convention of Virginia, April 17th, 1861

[*Ratified by a vote of 32,201 to 37,451 on May 1861*]

ARKANSAS

AN ORDINANCE to dissolve the Union now existing between the State of Arkansas and the other States united with her under the compact entitled "The Constitution of the United States of America."

Whereas, in addition to the well-founded causes of complaint set forth by this convention, in resolutions adopted on the 11th of March, A.D. 1861, against the sectional party now in power in Washington City, headed by Abraham Lincoln, he has in the face of resolutions passed by this convention pledging the State of Arkansas to resist to the last extremity any attempt on the part such power to coerce any State that had seceded from the old Union, proclaimed to the world that war should be waged against such States until they should be compelled to submit their rule, and large forces to accomplish this have by this same power been called out, and are now being marshaled to carry out this inhuman design; and to longer submit to submit to such rule, or remain in the old Union of the United States, would be disgraceful and ruinous to the State of Arkansas:

Therefore we, the people of State of Arkansas, in convention assembled, do hereby declare, and ordain, and it is hereby declared and ordained. That the "ordinance and acceptance of compact" passed and approved by the General Assembly of the State of Arkansas on the 18th day of October, A.D. 1836, whereby it was by said General Assembly ordained that by virtue of the authority vested in said General Assembly by the provisions of the ordinance adopted by the convention of delegates assembled at Little Rock for the purpose of forming a constitution and system of government for said State, the propositions set forth in An act supplementary to an act entitled 'An act for the admission of the State of Arkansas into the Union, and to provide for the due execution of the laws of the United States within the same, and for other purposes.' Were freely accepted, ratified, and irrevocably confirmed articles of compact and union between the State of Arkansas and the United States, and all other laws and every other law and ordinance, whereby the State of Arkansas became a member of the Federal Union, be, and the same are hereby, in all respects and for every purpose herewith consistent, repealed, abrogated, and fully set aside; and the union now subsisting between the State of Arkansas and the other States, under the name of the United States of America, is hereby forever dissolved.

And we do further hereby declare and ordain, that the State of Arkansas hereby resumes to herself all rights and powers heretofore delegated to the Government of the United States of America; that her citizens are absolved from all allegiance to said Government of the United States, and that she is in full possession and exercise of all rights and sovereignty which appertain to a free and independent State.

We do further ordain and declare, That all rights acquired and vested under the Constitution of the United States of America, or of any act or acts of Congress, or treaty, or under any law of this State, and not incompatible with this ordinance, shall remain in full force and effect, in nowise altered or impaired, and have the same effect as if this ordinance had not been passed.

[Adopted and passed in open convention on the 6th day of May A.D. 1861.]

NORTH CAROLINA

AN ORDINANCE to dissolve the Union between the State of North Carolina and the other States united with her, under the compact of government entitled "The Constitution of the United States"

We, the people of the States of North Carolina in convention assembled, do declare, and ordain, and it is hereby declared and ordained, that the ordinance adopted by the State of North Carolina in convention of 1789, whereby the Constitution of the United States was ratified and adopted, and all acts and parts of acts of the General Assembly ratifying and adopting amendments to the said Constitution, are hereby repealed, rescinded, and abrogated.

We do further declare and ordain, That the Union now subsisting between the State of North Carolina and the other States, under the title of the United States of America, is hereby dissolved, and that the State of North Carolina is in full possession and exercise of all those rights of sovereignty which belong and appertain to a free and independent State.

[Done in convention at the city of Raleigh, this 20th day of May, in the year of our Lord 1861, and in the eighty-fifth year of the independence of said State.]

TENESSEE

DECLARATION OF INDEPENDENCE AND ORDINANCE dissolving the federal relations between the State of Tennessee and the United States of America.

First. We, the people of the State of Tennessee, waiving any expression of opinion as to the abstract doctrine of secession, but asserting the right, as a free and independent people, to alter. Reform, or abolish our form of government in such manner as we think proper, do ordain and declare that all the laws and ordinances by which the State of Tennessee became a member of the Federal Union of the United States of America are hereby abrogated and annulled, and that all the rights, functions, and powers which by any of said laws and ordinances were conveyed to the Government of the United States, and to absolve ourselves from all the obligations, restraints, and duties incurred thereto; and do hereby henceforth become a free, sovereign, and independent State.

Second. We furthermore declare and ordain that article 10, sections one and two of the constitution of the State of Tennessee, which requires members of the General Assembly and all officers, civil and military, to take an oath to support the Constitution of the United States be, and the same are hereby, abrogated and annulled, and all parts of the Constitution of the State of Tennessee making citizenship of the United States a qualification for office and recognizing the Constitution of the United States as the supreme law of this State are in like manner abrogated and annulled.

Third. We furthermore ordain and declare that all rights acquired and vested under the Constitution of the United States, or under any act of Congress passed in pursuance thereof, or under any laws of this State, and not incompatible with this ordinance, shall remain in force and have the same effect as if this ordinance had not been passed.

[Sent to referendum on the 6th of May 1861 by the legislature and approved by the voters by a vote of 104,471 to 47,183, on the 8th of June 1861.]

MISSOURI

An act declaring the political ties heretofore existing between the State of Missouri and the United States of America dissolved.

Whereas the Government of the United States, in the possession and under the control of a sectional party, has wantonly violated the compact originally made between said Government and the State of Missouri, by invading with hostile armies on the soil of the State, attacking and making prisoners of the militia while legally assembled under the State laws, forcibly occupying the State capital, and, and attempting through the instrumentality of domestic to usurp the State government, seizing and destroying private property, and murdering with fiendish malignity peaceable citizens, men, women, and children, together with other acts of atrocity, indicating a deep-settled hostility toward the people of Missouri and their institutions; and

Whereas the present Administration of the Government of the United States has utterly ignored the Constitution, subverted the Government as constructed and intended by its makers, and established a despotic and arbitrary power instead thereof: Now, therefore,

Be it enacted by the general assembly of the State of Missouri, that all political ties of every character new existing between the Government of the United States of America and the people and the government of the State of Missouri are hereby dissolved and the State of Missouri, resuming the sovereignty granted by compact to the said United States upon admission of said State into the Federal Union, does again take its place as a free and independent republic amongst the nations of the earth.

This act to take effect and be in force from and after its passage. [Approved by the Missouri Legislature on October 31, 1861.]

KENTUCKY

Whereas, the Federal Constitution, which created the Government of the United States, was declared by the framers thereof to be the supreme law of the land, and was intended to limit and did expressly limit the powers of said Government to certain general specified purposes, and did expressly reserve to the States and people all other powers whatever, and the President and Congress have treated this supreme law of the Union with contempt and usurped to themselves the power to interfere with the rights and liberties of the States and the people against the expressed provisions of the Constitution, and have thus substituted for the highest forms of national liberty and Constitutional Government a central despotism founded upon the ignorant prejudices of the masses of Northern society, and instead of giving protection with the Constitution to the people of fifteen States of this Union have turned loose upon them the unrestrained and raging passions of mobs and fanatics and because we now seek to hold our liberties, our property, our homes, and our families under the protection of the reserved powers of the States, have blockaded our ports, invaded our soil, and war upon our people for the purpose of subjugating us to their will; and

Where, our honor and our duty to posterity demand that we shall not relinquish our own liberty and shall not abandon the right of our descendants and the world to the inestimable blessings of Constitutional Government: Therefore,

Be it ordained, that we do hereby forever sever our connection with the Government of the United States, and in the name of the people we do hereby declare Kentucky to be a free and independent State, clothed with all power to fix her own destiny and to secure her own rights and liberties.

And whereas, the majority of the Legislature of Kentucky have violated their most solemn pledges made before the election, and deceived and betrayed the people; have abandoned the position of neutrality assumed by themselves and the people and invited into the State the organized armies of Lincoln; have abdicated the Government in favor of a military despotism which they have placed around themselves, but cannot control, and have abandoned the duty of shielding the citizen with their protection; have thrown upon our people and the State the horrors and ravages of war, instead of attempting to preserve the peace, and have voted men and money for the war waged by the North for the destruction of our Constitutional Rights; have violated the expressed words of the constitution by borrowing five million of money for the support of the war without a vote of the people; have permitted the arrest and imprisonment of our citizens, and transferred the constitutional prerogatives of the Executive to a military commission of partisans; have seen the writ of habeas corpus suspended without an effort for its preservation, and permitted our people to be driven in exile from their homes; have subjected our property to confiscation and our persons to confinement in the penitentiary as felons, because we may choose to take part in a cause for civil liberty and Constitutional Government against a sectional majority waging war against the people and institutions of fifteen independent States of the Federal Union and have done all these things deliberately against the warnings and vetoes of the Governor and solemn remonstrance's of the minority in the Senate and House of Representatives: Therefore,

Be it further ordained, that the unconstitutional edicts of a factious majority of a Legislature thus false to their pledges, their honor, and their interest are not law, and that such a government is unworthy of the support of a brave and free people, and that we do therefore declare that the people are thereby absolved from all allegiance to said government and that they have a right to establish any government which to them may seem best adapted to the preservation of their rights and liberties.

[Adopted on the 20th of Nov, 1861, by a "Convention of the People of Kentucky"]

Authors Notes: Read these Ordinances of Secession very carefully! Each individual State, share their views and justifications for leaving the Union. And it paints a different picture than the propaganda that is taught in the Federal public schools. According to the Declaration of Independence, these Ordinances do fall in an alignment with the requirements to leave the Union of the United States of America. These secessions are a fact, and they are not trying to leave the Union or start a rebellion or start a Civil War. (NO) other State nor the Federal Government has any right to deny any individual State of self-government. Nor does anybody have to agree or approve the justifications against any sovereign State that wants to disband their relationship with other member States. The United States of America has (NO legal or Constitutional authority) to deny secession or undo the Constitutional Compact of those States, that had formed the nation of the Confederate States of America. The Socialist America of today is the by product and the actions by the United States Government of 1861. And we are now seeing the rotten fruits that it has brought forth. And while the American people remain ignorant enough to believe that they are still free! It clearly shows that they have no true concept as to what freedom truly is? If you are forced by submission and by bayonet and gun powder and forced by different forms of Reconstructions and Socialist transformation against your culture, identity, and history until you have fully been eliminated as a people and as a race! Then what is your definition of freedom? If the United States Military is fighting all of these wars around the world, while the American Empire is collapsing from within, then how could the military truly be fighting for your freedom? Who's freedom? Is it really for your freedom, or is it toward creating a New World Order?

CONFEDERATE STATES OF AMERICA

History of the Birth and Defense of the CSA

1. *JANUARY-1863*, At Murfreesboro, TN, both armies rest at the Battle of Galveston, TX. Confederates recapture important port city. Lincoln signs the falsified Emancipation Proclamation.
2. 1861-Battle of Murfreesboro, horrific fighting, over 24,000 C.S. & U.S. killed, wounded, or missing in action.
3. 1863-Despite his victory, Gen. Bragg withdraws the C.S. Army of TN from Murfreesboro.
4. 1863-Off of Charleston, C.S. blockade runner carrying important dispatches is captured by USS Quaker City.
5. 1861-After a main battle, minor fighting in several places near Murfreesboro, TN as Federal troops enters the city.
6. 1863-NY City Mayor Fernando Wood proposes that if the Union is dissolved, NY should become a free city, trading with both of the North and South.
7. 1861-At St. Augustine, FL. State Troops take control of Ft. Marion.
8. 1821—CS Gen. James Longstreet was born. 1863-C.S. Gen. Joseph Wheeler begins a week long raid at Mill Creek near Harpeth Shoals and Ashland, TN.
9. 1861-The sovereign State of Mississippi is the second State to withdraw her membership from the United States.
10. 1861-The sovereign State of Florida is the third State to withdraw her membership from the United States.
11. 1861-The sovereign State of Alabama is the fourth State to withdraw her membership from the United States. And the Naval battle between the CSS Alabama and the USS Hatteras took place of the cost of Galveston, TX.
12. 1864-Across the Rio Grande River in Brownsville TX, Federal troops enter Matamoras, Mexico to remove the U.S. Counsel because of heavy fighting between warring Mexican factions.

13. 1863-Federals capture the towns of St. Charles, Clare don, and Duvall's Bluff including Dec Arc, Arkansas. In 1865—U.S. Adm. Porter attacks Ft. Fisher.
14. 1864-Skirmishes had taken place at Shoal Creek, Al.
15. 1865-After heavy fighting, Federal forces had assaulted and capture Fort Fisher, N.C.
16. 1865-Off of Aransas Pass, TX, the C.S. schooner Mary Agnes, loaded with cotton bales, was destroyed by the USS Penobscot.
17. 1862-On the Tennessee River, Federal gunboats demonstrate against the Confederates holding of Fort Henry.
18. 1862-The Confederate Territory of Arizona is formed. In 1864-the western North Carolina, opponents of the Confederate conscription law held meetings. In1862-the Battle of Mill Springs.
19. 1807-Gen. Robert E. Lee was born. In 1861-the sovereign State of Georgia is the fifth State to withdraw her membership from the United States.1862-Battle of Mill Springs.
20. 1861-Mississippi secessionists take the Federal installations on Ship Island.
21. 1824-Lt. Gen Thomas Jonathan "Stonewall" Jackson was born.
22. 1862-Federal blockading ships attack Aransas Pass, TX.1864-A skirmish at clear Creek Arkansas.
23. Skirmish took place at Cowskin Bottom, Indian Territory.
24. 1861-Georgia State troops had taken control over the Federal arsenal in August.
25. 1865-The C.S. cruiser "Shenandoah" arrives at Melbourne, Australia.
26. 1861-The sovereign State of Louisiana is the sixth State to withdraw her membership from the United States.
27. 1863-Philadelphia Journal editor was arrested & charged with publishing anti-Union material. A violation of his freedom of speech and of the press.
28. 1825-Gen. George Pickett was born.
29. 1863-Federal ships bombard the Confederate Forces at Galveston, Texas. 1864-Confederates had attack the Federal steamer "Sir William Wallace" on the Mississippi.
30. 1861-At Mobile, Alabama U.S. Revenue Cutter "Lewis Cass" surrenders to Alabama officers. 1865-Skirmishes at the lake Verret and Richland Plantation, Louisiana.
31. 1865-Robert E. Lee is named as the Commander-in-Chief of the Confederate States Armies.

1. *FEBRUARY*-1861-Austin TX secession convention votes 166 to 7 in favor of Secession. 1865-Sherman begins his Carolina Campaign.
2. 1804-Gen. Albert S. Johnston was born. 1862-Minor skirmish in Morgan County, TN. 1863-The Union had ram "Queen of the West," that runs past the C.S. batteries at Vicksburg.

3. 1807-Gen. Joseph E. Johnston was born. 1863-Below Vicksburg, "Queen of the West" captures three Confederate vessels. In 1864-Maridian Campaign begins. In 1865-A skirmish at Hog Jaw Valley, Alabama.
4. 1861-At Montgomery Alabama, the Confederate States of America is organized at the 1st session of the Provisional Congress.
5. 1861-At the Secession Convention at Montgomery, a resolution is offered calling for the formation of a Confederacy of the States which had seceded from the United States.
6. 1833-J.E.B. Stuart was born. In 1862-On the Tennessee River, Fort Henry is surrendered to the Federals. 1863-The [Federal Government refuses a French offer of mediation between the U.S. & the C.S ...]
7. 1865-Federal cutters enter Galveston Harbor, TX & capture schooners Pet and Annie and Sophie & their cargo totaling 476 bales of cotton.
8. 1861-The Constitution of the Confederate States of America was unanimously adopted. The provisional Congress at Montgomery, Al. In 1862-The Battle of Roanoke Island had taken place.
9. 1861-Jefferson Davis and & Alexander Stephens was elected to be the first President and Vice-President of our beloved Confederacy, or Confederate States of America.
10. 1864-Fighting at Barber's Ford Camp Cooper, and Lake City, Fl.
11. 1812-Alexander H. Stephens was born at Crawfordville, GA. Stephens was the V.P. of the C.S.A., a U.S. Congressman and Gov. of the State of Georgia. He later died in Atlanta in 1883.
12. 1861-At Montgomery, the Provisional Congress of the Confederacy provides for a Peace Commission to the U.S ... They we're disrespectfully ignored by the U.S. President.
13. 1862-Beginning of the Federal attack on Ft. Donelson, on the Cumberland River.
14. 1862-At Ft. Donelson, Union ironclads begin its fierce exchange of fire power with the Confederate shore batteries.
15. 1862-Battle of Ft. Donelson. Despite the day-long fighting in which the Federals are nearly defeated, inept Confederate Generals Floyd and Pillow decide to surrender the next day. They must not have known the condition of their enemy or ells they wouldn't have surrender to them?
16. "Committee of Public Safety", pro-CS forces, seize US Army Military Post & Federal Arsenal San Antonio, TX. [Apologizing for no date.]
17. 1864-Off of the Charleston Harbor, SC, Confederate States Navy submarine "H.L. Hunley" becomes the first war submarine in the world Navel history to sink an enemy ship in combat. 1865-Columbia, South Carolina had surrender to the enemy.
18. 1861-At Montgomery, Alabama, and Jefferson Davis is inaugurated as our first Provisional President, of the Confederate States of America. [This became the finalization of the Birth, of a "New Nation".]

19. 1861-Lousisiana State Troops had seized the U.S. payments office in New Orleans. 1865-Sherman's men destroy most of Columbia, South Carolina, including the burning of all of the railroad property.
20. 1865-<u>The Confederate States House of Representatives authorizes the use of slaves as soldiers. C.S. Gen. Robert E. Lee had endorsed the idea.</u>
21. 1864-Fighting at Elli's Bridge, Prairie Station. West Point and Union, MS.
22. 1862-On the Texas Gulf Coast, the U.S. Navy is heavily shelling the town of Port Aransas.
23. 1861-The Confederates begin to evacuate Nashville, TN as the Federals approaches toward them. 1865-Gen. Joseph E. Johnston assumes command of the army of Tennessee.
24. 1864-Along the Texas Gulf Coast around Matagorda Bay, the Federal Army issues a conditional amnesty for all of the local residents.
25. In Nashville, TN is occupied by Union troops & remains that way throughout the war. [Apologizing for no date]
26. 1863-Below Vicksburg, Confederate blows up newly captured gunboat "Indianola," mistakenly believing they were under attack by a Federal ironclad.
27. 1863-The C.S.A. President Jefferson Davis, names three Confederate Commissioners to Washington in attempting negotiations with the U.S. Government. However, President Lincoln refused to recognize the Commissioners from the Confederate States and preferred (War), instead of Peace.
28. 1863-Near Ft. McAllister, GA, CSS Nashville destroyed by USS Montauk.
29. 1861-Not sure of the correct Month, however (GOD SAVE THE SOUTH,) written and Composed by, Earnest Halphin, which was published by Miller & Beacham, Baltimore MD. Was entered according to an Act of Congress, A.D. in Clerk's Office of the Dist, Court of MD, and has been the [Constitutional National Anthem of the Confederate States of America, to this very present day.]

1. *MARCH-1862*-President Jefferson Davis proclaims martial law in Richmond, & pro-Northern sympathizers are arrested.
2. 1861-Texas admitted into the Confederacy, Federal Revenue Cutter Henry Dodge was seized by Texas State Troops at Galveston.
3. 1863-Enrollment Act had passed. 1865-Texas Gulf Coast, USS "Quaker City" captures the CSS schooner "Telmico," loaded with 24 bales of cotton & 64 sacks of pecans. 1865-The U.S. Congress creates the Freedmen's Bureau.
4. 1861-Abraham Lincoln is inaugurated as the 16th President of the United States of America. And in the newspaper's editorials of the South, proclaim the possibility of war. 1862-Confederate States Troops entered

the City of Santa Fe, NM. 1865-The 2nd inaugural of the U.S. President Lincoln, and the falsifying at the Unions ballot box for his election …

5. 1862-Near Fayetteville, AR, C.S. General Earl Van Dorn's forces joins C.S. General Starling Price's in order to stop U.S. General Samuel Curtis.
6. 1862-Battle of Elkhorn Tavern (Pea Ridge), AR. C.S.A … The first day was moderate. C.S. General Van Dorn's forces flank the Federals during the night.
7. 1862-The Battle of Elkhorn Tavern continues at (Pea Ridge), C.S.A. Generals McCulloch & McIntosh had been killed in action.
8. 1862-Battle of Elkhorn Tavern, AR. C.S.A … On the third and final day of fighting, the causing results of the Federals driving out the Confederates from Pea Ridge.
9. 1862-Battle of the USS Monitor & the CSS Virginia. In Hampton Roads, Virginia C.S.A., two modern Ironclad's vessels battle to a draw. [The first Navel battle in World Navy History between two Nations, and it became a draw.
10. 1865-Conclusion of the three days of heavy engagements at Kinston, North Carolina C.S.A … 1865-A skirmish near Boyd's Station, Alabama C.S.A …
11. 1861 The [Confederate States Congress unanimously adopts the Constitution of the Confederate States of America.]
12. 1862-The U.S. Federal forces temporarily occupy Jacksonville, Florida C.S.A … In 1864-The Red River campaign begins. Also, U.S. Grant was promoted to command the U.S. forces. 1865-Skirmishing near Columbia and Macon, Mo. C.S.A.
13. 1865-<u>C.S. President Jefferson Davis signs a legislation in allowing Southern Negroes into the Confederate States Army. C.S. General Lee acts promptly and the first Black Troops in the uniform of the Confederate States Army was deployed in Richmond, Virginia C.S.A.</u>
14. 1863-The Feds gunboats are bombarding the Confederate positions at Port Hudson. Louisiana C.S.A …
15. 1863-The British ship "Britannia," runs the Federal blockade into Wilmington, N.C. C.S.A …
16. 1861-Jefferson Davis arrives in Montgomery, Alabama to accept the post of the first Provisional President of the newly organized C.S.A … Arizona withdraws its membership from the United States.
17. 1828-Gen. Patrick Cleburne was born. In 1864, C.S. forces had attacked the Federal occupation of Corpus Christi, Texas C.S.A … And in 1865-The campaign to capture the City of Mobile, Alabama C.S.A. begins.
18. 1861-In Texas, Governor Sam Houston refuses to take the oath of allegiance to the Confederate States of America. In 1862-Confederate States President Jefferson Davis Appoints, Judah P. Benjamin as the first Confederate Secretary of State.

19. 1864-Battle of Bentonville, N.C. C.S.A … The harsh fighting between Gen. Sherman's army and the C.S. forces.
20. 1865-Battle of Bentonville, with no heavy fighting and considerable skirmishing.
21. 1865-The battle of Bentonville is concluded with the last significant effort to halt Sherman.
22. 1817-Gen. Braxton was born.1864-after a heavy snow fall in the Nation's Capital of the Confederacy, the Confederate soldiers in Richmond VA, C.S.A. has engage in a (Huge Snowball Fight.)
23. 1862-The first battle begins in Kernstown, VA, C.S.A …
24. 1864-The Confederate States Calvary, under C.S. Nathan Bedford Forest, captures the Union City, TN C.S.A …
25. 1865—In Florida, fighting at Bluff Springs, the Cotton Creel, and Escambia River. 1865-The C.S. attacks the Union at Fort Stedman, in Petersburg, VA C.S.A …
26. 1862-The New Mexico campaign. Confederate and Federal troop's clashes with each other near Santa Fe at Apache Canyon.
27. 1864-The Camden Expedition, and fighting at the Branchville & Brooks Mill. Arizona C.S.A …
28. 1818-Gen. Wade Hampton was born. 1862-New Mexico campaign and the battle of Glorieta Pass. The major battle of the war in the far West occurs not far from Santa Fe. 1862-Taylor marches to reinforce Jackson.
29. 1865-Appomattox campaign begins near Petersburg, Virginia C.S.A … There is a heavy fighting near the junction of Boydton and Quaker roads.
30. 1862-The Federal forces are attacking Union City, Tennessee, and C.S.A … 1963-Skirmish at Tahlequah Indian Territory.
31. 1863-A skirmish at Clapper's Saw Mill.

1. *APRIL*-1865-The Appomattox Campaign. The Battle of five Forks, southwest of Petersburg.
2. 1865-The Petersburg-Richmond front begins to collapse. The Confederate States Government flees and was dispersed, because of the illegal invasion into Richmond. C.S. Gen A. P. Hill was killed near Petersburg.
3. 1865-The occupation of Richmond and Petersburg begins by the U.S. Federal Troops.
4. 1862-C.S. Gen. Albert S. Johnston's army marches from Corinth, Miss C.S.A. toward Pittsburg Landing, the Confederate State of Tennessee.
5. 1862-Gen. Albert S. Johnston's C.S. Army moves toward the Shiloh Church near Pittsburg Landing, TN C.S.A …
6. 1862-The Battle of Shiloh, TN C.S.A … The second largest of the war, since the unconstitutional invasion by the United States forces. The C.S. furious assault drives back the U.S. Federal Army.

7. 1862-The Battle of Shiloh. The U.S. Federal forces retakes and holds the field on the second day of fighting. The fall of Island #10, on the Mississippi River.
8. 1864-The Red River Campaign. The Battle of Mansfield, Louisiana. 1865-The Appomattox Campaign. Lee is cut off near the Appomattox Court House.
9. 1865-Lee surrenders 26,000 Confederate Americans under his command only, not the government of the Confederate States. The Northern Virginia Army under his command was surrendered at the Appomattox Court House.
10. 1806-Gen. Leonidas Polk was born.1865-At the Appomattox, C.S. Gen. Lee issues his last general orders as a soldier, bidding "an affectionate farewell," to his troops.
11. 1861-At the Confederate City of Charleston, Fort Sumter was forced to surrender. 1862-Near Savannah, the Federals surrender Fort Pulaski after being heavily shelled & hit over 5,000 times.
12. 1861-Southern Forces fires on Fort Sumter, South Carolina at 4:30 A.M …
13. 1861-The Federal garrison at Fort Sumter surrenders to South Carolina after 34 hours of bombardment.
14. 1865—Struck with grief by the destruction of the lives and the liberty of his Confederate American people & Nation. The actor (John Wilkes Booth) took vengeance into his own hands and shot and murdered the U.S. President Abraham Lincoln in Washington D.C … But what Booth didn't realize was this only cause more tyranny and oppression toward his occupied Confederate Nation. Two Wrongs do not make a Right! And vengeance is the Lord's!
15. 1863-CSS Alabama captures the second U.S. Whalers off the coast of Brazil. 1864-The U.S. ironclad Eastport is severely damaged by the Confederate torpedo on Red River.
16. 1863-Under heavy fire from the Confederate artillery, Porter's Federal fleet passes Vicksburg. 1864-Red River Campaign and the skirmishing at Grand Ecore, Louisiana C.S.A …
17. 1861-In Richmond. The future Capital of the Confederate States of America, the sovereign States of Virginia, held their Convention and adopts an ordinance by a vote of 88 to 55.
18. 1864-At Poison Springs, Arkansas C.S.A., the Confederates under Gen. John S. Marmaduke had attacked a Federal supply column capturing 198 wagons.
19. 1861-The Federal President Abe Lincoln declares a blockade against the ports of the Southern States, South Carolina, Georgia, of Alabama, of Florida, of Mississippi, of Louisiana, and of Texas. 1862-The battle of South Mills.
20. 1865-In Georgia, there are fighting at Rocky Creek near Macon Springs Hill, and at Mimms Mills on the Tobesofke Creek.
21. 1861-Col. Earl Van Dorn accepts command of the Confederate forces in Texas. His Volunteers capture three of the Union ships. The Mobil, the Fashion, and the United States.

22. 1861-Mr. Franklin Buchanan, Commandant of the Washington Navy Yard, resigns from the U.S. Navy and joins the Confederacy.
23. 1862-The Confederate Raiders capture several Federal vessels in Aransas Bay, Texas C.S.A ... 1863-A skirmish took place at Independence, Missouri C.S.A ...
24. 1862-Below New Orleans, the Federal fleet, under heavy fire, passes Fort Jackson and moves up the Mississippi, to engage with the Confederate gunboats.
25. 1861-At Saluria, in the Confederate States of Texas, seven companies from the First and Third and the Eighth U.S. Infantry Regiments had surrender to C.S. Col. Earl Van Dorn.
26. 1865-C.S. Gen. Joseph E. Johnston surrenders the Army of Tennessee near Durham Station, of the Confederate State of North Carolina.
27. 1861-The Federal blockade is extended to the Virginia and the North Carolina Coast. The Virginia Convention invites the Confederate States Government to make Richmond the seat for their National Government.
28. 1862-Confederates had surrendered Fort Jackson & St. Philip to the foreign invading Federals, and the Mississippi River is under the Federal control from the Gulf of Mexico to New Orleans.
29. 1861-The sovereign State of Maryland, votes against secession by 53 to 13 in a vote. 1862-New Orleans surrenders to the Union forces.
30. 1864-In Richmond, the Capital State of the Confederacy, Joe Davis, the child of the Confederate States President Jefferson Davis, was killed in an accidental fall off the veranda of the Confederate States White House.

1. *MAY*-1863-The Battle of Chancellorsville, VA. C.S.A. First fighting in Fredericksburg and in Salem Heights, including Marye's Heights.
2. 1863-The Battle of Chancellorsville, C.S. Stonewall Jackson's flank march was successful. Then later on, he was accidentally wounded by his own men.
3. 1863-The Battle of Chancellorsville. The failure of the Federal frontal assaults in Fredericksburg.
4. The Battle of Chancellorsville, and Salem Church, VA. CSA ... Apologies for no date!
5. 1862-The Battle of Williamsburg, VA C.S.A ... And the Battle of the Wilderness VA C.S.A. begins.
6. 1861-The Sovereign States of Arkansas and Tennessee voted to secede from the Union. [Confederate States President approves a State of War between the United States and of the Confederate States.] In 1864, the Battle of the Wilderness continues.
7. 1862-The Eltham's Landing, VA C.S.A ... 1864-the Northern section of Georgia, U.S. Gen. Sherman's three different Armies of 100,000 solders, began their march toward Atlanta.

8. 1862-The Valley Campaign and the Battle of McDowell VA are the victories of C.S. Gen. Stonewall Jackson. And fighting begins at the Spotsylvania Court House VA. C.S.A …
9. 1864-The Atlanta Campaign begins. And near Resaca, Georgia at the Snake Creek Gap. The Federal army fails to dislodge the entrenched Confederate Army by deciding to withdraw rather than to fight.
10. 1863-C.S. Lt. Gen. "Stonewall" Jackson dies. 1864-The Battle of Spotsylvania Court House, VA, C.S.A …
11. 1864-The Battle of Yellow Tavern, VA, C.S.A … C.S. Gen. "Jeb" is mortally wounded in this cavalry battle about six miles north of the Confederate Capital of "Richmond."
12. 1864-C.S. Gen Jeb Stuart dies. 1864-, at the Battle of "Bloody Angle," at Spotsylvania Court House. Also, in 1865, the last battle of the war fought at Palmito Ranch, near Brownsville, TX C.S.A …
13. 1863-Gov. Zebulon B. Vance of the Confederate State of North Carolina expresses concern over the desertions in the Army of the Confederate States.
14. 1864-The Atlanta Campaign. And the Battle of Resaca, GA C.S.A.
15. 1864-The Battle of New Market, VA C.S.A … The Atlanta Campaign and the Battle of Resaca. Armies meet head-on and the Confederates were driven back. Hood withdraws his Army during the night.
16. 1863-At Montgomery Alabama Confederate States Congress officially admits Tennessee, into the membership of the Confederacy. In 1863, the Battle of Champions Hill. The siege of Vicksburg begins. 1864, the Battle of Drewrys Bluff, VA C.S.A …
17. 1863-The Battle of Bib Glack River Bridge, MS C.S.A … Confederates under Gen. Pemberton withdrew to Vicksburg defenses.
18. 1863-The beginning of the Federal siege of Vicksburg. 1864—Heavy fighting took place at Spotsylvania Court House, VA. C.S.A …
19. 1863-Failure of a major Federal frontal assault on Vicksburg defenses.
20. 1861-The Sovereign State of North Carolina was the last member to withdraw her membership from the United States. 1864—Federal troops are occupying Cartersville, Georgia. C.S.A … After skirmishing had taken place at Etowah River.
21. 1863-The Federal siege of Port Hudson, Louisiana begins. 1865-under the Command of C.S. Lt. Waddell. The CSS Shenandoah enters the Sea of Okhotsk, looking for Yankee Whalers.
22. 1863-The siege of Vicksburg. A major Federal assault against the Confederate line fails. The former Confederate States President Jefferson Davis was unconstitutionally and unjustly imprisoned in the occupied State of Ft. Monroe, Virginia, C.S.A …
23. 1861-The Battle of Front Royal, VA. C.S.A … The Sovereign State of Virginia withdraws their membership from the Union.

24. 1861-For the first time, the United States sets foot upon Confederate States soil, as Federal troops enters Virginia, to occupy Alexandria.
25. 1862-First Battle of Winchester. 1864-Atlanta Campaign and the Battle of New Hope Church, Georgia, C.S.A … The Federals suffered heavy losses and their attack fails.
26. 1865-In New Orleans, the Confederate States General Simon B. Buckner meets Federal authorities and surrenders the Confederate Army of the Trans-Mississippi, the last significant Southern force still in the field.
27. 1863-At Port Hudson, Louisiana C.S.A., 13,000 men of the Federal army attacks the 4,500 Confederate defenders in the first actual assault on the post. After a heavy Federal loss, the attack fails.
28. 1818-The future C.S. Pierre G.T. Beauregard was born. 1864-Heavy fighting at Pickett's Mills and along the Confederate lines from Hew Hope Church to Dallas TX C.S.A …
29. 1865-With a few exceptions, the U.S. President Andrew Johnson grants amnesty and pardon to all who participated in the so-called-existing-rebellion.
30. 1862-Skirmish at Mill Creek, Missouri. C.S.A … 1863-A skirmish at Port Isabel, TX C.S.A …
31. 1862-The Battle of Fair Oaks, Virginia C.S.A … The Battle of Seven Pines, Virginia C.S.A … 1863-Fighting continues at Vicksburg, MS C.S.A., and Port Hudson LA C.S.A …

1. *June-1862*-Lee was appointed as Commander of the Army of Virginia. 1862-The Battle of Seven Pines, on its second day. 1864-The first day Battle of Cold Harbor.
2. 1864-The second day Battle of Cold Harbor.
3. 1808-the First President of a New Nation was born, "Jefferson Davis." 1864-The Third day Battle of Cold Harbor. Near the Nation's Capital of Richmond, Gen. Lee's Army repels a massive charge that cost the lives of 7,000 Federal solders in less than in one hour.
4. 1862-Along the Yazoo and Mississippi Rivers, the Southern Confederate planters had burn huge cotton stores to prevent the capture by the foreign invading federals.
5. 1863-Stuart hosts Grand Review of his cavalry. 1864-On Matagorda Island, TX. C.S.A … 13 Black members of the Union Corps de Afrique are hanged by military authorities after convictions for mutiny.
6. 1862-Memphis has surrendered. Brig, Gen. Turner Ashby was killed in action near Harrisonburg, VA. C.S.A …
7. 1862-In New Orleans LA. C.S.A …, the Union Gen. Butler has citizen William B. Mumford hanged, for tearing down the foreign Flag over New Orleans Mint.

8. 1861-The Sovereign State of Tennessee withdraws her membership from the United States. The Federals blockade at Key West, Florida. C.S.A … 1862-the Valley Campaign. A Confederate Victory at the Battle of Cross Keys, VA. C.S.A …
9. 1862-The Valley Campaign. The Battle of Port Republic. 1863-The Battle of Brandy Station, VA. C.S.A …
10. 1861-The First serious battle of the war was fought at Big Bethel, VA. C.S.A … 1864-At Brice's Crossroads, Mississippi, and C.S. Gen. N.B. Forrest leads his Calvary to a brilliant and classic victory.
11. 1864-Forrest's men follow and attack the beaten Federals as they struggle back toward the occupied city of Memphis, TN C.S.A …
12. 1862-On Peninsula in Virginia, the Brigadier Gen. "Jeb" Stuart begins the famous four-day reconnaissance known as the "Ride around McClellan."
13. 1862-C.S. Gen. Jeb Stuart's Troopers moved around McClellan's right flank, passing thru Hanover Court House and Fighting at Haw's Shop. VA C.S.A …
14. 1861-The skirmish at Seneca Mills, Maryland, U.S.A … The Atlanta Campaign & unknown General was killed at Pine Mountain, GA C.S.A …
15. 1863-The Battle of Winchester, VA C.S.A … The British House of Lords debates the seizure of British ships by U.S. vessels. 1864-The Petersburg Campaign begins.
16. 1862-The skirmish at Denmark, Arkansas C.S.A … And the Battle of Secessionville, James Island, SC C.S.A …
17. 1864-The Atlanta Campaign, in front of Marietta, Georgia C.S.A … along the side the mud creek. U.S. Sherman's Troops launch the attack on Confederate line.
18. 1862-In VA, skirmishing is taking place near Richmond on the Nine-Mile Road.
19. Off of Cherbourg France, the CSS Alabama was sunk by the USS Kearsarge. The siege of Petersburg has just begun.
20. 1863-19. 1864-Off of Cherbourg France, the CSS Alabama was The Vicksburg Campaign. The Confederate city comes under intense shelling from the Federal batteries.
21. 1862-The 2nd of three days of fighting at Des Allemandes Bayou, LA C.S.A … 1863-Fighting at Hudsonville MS C.S.A … Brashear City LA C.S.A … and Powder Springs Gap, TN C.S.A …
22. 1864-The Petersburg Campaign. The Confederate Forces of C.S. Gen. A.P. Hill's Corps stop the Union attempt to seize Weldon Railroad.
23. 1865-Ft. Towson C.S. Gen. Stand Watie-Native American Indian—surrenders his Indian Command in the last formal surrender of the large Confederate States military.
24. 1863-C.S. Gen. Longstreet's and A.P. Hill's Corps cross the Potomac and entered Maryland while enroute to PA U.S.A …

25. 1862-The Peninsular Campaign. Near the Confederate States Capital, of Richmond VA … A series of battles known as the Seven Day's Battles begins with fighting at the Oak Grove.
26. 1862-The Peninsular Campaign and the Seven Day's Battles. The Battle of Mechanicsville. And the Federals fall back from their advance toward Richmond. 1864-The Stoneman begins the Atlanta raid.
27. 1862-The Peninsular Campaign and the Battle of Gain's Mill, VA C.S.A … 1864-The Battle of Kennesaw Mountain, GA C.S.A …
28. 1863-C.S. Gen. Lee gives orders to Longstreet, Hill, and Ewell to march toward Gettysburg, PA U.S.A …
29. 1862-The Peninsular Campaign. The Battle of Savage's Station. 1864-Early marches toward Washington, D.C. U.S.A …
30. 1862-The Peninsular Campaign. And the Battle of White Oak Swamp.

1. *JULY*-1862-The Peninsular Campaign. The Battle of Malvern Hill. 1863-The Battle of Gettysburg begins.
2. 1863-The Battle of Gettysburg, PA U.S.A. The second day of fighting at Little Round Top, and Big Top, Devil's Den, Wheatfield and Peach Orchard, Cemetery Hill and Culp's Hill.
3. 1863-The Battle of Gettysburg ends with C.S. Pickett and Pettigrew charge, the "High Tide of the Confederacy."
4. 1863-Vicksburg surrendered to the Feds giving them control of Mississippi River.
5. 1861-The Battle of Carthage, Missouri C.S.A … Confederate victory halts the Federal advance into Southwest Missouri.
6. 1861-CSS Sumter releases seven captured vessels at Cuban Port. 1863-Fighting at various locations as C.S Lee's Army withdraws from Gettysburg toward the Potomac.
7. 1865-In Washington D.C., Four accused [Lincoln assassination] prisoners was executed by the hanging on the Arsenal Grounds at Old Penitentiary Bldg.
8. 1863-The surrender of Port Hudson, Louisiana C.S.A … The last Confederate garrison in action, on the Mississippi River.
9. 1864-The Battle of Monocracy, Maryland U.S.A … And the advancing on toward Washington, D.C., by C.S. Gen. Jubal Earl's Infantry reaches Frederick and routed the Union defenders.
10. 1861-The Confederate States Government signs a treaty with the Creek Indians. 1863-The beginning of the U.S. Federal siege of Battery Wagner in Charleston Harbor.
11. 1863-The first major Federal assault on the Battery Wagner in Charleston harbor.
12. 1864-The Confederate Calvary under C.S. Jubal Early invaded the suburbs of Washington, D.C. U.S.A … 1864-The skirmish at Campbellton, Georgia, C.S.A …

13. 1821-Birthday of the future C.S. Lt. Gen. Nathan Bedford Forrest (1821-1877.) A self-made man who became 'The foremost Cavalry Officer" produced in our Northern Continent of America. 1861-Union forces secure the Western section of Virginia C.S.A …
14. 1862-C.S. Gen John H. Morgan reaches the town of Cynthiana, Kentucky C.S.A. with his Calvary Raiders. Union Citizens of Southern Indiana and Ohio are in an uproar as Morgan comes nearer.
15. 1862-At Vicksburg VA C.S.A., nearly completed Confederate States ironclad (Arkansas) attacks & badly damages three U.S. Federal vessels.
16. 1862-In Paris, France, the Confederate States Commission John Slidell meets Napoleon the Third and requests France's formal recognition of the Confederacy. And France had declined the offer.
17. 1863-Morgan's Raiders ride thru the suburbs of Cincinnati, U.S.A., heading east toward the Ohio River.
18. 1861-First Manassas and the heavy skirmishing along Bull Run. 1863-The Battle of Fort Wagner.
19. 1863-At Buffington Island on the Ohio River, C.S. Morgan's Raiders are cut to pieces by superior Union Forces as Morgan himself, escapes.
20. 1864-The Atlanta Campaign. The Battle of Peachtree Creek, Georgia, and C.S.A … Confederates suffer 4,796 casualties in only within a few hours.
21. 1861-The Battle of Manassas, Virginia, C.S.A … Confederates have routed the Federal Army in the first battle of the war. First Battle of Bull Run.
22. 1864-The Atlanta Campaign and the Battle of Atlanta, C.S.A … C.S. solders still hold Atlanta after suffering up to 10,000 casualties of nearly 40,000 engaged.
23. 1863-Skirmishing at Snicker's Gap and Gaines Cross Roads, Virginia C.S.A …
24. 1864-Confederate State of Virginia and the second Battle of Kernstown. C.S. solders inflict heavy losses.
25. 1863-A skirmish at Brownsville, Arkansas and Williamsburg, Kentucky, C.S.A … 1862-A skirmish at Benton and Pleasant Hill, Missouri, C.S.A …
26. 1861-Near Mesilla, New Mexico Territory and the Federals had surrendered Fort Fillmore, to a smaller Confederate Forces.
27. 1864-The Atlanta Campaign. War criminal U.S. Sherman orders Cavalry to cut railroads south of the City.
28. 1864-The Atlanta Campaign. The Battle of Ezra Church, Georgia C.S.A … Confederates suffer 5,000 casualties after repeated attacks against entrenched U.S. Federal Troopers.
29. 1863-The CSS Alabama sails out of England. In 1864—C.S. Gen. Jubal Early's Cavalry cross the Potomac west of Williamsport and enter the United States of Maryland and Pennsylvania.
30. 1864-At Petersburg, Confederate State of Virginia, and the Battle of the Crater occurs after a Federal mine exploded. 1864-Confederate States Cavalry under Col. John S. "Rip" Ford recaptures Brownsville Texas.
31. 1863-Fighting at Kelly's Ford, Virginia C.S.A … 1864-Fighting near Ft. Smith Arkansas C.S.A …

★ GOD SAVE THE SOUTH ★

1. *AUGUST*-1861-C.S. Troops skirmish with American Apache Indians near Ft. Bliss, TX C.S.A., before they had invaded New Mexico, U.S.A …
2. 1862-Skirmishes at Jonesboro, Arkansas and Austin, Mississippi C.S.A … 1863-skirmish in the Confederate State of Stumptown, Missouri, C.S.A …
3. 1864-The Atlanta Campaign. The U.S. Federals had crossed the Utoy Creek, moving slowly toward the city. And fighting at Mulberry Creek, Jug Tavern, Sunshine Church and Frogtown.
4. 1862-Fort Bliss, Confederate State of Texas, was burned by Confederate units of Sibley's brigade as they retreated from the territory of New Mexico.
5. 1862-Major engagement at Baton Rouge, LA C.S.A … 1864-The Battle of Mobil Bay, in the Confederate State of Alabama.
6. 1864-At Wilmington, NC C.S.A … The CSS Tallahassee runs past a U.S. Federal blockading fleet and heads north to begin raiding northern shipping, destroying 30 ships in two weeks.
7. 1863-Near Fort Fillmore, New Mexico Territory, the Feds defeated C.S. Gen. Sibley's Army of New Mexico. 1864-Surrender of Fort Gains in Mobil Bay to the Union.
8. 1863-C.S. Gen. Robert E. Lee offers his resignation as the Commander of the Army of Northern Virginia. The offer was rejected by the First President of the Constitutional Republic of the Confederate States of America, Jefferson Davis.
9. 1862-The Battle of Cedar Mountain, VA C.S.A … 1864-In England County TX C.S.A., two Confederate Cavalrymen were killed and three were wounded in a fight with forty American Comanche's.
10. 1861-The Battle of Wilson's Creek, Missouri C.S.A … Confederate American soldiers are victorious in a major battle of war, in the Confederate State of Missouri.
11. 1861-Near Fort Bliss, Texas, C.S.A … American Apache Indians attack a Confederate patrol of Company D, 2nd Texas Mounted Rifles.
12. 1864-Near Brownsville, Texas, and C.S.A … U.S. Federals captures British schooner "Flying Scud," after she unloaded 65,000ibs of gunpowder and seven tons of cavalry horseshoes.
13. 1862-A large Union American force drives C.S. Morgan's Raiders out of Gallatin, TN C.S.A …
14. 1861-C.S. Brig. Gen. Paul O. Hebert appointed Commander of all Confederate States troops in Texas.
15. 1862-A skirmish at Clarendon, Arkansas, C.S.A … In 1863-A skirmish at Bentonville, Arkansas, C.S.A …
16. 1862-The beginning of a three day Federal bombardment of Corpus Christi, Texas, C.S.A … In 1864-The CSS Tallahassee captured five enemy vessels off the coast of New England, U.S.A …
17. 1862-The fighting at Flat Lick, London, and Mammoth Cave, Kentucky, C.S.A … And the uprising of the Native American Sioux Indians.

18. 1864-The Petersburg Campaign, and the Battle for Welcome Railroad. The beginning of a three day's intensive fighting.
19. A skirmish near Antioch Church, Alabama, C.S.A …
20. 1864-The Atlanta Campaign. U.S. Federal Calvary marched on Macon and Western Railroad and fighting at Lovejoy's Station.
21. 1821-C.S. Gen. William Barksdale was born. 1863-A skirmish at Coldwater, Mississippi, C.S.A … 1864-A skirmish at Grubb's Cross Roads, Kentucky, C.S.A …
22. 1862-A skirmish at Catlett's Station, Virginia, C.S.A … 1863-A skirmish at Big Creek Missouri, C.S.A … 1863-A skirmish at Stafford Court House, Virginia, C.S.A …
23. 1862-Off of the Port Aransas, Texas, and C.S.A … The U.S. Arthur captures a Confederate schooner "Water Witch," and her cargo of 3750 pounds of gunpowder.
24. 1863-C.S. Mosby's Raiders active of the north of Rappahannock River. 1864-A skirmish at Mud Town, Arkansas, C.S.A …
25. 1864-The Battle of Ream's Station, Virginia, C.S.A … 1864-The C.S. schooner "Mack Canfield," and cargo of 133 bales of cotton was captured near Brownsville, Texas C.S.A …
26. 1862-The beginning of the second Manassas Campaign. The C.S. Cavalry enters Manassas Junction and captures the rail point, prisoners, and supplies.
27. 1862-The Second Manassas Campaign. Troops under C.S. Gen. Stonewall Jackson destroys the U.S. Federal stores and facilities at Manassas Junction.
28. 1861-Fort Hatteras falls. 1862-The Second Manassas Campaign. Fighting at Groveton. An Accused Confederate American spy (Belle Boyd,) was released from the old prison in Washington for lack of evidence.
29. 1862-The Battle of Second Manassas, VA C.S.A … The second Battle of Bull Run. Union Federals drive against C.S. Gen. Stonewall Jackson's troop's ends in failure.
30. 1862-The Battle of Second Manassas, Virginia, C.S.A … The Second Battle of Bull Run. C.S. Gen. Robert E. Lee's Army was victorious. The Battle of Richmond, KY C.S.A … C.S. Gen. Kirby Smith has an impressive victory.
31. 1864-The Atlanta Campaign.

1. *SEPTEMBER*-1862-The Second Manassas Campaign. Fighting at Chantilly, VA C.S.A … 1862-Second Manassas Campaign. The fighting at Chantilly, VA C.S.A … 1863-In the Confederate State of Alabama, skirmishes at Davis, Neal's, and Tap's Gap.

2. 1864-The Atlanta Campaign. U.S. Federal Forces occupied the city after C.S. Forces withdrew the previous day. The city was looted and burned after surrendering.
3. 1861-Confederate States Forces enter Kentucky and Tennessee C.S.A … Movement ends "Neutrality' of Kentucky and many of repercussions.
4. 1864-Engagement at Hog Eye, Arkansas, and C.S.A … 1864-C.S. Gen. John Hunt Morgan was killed at Greenville, Tennessee C.S.A …
5. 1861-Editorial in Charleston "Mercury" calls for Confederate offensive against Washington to force the United States 'to defend themselves." 1863-Great Britain seizes Confederate States ships, and shipyard.
6. 1861-U.S. Gen. Grant moves into Paducah. 1864-The beginning of the eighth major bombardment of the civilian population in Charleston, SC C.S.A … Almost 600 rounds was fired against the Confederate defenders of Ft. Sumter.
7. 1862—C.S. Gen. R.E. Lee's Army of the Northern Virginia concentrated. At Frederick, MD U.S.A … 1863-U.S. Federal expedition to invade TX C.S.A., arrives off the Sabine Pass.
8. 1863-The Battle of Sabine Pass, Texas C.S.A … Lt. Dick Dowling and the 47 Texas repel the entire foreign Union Federal invasion forces.
9. 1863-The U.S. Federal Army enters Chattanooga, TN C.S.A., after C.S. Gen. Bragg abandons the city. 1864-A skirmish at Hodges Plantation, Louisiana C.S.A …
10. 1863-C.S. Gen. Joseph Wheeler was born. 1861-The engagement at Carnifix Ferry, of the Western part of Virginia. The U.S. Federal forces fails, to break the line of the Confederate Americans, but the C.S. Gen Floyd decides to withdraw during the night, and a Union victory at Cheat Mountain.
11. 1861-C.S. Gen. R.E. Lee begins the five-day Cheat Mountain, VA Campaign, ending the Confederate defender's withdrawal.
12. 1861-U.S. Gen. Sterling Price's Army attacks Lexington, Missouri C.S.A …
13. 1863-While attending Church services at Rodney, Mississippi C.S.A., twenty crewmen of the USS Rattler were captured by the Confederate States Cavalrymen.
14. 1862-The Battle of South Maintain and Crompton's Gap. Maryland U.S.A … A severe fighting throughout the entire day results in a real heavy casualty for both sides of the nation's armies.
15. 1862-12,000 prisoners at Harper's Ferry were captured by C.S. Gen. Stonewall Jackson's command.
16. 1864-From Verona, Mississippi C.S.A., C.S. Gen. Forrest leads 4500 cavalry and mounted infantrymen on a month raid against the foreign invaders in the northern part of Alabama, and the middle section of Tennessee C.S.A …
17. 1862-The Battle of Antietam (Sharpsburg,) Maryland U.S.A … The bloodiest day, in both American Nations history.

18. 1862-C.S. Gen. Lee withdraws from Sharpsburg after dark. Thousands of dead heroics remains on the battlefield.
19. 1862-The Battle of Iuka, Mississippi C.S.A ... 1863-The Battle of Chickamauga of the first day. 1864-The third battle of Winchester, VA C.S.A ...
20. 1861-The United States forces surrenders at Lexington, Missouri C.S.A ... 1863-The second day Battle of Chickamauga. 1864-A skirmish near Fort. Cottonwood, of the Arizona territories, of the Confederate States.
21. 1863-With the returning from defeat at Chickamauga, the Federals still occupy a strong defensive position in and around Chattanooga, Tennessee C.S.A ...
22. 1864-The Battle of Fisher's Hill. Virginia C.S.A ... With the following of his advance on the U.S. Capitol, Washington D.C., The Confederate States General Jubal Early's forces are defeated in the Shenandoah Valley.
23. 1862-The U.S. forces burns Randolph, Tennessee C.S.A ... C.S. General Forrest's troops skirmishes at Athens, Alabama C.S.A ...
24. 1864-Union forces burn Confederate American barns, crops, and other civilian property in the Shenandoah Valley.
25. 1863-In the New Orleans area, cases of yellow fever and some deaths are reported among crews of steamers and other vessels.
26. 1863-Inn the Trans-Mississippi, C.S. General Kirby-Smith urges all citizenry to protect the State from the foreign invasion of the Federal Union by fighting from the "thickets, gullies and streams."
27. 1863-The Confederate States raises the age limit conscription of troops to 45. 1864-The Confederate guerrilla leader "Bloody Bill" Anderson attacks Centralia, Missouri C.S.A ...
28. There's fighting in Polk County and Caledonia, Missouri. During the time of General Sterling Price's Invasion. "Apologize for no date."
29. 1864-The Siege of Petersburg and the Battle of Fort Harrison. The Federal Army Captures the fort after very heavy fighting.
30. 1864-The Siege of Petersburg, Virginia C.S.A ... And heavy fighting at Peeble's Farm.

1. *OCTOBER*-1864-C.S. General N.B. Forrest's Cavalry skirmish with the Union garrisons at Athens and Huntsville, Alabama. Now, near Petersburg, Virginia, fighting took place at Peeble's Farm.
2. 1864-Fighting took place at Fairburn, Flat Rock, Sand Mountain and Powder Springs, Georgia, C.S.A ...
3. 1862-The Battle of Corinth, Mississippi. And C.S. Van Dorn and Price inflicts severe loses on the U.S. troops.

4. 1862-The second day of Battle of Corinth with the Confederate Americans withdrawal from an important rail center.
5. 1864-The Atlanta Campaign, and the Battle of Allatoona, Georgia C.S.A … With heavy casualties on both sides in an unsuccessful Confederate Americans attack against the Federal Americans in holding the railroad pass.
6. 1864-The USS Virginia captures a British schooner "Jenny," with 150 bales of cotton on the Texas Gulf Coast off of Rio Grande.
7. 1863-Fighting at Evening Shades, Arkansas C.S.A … 1864-The sea raider CSS Florida was captured at Bahia, Brazil.
8. 1862-The Battle of Perryville, Kentucky C.S.A … The Confederate forces was halted after a bloody fighting in Kentucky.
9. 1862-C.S. General J.E.B. Stuart leads 1,800 Confederate States cavalrymen on a raid into Pennsylvania, U.S.A … for several days.
10. 1864-The Federal troops and gunboats engage the C.S. General Nathan Bradford Forrest's cavalrymen on the Tennessee River at Eastport, Mississippi with the Confederates inflicting serious damage to three of the vessels.
11. 1862-C.S. General J.E.B. Stuart's cavalrymen begin circling the unmoving Union Army cutting the telegraph wires and destroying its military equipment.
12. 1861-Enroute to England, the Confederate States Commissioners, Mason and Slidell ran the Charleston blockade on the steamer Theodora. 1865-By the Presidential proclamation, martial law had ended in Kentucky.
13. 1864-In North West Texas near Fort. Belknap, a Confederate cavalryman of Col. James G. Bouland's "Border Regiment" begins a fierce two-day engagement with several hundred Comanche and Kiowa Indians.
14. 1863-Fighting is accruing at Bristoe Station, Virginia 1864-NearBrownsvilleTexas, Confederate cavalrymen had attacked an encamped Federal force.
15. 1863-The Confederate States Navy submarine "H.L. Hunley" sinks a second time during a practice dive, and Hunley and seven men are killed in Charleston Harbor, South Carolina C.S.A …
16. 1863-Skirmishes at Grand Choteau in Louisiana C.S.A … Fort Brooke in Florida and Pungo Bridge landing in North Carolina C.S.A …
17. 1863-On Hillsborough River in Florida, the landing parties from USS Tahoma and Adela had boarded and destroy the cotton-laden blockade runners known as the Scottish Chief and Kate Dale.

18. 1864-In Liverpool England, at St. George's Hall, pro-Southern ladies of Great Britain held a benefit for the Confederate American soldiers.
19. 1964-The Battle of Cedar Creek, VA. C.S.A., Maj. Gen. Stephen D. Ramseur is mortally wounded in the last major battle of the war in the Shenandoah Valley.
20. 1863-Fighting at the Barton's & Dickson's Station and Cane Creek, Alabama, including the Treadwell's Plantation, Mississippi C.S.A …
21. 1861-The Battle of Ball's Bluff. 1864-Missouri, as Price's Confederates are leaving Lexington, they defeated the Federal Union on the Little Blue, and the U.S. withdrew from Independence.
22. 1864-In the aftermath of the Atlanta Campaign, Hood's Army of Tennessee, moves West across Alabama enroute to Tennessee.
23. 1864-The Battle of Westport, Mississippi C.S.A., C.S. Brig. Gen, Turner Ashby's birthday in Virginia, (1828-1862.)
24. 1864-After his Missouri raid, Maj. Gen. Sterling Price and his army retreats south along the Missouri and Kansas State's borders.
25. 1864-Elements of Lt. Gen. Hood's Army attacks the U.S. Army at Round Mountain, near Turkey town, Alabama C.S.A …
26. 1864-The Confederate American Guerrilla "Bloody Bill" Anderson was killed near Richmond, Missouri C.S.A …
27. 1864-The Siege of Petersburg. The Federal aggressors launch an offensive against the South Side Railroad, Petersburg's lifeline.
28. 1864-C.S. Lt. Gen. John B. Hood's Army demonstrates against the U.S. garrison in Decatur, Alabama C.S.A …
29. The Federal Union batteries fires 2,691 of shells into the Confederate States Fort of (Fort Sumter,) and killing 33defenders of our liberty.
30. 1863-Action took place near New Bern, North Carolina C.S.A … The Federal invaders artillery continues pounding the Confederate American soldiers in Fort Sumter at Charleston, South Carolina C.S.A …
31. 1863-The Confederate forces at Fort Sumter endures the third day of tremendous shelling by the United States heavy artillery. And a skirmish takes place in Barton's Station, Alabama C.S.A …

1. *NOVEMBER*-1861-At Springfield, Missouri, the U.S. Gen. Fremont signs an agreement with the Confederate States Commissioners to exchange prisoners of war. Fremont also agrees to release those arrested for political dissent.

2. 1861-Loaded with 2000 bales of cotton, British steamer "Bermuda" runs thru the Federal blockade and escapes from Charleston, South Carolina C.S.A …
3. 1813-C.S. Gen. Jubal A. Early was born. 1863-At Charleston, South Carolina, and the U.S. Federal artillery fire is bombarding Fort Sumter, with 661 rounds. Heavy fighting in Louisiana at the Bayou Bourdeau and Carrion Crow Bayou.
4. 1864-C.S. Gen. N.B. Forrest attacks and bombards Johnsonville, Tennessee C.S.A., destroying Federal gunboats and transports including storage warehouses, and causing over 2 million dollars in damages.
5. 1861-C.S. Gen. Robert E. Lee is named Commander of the new Confederate Depart of S.C., GA, & E. FL.
6. 1861-Jefferson Davis is elected as the President of the Confederate States. 1865-The Confederate States Third National flag was officially lowered for the last time in Liverpool England, when the sea-raider CSS Shenandoah strikes her colors. However, constitutionally speaking, and according to the Declaration of Independence, the Third National is still the legal national flag of the occupied Confederacy, in the American empire.
7. 1861-The Union forces captures Port Royal. 1863-Severe fighting erupts on the Rappahannock River at Kelly's Ford and Rappahannock Station.
8. Mr.Wilkes seizes as Confederate Commissioners. 1863-Off of the Texas coast at the mouth of the Rio Grande, British schooner "Matamoros" is by the CSS Virginia.
9. 1825-C.S. Gen. Ambrose P. Hill was born. In 1861-The Federal invaders captures Beaufort, South Carolina. 1862-Theirs fighting at Silver Springs and Lebanon, Tennessee C.S.A … 1864-U.S. President Lincoln was re-elected for the second term as President of the United States. His second election as being legal is very questionable.
10. 1863-In Arkansas C.S.A., in an attempt to repress Confederate guerrilla activity, and there are Federal cavalry expeditions North West portion of the State.
11. 1864-At Rome, Georgia C.S.A., the Yankee invaders tears up the railroad tracks, local mills, and foundries.
12. 1861-The Confederate States blockade runner, "Fingal," bought in England, arrives in Savannah with military supplies.
13. 1862-Skirmishes at Holly Springs, Mississippi and at Nashville, Tennessee C.S.A., including Sulphur Springs, Virginia C.S.A …
14. 1863-Off the Texas coast at the mouth of the Rio Grande, the USS Granite captures the CS blockade runner "Terista" and her cargo of 298 bales of cotton.
15. 1861-The Trent Affair. The USS San Jacinto reaches Monroe, VA. C.S.A., with prisoners Mason and Slidell. 1864-US General Sherman begins his 'Extermination March" toward the sea.

16. 1861-The Trent Affair continues. The Yankee politicians of the United States made a statement that the said affair was a violation of international law that Mason and Slidell should be released.
17. 1863-On Mustang Island, Texas C.S.A., 110 Confederate American soldiers were captured at Camp Semmes and had been transported to New Orleans as prisoners of war.
18. 1864-In the Confederate States of Georgia, US General Sherman's genocide and other war crimes against the Confederate Americans continues, as the Union troops move between Ocmulgee and the Oconee Rivers.
19. 1861-At Round Mountain, Indian Territory. Texas Confederates and Confederate Cherokees attack the Union Creek Indians as they are fleeing toward Kansas. 1863-The U.S. President delivers his political speech of the Gettysburg Address.
20. 1864-Fighting has taken place at Clinton, East Macon, Walnut Creek, at Griswoldville, Georgia.
21. 1864-C.S. General John B. Hood's Confederate States Army of Tennessee with more than 30,000 infantry and 8,000 cavalry leaves Florence, Alabama C.S.A., and heads toward the Confederate State of Tennessee.
22. 1863-On the Texas Gulf coast, heavy fighting is occurring at Cedar Bayou, between St. Joseph's and Matagorda Islands.
23. 1863-The Battle of Chattanooga, Tennessee begins. U.S. General Grant's first attempt to break the Confederate States siege.
24. 1863-The Battle of Chattanooga. The Union and Confederate force strengthens their positions after the Battle of Lookout Mountain.
25. 1864-The Battle of Chattanooga. The Battle of Missionary Ridge, Tennessee C.S. of A. The foreign invading Federals were finally able to break the line of the defenders of liberty, after two hours of fierce fighting.
26. 1864-In Columbia, Tennessee C.S.A., C.S. Hood's Tennessee Army arrives in front of the lines of the invaders just south of Duck River.
27. 1864-In the Confederate State of Virginia, the U.S. Army transport ship "Greyhound," is sunk by a Confederate torpedo on James River.
28. 1861-Missouri has been officially admitted into the Constitutional Republic of the Confederate States of America.
29. The Knoxville Campaign, and C.S. General Longstreet, launches an unsuccessful attack on the Union Federals at Fort Sanders.
30. The Battle of Franklin, Tennessee C.S.A …

1. *DECEMBER*-1861-A skirmish at Camp Goggin, and Whipporwill Creek, Kentucky C.S.A …

★ GOD SAVE THE SOUTH ★

2. 1861-Near Newport News, Virginia C.S.A., the Confederate States Patrick Henry is damaged from engaging with four of the United States gunboats for two hours.
3. 1863-Off of the Texas coast, the USS London captures the Spanish schooner "Raton Del Nilo," and her cargo of wine, coffee and percussion caps.
4. 1862-Confederate States General Joseph E. Johnston assumes overall command in the western parts of the Confederacy.
5. 1862-At Coffeeville, Mississippi Central Railroad was defended by the Confederate States forces against the United States cavalry.
6. 1833-C.S. General John S. Mosby was born. 1865-The 13th Amendment was passed by Congress, within the Constitution of the United States of America. 1889-The last breath of our first Constitutional President of the Confederate States of America, Jefferson Davis, had taken place in the occupied New Orleans, LA. C.S.A …
7. 1862-The Battle of Prairie Grove, Arkansas C.S.A., after a bitter fighting, the Federals still maintain control of the North West of that sovereign State.
8. 1860-The U.S. Secretary of the Treasury Howell Cobb resigns. The Georgia native will become a Confederate States Major General by 1863, rendering valuable service to the 'New Nation of the Confederacy." 1863-The "New American Caesar-Abraham Lincoln," makes the proclamation of Amnesty toward any Confederate American that would yield to the will of the New Centralized Nation, of Democracy of the United States and their Reconstruction enslavement programs.
9. On the South Carolina and Georgia Coast lines, Southern planters burns the cotton to prevent it from falling into the hands of the illegal alien invaders. [Apologize for no date.]
10. 1861-An act of the Confederate States Congress in the Capital of Richmond, Virginia, admit the Sovereign State of Kentucky into this New Confederate Nation. Thus, completing the thirteen States, which the "thirteen stars" is a symbolic symbol of liberty and freedom during the Colonel War for Independence, or the Revolutionary War.
11. 1861-Already suffering under the blockade of submission by the Union Navy, Charleston, South Carolina C.S.A., is struck by a disastrous fire that sweeps through the business district.
12. 1862-In Mississippi, the USS Cairo, strikes a C.S. torpedo in the Yazoo River, the first U.S. ship to be sunk in this way.
13. 1861-The Battle of Fredericksburg, Virginia C.S.A., with over 186,000 Confederate American troops engaged in fighting. 1862-The Battle of Fredericksburg. 1864-Fort McAllister had surrendered.
14. 1862-At Fredericksburg, the Yankee Army withdraws after being severely beaten in the previous day's assaults.

15. 1864-The Battle of Nashville, Tennessee C.S.A … Our outnumbered Confederate defenders are driven from their main defensive lines.
16. 1864-The Battle of Nashville. The Confederate States Army of Tennessee was shattered by overwhelming forces of the U.S. forces.
17. 1860-In Columbia, the South Carolina Secession Convention issues a resolution in favor of their Sovereign State in seceding from the membership of the Federal Union known as the United States of America.
18. 1862-In Lexington, Tennessee C.S.A., C.S. Nathan Bedford Forrest's Cavalry was defeated by a Federal Cavalry force. 1863-Minor fighting at Beans Station at Rutledge, Tennessee C.S.A …
19. 1862-C.S. General Nathan Bedford Forrest attacks U.S. General Grant's supply line by striking the railroads near Jackson, Tennessee C.S.A … 1863-The naval forces destroy a Confederate supply base at St. Andrews, Florida C.S.A …
20. 1860-By a vote of 169 to 0, South Carolina adopts an Ordinance of Secession, and their membership in the Union was dissolved.
21. 1862-C.S. General John Hunt Morgan launches another cavalry raid on the Union supply lines in Kentucky.
22. 1862-Morgan's Confederates, crosses the Cumberland River on their Kentucky raid.
23. 1862-Skirmish near Helena, Arkansas. 1863-Fighting at Culpepper Court House, Virginia and Corinth, Mississippi C.S.A …
24. A skirmish near Dandridge, Tennessee C.S.A … [Apologize for no date.] 1864-The United States begins bombardment upon the Confederate States "Fort Fisher," in North Carolina.
25. 1863-The Federal troops enters the Gulf Coast town of Port Lavaca, Texas C.S.A …, after taking what they want, the United States begins burning the business districts of the civilian town.
26. 1860-In the Charleston Harbor, South Carolina Militia seizes the castle Pinckney.
27. 1862-A skirmish at Dripping Springs, Arkansas C.S.A … 1863-The Confederate States Congress abolishes substitution for military service.
28. 1862-The Vicksburg Campaign. The Battle of Chickasaw Bayou. 1863-On the Matagorda Peninsula in Texas C.S.A., there is heavy fighting between the Cavalrymen of Texas and the infantrymen of the State of Maine.
29. 1863-While landing on the Texas Matagorda Peninsula, twenty of the Confederate American soldiers of the Matagorda Bay force, freezes to death when the Federals swamps their boats, and the Federals fires on the survivors.
30. 1862-The USS Monitor had sunk off the coast of Cape Hatteras, N.C. C.S.A … 1863-A skirmish at Augustine, Florida C.S.A … 1864-A skirmish at Leighton, Alabama C.S.A …

31. 1862-The Battle of Murfreesboro, Tennessee C.S.A … The Confederate defenders and the Federal invaders fought the whole day.

CLOSING STATEMENT: While these highlights do not share the deeper part of how this war came so **"close,"** as an **"act of genocide against our people,"** and in destroying and enslaving our New Nation. It does; however, give you an idea as to the seriousness in the defense of our liberty, our Republic, our people, and our family.

A SHORT HISTORY OF THE 49TH REGIMENT OF THE NORTH CAROLINA TROOPS

The 49th Regiment North Carolina Troops (49th) was organized in March of 1862 from ten (10) separate rifle companies raised in the Piedmont region of NC. Many of the recruits were members that had enlisted earlier in the war, but for the lack of weapons were not able to be mustered into service. The rank and file contained a population wholly of volunteers second to one for self-reliance, integrity, just respect for authority and modest worth and courage. Many of them were descendants of the people who made the Hornet's Nest of North Carolina a fortress of independence and a terror to their country's invaders.

The 49th was placed under the command of Colonel (future General) Stephen Dodson Ramseur, a rising star in the Confederacy and whose exploits are well known to all the people in NC. After a short time of drill and instructions, the 49th was sent to the Capital of Richmond, where they participated in the Seven Battles. The regiment was placed in Ranson's Brigade and under Ramseur's leadership who was gravely wounded. Colonel Lee McAfee assumed command of the regiment and held that post until the 49th had surrendered at Appomattox. The great C.S. General Robert E. Lee decided to follow up his victory at Richmond and second Manassas with an invasion into Maryland. The 49th participated in the capture of Harpers Ferry and were then hurried to Sharpsburg where they held off a Union assault. The 49th along with the rest of the brigade had the honor of retaking and holding the famous "West Woods." After returning to Virginia, the unit was in the battle of Fredericksburg. The 49th was subjected by too much cannonading & infantry fighting including with many casualties.

Ransom's Brigade was recalled to Eastern NC with the expressed purpose of protecting vital Petersburg, Weldon, and Wilmington Railroad. This railroad was the Confederate States General (Lee), most important supply line and with the Eastern North Carolina being occupied by the U.S. Federal troops, it was essential to keep this railroad open.

On brigade was not nearly large enough to secure this vital supply line. And mostly during 1863, it was founded that the 49th along with the brigade was constantly on the move to give the impression of a much larger force. One day they would appear at one end of the line and the next there showing up at the other end. Strategically speaking, the 49th was the right wing of the Army of Northern Virginia. Ransom's Brigade was the most important force in this section for many months; and, occupying in quick succession Weldon, Warsaw, Kenansville, Goldsboro, Kinston, Wilmington & Greenville, they we are always on hand to confront any movement by the foreign invaders in that region.

Occasionally, a sharp brush with the enemy's forces was necessary to warn them of the foe that would be in their path. From New Bern, Plymouth and Washington, in Eastern North Carolina, and from Norfolk and Suffolk, in Virginia, the Federals would send out expeditions; but, in each instance, no great distance would be traversed before they were confronted by Ransom's Brigade. During this period, the 49th along with the brigade recruited and drilled almost at a constant pace so that when the brigade was transferred to the command of General P.G.T. Beauregard's command in the spring of 1864, it is probable that there was not in the Confederate American service any brigade, containing a greater number of effective, well-trained, veteran soldiers.

In May of 1864, Union General Butler moved on to Drewry Bluff with the Nation's Capital of the Confederate States (Richmond) as his objective. When the brigade containing the 49th had reached Petersburg, Butler had already captured Richmond pike. The brigades of Ransom and Hargood under the command of that sterling North Carolina, Robert F. Hoke were thrown into the fight by causing the foreign invaders (Federals) to retire to the other side of the pike. At a half-way house, Hoke offered the battle, but the enemy had slowly retired before him and the way was opened to Drewry Bluff for the reinforcements to Beauregard. As soon as Ranson's Brigade arrived they were ordered to the right of the line.

The 49th had barely reached there and occupied the works when the first assault of the Battle of Drewry Bluff was made. The 49th held the extreme right and was subjected to a galling fire as the U.S. Federals tried to turn that flank, but skirmishers held them at bay under the command of Cicero Durham known as the "Fighting Quartermaster." The 49th had lost 11 patriots and a considerable number of wounded in this continual engagement of freedom during the evening of the 13th of May. The 14th and 15th were spent repelling the repeated charges of the enemy upon the line. And severe loss was in was inflicted upon them in each attempt.

★ JOHN THOMAS NALL ★

The mourning of the 16th of May was obscured by a dense fog. And C.S. General Beauregard moved his entire army forward for an attack with the left wing under the immediate command of C.S. General Ransom. Ransom struck the foreign enemy on their extreme right, carried their works, and turned their flank. Blow after blow fell thick and fast into U.S. Butler's Army. All parts of his line were heavily pressed. And Colonel McAfee being wounded, the regiment was commanded by Major James T. Davis. He ordered Captain Chambers of Company C to throw his company out as skirmishers at an oblique right angle and their help the works in front of the 49th were readily taken.

In action that day, the 49th suffered heavily in casualties to officers and men. The next day the regiment continued the pursuit of Butler's army and assisted in his "bottling up" at Bermuda Hundreds. On the 4th of June, the brigade had crossed the James River at Drewrys Bluff and went into the trench lines in front of Petersburg. Hastily rifle pits were thrown up and now commenced Beauregard's magnificent grapple with Grant's Army until Longstreet's command could arrive. With scarcely more than 5.000 men and 18 pieces of artillery he kept Grant's Army, from coming up from City Point, in check all day and night of the 17th of June.

For the next nine months the 49th occupied with the brigade in different parts of the trench lines in front of Petersburg. During this period, they were subjected sun and storm. Heat and cold, with scant food and insufficient supplies, the ranks thinning hourly from the deaths, wounds and of the sickly, and depressed by the gathering gloom of the falling fortunes, through the dark, and bitter foreboding winter of 1864-65. The men of the 49th were faithful unto the end; never faltering in the performance of any duty. And never failing to meet and resist the foes against liberty. On the 30th of July, U.S. General Grant had surprised the Confederate American Army in the Battle of the Crater. The 49th was on the flank of the attack and held the breach until re-enforcements could be brought up to stabilize the situation. Colonel McAfee commanded Ransom's Brigade during this attack.

The 49th participated in the ill-fated attack on Fort Steadman and this defeat signaled the beginning of the end. Union General Sheridan attacked on the extreme right of the Southern lines at Five Forks and although offering stubborn resistance, the 49th was overwhelmed by superior numbers being attacked on three sides. Most of the 49th were captured at this battle. C.S. General Lee then ordered a retreat and on April the 9th of 1865, what was left of the 49th was unfortunately surrendered at Appomattox Court House. On that black day, 11 officers and 23 NCOS and Privates were forced to surrender. It was a very inglorious ending to a very noble fighting unit-The 49th North Carolina …

THE CONFEDERACY IS LIBERATED

Occupation forces Capitulate

*NEW CONFEDERATE STATES
PRESIDENT IS INSTALLED*

The President-elect, George Randolph Calcurry, took his office while standing on the very same spot. Marked by a star, on the top step of the Capital entrance in Montgomery, Alabama, where the oath was administered to our first President. From there he was flown by helicopter, under a Confederate military escort to Irwinville, Georgia, where President Davis was captured on the 10th of May 1865. He gives a moving speech about how President Davis being captured and that it did not mark the end of the Confederacy, but rather the beginning of a long journey to the present day.

The President and the First Lady of the Confederacy was flown to a prepared landing site near Stone Mountain Park the next morning after a restful night at the home of a Confederate patriot in Irwinville. The arrival of the President and the First Lady of the Confederacy at Stone Mountain by motorcade was marked by the largest crowds that have ever been seen in the State.

And Confederate flags so numerous it was more like, a sea of flags. The National Guard having been dissolved a month earlier was now replaced by the Georgia Confederate Armed Forces, which lined the streets for the safety of the first family. It was at Stone Mountain that our President made an announcement of what will go down in history as the Confederate Declaration of Liberty. Wherein he states, "That it was for us of this generation, and for generations yet to come, to live out the true meaning of the Cause for which our forefathers died and for which so many families sacrificed."

The President also declares before the world's media, "The Confederate States of America shall return to Richmond Virginia." In Virginia, the first family would be met by the largest parade of arms in history of this continent, as over 400,000 troops await his arrival! That sense of history which has bound us together as a distance and separate people and had made this hour in history possible. As the President's airplane lands in Richmond, the Confederate Congress is ready in secession, racing through the myriad of bills that had been pre-planned during the previous months, bills long delayed during the years under conquest and occupation.

The President's motorcade passed around the city from the airport in order to make their official entry down Monument Row, heading directly for the reviewing platform, from which the Confederate States Armed Forces will salute their Commander-in-Chief, in a pass and review parade the likes of which would never be witnessed again. From every Confederate State they came; old and the young, the historic and the modern. They paraded through the heart of Richmond and on that day, they could be seen by the nations of the earth who are represented as "Confederate Foreign Legionnaires," from such places as Sweden, Poland, France, Spain, Germany, and Italy. Confederate units from, South America, Canada, and Asia. History would not recall such an outpouring again.

The rise of the Confederate States of America is more than the rebirth of a single nation. It is a victory of truth; the rebirth of liberty, and in this, the world shares our joy. Yet in all the outburst of that day, the tenderness moment had to have been when a small boy dressed in a Confederate Officers uniform, escorted by armed troops, slowly approached the President, and one by one handed him four items. The Holy Bible that was used by Jefferson Davis, the original Confederate States Constitution, the Sword of General Robert E. Lee, and the last previous National flag which flew over the Confederate States Government in 1865. These items were destined to be present in later years, at the newly planned Confederate Military Institute, as a reminder to future officers of the price of liberty. Inscription in bronze are the words "Least we forget, and history repeats itself!"

-We Dare to Dream-**********

By: Thomas E. Guinn.

★ GOD SAVE THE SOUTH ★

JESSE HELMS
1921-2008

★ ★ ★
YOU'RE A CONFEDERATE ... BUT DON'T KNOW IT?

Most of the political problems in this country will not be settled until more folks realize the South was right. I know that goes against the P.C. edicts, but the fact is that about the Constitutional Republic, the Confederate leaders were right, and the Northern Republicans were wrong. Many people today even argue the Confederate position without realizing it.

For example, if you argue for strict construction of the Constitution, you are arguing the Confederate position; when you oppose pork-barrel spending, you are arguing the Confederate position; and when you oppose protective tariffs, you are arguing the Confederate position; but that is not all. When you argue for the Bill of Rights, you are arguing the Confederate position, and when you argue that the Constitution limits the power and jurisdiction of the federal government; you are arguing the Confederate position.

One of the things that gets lost when you adopt to the politically correct oversimplification that the "War Between the States" was a Civil War," all about slavery is a whole treasure load of American political history. It was not a "Civil War." A "Civil War" is when two or more factions contend for control of one government. At no time did the South intend or attempt to overthrow the government of the United States. The Southern States simply withdrew from what they correctly viewed as a voluntary Union. They formed their own Union and adopted their own Constitution.

The U.S. government remained intact. There were just fewer States, but everything else remained as exactly as it was. You can be sure that, with as much bitterness and hatred of the South that there was in the North, the Northerners would have tried Confederates for treason if there had been any grounds. There weren't, and the

South's worst enemy knew that Abraham Lincoln's invasion of the South was entirely without any Constitutional authority.

And it's as plain as an elephant in a Tea Party, that Lincoln did not seek to preserve the Union to end slavery. All you must do is read his first inaugural address. What Lincoln did not want to lose was tax revenue generated by the South. As Northern States gained a majority in both houses, they began to use the South as a "Cash Cow." Here's how it worked. Most Southerners who exported cotton bartered the cotton in Europe for goods. When the protective tariffs were imposed, that meant that Southerners had to pay them. To make matters worse, the North would then use the revenue for pork-barrel projects in their States. The South was faced with either paying high tariffs and receiving no benefits from the revenue or buying artificially high-priced Northern goods.

Southerners opposed pork-barrel spending. Their correct view was that, because the Federal Government was merely the agent of all of the States, whatever money it spent, should be of equal benefit. Their position on public lands was that they belonged to all the people, and the Federal Government had no authority to give the lands to private interests. Northerners had announced that they would not be bound by the Constitution. What you had was the rise of the 'Modern Nationalism,' fighting the original Republic, founded by the American Revolution. So, regardless where were born, you may be a Southerner, "philosophically speaking."

By: Charley Reese.

✯ ✯ ✯
A MESSAGE FROM THE PRESIDENT OF THE CONFEDERATE SOCIETY OF AMERICA

My Fellow Americans:

In my many discussions with other leaders within the movement, I have often stated my belief that many of the problems associated with modern America are a direct result of the outcome of The War for Southern Independence, more commonly referred to as The American Civil War. The defeat of the Southern armies in the field not only sounded the death knell of the State Sovereignty, but dramatically increased the pace of the transformation from the Old Republic based upon the principles of self-interest to the American Empire, committed not only to the "Reconstruction" of the South, but of the world as well.

Although the U.S. Constitution allocated certain restrictive powers to the General Government, it undeniably enthroned the Sovereign State as master of the Republic and the legitimate avenue through which the voices of the people would be made manifest. Following the war, the Reconstruction Acts as well as the 13th, 14th & 15th Amendments-whose passage was made possible via the disenfranchisement of the Southern States and a direct political assault on the office of the President itself-the balance of power was deceitfully and illegally shifted to the General Government.

As a result, the status of the individual shifted from the status of master to slave groveling at the foot of Uncle Sam for the scraps from a tax system that enshrines federally mandated programs, regulations and the ability to indoctrinate the people through rigidly controlled education system. And the most ludicrous part of this whole system is that the money, and the power with which the General Government dominates the States, is almost eagerly, donated from the slaves themselves.

★ GOD SAVE THE SOUTH ★

The people of this nation have been led to believe that they live within a free country; but the harsh and obvious truth is that we are deeply immersed in (democratic) socialism, in which is seen as "good" for the masses outweighs the concerns of the individual (including those little nuisances we know as "Rights.") Our Founding Fathers were very clear in explaining their concerns, fears, and apprehensions of so-called 'democracies:' for all 'democracies' ultimately fail because by systematically depriving the people of their freedoms, they stifle individual creativity and productivity. A look at the history of the Soviet Union may provide a dark and ominous glimpse into the future of America.

Ah, it is however, a future not yet set-in stone. But there is much work to be done and the days grow short. Therefore, the Confederate Society of America (CSA) and other organizations are gathering the people and the resources necessary to both convert the populace to our Cause while simultaneously engaging the enemies of freedom on all fronts.

While it is true that the CSA is a Southern Nationalist organization, our efforts are not confined to the South of the Mason-Dixon Line. We are as committed to the principles, convictions and laws as outlined and enumerated in the original Constitution as any Americans. While others wish to define us as a "racist" or "extremist," we are nothing as much as simple folks looking for the freedom to live raise a family and work as we see fit. We believe there is, but one God and his residence is not Washington D.C.

Further, our commitment to "equality before the law" and to the rights of all is why we eagerly invite all people to come and join us. Our Mission Statement and our By-law are self-explanatory and encapsulates who we are.

And we are proud of who we are. We make NO excuses. In short, we are Confederates in the mold of our ancestors of 1860, holding to those beliefs and common goal that gave our lives meaning and direction before it was taken by force of arms in the Second American Revolution (also known as the American Civil War.) No matter how loud our enemies' blather, we are too proud to wear hoods, we do not burn crosses, we do not lynch blacks, and we do not seek to reinstitute slavery! What we do wish "*is too be left alone.*" It is our belief that within our enemies lies the true danger to American freedom.

We are NOT rebels! We are Patriots! We will NOT be intimidated, and we will NOT go away. Y'all have eyes to see that something is not right; ears with which to hear the cries of the innocent; and noses which tell you that something stinks in this land that 'everything' is NOT right! When God is cast out, the very purpose of our being and as a people and as a country is gone. We must as a people, bow down, ask forgiveness, and restore the biblical God to His rightful place in America and in our hearts. I ask all that believe as we do to come, join the CSA and let the Yankees quiver once more before the cacophonous "Rebel Yell" as the legions of Dixie arise to reclaim their homes, their nations and their God.

God Save the South—For so goes The South—So Goes the Republic!

Deo Vindice,

Craig Maus/ October 29th 2001/ President of the Confederate Society of America. www.deovindice.org/—*All Internet Address within this book can change without any notice-sorry for any inconvenience!*

★ ★ ★

THE CONFEDERATION VS FEDERAL AUTOCRACY

I have been travelling the back roads of our Southland for the last two months, stopping whenever & wherever to speak with our people. I have made this a matter of practice ever since I attended my first Southern Conference back in 94'. It was a rewarding experience. Additionally, it helps me to re-charge my battery's as I am reminded that hope for a Confederate restoration is entirely possible.

There on those back roads within that same Southern Frontier of yesteryear remains those Confederates of old. A little more weathered and older, like me, but mindful of the lies, waste, disobedience, and colossal theft brought upon this country & her people by a Federal Demagogue that has transitioned us from a Nation of Independence to a Nation of Dependence.

Washington serves NOT you or I, but themselves. They have conspired & transformed this land called home into an Autocratic Democracy and from those Hallowed Halls wherein the Framer's created & provided us with a Republic of Sovereign States. The brute force being exhibited and played out in full sight by the Washington establishment on daily & regular bases can No longer be denied. There is NO longer a 'system' of checks and balances. Obama is now the residing Federal Autocrat. His 14 czars', stooges in Congress, 'Citizen Police' and the real power brokers who control him, are the stark reality of every Confederate claim we have made

We and those before us warned y'all what would come about, dating back & resulting from their illegal invasion of our legal & just Christian Confederate Government in 1861. The 'state-run' media will neither elaborate nor remotely call attention to ANY of their present-day activities much less those events of 145 years ago when the Devil came a calling in Dixie.

★ JOHN THOMAS NALL ★

Everything has been homogenized and marginalized to distract us from the painful obvious. Federal obliteration steals our money and gives it to those who support them no matter what, as that is their tablet for sustenance & existence. Further, they use our money to graduate our children from their schools of non-thought who ultimately become tomorrow's teachers & politician's. It is never-ending self-greasing wheel and we have become the enslaved and they have become the consummate Federal Overseer. Nonetheless, there on MANY on those back roads who know full well of what was going on-they are <u>our people, a people who remain in waiting.</u>

They are a decent and beautiful people, full of life with a passionate love for God and Country. They know the real deal and will spit in the eye of the oppressor if given the chance to do so again. They are the Sheppard's of the faith and they have NOT forgotten their identity and thy seed from which they came-they remain vigilant-they are our God-Fearing Confederate's. They will not speak to just anyone but will speak to someone who <u>they decide</u> is trustworthy.

And when that 'conversation' comes to fruition, it is as though a vacuum of 20 kilotons has been unleashed. It is a Power of Faith that NO ruling body can ever hope to conquer. They are massing my friends and they have kept their 'powder dry and hidden' over these many years. It was on one of these trips through the heartland, in Locust, North Carolina, that I came upon an auction on an early Saturday morning. A farmhouse was being sold and the owner had recently passed. Her siblings could no longer take care of the 16-acre farm and thus, sadly, it was going up for auction. I pulled in, and it was still very early & the crowd that had gathered was still small. I chatted with the local folks and then took my leave and walked the property.

It was as though time had stood still there at that ole farmhouse. I came upon the Family Graveyard. Before entering, I ask for God's permission to enter, as it was with total respect for those laying in peace in their land. I did not want my visitation to be viewed or construed as an intrusion or perceived as a violation bordering on nothing more than 'curious encroachment."

That is NOT my way. Permission & Respect, <u>unlike the Federal,</u> is always absolute among any Confederate. There were three centuries of family buried there. From small children to adults. In the corner of the sacred ground, there was a tombstone of a Confederate soldier. It read:

[John Quincy Lambert Corp Co H 42 Regt NC TROOPS
Confederate States Army APR 15th 1841 MAR 15th 1906]

In my moment of private reflection and solitude, I could only provide to a former soldier what another ex-soldier could offer, a well-deserved and humble SALUTE, accompanied with a simple and sincere THANK YOU ON A JOB <u>EXCEEDINGLY WELL DONE!</u> My thoughts were broken as I realized that an older man had been standing alongside me, without so much as even being aware.

He looked at me and said, "Y' all kin?" I replied, "No sir, just an appreciative person for that which this man, along with so many others, tried to accomplish and preserve." He said, Amen!" I said, "Do y'all think anyone will really know the true reason's for why they fought?" He said, "I don't know, but one thing's for sure fer sure … if they could rise up, I KNOW they would do it all over again!"

I asked him his name. "Ned Honeycutt, young fella, Ned Honeycutt." We shook hands and as quickly as he appeared, he was gone. You see folks; Confederates are naturally mindful and respective of others. We recognize and respect the sanctity of individuality. All we ever wanted was peace and natural harmony to prevail. Confederates understand the rudimentary difference between right and wrong and good and bad.

We understand the difference between legitimate and illegitimate … and we also know the difference between honesty and treachery and the tragedy that is the natural consequence when evil overtakes good in the name of the public good. We are a devoutly Christian People who believe in God's theater and it is for all these reasons and more, "that we will probably have to do it again' if we are to save ourselves.'

There are hundreds of thousands of Ned Honeycutt's out there who, no matter the time passed, know what is going on. We, in my humble opinion, have entered the "Final Hours" of our existence. The Federal Government, despite All they have extolled from us, cannot hide what exists in those History books of old. Those Books still hold their treacherous feet to the fire, although they will deny their credibility and will leave the written words which formulated our very existence to their cronies within the judiciary to 'decipher' and judge in the contemporary … thus reducing them to 'theory' and no longer representative by THEIR standards.

It is no less similar than having the Devil tell us that Christ was but a mere myth! They have become our Jailor's and have long since abrogated from representation. They are incapable of representation for they have morphed into a solitary state of their own making and we are simply the providers for them to feast & salivate upon. They, along with their various fifth columns depict us continuously as (rednecks, racists, yahoos) and a variety of names whose sole purpose & design is to strip us from any of our former identity & credibility. At any other time in previous World History, it is a tactic known and referred to as vanquishing your former enemy. Rendering him to a point of persona non grata without so much as a claim of legitimacy. We call for accountability and they provide paltry excuses for their continued onslaught and misbehavior designed to gratify themselves at our expense.

This is not new to us for we have been forced to live as a conquered Country and People for over 145 years. But it is new to the rest of America because they don't know any better and are still trying to figure out just what in the hell has happened! John Quency Lambert of the 42nd North Carolina knew what it was ALL ABOUT, as did his other 325,000 Brethren who fought and died for our Right of Sovereignty & Independence to exist. He was but 20 years old and he knew the difference! How many 20-year-old people of today do you know who have the slightest clue to what it was all about? And if things continue as they are, what, or better asked, who will be there for your children and grandchildren in the next 145 years to teach them the difference between God & Country and the debauchery created by the Federal incarnate? In whose name and purpose will they be sacrificed to? The 'Federal Beasts' insatiable appetite for control & advancement of their ONE WORLD ORTHODOXY of the masses has NO boundaries or limitations? In what capacity will they serve the Federal Beast, since any province of original being willed have been carved from them in a manner leaving them much in the same condition as a patient who has undergone a lobotomy … for they will have nothing else?

Time is hastening and the only thing remaining absolute is ourselves … All else has been sold or given away via acts of Federal intervention/ legislation, cloaked in political correctness & designed to cover the real political expediency & design of their maddening ways. Their time clock has stepped up & they are devouring this nation & us almost daily … If it were not as real, one could argue that it has become almost 'fashionable'!

Our 'elected' politicians do not have a clue and if you ever listen to any of them, they do not make a lick a sense at all! They are the blind leading the decapitated and what is scarier, is they are making the rules without so much as a backbone to substantiate any of their incoherent actions. Hell, they don't even bother to read what they enact into law anymore!

All Roads Have Always Leaded To 1865! When the South lost, this entire Nation lost … But only we knew it at the time! The question is just how many others have come to figure that out at this very present? For God, Family and the Confederacy,

By; Craig Maus: President of the Confederate Society of America, and a proud member of the Confederate Alliance of Organizations. This subject was in reference to [The Eve of Destruction of Part eight-The Final Hours.] For more information about the Confederate Society of America, web search for <u>www.deovindice.org</u>/. 19th June 2009.

THE COMMUNIST REVOLUTION OF 1861 AGAINST THE UNITED STATES AND AGAINST THE CONFEDERATE STATES OF AMERICA

After the Declaration of Independence in 1776, our first founding fathers begin putting together a more cohesive contract of government between the various Sovereign States of America. This was called Articles of Confederation which was ratified on March 1st, 1781. Eight decades later, with the election of Abraham Lincoln, a man determined to destroy State's Rights and the Confederacy of our second founding fathers, seven Southern States secede from the United States "(the Union.)" On March 4th, 1861 the first Provisional Congress was convened and formed the Confederate States of America, to preserve the dream of our first founders that created the Republic of the United States.

Six weeks later on April 15th, 1861, Abraham Lincoln Declared War on the Southern States after manufacturing an excuse by sending troops on April 4th, 1861 to fortify Ft. Sumter, South Carolina, within the New Southern Nation. Lincoln did not bother to get Constitutional permission from Congress for his Declaration of War.

Southern Statesmen knew that Abraham Lincoln and his new Republican Party were corrupt men who intent upon continued plundering of the Southern States, through unfair tariffs, but it was even worse than most suspected. They did not know that the (Communist "Karl Marx") was corresponding with Lincoln and encouraging the war against the South. A Confederacy of State Republics is opposite of a Communist or Federalist type of a Centralized ("Union.").

★ ★ ★

THE LINCOLN PUTSCH: AMERICA'S BOLSHEVIK ASSISISTED REVOLUTION

Union General Franz Sigel had been a leader in the Communist Revolution of 1848, a revolution fought to destroy the individual State governments of Germany and France, and forcibly unite them under an all-powerful Central, Socialist government. That revolution had failed and Sigel, along with thousands of other "Forty-Eighters," fled Europe for America, bringing their revolutionary Socialist ideas with them. Karl Marx fled to London under the protection of the rich Friedrich Engels. During Lincoln's War against the South, Lincoln's German troops declared "I fight mit Segel."

Carl Schurz, another Forty-Eighter, had met Karl Marx at the Democratic Club in Cologne. Schurz delivered the votes of 300.00 German immigrants to Lincoln in 1860. It was Schurz's ideas and influence that eventually held sway with Lincoln and encourage the invasion of the Confederacy and resulted in the Emancipation Proclamation allegedly freeing slaves in the Confederacy Territory, but not freeing any slaves in Yankee Territory. Meanwhile, Lincoln executed hundreds of Blacks in New York for refusing to join the Yankee Army as well as crushing opposition to his war by Northern newspapers.

German and other European Communist refugees in America were instructed to support Lincoln's invasion of the South. The extremely pro-Union, anti-Southern writings of Marx and his colleague Engels echo the attitude of his German followers. <u>(It is worth nothing that Lincoln has long been a hero in the Communist world including in the U.S.S.R. and there was the (Communist "Abraham Lincoln Brigade" in the Spanish Civil War.)</u>

The preponderance of German-born officers and men in the Union armies is overwhelming. It is estimated that in 1860 there were approximately 1.204.075 Germans in the States. Of the total of those serving, at least 36.000 served under German officers. If the total number of German troops is assumed to be 216.000 and we accept that the total of all foreign-born troops was nearly 500.000.

Most of the same super rich bankers and royal families who were secretly behind the Karl Marx and his Communist movement in the attempt to take over Europe in 1848 were behind the successful Communist Revolution of 1861 in America to crush the Confederate States of America and at the same time to establish complete (Centralization of Government in Washington D.C.) Movements like the Confederacy are a threat to all empires. Mega-States, regardless of their personal differences, must hang together to maintain the myth of omnipotent government.

However, many communists then as well as today have no idea that a group of elitist families largely control the entire international movement for their own ultimate benefit of forming a (New World Order) plantation of worker-slaves who have only an illusion of freedom and liberty.

Bibliography: Engle, Stephen, Yankee Dutchman (Fayetteville, AR: Univ. of Arkansas Press, 1993)

Foner, Eric, Politics and Ideology in the Age of the Civil War (Oxford Univ. Press, 1980)

Levine, Bruce, The Spirit of 1848 (Urbana, Ill. Press, 1992)

Logsdon, "The Civil War-Russian Version (III): The Soviet Historians," in Civil War History, Dec. 1962

Lonn, Ella, Foreigners in the Union Army and Navy (Baton Rouge: LSU Press, 1951)

Luebke, Frederick, Ethanic Voters and the Election of Lincoln (Lincoln, NB: Univ. of Neb. Press, 1971)

Marx and Engels, the Civil War in the U.S. (New York: International Publishers, 1971)

Wersich, Rudiger, Carl Schurz (Munich: Heinz Moos Verlag, 1979)

Wittke, Carl, Refugees of Revolution (Philadelphia: Univ of Pa. Press), 1952)

The Utopian Communist: A Biography of Wilhelm Weitling (Baton Rouge: LSU Press, 1950)

Zucker, A.E., ED., the Forty-Eighters (New York: Columbia Univ. Press, 1950)

LINCOLN'S SOCIALIST LEGIONS

(Yankees and Socialist-Birds of a feather)

During the War of Northern Aggression, it has been reported that over 180.000 Germans fought in the Union Armies. This number was buttressed by thousands of Austrians, Hungarians, Poles, Czechs and Irish. The majority of these were probably honest, hardworking people. Yet the question must be asked-with a population of around 22 million in the North as opposed to 9 million in the South-why did the North have so many foreign troops in her armies?

Francis Springer, in his book "War for What?" puts the number even higher. He noted: "It seems strange that the North, with such vast human resources, should find it necessary to resort to recruiting men abroad. The 1860 census shows 4.100.000 foreign born in this country, mostly in the North, but there were 500.000 men in the Northern Army of foreign birth, or 90.000 more than 10% of the foreign population, indicating that 90.000 Northern soldiers, and probably more, were recruited abroad."

Author William Burton, in his book "Melting Pot Soldiers" deals with the foreign soldiers in the Yankee Armies. He quotes a correspondent for the "London Daily Telegraph" as stating that the foreign soldiers in the Union Armies has scant use for the abolitionist and their "Holy Crusade." German immigrant Valentin Bechler, according to Burton, told his wife "I wish all abolitionists were in Hell." One of the carefully concealed facts over the decades about Mr. Lincoln's Armies is that he had an amazing number of European Socialists under uniform during the war. Only recently has information regarding this started to service. Up until a few years ago it was one of the most studiously ignored facts and aspects of the War. "Establishment Historians," (or maybe we should label them "Hysterians" in their messianic quest to give us the "Correct Spin" on the War and the reasons for it just knew in their hearts that we didn't need this kind of information, so they labored mightily to make sure were not exposed to it.

★ GOD SAVE THE SOUTH ★

It has been reported that as many as 5.000 European Socialist and Communists from the failed 1848 Socialist revolts in Europe served in the Union Armies in one place or another. Some sources have placed that number closer to 10.000. After these Socialists failed in their revolutionary aims in Europe in1848-49, many came to America.

A good portion of them felt that they failed to do Europe in 48 and 49 might just be accomplished here in America during the War of Northern Aggression. In "Forty-Eighters in the Union Armies" is has been stated: "The failure of their revolutionary hopes in Europe did not prevent them from taking up arms again in 1861 to defend the very principles they had fought for in 1848 and 1849; Union, Freedom, and Democracy." Please go back and reread that last quote. Let it sink in.

These European Socialists viewed the War of Northern Aggression as an extension of their Socialist hopes for Europe. If you consider that fact, the entire scope and reason for that War, from the Yankee perspective, takes on a whole meaning. No longer was it a struggle to "Preserve the Union as given to us by the founding fathers, rather it was a struggle to preserve and extend the influence of European Socialism in America. Author William Burton has revealed the August (von) Willich, the "Communist with a heart" … was not reluctant to lecture his soldiers on the virtues of Socialism."

If we have a record of one instance of that being done, one wonders how many other places it occurred that have gone unreported. One amazing thing about these European Socialist and Communists is how many of them managed to end up with high-ranking positions in the Union Armies. I will list a few here so you get the idea.

1. Franz Sigel-Major General.
2. Carl Schurz-Major General.
3. August (von) Willich-Major General.
4. Sandor (Alexander) Asboth-Brigadier General on Fremont's staff.
5. August Becker-called "Red Becker (on account of his political leanings?-Chaplain for the 8th New York.
6. Lugwig (Louis) Blenker-Brigadier General of volunteers.
7. IsdorBush-Captain of Fremont's staff.
8. Johann Fiala-Lt. Colonel and topographical engineer on Fremont's staff.

Scores of other Socialists and Communists could be listed if space permitted, but I think you begin to get the idea. The ethnic and ideological makeup of Mr. Lincoln's Army has yet to be fully exposed. If we are to try to understand the War from a Yankee perspective, we must, at all cost, take the strong Socialist influence exerted on Mr. Lincoln's Army into consideration.

The fact that so many European Socialist and Communists looked upon Mr. Lincoln's War of Aggression as an extension of their own aggressive aspirations and political desires should begin to speak volumes about the true nature of the Union Cause-no matter what the "Hystery books" tell us, Mr. Lincoln was known to be friendly to the cause of Socialism. Establishment historian James McPherson has admitted that Mr. Lincoln championed the cause of the leaders of the 48 revolts in Europe.

In 1848 he was all in favor of secession (for the Socialists in Europe,) but in 1860 he was adamantly opposed to it for Christian Southerners. That fact, alone should give you some indication as to where Mr. Lincoln was really coming from and it should help to explain why, in 1861, the Socialists flocked to own his "Holy Cause."

By: Al Benson Jr.

13th June 2005 The Copperhead Chronicle
[http://thecopperhead.blogspoy.com/]

EVER WONDER WHERE THE LINCOLNITES GET THEIR ARGUMENTS? LOOK NO FURTHER THAN KARL MARX

I was reading some articles online and came across some pro-Northern writings by the father of Communist thugs and big Centralized government himself, Karl Marx, it turns out was one of the biggest advocates and defenders in the British newspapers during the 1860's. He also thought very highly of Lincoln. Perhaps the most shocking thing about it all is the strong similarities between the arguments Marx put forth on behalf of the North in the 1860's and the arguments the Lincoln defenders put firth today. They are often identical! See for yourself-

MARX ON THE CAUSES OF THE WAR

"It is above all to be remembered that the war did not originate with the North, but with the South. The North finds itself on the defensive. For months it had quietly looked on while the secessionist appropriated the Union's Forts, Arsenals, Shipyards, Custom Houses, Pay Offices, Ships and *Supplies of Arms insulted its flag and took prisoner bodies of its troops. Finally, the secessionists resolved to force the Union government out of its passive by a blatant act of war, and solely for this reason proceeded to the bombardment of Fort Sumter near Charleston."*- Karl Marx, On the North American Civil War, October 20th 1861.

(NOTE: The firing upon Fort Sumter occurred one day prior to the arrival of a war fleet tasked specifically by Lincoln to increase the fort's garrison by force if necessary.)

"*Naturally, in America everyone knew that from 1846 to 1861 a free trade system prevailed, and that Representative Morrill carried his protectionist tariff through Congress only in 1861, after the rebellion had already broken out. Secession, therefore, did not take place because the Morrill tariff had gone through Congress, but, at most, the Morrill tariff went through Congress because secession had taken place.*"-Karl Marx. On the North American Civil War, October 20th, 1861.

(NOTE: Marx's dates are incorrect. The Morrill Tariff Bill passed the U.S. House on May 10th 1860. The Act's Senate approval came on March 2nd 1861.)

"*A strict confinement of slavery within its old terrain, therefore, was bound according to economic law to lead to its gradual effacement, in the political sphere to annihilate the hegemony that the slave States exercised through the Senate, and finally to expose the slaveholding oligarchy within its own States to threatening perils from the poor Whites. In accordance with the principle that any further extension of slave Territories was to be prohibited by law, the Republicans therefore attacked the rule of the slaveholders at its root.*"-Karl Marx, On the North American Civil War, October 20th, 1861.

(NOTE: Marx's characterization of Lincoln's policy regarding the non-extension of slavery as a supposed tool to end the institution as an argument shared and forwarded by many modern Lincoln supporters.)

"*The whole movement was and is based, as one sees, on the slave question. Not in the sense of weather the slaves within the existing slave State should be emancipated outright or not, but whether the twenty million free men of the North should submit any longer to an oligarchy of three hundred thousand slaveholders; whether the vast Territories of the Republic should be nurseries for free States or for slavery; finally, whether the national policy of the Union should take armed spreading of slavery in Mexico, Central and South America as its device.*"-Karl Marx, On the North American Civil War, October 20th 1861.

(NOTE: In this passage Marx argues that the entirety of the dispute was the slavery question and nothing more.)

MARX ON THE VALIDITY OF SECESSION:

"*, if the North and South formed two autonomous countries, like, for example, England and Hanover, their separation would be no more difficult than was the separation of England and Hanover. "The South," however, is neither a territory closely sealed off from the North geographically, nor a moral unity. It is not a country al all, but a battle slogan.*"-Karl Marx, On the Civil War in the United States, late October 1861 (follow up to the October 20th editorial)

★ GOD SAVE THE SOUTH ★

"The advice of an amicable separation presupposes that the Southern Confederacy, although it assumed the offensive in the Civil War, at least wages it for defensive purposes. It is believed that the issue for the slaveholders' party is merely one of uniting the territories it has hitherto dominated into an autonomous group of States and withdrawing them from the supreme authority of the Union. Nothing could be more false ... What the slaveholders, therefore, call the South, embraces more than three-quarters of the territory hitherto comprised by the Union. A large part of the territory thus claimed is still in the possession of the Union and would first have to be conquered from it ... The war of the Southern Confederacy is, therefore, not a war of defense, but a war of conquest, a war of conquest for the spread and perpetuation of slavery."-Karl Marx, On the Civil War in the United States, late October 1861 (follow up to the October 20th editorial)

(NOTE: In this passage, Marx claims the existence of a Confederate plot to increase their territory by drawing the Border States into secession through war-a popular argument among Lincoln supporters.)

MARX ON COMMUNIST SUPPORT OF THE NORTH:

"The workingmen of Europe feel sure that, as the American War of Independence initiated a new era of ascendancy for the middle class, so the American Antislavery War will do the working classes. They consider it an earnest of the epoch to come that it fell to the lot of Abraham Lincoln, the single-minded son of the working class, to lead its country through the matchless struggle for rescue of an enchained race and the reconstruction of a social world."-Karl Marx, on behalf of the International Workingmen's Association, letter to Abraham Lincoln on congratulating him on the reelection as President of the United States, January 28th, 1865.

"From the commencement of the titanic American strife the workingmen of Europe felt instinctively that the—Star Spangled Banner-carried the destiny of their class."-Karl Marx, letter to Abraham Lincoln congratulating him on his reelection as President of the United States, January 28th 1865.

MARX ON ABRAHAM LINCOLN:

"Sir: We congratulate the American people upon your re-election by a large majority."-Karl Marx, Letter to Abraham Lincoln congratulating him on re-election as President of the United States, January 28th 1865.

"[Lincoln was] one of the rare men who succeed in becoming great, without ceasing to be good. Such, indeed, was the modesty of this great and good man, that the world only discovered him a hero after he had fallen as a martyr."-Karl Marx, Address of the International Working Men's Association to President Johnson, 1865.

From the GOP Capitalist on Aw-shucks! Southern News & Links 2003.

COMMUNIST SUPPORT FOR THE UNION AND FOR "RECONSTRUCTION"

For at least a decade I have been writing and talking about the Socialist and the Communist support for Lincoln, the Union, and the radical "reconstruction' revolution after the War of Northern Aggression and ceased. This is something the 'historians or should we label them 'hysterians' have only dared allude to in passing, except for the Socialist historian James McPherson, who openly admits that Lincoln had the support of Marx and those of his ilk. [Yet the Communist themselves have, for years, admitted their support for the Union.]

In a book published by Communist publishing house, Reconstruction-the Battle for Democracy, written by James Allen and published way back in 1937, Communist support for the Union side in the War is clearly mentioned.] Allen has written of "German Workers' groups" that aided in the Abolitionist Movement. He has said: *"Many of their members enlisted in the Northern Army and a number of them led regiments which they themselves recruited."*

The Communist Club especially was active in the Abolition movement; some of its members even joined the "Radical Wing of the Republican Party." Several years back, Communist theoretician Herbert Apthecker wrote a book called, if I recall it correctly, Abolitionism: A Revolutionary Movement. Mr. Apthecker had glowing praise for the Abolitionist Movement and its goals. Now maybe you know why. Allen noted, on page 25 of his book *"Many Socialist leaders and German émigrés of the 1848 revolution, among them, Joseph Weydemeyer, who was a close friend of Karl Marx, served as officers in the Union army."*

So, the Communist were involved with the Abolitionist Movement, they supported Lincoln and the Union cause, and they also supported the radical abolitionists who, after the war was over, instituted the horrible and shameful *"reconstruction"* program, which was aimed at humiliating and prostrating the South completely. And "reconstruction was aimed at destroying the theological base of the South as well as all the rest.

Allen felt that most American historians really tarnished the good images of such notables as Thaddeus Stevens and Charles Summer because they only dealt with the vituperative hate these men harbored for the South." He observed: *"One looks in vain to find in the writings of most American historians' recognition of the revolutionary character of the period following the Civil War."* Sort of makes you wonder why, doesn't it? As much as I hate to agree with a Communist on anything, this guy had this aspect of *"reconstruction"* accurately pegged. *"Reconstruction" was truly "another revolution"* in the words of Bakunin, the Russian anarchist.

It changed America for the worst, and we are, even in our day, reeling from the problems it has created, to the extent that we now live in what many consider to be 'post-America' in the sense that the original system given to us by our founders no longer exist. It has been replaced with a system that was, and is, truly revolutionary in nature and intent. Allen has told us that Thaddeus Stevens and Charles Sumner were the *"leading representatives of the Parliamentary Left."* I cannot argue with him there, either.

Claude Bowers, writing in The Tragic Era back in 1929 had accurately noted that the *"reconstruction" years were "years of revolutionary turmoil."* He recognized that fact, but because he refused to come from where the Communist were coming from, such well-known Communist as W.E.B. DuBois and others sought to defame his book, and even to this day they continue to rent about how horrible Bowers "book of reconstruction' is. They do not like Bowers because he dared to tell the truth about what happened to the South during 'reconstruction.'

Bowers wrote of the perpetrators of 'reconstruction' that *"The story of this revolution is one desperate enterprise's, by daring and unscrupulous men, some of whom had genius of a high order. In these no American can take pride. The evil they did lives after them. They changed the course of history …"*

A few years back, I wrote a little booklet called 'The Marxist Revision of Reconstruction-paving the way for the Civil Rights. Somehow, it caught the notice of some left-wingers somewhere and was mentioned with derision in a publication called 'Z Magazine' back in 1996, I think. In it I attempted to explain how the Marxists had tried to make 'reconstruction' appear as a glowing, positive event in our history and how they tore down those who opposed it.

By the Editor of: Al Benson, Jr. of the Copperhead Chronicles.

For more information about the Copperhead Chronicles and Mr. Al Benson, visit the website (www.albensonjr.com).

★ ★ ★
LINCOLN'S WAR: CONFLICT?

This article first appeared in the October 1997 issue of 'Chronicles': A Magazine of American Culture. It was adapted from a book manuscript.

"[T]he contest is really for an Empire on the side of the North, and for Independence on that of the South, and in this respect we recognize an exact analogy the North and the Government of George III, and the South and the Thirteen Revolted Provinces. These opinions ... are the general opinions of the English Nation."

"The preservation of the Union is the supreme law." Andrew Jackson, December 25, 1832.

The Civil War was the greatest tragedy ever to befall the nation. Brother slew brother. Six hundred thousand of America's best and bravest died of shot, shell, and disease. The South was bled to death, invaded, ravaged by Union armies, occupied for a dozen years. Under Federal bayonets, her social and political order was uprooted and the *Eleven States* that had fought to be free of the Union were *"Reconstructed"* by that Union. America's South would need a Century to recover.

Thirteen decades after Appomattox the questions remain: Was *it "an irrepressible conflict?"* Was it a necessary war? Was it? As Churchill write, *"the noblest and least* avoidable of all the great mass-conflicts of which till then *there was a record"*? Was it a just war? What became of the great tariff issue that had divided and convulsed the nation equally with slavery in the decades before the war? Are there lessons for us in this most terrible of tragedies where all of the dead were Americans?

After any such war, it is the victor who writes the history. That has surely been true of the Civil War. Among the great myths that are taught to American school children has been that the *"Great Emancipator,"* Abraham

Lincoln, was elected to free the slaves from bondage, that America's *"Civil War"* was fought to end slavery in the United States.

This is a fable. Even the name given this terrible was is wrong. A Civil War is a struggle for power inside a nation like the 'War of the Roses,' or the horrible 'War between Bolsheviks and the Czarists in Russia' and *"Reds and Whites,"* after Lenin's October Revolution. The combatants from 1861 to 1865 were not fighting over who would govern the United States. The South had never contested Lincoln's election. The South wanted only to be free of the Union.

The war was not over who would rule Washington, but who would rule in South Carolina, Georgia, and the five Gulfs States that seceded by the time of Fort Sumter. From the standpoint of the North, this was a War of Southern Secession, a War to Preserve the Union. To the South this was the War for Southern Independence.

THE BIRTH OF A MYTH:

At Gettysburg Battlefield, on November the 19th 1863, three years after Lincoln's election, the Great Myth was born. There, Abraham Lincoln had declared that the war had been, all along about equality.

"Four score and seven years ago our fathers brought forth on this continent, a new nation, conceived in Liberty, and dedicated to the proposition that all men are created equal. Now we are engaged in a great Civil War, testing whether that nation or any nation so conceived and so dedicated, can long endure."

But four score and seven years before Lincoln spoke was in 1776. The *"New Nation"* may have been *"conceived"* in 1776. But it was not born until 1788 after the Ninth State had ratified the Constitution. In that Constitution, freemen, Black and White, were equal. But slavery, the antithesis of equality, was protected. By Benjamin Franklin's compromise, slaves were to be considered as three-fifths of a person for purposes of representation in the House.

Painful to concede, it is more truthful to say that slavery, the essence of inequality, was embedded in the Constitution of the New Nation. Moreover, in reaching back to 1776, Lincoln had invoked, in defense of a war to crush a rebellion, the most powerful brief ever written on behalf of a rebellion. *The Declaration of Independence is not about preserving a Union. It is a Declaration of Secession; it is about the "Right of the People to alter or to abolish" one form of government* "*and institute a new Government, laying its Foundation on such Principles, and organizing its Powers on such Form, as to them shall seem most likely to affect their Safety and Happiness.*"

It is about a person's right *"to dissolve the political bands which have connected them with another, and to assume among the Powers of the Earth, the separate and equal Station to which the Laws of Nature and Nature's God entitle them."* Lincoln's words, eloquent as they are, are the sheerest audacity. As Garry Wills writes approvingly. Lincoln, at Gettysburg, performed of the most daring acts of open-air sleight-of-the-hand ever witnessed by the unsuspecting. Everyone in that vast throng of thousands was having his or her intellectual pockets picked. The crowd departed with a new thing in its ideological luggage that the (New Constitution) Lincoln had substituted for the one they brought there with them.

They walked off, from those curving graves on the hillside, under a changed sky, into a [different America.] Lincoln had revolutionized the Revolution, giving people a new past to live with that would change their future indefinitely. On reading Lincoln's address, many, North, and South, were astounded. In suggestion the terrible war had all along been about equality, what was the President talking about?

Quoting the Constitution back to the President, the Chicago Times charged Lincoln with betray in both that sacred document he had taken an oath to defend and the men who had died for it. It was to uphold this Constitution, and the Union created by it, that our officers and soldiers gave their lives at Gettysburg. How dare he, then, standing on their graves, misstate the cause for which they died, and libel the Statesmen who founded the government?

Even as Lincoln spoke, slavery was still legal in Washington, D.C., the seat of government, as well in Maryland, Missouri, Kentucky, West Virginia, Delaware, and the areas of Tennessee that had remained loyal. The Emancipation Proclamation of January 1st, 1863 only the slaves in those States that were still in rebellion. All other slaves remained the protected property of their masters. Prime Minister Palmerstone noted in amusement that Lincoln had undertaken to abolish slavery where he had no power to do so, while protecting slavery where he had the power to destroy it.

Indeed, when issuing the Proclamation, Lincoln confided to his Secretary that he had done so only as a [military necessity] after the defeats of First and Second Manassas, Jackson's valley Campaign, the Seven Days battle, Chancellorsville, Fredericksburg, and the stalemate at Antietam:

Things had gone on from bad to worse, until I felt that we had reached the end of our rope on the plan of operation we had been pursuing; that we had about played out our last card, and must change our tactics, or lose the game. I am now determined upon the adoption of the *Emancipation Policy.* Far from universal celebration, the Emancipation Proclamation was regarded by many, even in abolitionist England, as cynical and awful weapon of war, settled upon by Lincoln in desperation. As Sheldon Vanauken points out in the Glittering Illusion: English Sympathy for the Southern Confederacy (1989):

[T]he Confederate States was winning the war. Only a few days before, Lee had smashed Burnside at Fredericksburg. The Proclamation freed all the slaves within the Confederate lines ... These slaves were grouped on the isolated plantations, controlled for the most part by the women since their gentlemen were off to the War. The only possible effect of the Proclamation would be the dreaded servile insurrection (that which John Brown was hanged for inciting.)

Either it is a slave uprising-or nothing. So, as the Englishmen saw it. Lincoln's insincerity as regarded as proven by two things: his earlier denial of any lawful right or wish to free the slaves: and his not freeing the slaves in *"loyal"* Kentucky and other United States areas or even in Confederate areas occupied by the United States troops, such as New Orleans.

It should be remembered that [in England] the horrors of the Indian mutiny, as well as the slave uprising in St. Domingo, were very much in everyone's memory. The effect of the Proclamation upon many in the Union ranks was the same. They had gone to war not to free the slaves but to preserve the nation! As James McPherson writes in, "What They Fought For"-1861 to 1856.

Plenty of soldiers believed that the Proclamation had changed the purpose of the war. They professed to feel betrayed. They were willing to risk their lives for the Union, they said, but not for Black freedom ... Desertion rates rose alarmingly. And many soldiers blamed the Emancipation Proclamation for it. Closing his address, Lincoln spoke of the duty imposed on Americans by those who had fallen on the great battlefield.

We "here highly resolve," he said, in his immortal words, *"that these dead shall not have died in vain-that this nation, under God, shall have a (new birth of freedom)-and that government of the people, by the people, for the people shall not perish from the earth."*

If Southerners found this incredible, it is understandable. The Confederates had never sought to cause the Government of the United States to *"perish from the earth."* It was the Union that was seeking to cause the Confederacy and their governments of the eleven Southern States to *"perish."*

Had the South wanted the government to "perish from the earth," the Confederate Army could have marched into Lincoln's Capital after the First Battle of Bull Run in June of 1861, when the Union Army had been sent up the road to Washington in a wild retreat. The South did not want this; the South wanted only to be free.

While Lincoln surely knew his eloquent words would be noted, and remembered, he could not have known his brief remarks would become the most famous address in American history. Nor is there evidence that Lincoln, at this moment, deliberately enlarged the war aims of the Union. But at Gettysburg, the war aims of the Union were enlarged, dramatically. In that address, they do go beyond anything Lincoln enunciated before the war began.

Indeed, if racial equality was Lincoln's and the Union's goal, then Lincoln himself was a changed man. For the Abraham Lincoln of 1861 was no champion of any political or social equality.

"We Cannot Make Them Equals"

The Lincoln Americans know the father figure with the wise and wonderful wit, who came out of Illinois to free the slaves and believed in racial equality-who has marched with Martin Luther King Jr.-, would be unrecognizable to his contemporaries. While Lincoln as early as 1854 had condemned slavery as a *"monstrous injustice,"* and bravely took the antislavery side in senatorial campaign debates with Stephen A. Douglas, here is the Republican candidate for the United States Senate on the stump, in Charleston, Illinois on September 18th, 1858, after he had been baited by the *"Little Giant"* to explain where he stood on marriage between the races, and on social and political equality:

"I will say then that I am not, nor ever have been in favor of bringing about in any way the social and political equality of the White and the Black races,-that I am not nor ever have been in favor of making voters or jurors of Negroes, nor of qualifying them to hold office, nor to intermarry with White people; and I will say in addition to this that there is a physical difference between the White and Black races which I believe will forever forbid the two races living together on terms of social and political equality.

And insomuch as they cannot so live, while they do remain together there must be the position of superior and inferior and I as much as any other man am in favor of having the superior position assigned to the White race."

Four years before, at Peoria, on October 16th, 1854, Lincoln confessed to his ambivalence as to what should be done about slavery, and with the freed Black men and women were slavery were abolished:

"If all earthly power were given to me, I should not know what to do, as to the existing institution. My impulse would be to free the slaves and send them back to Liberia, -to their own native land ... [But Free] them, and to make them politically and socially, our equals? My own feelings will not admit of this; and in my mind we both well know that those of the great mass of White people will not ... A universal feeling, whether well or ill-founded, cannot be safely disregarded. We cannot, then, make them equals."

Three years later, in June of 1857, in Springfield, Lincoln was still entertaining the idea of repatriating the freed slaves back to their native continent: *"Such separation, if ever affected at all, must be affected by colonization; what colonization most needs is a hearty will ... Let us be brought to believe it is morally right ... to transfer the Africans to his native clime, and we shall find a way to do it, however the task may be."*

In urging colonization Lincoln was echoing men of far greater learning and higher station, such as Jefferson and Madison. In 1829, the author of the Constitution became President of the American Colonization Society—founded by John Randolph and Henry Clay after the War of 1812-in the belief that its plan would be able to return the slaves back to Africa, represented the most sensible way out of that long-festering crises."

Clay, Lincoln's idol, advocated returning the slaves to Africa throughout his public career. In eulogizing Clay in Springfield on the 6th of July of 1852, Lincoln celebrated his hero's lifelong association with the American Colonization Society, and quoted Clay's 1827 address to that society:

"There is a moral fitness in the idea of returning to Africa her children, whose ancestors have been torn from her by the ruthless hand of fraud and violence. Transplanted in a foreign land, they will carry back to their native soil with the rich fruits of religion, civilization, law and liberty."

In a hearty approval of Clay's words, Lincoln declared:

"The suggestion of the possible ultimate redemption of the African race and the African continent was made twenty-five years ago. Every succeeding year has added strength to the hope of realization. May it indeed be realized!"

Gradual repatriation and return of all the slaves to Africa, said Lincoln in the closing words of his long eulogy, would be a "glorious consummation"—Henry Clay's greatest contribution to his country. Lincoln's words in the decade prior to his Presidency are jolting to the modern era. But all they tell us is this: on racial equality, Lincoln in 1858 was a man of his time and place. Like almost all White males of his age, he believed the races should remain separate. This is confirmed by his admirer General Donn Piatt, who thought Lincoln *"the greatest looming figure up in our history."*

After meeting with the President-elect in Springfield, Piatt wrote on the eve of Lincoln's departure for Washington: *"Expressing no sympathy for the slave, [Lincoln] laughed at the Abolitionists ... We were not at a loss to get at the fact, and the reasoning for it, in the man before us. Descended from the poor Whites of a slave State, through many generations, he inherited the contempt, if not the hatred, held by that class for the Negro. A man must be measured against his time. As Lincoln himself said in his Second Inaugural: "judge not that we be judged."* Lincoln's position on slavery—that it was evil, that he would have no part of it—was that of a principled politician of courage.

As for his views on racial equality, they were views of almost of his countrymen. But if Lincoln did not go to war to make men equal, did he go to war to make men free to end the evil of slavery? For to answer the question, "Was this a just war? We have to understand as to why both sides had fought.

LINCOLN'S CONFESSIONS TO THE SOUTH:

Unlike the Lincoln of Gettysburg in 1863, the Lincoln who slipped into Washington in disguise in the dead of the night in the winter of 1861 did not have the least intention of freeing any slaves. Nor did the South have any reason to fear Lincoln would, or could, abolish slavery. The Supreme Court was Southern dominated, led by Chief Justice Roger Taney of the 1857 Dred Scoot decision. There was no threat to slavery from that quarter. And, during the campaign of 1860, Lincoln repeatedly assured the South he was no Abolitionists.

In the first paragraphs of his inaugural Address, Lincoln repeated his assurances that he would make no attempt to abolish slavery. Apprehension seems to exist among the people of the Southern States, which by the accession of a Republican Administration, their property, and their peace, and personal security, are to be endangered. There has never been any responsible cause for such apprehension. Indeed, the amplest evidence to the contrary has all the while existed and been open to their inspection. It is found in nearly all the published speeches of him who now addresses you.

I do but quote from one of those speeches when I declare that *"I have no purpose, directly or indirectly, to interfere with the institution of slavery in the States where it exists. [I believe I have no lawful right to do so,] and I have no intention to do so. Those who nominated and elected me did so with full knowledge that I made this, and many similar declarations, and had never recanted them."*

His party's platform, said Lincoln, endorsed the *"inviolate" right of each State to "control its own domestic institutions.* "In excoriation of John Brown's raid, Lincoln noted in his Inaugural that, in their 1860 platform, Republicans *"denounce the lawless invasion by armed forces of the soil of any State or Territory, no matter under what pretext, as among the gravest of crimes."*

South Carolina had seceded on the grounds that the United States was failing to uphold the fugitive slave provision of the Constitution. But, Lincoln assured Southerners their escaped slaves would be returned to them: There is much controversy about the delivering up of fugitives from service or labor. The clause I now read is as plainly written in the Constitution as any other of its provisions:

"No person held to service or labor in one State, under the laws thereof, escaping into another, shall, in consequence of any law or regulation therein, be discharged from such service or labor, but shall be delivered up on claim of the party to whom such service or labor may be due."

It is scarcely questioned that this provision was intended by those who made it, for the reclaiming of what we call fugitive slaves; and the intention of the lawgiver is the law. All members of Congress swear their support to the whole Constitution—to this provision as much as to any other. To the proposition, then, that slaves whose cases come within the terms of this clause, *"shall be delivered up,"* their oaths are unanimous. Now, if they would make the effort in good temper, could they not, with nearly equal unanimity, frame and pass a law, by means of which to keep that unanimous oath?

[Emphasis added]

Lincoln is calling here for a new federal fugitive slave law to reinforce Congress' Constitutional obligation that escaped slaves *"shall be delivered up"* to their masters. In capturing and returning fugitive slaves, said Lincoln, some observers favor State authority. But, he asked: What is the difference?

"If the slave is to be surrendered, it can be of but little consequence to him, or to others, by which authority it is done."

The issue on which Republicans were united was that the extension of slavery to the new States should be halted. Lincoln did not back down from this position in his Inaugural Address. But, he did offer a guarantee to the South that where slavery existed, it could be made a permanent institution, by a new Constitutional amendment.

"One section of our country believes slavery is right, and ought to be extended, while the other believes it is wrong, and ought not to extend it. This is the only substantial dispute … I understand a proposed amendment to the Constitution … has passed Congress, to the effect the federal government, shall never interfere with the domestic institutions of the States, including that of persons held to service. To avoid misconstruction of what I have said, I depart from my purpose not to speak of a particular amendment, so far as to say that, holding such a provision to now be implied Constitutional law, I have no objection to its being made express, and irrevocable."

Thus, in this final concession, Lincoln says he would not oppose a Constitutional amendment to make slavery permanent in the fifteen States where it then existed. The first Thirteenth Amendment to the Constitution Abraham Lincoln endorsed, then, did not end chattel slavery, but would have authorized chattel slavery forever. No true Abolitionist could have been other than be horrified by Lincoln's first Inaugural Address.

Is there a moral defense of Lincoln's offer to make permanent an institution that all now agree was odious and evil? Only this:

"If it was not wrong for the founding fathers to accept slavery as a price of a Constitution to be established in the United States, it cannot be wrong for Lincoln to reaffirm the founding fathers' concession—to repair and restore his fractured country. In appeasing the South on slavery, Lincoln was being faithful to his duty as President to unite his divided nation. He was also being true to his belief that, if slavery were restricted to where it existed, it would wither and die."

JOHN THOMAS NALL

At the dedication of Freedmen's Monument in Washington in 1876—a sculpture depicting a slave on his knees looking up in gratitude into the benevolent face of the Great Emancipator—Frederick Douglass stunned an audience including President Ulysses S. Grant by calling Lincoln *"the White man's President, entirely devoted to the welfare of White men." "View from the genuine abolition ground,"* Frederick Douglass went on, *"Mr. Lincoln seemed tardy, cold, dull, and indifferent; but measuring him by the sentiment of his country ... he was swift, zealous, radical and determined."* A not so unfair assessment.

Did slavery cause the war? In 1927, historians Charles and Mary Beard produced their famous and first in-depth study of American history, 'The Rise of American Civilization'. It captivated scholars and laymen alike. After carefully examining the facts concerning slavery and the Civil War, they concluded:

"Since, therefore, the abolition of slavery never appeared in the platform of any great political party, since the only appeal ever made to the electorate on that issue scornfully repulsed, since the spokesmen of the Republic [Lincoln] emphatically declared that his party never intended to interfere with slavery in the States in any shape or form, it seems reasonable to assume that the institution of slavery was not the fundamental issue during the epoch preceding the bombardment of Fort Sumter."

To those yet contend that Lincoln and the Union went to war *"to make men free,"* [how do they respond to the fact that when the war began, with the firing on Fort Sumter, there were more slave States inside the Union (Eight) than, in the Confederacy (Seven)? Four Southern States, Virginia, North Carolina, Tennessee, and Arkansas had remained loyal. They did not wish to secede; they did so only after Lincoln put out a call for 75,000 volunteers for an army to invade and subjugate the Deep South.

That army would have passed through the Upper south, which would have (*joined a war against its kinfolks.*) This Upper South would not do so. It was Lincoln's call to war against the already seceded States in the Deep South that caused Virginia, North Carolina, Tennessee, and Arkansas to leave a Union in which they had hoped to remain. Jeffrey Hummel notes in Emancipating Slaves, Enslaving Free Men (1996):

"Previously unwilling to secede over the issue of slavery, these four States of [Virginia, North Carolina, Tennessee, and Arkansas] were now ready to fight for the ideal of voluntary Union. Out in the Western territory ... the sedentary Indian Tribes ... Cherokees, Choctaws, Creeks, and Seminoles ... also joined the rebellion ... Lincoln [by calling up militia] had more than doubled the Confederacy's White population and material resources."

Before Fort Sumter, the Confederacy sent emissaries to discuss a compromise. Lincoln refused to meet with them, lest presidential meeting confer legitimacy on a secession he refused to recognize. Against the advice of army Chief General: Winfield Scott, Secretary of State: William H. Simon Cameron, and Secretary of the Navy: Gideon Welles, all of whom advocated evacuating Fort Sumter, he sent in the [Star of the Sea] to resupply the fort. Viewing this as a provocation, the Southerners fired on the fort, and the American flag, and the Great American War was on.

And Southerners were perhaps not mistaken in their belief that Lincoln had provoked the conflict. As the President wrote with quiet satisfaction to his Assistant Secretary of the Navy: Gustavus Fox, Commander of the expedition to Fort Sumter, on May 1st, 1861: *"You and I both anticipated that the cause of the country would be advanced by making the attempt to provision Fort Sumter [sic], even if it should fail; and it is no small consolation now to feel that our anticipation is justified by the result."* Like Polk before him, and Wilson and Franklin Roosevelt after him, Lincoln had maneuvered his enemy into firing the first shot.

DID THE SOUTH HAVE A RIGHT TO SECEDE?

In the modern are, one reads more and more that the great Southern Leaders were *"traitors."* Robert E. Lee, Thomas J. *"Stonewall"* Jackson, and Jefferson Davis, all heroes of the Mexican War, however, were no more less traitors than Washington, dams, and Jefferson were traitors to Great Britain. At West Point, which George E. Pickett, Stonewall Jackson, and Joe Johnson attended, the constitutional law book, that all three Confederate Generals had studied, A view of the Constitution of the United States, by William Rawle—a Philadelphia Abolitionist and Supreme Court Justice—taught that the States had a right to secede:

"To deny this right would be inconsistent with the principle on which all our political systems are founded. Which is, that the people have in all cases, a right to determine how they will be governed."

Union Officers had studied Rawls as well. Indeed, the idea of State's Rights to nullify federal law, and of the right to secede if the issue were truly grave, had a long, distinguished history in America. In the Kentucky and Virginia Resolutions of 1798 and 1799, Jefferson and Madison, authors respectively of the Declaration of Independence and the Constitution—enrage at the jailing of editors under the Alien and Sedition Acts argued that the States had a right to nullify patently unconstitutional federal laws.

★ JOHN THOMAS NALL ★

Between 1800 and 1815, three serious attempts were made by New England Federalists to secede—at the time of the Louisiana Purchase in 1803, Jefferson's Embargo Act of 1807, and Madison's War of 1812. The secessionist leader was a Revolutionary War hero and a member of Washington's Cabinet, Massachusetts Senator Timothy Pickering. The Federalist causes mirrored South Carolina's causes: what they saw as an intolerable regime, interference with trade, incompatibility with alien peoples (Germans and Scotch-Irish,) and a conviction the Union was being run for the benefit of the South, said Pickering in 1803: *"I will rather anticipate a New Confederacy from the corrupt and corrupting influence and oppression of the aristocratic Democrats of the South."*

By a twist of fate, Jefferson's rival, Alexander Hamilton, who had made Jefferson President in 1801 by persuading his allies to abandon Aaron Burr in the House of Representatives in the tie election of 1800, probably saved the Union. (Federalist had conspired with Burr in 1804 to support him for governor, if Burr would lead New York into a New England Confederacy.)

But the revilements of Burr by Hamilton, as venal, corrupt, dictatorial, and dangerous, persuaded New Yorkers, by 7,000 votes, to reject him. Burr challenged Hamilton to a dual and killed him. Revulsion at the death of the patriot-statesman aborted the Federalist's plot. In anticipation of John C. Calhoun's nullification, Massachusetts legislature in 1807 denounced Jefferson's embargo, demanded that Congress repeal it, and declared the Enforcement Act "not legally binding. "Many merchants ignored the law; and the New England authorities looked the other way.

At the Hartford Convention of 1814, New Englanders, enraged by Madison's war with England when the Mother Country was in a death struggle against the dictator Napoleon, and by the interruption of their trade, threatened to secede and reassociate with Great Britain. In 1832, South Carolina *"nullified"* a tariff law it believed was bleeding the South to death and asserted a right to secede. In 1843, when Tyler was driving for annexation of Texas, a vast territory that might be broken into five States, tilting the political balance of power in favor of the slave States.

John Quincy Adams thundered that the annexation of Texas would justify Northern secession. And, in 1848, a freshman Congressman critic of the Mexican War spoke of the inherent right of States to secede: *"ANY PEOPLE ANYWHERE, BEING INCLINED AND HAVING THE POWER, HAVE THE RIGHT TO RISE UP, AMD SHAKE OFF THE EXISTING GOVERNMENT, AND FORM A NEW ONE THAT SUITS THEM BETTER. THIS IS A MOST VALUABLE, A MOSTSACRED RIGHT, WHICH WE HOPE AND BELIEVE, IS TO LIBERATE THE WORLD. NOR IS THIS RIGHT CONFINED TO CASES IN WHICH THE WHOLE PEOPLE OF AN EXISTING GOVERNMENT MAY CHOOSE TO EXERCISE IT. ANY PORTION OF SUCH PEOPLE, THAT CAN, MAY MAKE THEIR OWN, OF SO MUCH OF THE TERRITORY AS THEY INHABIT*

★ GOD SAVE THE SOUTH ★

... IT IS A QUALITY OF REVOLUTIONS NOT TO GO BY OLD LAWS; BUT TO BREAK UP BOTH AND MAKE NEW ONES" These are the words of Abraham Lincoln, January 12th 1848.

WHY DID THE SOUTH SECEDE?

If Lincoln did not threaten slavery, why than did the Deep South secede? Answer: By 1861, America had become two nations and two peoples. The South evolved into a separate country. While moderates like Lee wanted to remain in the Union, Southern militants had concluded that, with the election of Lincoln, the North had won the great struggle for control of the national destiny. The South had given the Union most of her Presidents, her Supreme Court Justices, and her Speakers of the House. But, the South would never again determine the nation's direction.

This first Republican President had not received a single electoral vote from any Southern State; in the ten Southern States he had not received a single vote. Lincoln owed the South nothing; but he owed everything to her enemies, to the admirers of John Brown, to the Northern industrialists who had Lincoln's commitment to a protective tariff that the South believed threatened its ruin.

After decades of troubled and unhappy marriage, for the Deep South, Lincoln's election was the final blow. They had decided, irrevocably, on a divorce. Thus, six weeks after Lincoln's election, December the 2nd of 1860, South Carolina seceded. By February, the 1st a month before Lincoln's Inauguration, South Carolina had been followed out of the Union by Georgia, Florida, Alabama, Mississippi, Louisiana, and Texas. In these States, the Federal forts, Post Offices, Customs Houses, and Military Posts had been occupied.

Federal employees and troops had been sent packing. Yet, by the day of Lincoln's Inauguration, four months after his election, there was no war. Why not? Because President James Buchanan did not believe the Federal government had a right to use military force to compel the States to remain within the Union. If the Union was not voluntary, it was not a true Union. To our 15th President, coercion was unconstitutional. As Professor Woodrow Wilson wrote in *"Division and Reunion,"* Buchanan *"believed"* and declared that secession was illegal; but he agreed with his Attorney General that there was no Constitutional means or warrant for coercing a State to do her duty under the law. Such, indeed, for the time, seemed to be the general opinion of the country. Most Northern newspapers agreed.

As early as November 13th, 1860, the Daily Union in Banger, Maine, defended the South's right to secede, asserting that a true Union *"depends for its continuance on the free consent and will of the sovereign people"* of each State. *"[W]hen that consent and will is withdrawn on either part, their Union is gone."* If military force is used, then a State can only be held *"as a subject province,"* and can never be a *"Co-equal member of the American Union."*

Horace Greeley wrote in the New York Daily Tribune, December 17th 1860, *"The great principle embodied by Jefferson in the Declaration is that governments derive their just power from the consent of the governed."* If the Southern States wished to depart, *"they have a clear right to do so."* And, if tyrannical government justified the Revolution of 1776, *"we do not see why it would not justify the secession of Five Million of Southrons from the Federal Union in 1861."*

Many Northerners and Abolitionists were delighted to see the Deep South State's gone. Abolitionist editor William Lloyd Garrison had spoken for many when he writes that the original Constitution, protecting slavery, had a *"covenant with death"* and an *"agreement with Hell."* In April 1861, Greeley wrote that "nine out of ten of the people of the North were opposed" to using force to return South Carolina to the Union. General Scott, hero of the Mexican War and Commander of the U.S. Army, said of the *"wayward sisters … let them go in peace."* Ironically, the *"wayward sisters"* were like fugitive slaves. They were trying to break free of Father Abraham's house, but he would not let them go.

Absent Abraham Lincoln, there might have been no war. But, without Lincoln, there might also be no United States today. Unlike Buchanan, the new President would accept war, raise an army of a [million men], and fight the bloodiest struggle ever on the American Continent, rather than let the South go. The Confederate firing on Fort Sumter may have been the spark that ignited the conflagration, but the real cause of the war was the iron will of Abraham Lincoln, as resolute a Unionist as was Andrew Jackson, who also would have accepted war rather than let South Carolina secede.

Thus, as the Mexican War had been *"Jimmy Polk's War,"* this was *"Mr. Lincoln's War."* To win it, the President would assume Dictatorial Powers, Suspend the Constitutional Right of Habeas Corpus, overthrow Elected State Legislatures, arrest and hold without trail for thousands of political prisoners, shut down opposition newspapers, and order army after army into the South to give his *(New Nation "Birth of Freedom")* and a [New Baptism of Blood and Fire.]

★ GOD SAVE THE SOUTH ★

When mobs rioted against the draft in July of 1863, looting and pillaging New York City, lynching Blacks, they saw as threats to their jobs and the cause of war, Lincoln ordered units detached from Mead's army. When the veterans of Little Round Top and Cemetery Ridge entered the city, a witness described the action:

"Streets were swept again and again by grape [shot], houses were stormed at the point of a bayonet, rioters were picked off by sharpshooters as they fired on the troops from housetops; men were hurled, dying or dead, into the streets by the thoroughly enraged soldiery; until at last, sullen and cowed and thoroughly whipped and beaten, the miserable wretches gave way at every point and confessed the power of the law."

Estimates of the dead ranged from 300 to a 1,000.

Lincoln meant to enforce the draft law. There are no reports of commissions to investigate the "root causes" of "urban disorder." Though he has come down to us as a kind and country homespun, backwoods humorist, there is truth in the depiction of Lincoln in Gore Vidal's novel, where the President is seen through the eyes of a marveling Secretary of State:

"For the first time, Seward understood the nature of Lincoln's political genius. He had been able to make himself an absolute dictator without ever letting anyone suspect that he was anything more than a joking, timid backwoods lawyer …"

No tougher, more resolute of a man that has ever occupied the White House. As the historians Samuel Eliot Morison and Henry Steel Commager have written. Abraham Lincoln was a dictator from the standpoint of the American Constitutional Law and practice; and even the safety of the Republic cannot justify certain acts committed under his authority … A loyal mayor of Baltimore, suspected of Southern Sympathies, was arrested and confined in a fortress for over a year, a Maryland judge who had changed a grand jury to inquire into illegal acts of government officials was set upon by soldiers … beaten and dragged bleeding from his bench, and imprisoned.

To this Lincoln pled, military necessity, the imperative of preserving the Union:

"Are all the laws but one to go unexecuted, and the government itself go to pieces, lest that one be violated?"

To those who denounced him as a [tyrant] for ignoring due process in crushing sedition, Lincoln made no apology:

"Must I shoot a simple-minded boy who deserts, while I must not touch a hair of the wily agitator who induces him to desert?"

THE FIRST EMANCIPATION PROCLAMATION

That preserving the Union, not ending slavery, was Lincoln's agenda is evident from the first year of the war. In the summer of 1861, General John C. Fremont, Republican candidate for President in 1856, was in command in Missouri. In a daring move, Fremont drew a line across the State, separating the pro-Confederacy region from the Union side, and issued an order.

"Any civilian caught carrying a weapon north of the line would be shot. Any man aiding the secessionist cause was to have all his slaves instantly emancipated."

An instant National hero to Abolitionists and Free soliers in the United States and Great Britain, the General sent his orders to the President for approval. But, Lincoln, desperate to keep pro-slavery Kentucky in the Union, told Fremont to withdraw it. Fremont refused, insisting he would not comply unless Lincoln issued a direct order. Lincoln issued the order.

The General's wife, impulsive and high-strung Jessie Benton Fremont daughter of the great Missourian Thomas Hart Benton, who had married the dashing Lieutenant Fremont when she was 16 of age, undertook a journey to Washington, carrying a written plea from her husband. When she arrived in the Capital, exhausted after days of day-and-night travel in a dirty coach over rough roads, she sent a brief note to the White House—where she had played as a girl in the days of Andrew Jackson—to set up an appointment to deliver the letter. A response came back that very night: *"Now, at once, A. Lincoln."*

When Lincoln received her in the Red Room, Jessie Fremont lectured the President on the difficulty of conquering the South with arms alone. She urged to appeal to the British Nation and the world be declaring emancipation to be the Union's Cause.

"You are quite a female politician," an irritated Lincoln responded. Mrs. Fremont walked out of the White House and wrote in her diary:

"I explained that the General wished so much to have his attention to the letter sent, that I had brought it to make sure it would reach him. He [Lincoln] answered not to that, but to the subject his own mind was upon, that "it was (war for a Great Nation idea, the Union) that General Fremont should not have dragged the Negro into it …"

Jessie Fremont had clearly upset Lincoln. When a confidante of the President saw the General's wife the next day, he was irate. *"Look what you have done for Fremont; you made the President his enemy!"*

The Chicago Tribune denounced Lincoln for reversing General Fremont's Emancipation Proclamation. Lincoln's action takes away the penalty for rebellion, charged the Tribune on September the 16th. *"How many times"*, asked James Russell Lowell, *"are we to save Kentucky and lose our self-respect?"* In Connecticut, indignation had risen to fury. Senator Ben Wade of Ohio wrote "in bitter execration."

"The President doesn't object to Gen. Fremont's taking the life of the owners of slaves, when found in rebellion, but to confiscate their property and emancipate their slaves he thinks is monstrous."

But Lincoln's policy was not the Emancipation. It was to return the South back into the Union, even if it meant appeasing the South on slavery. As Lincoln write Greeley in his famous letter of August the 22nd of 1862.

"My paramount object in this struggle is to save the Union and is not either to save or destroy slavery. If I could destroy slavery without freeing any slave, I would do it."

Lincoln, however had already settled on his decision to issue the Emancipation Proclamation and had so informed his Cabinet.

DID TARIFFS CAUSE THE WAR?

In for Good and Evil: The impact of Texas upon the Course of Civilization, historian Charles Adams refers to John C. Calhoun's 1832 Warning about the great sectional division, that Calhoun had seen coming on the horizon: Federal import tax laws were, in Calhoun's view, a class of legislation against the South. Heavy taxation on the South raised funds that were spent in the North. This was unfair. Calhoun argued further that high import taxes would force Southerners to pay either excessive price for Northern goods or excessive taxes.

Competition from Europe was crushed, thereby giving Northerners a monopoly over Southern markets. Federal taxation had the economic effect of shifting wealth from the South to the North—not unlike what the OPEC Nations have been doing to the oil-consuming Nations since 1973. After Lincoln's election, South Carolina, Georgia, Florida, Alabama, Mississippi, Louisiana, and Texas did not wait to see how he would govern. All had seceded before his inauguration. They knew what lay ahead.

For, even before Lincoln took his oath in early March, the first of the Morrill tariffs had been passed and signed by President Buchanan, raising tariff rates to the levels not seen in decades. Consider the situation of the South: As the South purchased two-thirds of the nation's imports, and tariffs were the prime source of tax revenue, the South was already carrying a hugely disproportionate share of the federal tax load. By raising tariffs, Congress, in Southern eyes, was looting the South. Southern imports would cost more, while the rising tariff revenue would be sent North to be spent by the Republicans who reviled the South's alternative: buy Northern manufactures instead of British. Either way, more of the South's wealth was heading North.

Dixie was unwilling to sit by, and watch Lincoln's customs Officers haul their fattening satchels of duty revenue out of Southern ports, up to Washington, to be spent somewhere else, by a President who had not won a single Southern electoral vote. As the historian Adams writes,

The Morrill Tariff ... was the highest tariff in U.S. history. It doubled the rates of 1857 tariff to about 47 percent of the value of the imported products. This was Lincoln's big victory. His supporters were jubilant. He had fulfilled his campaign and IOU's to the Northern Industrialists. By this act he had closed the door for any reconciliation with the South. In his inaugural address he had also committed himself to collect customs in the South even if there were secession.

With slavery, he was conciliatory; the import taxes he was threatening. Fort Sumter was at the entrance to the Charleston Harbor, filled with Federal Troops to support U.S. Customs Officers. It was not too difficult for the angry South Carolinians to fire the first shot. Believing herself being an exploited region in a country where the newly empowered Republicans despised her, Dixie decided to leave. But there was a powerful reason the industrialized North could not let her go. The (free-trade Confederacy, had written into its Constitution a permanent prohibition against all protective tariffs: *"nor shall any duties or taxes on importations from foreign nations be laid to promote or foster any branch of industry."*

★ GOD SAVE THE SOUTH ★

To the Northern manufacturers free-trade South spells ruin. Imports would be diverted from Baltimore, New York, and Boston where they faced the Morrill Tariff to Charleston, Savannah, and New Orleans where they would enter duty free. Western States would use the tariff-free from Southern ports to bring in goods from Europe. So, would many Northerners. On the very eve of war, March 18th, 1861, the Boston Transcript wrote:

"If the Southern Confederation, is allowed to carry out a policy by which only be a nominal duty is added upon the imports no doubt the business of the chief Northern cities will be seriously injured thereby."

The difference is so great between the tariff of the Union and that of the Confederate States, that the entire Northwest must find it to their advantage to purchase their imported goods at New Orleans rather than New York. In addition to this, the manufacturing interest of the country will suffer from the increased importations resulting from low duties … The … [Government] would be false to all obligations if this State of things were not provided against.

Adams describes the political and economic crisis the North would have confronted, living side-by-side with free-trade a Confederacy:

"This would compel the North to set up a chain of Customs Stations and Border Patrols from Atlantic Oceans to the Missouri River, and then some. Northerners would clamor to buy duty-free goods from the South. This would spell disaster for Northern industrialists. Secession offered the South not only freedom from the Northern tax bondage but also an opportunity to turn from the oppressed into the oppressor. The Yankees were going to squirm now!

Nor was Lincoln unaware of the dread prospect. In his First Inaugural Address, where he had been a portrait in compromise on slavery, promising "no bloodshed or violence" against the seceding States, he made an exception:

"The powers confided to me, will be used to hold, occupy, and possess the property, and places belonging to the government, and to collect the duties and imposts; but beyond what may be necessary for these objects, there will be no invasion—no using of force against, or among the people anywhere. [Emphasis added.]"

A message to the Confederacy from Abraham Lincoln:

"You may keep your slaves, but you cannot keep your duty-free ports!"

British intellectuals like John Stuart Mill blithely declared, *"Slavery the one cause of the Civil War."* But, as Adam's writes, others in Britain put the cause elsewhere:

In the British House of Commons in 1862, William Foster said he believed it was generally recognized that slavery was the cause of the Civil War. He was answered from the House with cries, *"No, no!* And *"The Tariff!"* It is quite probably the British commercial interests, which dominated the House of Commons, were more in tune with the economics of the Civil War than the intellectuals and writers.

The tariff was *"a prime cause of the Civil War."* Writes historian John Steele Gordon, author of Hamilton's Blessing. But, while the tariffs were a cause of sectional rancor and division, and one of the reasons for secession Lincoln never discussed the tariff in depth after his speech in Pittsburgh before the inauguration. Henry Carey, the great protectionists, never forgave Lincoln, whom he had supported to the hilt, for the omission. And given Lincoln's devotion to the Union—the cause to which he subordinated all others—it would seem that, for him as for Andrew Jackson, the tariff was not the end, but the means to the end: a greater, more glorious Union. Mary Rothbard was not too far off when she wrote that Abraham Lincoln *"made a god out of the Union."*

THE SOUTH'S FATAL DEPENDENCY

Though the abolition of slavery was not why Lincoln went to war, slavery and the South's dependency on trade for the necessities of national life were the South's undoing in that war. Slavery had kept the South in mercantilist bondage. Eighty years after Yorktown, the South was still shipping raw materials to Britain for manufactured goods. Had slavery been abolished, the Deep South would have been forced off her dependence on cotton, tobacco, and rice. Given her natural resources, the capacities of her people, Black and White. The South would have developed alongside the North and west instead, it was in the North where 90 % of the manufacturing was done, where warships were built, cannons were forged, locomotives were constructed, and most of the railways laid. From the War's outset, the position of the South to the North was like the Colonies of Great Britain in the Revolution.

With its fleets, the North quickly imposed a naval blockade, and sliced the Confederacy in two at the Mississippi. Dependent on trade, the South saw her cotton and tobacco rot in the warehouses, and her trade dried up. The South's slaves, unlike Northern immigrant labor, could not be used to produce [Weapons of War.] Slavery and the agrarian character of the South tied them to the land. There may be truth in what Henry Carey wrote:

★ GOD SAVE THE SOUTH ★

"Had the policy advocated by Mr. Clay, as embodied in the tariff of 1842, been maintained, there could have been so secession, and for the reason, that the Southern mineral region would long since have obtained control of the planting one."

Without slavery, the South's Statesmen would not have been forced to use their brilliance in defending an institution the South's greatest men-Washington, Jefferson, Madison, Jackson, Lee—knew not be reconciled with the ideals in which they believed. Southerners were bound to a system they inherited at birth. Because that system depended on three and a half million slaves, the South had to submit to the abuse from moral postures from the North who ignored the exploitation of immigrant labor and could not care less about. Eventually the South had to leave a Union their fathers helped to create, and fight to their defeat and ruin in an independence struggle made almost impossible of victory because they had relied too long on the land neglected the "Work Bench" Jefferson and Randolph had so detested.

One cannot read the story of that four-year struggle without coming away with boundless admiration for the bravery of the Southern soldiers, the perseverance of her people, and the brilliance of her Generals. From Bull Run to Antietam, Gettysburg to Appomattox, the men of gray wrote a [Chapter in Glory] that will bring tears to men's eyes if they have hearts.

And Mr. Lincoln? Unquestionably, the war changed the man. The President-elect who arrived in Washington anxious to appease the Southern slave-owners, that ambivalent man of whom Richard Hofstadter wrote that his mind on the Negro was a *"house divide against itself,"* seemed by the war's end, to become a remorseless Abolitionist. At Gettysburg, weather he had intended it or not, Lincoln had succeeded for all time in *"ennobling"* the Northern cause and immortalizing himself. In those, haunting, and memorable words, Lincoln had proclaimed that the war, all along had been the equality of man.

Antietam, the Battle of the Wilderness, the March to the Sea, had hardened Lincoln. Unlike the conciliatory rhetoric of his First Inaugural, his second rings like the final warning of impending judgment from an Old Testament prophet. In that Second Inaugural, the armies of Sherman and Grant have become instruments of God's will. This Inaugural could have been delivered by John Brown:

"Fondly do we hope-fervently do we pray-that this mighty scourge of war may speedily die. Yet, if God wills that it continues, until all the wealth by the bondman's two hundred and fifty years of unrequited toil shall be sunk, and until every drop of blood drawn with the lash, shall be paid by another drawn with the sword, as was said three thousand years ago, so still it must be said, "the judgments of the Lord, are true and righteous altogether."

The war had not been about slavery when it began. But, by its end, Abraham Lincoln had declared it to be so. And it was. And the terrible and tragic manner of his death affirmed it forever.

WAS THE CAUSE JUST?

Was the Great War a just Cause?

For the South, the Issue comes down to a single question: Did the South have the right to secede from the Union? For, if the South had a right to secede—as the Colonies had a moral and legal right to break away from the British Empire—then the South and the right to fight for that independence, and to resist a Union invasion and a forcible return at the point of the Union bayonets.

On that first question, the South in 1861 had at least as strong a case for secession as the Federalist of the Hartford Convention, or ex-President John Quincy Adams, who threatened President John Tyler with secession if Texas were admitted into the Union. By the Jeffersonian test, that, to be legitimate, a government must rest upon the consent of the governed, the Confederacy had legitimacy by the time of Fort Sumter. What the Union took back in 1865 was not [Free Men and States,] but defeated rebels and a Conquered province.

In 1861, it had been an open question whether a State had a right to secede. The question was submitted to the arbitrament of the sword and settled only at Appomattox. But, of all the wars that America has ever fought, *"vital interests"* were at risk in the Civil War. Had South Carolina, Georgia, and the Gulf States broken away, British and French would have moved in to exploit the Southern free-trade zone to undermine the Northern industries and wean the West away from the Union. Indeed, during the war, Napoleon III installed a puppet regime in Mexico in a violation of the Monroe Doctrine, and the British were moving troops into Canada. The first secession would not have been the last.

Fragmentation of the nation was at hand. As a private in the 70th Ohio had wrote in 1863:

"Admit the right of the seceding States to break up the Union at pleasure ... how long will it be before the new Confederacies created by the first disruption shall be resolved into still smaller fragments and the continent became a vast theater of a Civil War, military license, anarchy and despotism. Better settle it at whatever the cost and settle it forever."

★ GOD SAVE THE SOUTH ★

With the Deep South gone, the United States would have lost a fourth of its territory, its window on the Caribbean and the Gulf, its border with Mexico, and its port in New Orleans—the outlet to the sea for the goods of Missouri, Illinois, Iowa, and the Middle West. The South would have begun to compete for the allegiance of New Mexico and Arizona; indeed, rebellions arose in both areas and had to be put down by Union troops.

To Lincoln, secession meant an amputation of his country that would destroy its élan and moral. Disunion was intolerable. Where Jackson said it directly *"Disunion is Treason,"* and *"preservation of the Union … the highest law,"* Lincoln used his rhetorical powers to elevate the cause to one of universal values. But his goal was the same as Jackson's.

Lincoln was the indispensable man who saved the Union. He accepted war and may have provoked war to restore the Union. In the end, that war freed the slaves. *"At last, the smoke of the battlefield had cleared away the horrid shape which had cast its shadow over the whole continent had vanished and was gone forever."* Wrote England's John Bright. But was war necessary to free the slaves, when every other nation in the hemisphere, save Haiti, freed its slaves peacefully. Without the *"total war"* Lincoln's Generals like Sherman and Sheridan unleashed on the South? To Lincoln, then belongs the credit of all the good the war did, and full responsibility for the war cost. While the men of government had one set of reasons for going to war, the men who marched into the guns had another: patriotism, love of country. They fought, as Macaulay said, because men always fight, *"for the ashes of their fathers and the temples of their gods."*

We are fighting against *"traitors who sought to tear down and break in fragments the glorious temple that our fathers reared with blood and tears,"* a Michigan private wrote to his younger brother. A month before he fell at Gettysburg, a Minnesota boy wrote home that he was willing to give his life *"for the purpose of crushing this g-d—rebellion and to support the best government on God's footstool."*

In the war's last days, a Union soldier captured a wounded rebel and was astonished by the man's ferocity. *"Why do you keep fighting like this?"* he demanded. *"Because you're here!"* the rebel replied.

By: Patrick J. Buchanan—February 13th, 2009.

This article first appeared in the October 1997 issue of Chronicles: A magazine of America Culture. It was adapted from a book manuscript.

ABRAHAM LINCOLN'S CIVIL WAR AGAINST NEW YORK
/PART ONE/

Fernando Wood, the former mayor of New York City, summed up the reality of what provoked the North to rise. He said that the United States was in the midst of two revolutions: *"One, at the South, with the sword, and the other at the North, by Executive and legislative usurpation ... Taking advantage of the popular enthusiasm in behalf of the Union, it has, under the pretext of furthering this holy object, gradually fastened the chains of slavery upon the people."*

The Democratic Party was devoted to peace and reconciliation with the Confederacy. Its platform, like the South's, defended State sovereignty by thwarting the powerful (centralized national government) advocated by the Republicans. Horatio Seymour, New York's Democratic governor before and during the war, spoke about Southerners being heroic and loyal to the Union in the past, to end the sectional conflict:

"Upon whom are we to wage war? Our own countrymen, who's ... courage has never been questioned in any contest in which we have engaged. They battled by our side with equal vigor on the Revolutionary struggle, in the last war with Great Britain (War of 1812) and in the Mexican conflict. Virginia sent her sons, under the Command of Washington, to relief of beleaguered Boston. Alone, the South defeated the last and most desperate efforts of the British power to divide our country, at the battle of New Orleans."

Seymour tried to negotiate a peaceful settlement, but when that had failed; he blamed the war fever on the Republican philosophy in areas outside their Constitutional authority. General William Tecumseh Sherman, in a speech to Congress, clarified the magnitude of the Northern war when he stated that the Union army had three million men in the field, and that half of them were fighting the war against the loyal States.

★ GOD SAVE THE SOUTH ★

NEW YORK CITY: BIGGEST BATTLE OF WAR

This turmoil erupted in July 1863 into a bloody battle between New York's Citizens alongside the State militia, and the Federal government's regular forces. History books call this the 'Draft Riot,' as if this was a spontaneous outburst against conscription. That term disguises the magnitude of this well-planned defiance against Lincoln's brutal policies against the North. This 'riot' was a brilliant military defense of the Empire State against the invasion of its sovereignty.

It was the 'Battle of New York City,' the longest engagement of the entire war and the only unban battle. It surpassed Gettysburg in length of time, geographic scale, and approached it in casualty numbers. It more resembled the house-to house fighting at Stalingrad or Berlin in the Second World War. As a result of New York's insurgency, Lincoln inflicted a harsh occupation program on it, while the war raged in the South.

This contradicts the myth that Abraham Lincoln was a moderate who opposed the radical Republican plan to impose a (reconstruction of vendetta upon the defeated Confederacy.) This myth presupposes that had Lincoln lived the seceded States would have returned to the Union painlessly. Yet, Lincoln imposed a tyrannical military dictatorship over New York during the war, and it remained into peacetime. This paralleled the treatment for the post-war South; with Boss Tweed's 'carpetbag' style regime and its incredible corruption and frenzied spending; changes and / or proposed changes in New York's Constitution, like those alterations in the conquered States, designed to centralize power in the Republican Assembly. Long after the bloodshed had ceased, there were still, military trails for New York's civilians, coinciding with that kind of false justice in the South.

VALLANDIGHAM'S ARREST LEADS TO INSURRECTION

Clement Vallandigham was a Congressman from Ohio and a nationally prominent Democrat. In May 1863, he made a speech in attacking the Lincoln Administration's conduct in the war. He was arrested, convicted by a military tribunal, although a civilian, and deported into the Confederacy. Vallandigham provoked this extreme reaction by assailing Lincoln's autocratic powers: As inexorable in its character as that of the worst despotism of the Old World of ancient or modern times.

When an attempt is made to deprive us of free speech and a free press, the hour shall then have come when it will be the duty of freemen to find some other efficient mode of redress. Governor Seymour said this about Vallandigham's arrest:

"If this proceeding is approved by the government and sanctioned by the people, it is not merely a step toward despotism, it establishes a military despotism." Then John Mullaly, a prominent Democrat in New York, gave this call to arms: *"While we have such a governor as Horatio Seymour …*

there is not a man that needs to be afraid of being carried off as Vallandigham has been … There was one State out of which Vallandigham could not have taken, except over the bodies of thousands of armed Citizens."

CONSCRIPTION: THE FINAL STRAW

Unconstitutional arrests, attacks on freedom of speech confiscation, etc, put the Citizens of New York on a collision course with Lincoln, but with the spark that provoked the War Between the States and the Federal government was the assault on State sovereignty. This was manifested by the radical transition from permitting each State to administer the bringing of men into the military system within its jurisdiction, to the nationalizing of conscription. In March 1863, with the war going badly, voluntary enlistments drooped dramatically. Congress enacted a Conscription Bill to coerce men into armed forces.

The reaction to this was immediate. Governor Seymour believed this would prove an 'unfortunate as a policy.' He asked Lincoln not to put the draft into effect not until its legality could be determined.

"I do not dwell upon what I believe would be the consequence of a violent, harsh policy before the Constitutionality of the act is tested. You can scan the immediate future as well as I." The Democratic Party passed a resolution concerning the Conscription Bill: *"It is subversive to the Rights of State governments and designed to make them dependencies and provinces, to be ruled by military satraps, under a great, consolidating, usurping, central despotism."*

Then Abraham Lincoln's bureaucrats sent New York its draft quota. Horatio Seymour wrote several furious letters to the President: *"If the comparison is made between cities of different States, the disproportion of men demanded from New York and Brooklyn (both Democratic Cities,) is still more startling. While in these cities 26% of the population is enrolled, in Boston (a Republican City) only 12.5% or less than half the ratios are liable to be drafted."*

Lincoln than backed down. The quotas were more equitably distributed, but the conflict had reached the point of no return. J.A. McMasters, editor of the Freemen's Journal, said that the time for deliberation had gone, and the time for action had come 'by fighting', not by street fighting, not disorganized opposition. They should organize by tens and hundreds, by companies and regiments, and they should send to their governor for commissions as soon as their regiments are formed.

NEW YORK vs. FEDERAL INVASION

On Saturday morning, 11th July 1863, the actual drawing of the draftee names began. At 5 A.M. it was already hot and overcast. A long column of citizens-soldiers moved from the lower East Side, across Broadway, to 9th Avenue, armed with iron bars. Bludgeons and bats. Armed women were among them. Small groups split off and smashed into the hardware stores to get guns and rifles. Another column poured down Lexington Avenue to the Bull's Head Hotel on 43rd Street. The office of the American Telegraph Company. From here messages could be sent to Washington, warning of the uprising.

The office was destroyed. Another formation swarmed over the Harlem and New Haven Railroad tracks. The American Telegraph's transmission lines were alongside. They were cut. Communications with the outside world and the police precincts went dead, delaying aid. Simultaneously the citizens-militia entered the railroad yards and depots, stopping all service. They moved against the major police stations, isolating them. Police headquarters on Mulberry Street was placed under siege. The 23rd Precinct Station House on East 88th was burned. The 16th Precinct on East 22nd Street, wrecked. The 5th Precinct at Baxter Street, surrounded.

Much further uptown, the Harlem River Bridge was burned to stall the Federal reinforcements. It was soon obvious to the Republicans that this was not a riot, but a well-planned military operation. Navy Secretary Gideon Welles wrote in his diary: *"There is, I think, indubitable evidence of concert in these riotous movements, beyond the accidental and impulsive outbreak of a mob or mobs, Lee's march into Pennsylvania, the appearance of several rebel steamers off the coast, the mission of A.H. Stephens (the Confederate States Vice President) to Washington, seem to be part of one movement, have one origin, are all concerted schemes between the rebel leaders and the Northern sympathizer friends."*

The New York Tribune, Republican newspaper, reported that *"no person who carefully watched the movements of this mob, who noticed their careful attention to the words of a certain tacitly acknowledge leaders, who observed the unquestionably preconceived regularity with which they proceeded from one part of their infernal program to the next*

... can presume to doubt that these men were acting under leaders who had carefully elaborated their plans." Sunday, at 6 A.M ... Another large body of New Yorkers-massed along Second Avenue. One section moved against the Union Steam Works, a weapons factory for the Federal Army, on 22nd Street. Thousands of rifles were in that building. A second attack was aimed at 21st Street; the New York State Armory. The Police held the armory. Ten thousand New Yorkers charged them.

The police retreated. To block reinforcements to the armory, the 18th Precinct on 22nd Street was also assaulted; it officers routed. Further downtown, New York's militia headed for the City Hall area and the offices of the Tribune. Simon Gay, the managing editor, saw the approaching force and said: *"This is not a riot, but a revolution."* The New Yorkers wrecked the Tribune's facility but the police counter-attacked, drove them back out, and the newspaper printed its next edition. Fifty thousand New Yorkers were now in the streets.

DIVERSIONARY ATTACKS HIT OUTLUING TOWNS

To divide the police and the Union Army strength away from the main battle area in New York City. Other attacks were staged in Brooklyn, Staten Island, and the Bronx. On Staten Island there was an assault on the military drill room of the Tompkins Lyceum in Stapleton. A detachment of 200 took 30 rifles. A second drill room near Stapleton landing was sacked and weapons taken. Then a railroad car barn of the Staten Island Railroad was burned at the Vanderbilt Landing Depot. This was to slow the Federals and police reinforcements.

Two companies of New York's Regiment were diverted from lower Manhattan to Staten Island, along with two Federal companies and 300 policemen. At Clifton, as they disembarked, one company was sniped at by a citizen concealed in the surrounding woods. They fired back. The citizens charged, took the soldier's weapons, crushed one's head, disemboweled a second, and bayoneted others. In Brooklyn, military activity pinned down a considerable portion of the police force when they were desperately needed in New York City.

The Metropolitan Police District (which encompassed both Cities) had about 2,000 men. At least half remained in Brooklyn as long as a threat existed there. One such attack was on two huge floating grain elevators in the bay off of Atlantic Basin. The elevators had been loading grain as food for the Union Armies. They were set on fire at night. The flames were visible to all of Brooklyn. This gigantic blaze drew firemen and police away from the major zone. A huge crowd gathered. It seemed they were just fascinated by the fire, but they attacked the pier where the elevators were docked 'like zouaves charging an enemy's breastworks.'

Firemen, police, and security guards only survived by escaping on small boats in the river. The Brooklyn Navy Yard was a logical target. Four howitzers were placed at one gate, four cannons along the flushing Avenue wall, and more artillery covered the main entrance. Soldiers and sailors were withdrawn from other locations to reinforce this critical base. It was not assaulted. In the Bronx, at Morrisania and the West Farms sections, citizens-militia burned the enrollment offices. At Westchester Square they demolished the telegraph offices and at William Bridge and Melrose, ripped up the rails on the New Haven and Harlem railroad.

POLICE AND TROOPS COUNTER-ATTACK

The initial clash between New Yorkers and the Union Army occurred on the first day. Fifty 'invalid Corps' troops met the New Yorkers on Third Avenue. The Invalid soldiers had been wounded in earlier battles and were unfit for front line service. At first, they fired blanks at the New Yorkers. This did not stop them. This switched to live rounds. Six New Yorkers fell, but the rest surged forward, killing several soldiers, and taking their weapons. Because of the cuts in communications, it took thirteen hours for two Companies of regular US infantry, stationed in the harbor, to arrive in the City. Mayor Opdyke sent an urgent telegram to secretary of War Stanton, asking that all New York regiments to return to the City from Gettysburg where they had just been fighting.

At the Steam works weapons factory, 150 New York State militiamen who were still loyal to the Federal government, confronted the citizens. It seemed the loyalist would not fire on their own people, but they did; grapeshot from artillery. Six rounds and the street were littered with the dead and dying. The police supported the loyal militia by attacking the Steam works from a different direction. They charged forward but were trapped in a hail of bullets and bricks from snipers on the rooftops.

The police poured into these buildings. They rushed to the roofs, in hand-to-hand fighting; both sides were hurled to the streets below. The citizens-militia retreated from the Steam works, to regrouped, and attacked again. The loyalists and police gave ground. The citizens took the factory, and it became their headquarters. Later, the police with the loyalist reinforcements, once again they rushed forward, and gained a foothold on the first floor and in a room-to-room, floor-to-floor combat, slowly they took back the Steam works. There were many shipyards along the East and Hudson Rivers, most of them had engaged in the building of military vessels for the Navy.

The New Yorkers had attacked Webb and Allen, one of the biggest, where the 'Dunderberg,' an iron-clad ram, was near completion. The 7th New York Regiment defended the facility. Their concentrated fire drove the citizen-militia back. Simultaneously a column of citizens attempted to seize the ferry terminal on Fulton Street to deny this landing site to the Union reinforcements. It was already defended the Federal troops. Here the citizens were also beaten off. The Police headquarters at Mulberry Street was still under siege. Thomas Acton, head of the Metropolitan board of Police Commissioners, ordered all police reserves to relieve the blockade, along with a company of Zouaves. 'Then the howitzer battery was ready.

But a mob could learn to be ready, on the order to fire, the mob flung themselves flat on the pavement or scattered into doorways on both sides of the Street. In the interval between rounds of canister screaming harmlessly down First Avenue, an answering rattle of musketry began to grow from the windows and rooftops; these sharpshooters concentrated their fire on the officers. The troops were trapped, and because they did not have the training to fight their way out or clear the buildings, they died.

The mob routed the Zouaves. The mob captured the artillery and turned it on the troops.' Then, two companies of police struck the citizen-army in the rear, at Fourth Street and Broadway. It led to more hand-to-hand fighting; they surged back-and-forth. The New Yorkers were routed, retreating up Broadway, which *"looked like a battlefield, thickly strewn with prostrate forms."*

INVADING US ARMY COUNTER-ATTACKS

On the third day, the 47th New York Regiment reached the battle from Gettysburg. Edwin Stanton informed Mayor Opdyke that another 'five regiments are under orders to return to New York.' Then Stanton telegraphed that 'eleven New York regiments have been relieved and will be forwarded to New York as fast as transportation can be furnished.' Stanton had chosen New Yorkers to kill New Yorkers. At noon of the third day, after having been driven back from Webb and Allen, the citizen-militia retreated until they reached barricades of cobblestones along the 9th Avenue. There the police and the Union army combined to dislodge them. Connecticut troops poured on a withering fire which allowed the police to overwhelm the defenders.

Governor Seymour came into the city and found that he not only had to deal with his efforts to force the Union army to withdraw but also with the Republican leaders. They were intent on inciting the New Yorkers to greater lawlessness. This would force General Wool, who commanded the Department of the East, to declare martial law. That would end Democratic Party rule and civil law and government in New York. It would be replaced by a military justice administered through the Republican administration. Martial Law would depose Horatio Seymour and require a military governor to control all future elections.

When General Wool refused to declare martial law, the Tribune called him an imbecile. Wool was immediately replaced by General Dix who was more compliant but the battle ended before he could initiate such extreme measure. As the tide turned and the Federal forces pushed the citizen-militia back, Governor Seymour, with a cavalry escort, entered City Hall Park. It was filled with infantry. Seymour spoke to the New Yorkers, asking them to stop fighting. He realized that the battle was lost and to continue meant needless laughter and permanent Federal control of the State:

"My friends, I come ... from a kind regard for the ... welfare of those, who under the influence of excitement and supposed wrong, were in danger of not only inflicting serious blows to the good order of society, but to their own interests ... I beg of you to listen to as your friend and friends of your families." Seymour told the citizens that he had sent his personal adjutant-general to Washington to stop the draft. The New Yorkers threw down their weapons and dissipated into the wreckage of the city.

After four days the battle was over. Union troops remained in control of the city. More soldiers were brought in, as part of a continuing army of occupation. Secretary of War Stanton sent this telegram to General Dix:

"We are sending you 10,000 infantry and 3 batteries of artillery. These are picked troops, including the regulars. If you need cavalry, we can, perhaps, send you 500.

This tremendous battle did not make Lincoln more willing to compromise on conscription. He announced that the draft would continue immediately, under General Dix, who provoked another confrontation with Horatio Seymour. Dix telegraphed the governor that since the enrollment *"will probably be resumed in this city, at an early date, I am desirous of knowing whether the military power of this State will be relied upon to enforce the execution of the law, in case of forcible resistance to it ... [so that] I need not ask the War Department to put at my disposal for the purpose, troops in the service of the United States."* Seymour wrote back that he had appealed to Lincoln to not resume conscription until the constitutionality could be tested. Lincoln refused to postpone it. August 14th was the day the draft resumed. Dix requested more Federal troops. Seymour again refused to comply, warning that enforcement would *"excite popular resistance"* and clarifying that the New York authorities would not carry out this [national law.] Conscription proceeded under the bayonets of this large Union army presence.

★ JOHN THOMAS NALL ★

CONCLUSION ...

"It has never been known as to how many had perished in those awful days. According to the lowest estimate, some 1,200 of the rioters must have been killed and five to six times that number wounded; but they hid their loses as far as possible and disposed of their dead in silence and darkness."

This means that the citizen-militia suffered about 8,400 casualties. And as a standard rule, an attacking army takes three times as many killed and wounded as the defenders. Then, the Union army and police had losses of 25,200. The combined total of the 33,600 is higher than the greater slaughter at Antietam and close to those at Gettysburg.

This battle radically altered political climate of New York, its [Constitution was shredded,] and the long-term consequences continue to be felt into the 21st Century, since Abraham Lincoln viewed New York as another Confederate State that had to be taught a lesson through reconstruction. To achieve this, its elections had to be manipulated through terror, as was voting in the occupied Southern States.

So, New York was invaded a second time by land, with a huge amphibious assault waiting on the New Jersey waterfront, to be launched in case another extra force was necessary. This was in 1864, during the Presidential election. With the pools controlled by the army, a Republican victory was assured. Horatio Seymour was deposed, and Lincoln re-elected. But, all that, dear reader, is the subject of another story on another day.

By: John Chodes

ENDNOTES

1. *Sidney David Brummer, 'Political History of New York State during the Period of the Civil War' (New York: Columbia University and Longmans, Green & Company, Agents, 1911) P.306.*
2. *Thomas M. Cook and Thomas Knox, editors, 'Public Records of Horatio Seymour' (New York.—I. W. England, at the offices of the New York.-I.W. England, at the offices of the New York 'Sun,' 1868) p.25*
3. *New York 'Herald,' 8th March 1863.*
4. *New York 'Herald,' 19th May 1863.*
5. *New York 'Tribune,' 26th May 1863.*
6. *Brummer, P. 328.*

7. *New York 'Herald,' 3rd April 1863.*
8. *James B. Fry, 'New York and the Conscription of 1863. A Chapter in the History of the Civil War' (New York.-G.P. Putnam's-The Knickerbocker Press, 1885) P.57.*
9. *Brummer, P. 312.*
10. *James McCague, 'The Second Rebellion: The story of the New York City Draft Riots of 1863.' (New York: The Dial Press, 1968) P. 107.*
11. *Ibid. P. 104.*
12. *Ibid. P. 105.*
13. *Brooklyn 'Eagle,' 16th July 1863.*
14. *McCague, P. 148.*
15. *Ibid. P. 148.*
16. *Ibid. P. 130 and P. 145.*
17. *Thomas M. Cook and Thomas Knox, P. 128.*
18. *Morgan Dix, 'Memoirs of John Adams Dix,' Vol.1 (New York: Harper & Brothers, 1883) P. 86.*
19. *Ibid. P.77.*
20. *Ibid. P. 76.*
21. *Ibid. P. 75.*

Mr. John Chodes is a former Chairman of the League of the South's New York Chapter.

ABRAHAM LINCOLN'S CIVIL WAR AGAINST NEW YORK
/PART TWO/

(Continued from the Last Page)

The issue that provoked New York, Pennsylvania, Ohio, Illinois, Indiana, and Wisconsin into insurrection was: The arrests of 38'000 civilians as traitors, and their convictions by military tribunals. Including the fact, they were being jailed in military prisons without the benefit of a (Writ of Habeas Corpus or a jury trial.) And many were mostly Democrats. Their property was confiscated, and many disappeared forever without a trace. Oppositional newspapers were closed, and their editors imprisoned. The movement for an armed confrontation escalated with the arrest, and the conviction and deportation of the nationally prominent Ohio Democratic Congressman; Clement Vallandigham.

He dared to publicly condemn Lincoln's methods against his political rivals. New York, the most populous State in the Union, began to arm and trains its militia and citizens in a secret defiance. The event that was the straw that broke the New Yorker's back was the [Conscription Bill.] This law nationalized the drafting of men into the army. The Democrats, as advocates of State sovereignty were opposed to Washington's interference in the process. Horatio Seymour, the New York's Democratic governor, had refused to participate in this Federal coercion until the legality of this law could be tested by the Supreme Court. Abraham Lincoln would not wait. With that response, New Yorker's launched a daring large-scale attack on governmental and military facilities to preempt the inevitable invasion by the Union army, which had intended to enforce the draft.

★ GOD SAVE THE SOUTH ★

The resulting four days of carnage in the New York City Streets in July of 1863 was the longest battle of the entire war. It was the only major urban conflict, with enormous casualties only surpassed by Gettysburg. The Union forces with superior numbers finally won, and New York was occupied like a conquered Confederate [State]. This tremendous struggle was recently presented in a fictionalized and intentionally misleading way in the hit movie, (Gangs of New York).

This set the State for the next phase: A second invasion with different objectives. Election of 1864; Prelude to the Second Invasion and in August 1864, Lincoln was told by the Republican leaders that his November re-election prospects were hopeless. Horace Greeley, the editor of the New York Tribune, one of the major Republican newspapers, wrote that Lincoln that if the election were held in August, the Democrats would carry New York by a 100,000 majority.

General Benjamin Butler was one of the most controversial officers in the Union army. He had political ambitions as a Republican and in the final phase of the national campaign, Butler divided his time between fighting and writing speeches for Lincoln, which were read at political rallies. For a New York convention he wrote that the voters who supported the would be acting in a way of more detrimental to the country and beneficial to the rebellion than if they placed themselves actively in arms, side-by-side with the rebels in the field. As a reward for his loyalty to the Republican cause, Butler was called to Washington for a new military assignment.

The election was only weeks away. He met with Edwin Stanton, the Secretary of War. Stanton wanted a stronger military presence in New York, particularly at the polling places to guarantee a Republican victory for Lincoln, who was opposed by the Democrat. General George McClellan and Stanton also hoped to depose Horatio Seymour for Reuben Fenton, the Radical Republican, and Butler would command that force.

Choosing Butler for this operation indicated the contempt that Lincoln's administration had for New York. It was viewed as just another rebel stronghold to be crushed. Earlier in the war, Butler had stirred considerable resentment, even in the North. When he oversaw Federal troops, during occupation of New Orleans. He was replaced because of his high-handed behavior. His first widely publicized act was the summary execution of William Mumford, who pulled down the United States flag from the New Orleans mint.

Then Butler generated more bad press when he rounded up many New Orleans residents and exiled them to a barren Ship Island in the Gulf of Mexico. Butler growled and scowled, swaggered, and bulldozed. He suppressed newspapers, and then came his infamous 'Woman Order.' Ladies began pouring the contents of chamber pots on members of his staff as they walked beneath their windows. Butler decreed:

"Hereafter, when any female shall by word, gesture of movement insult or show contempt for any officer or soldier of the United States. She shall be regarded and held liable to be treated as a woman of the town plying her avocation."

This had negative repercussions in the Northern Press. England's newspapers denounced his actions. Even the Prime Minister, Parlmerston had protested. Butler's excessively harsh confiscations and trade restrictions also aroused strenuous objections from foreign consuls. All this resulted in Butler being called 'Beast'. In December 1862, U.S. Secretary of State: William Seward, recalled him back home in Massachusetts. Butler said:

"I have not erred too much in hardness … There is no middle ground between loyalty and treason".

BUTLER TAKES COMMAND OF NEW YORK

When Butler arrived in Washington for his new assignment, Stanton gave him an overstated report about conditions in New York, to disguise the truth that Butler's role in that city was to steal the election for Lincoln by raw force and terror. In his memoirs Butler described his meeting with Stanton, who said: *"Read these papers, general"*. I carefully read the papers … In substance they stated that there was an organization of troops to be placed under the command of (Union General) Fitz John Porter; that there was to be inaugurated in New York, a far more widely extended and far better-organized riot, than the draft riot in July 1863; that the whole vote of the city was to be deposited for McClellan … that the Republicans were to be driven from the polls; that there were several thousand rebels in New York who were to aid in the movement; and that Brigadier John A. Green, who was known to be the confidential friend of the governor (Horatio Seymour) was to be present, bringing some forces from the interior from the State to take part in the movement. Butler asked Stanton: *"What do you want me to do?"* Stanton replied: *"I want you to go down there and take command of the department of the East, relieving General Dix, and I will have sent to you from the front, a sufficient force to put down any insurrection,"* … He then asked what troops I wanted, and I said: *"About 3'000 men will be enough, but a larger force may be better for over-awing an outbreak."*

Stanton said:

"*I suppose you will want your Massachusetts troops sent.*" Butler: "*Oh, I said, "Not Massachusetts men to shoot down New Yorkers. That will not do. I have as faithful. Loyal, good soldiers in my New York regiments as there are in the world, and I can fully rely on them.*"

Butler moved into his New York headquarters at Hoffman House on November the 4th. The election would be on the 8th. Butler: 'That day Major-General Sanford, commanding the divisions of State militia in the City of New York, called upon me and said that he proposed on the day of election to call his divisions of militia to preserve the peace. I told him that could not be done without his reporting to me as his superior officer …

He could not agree to that. I then told him that I did not need his divisions, and that I did not think it would be advisable to have the militia called out; that if they were called out, they would be under arms, and in case of difficulty it was not quite certain which way all of them would shoot … He was very obstinate about it, and said he should call out the militia. Well, said I, "If there are to be armed forces that do not report to me, and are not under my orders, I shall treat them as enemies … And from the reported doings of Governor Seymour in the center of the State in organizing new companies of militia, which I believe to be a rebellious organization.

I may find it necessary to act promptly in arresting all those whom I know are proposing to disturb the peace here on Election Day. Then Butler issued a harsh military order designed to intimidate voters. The Albany editorialized:

"*We will not characterize, as it deserves, the conduct of the administration in sending to New York on the eve of the election with a man like Butler … His career in the army is calculated to arouse bitter indignation.*" Many Republicans doubted the wisdom of sending Butler to New York.

LINCOLN'S FRAUD SCHEME FOR SOLDIER's VOTES

In April of 1863, Governor Seymour addressed the Albany Legislature concerning 'the question of the method by which those of our fellow citizens who are absent in the military and naval service of the nation may be able to enjoy their right of suffrage … The constitution of this State requires the elector to vote in the election district in which he resides; but a law can be passed whereby the vote of an absent citizen may be given by his authorized representative.

Instead, the Republican Legislature passed a law which they knew to be unconstitutional, and which they knew that Governor Seymour would be compelled to veto, for the purpose of making it seem he was opposed to the soldiers voting. Horatio Seymour did veto it, saying:

"The bill is in conflict with vital principles of electoral purity and independence ... The bill not only fails to guard against abuses and frauds, it offers every inducement and temptation to perpetuate them by those who are under the immediate and particular control of the General Government. The Government has not hesitated to interfere, directly, with local elections, by permitting officers of high rank to engage in them in States of which they are not citizens."

In March of 1864, a Constitutional Amendment was passed by the people, after being accepted by Seymour, enabling soldiers to vote in the field. In September of 1864, Seymour instructed commanders to give their troops the absentee ballots, but the Republican Secretary of the State of New York: Chauncey Depew refused to distribute the forms to the officers.

Then Lincoln's aides seized the agents who were transmitting the New York soldier's ballots, charge them with fraud, or took their ballots and either held them until after the election or secretly changed the forms to show a Republican chose. The agents, Col. Samuel North, Major Levi Cohen and M.M. Jones, were brought before a secret military tribunal which charged them with being Confederates and employees of Governor Seymour, in the Fraud plot. Thousands of other ballots, which had been deposited in the mails, were detained in the Post Offices until after the election.

To prevent detection of this crime, the post marks were altered. In some instances, when the soldiers returned home to vote in person, and they discovered that their Democratic ballots had become Republican votes. The Albany Argus editorialized: In the history of outrage and crime which makes up the Lincoln administration, there is no darker deed than this! It reveals the terror and desperation of the Washington junta.' Horatio Seymour appointed three prominent Democrats as Commissioners to proceed to Washington to inquire about the arrests and voting deceptions. They reported that there were irregularities and gave a harrowing account of the treatment of the three prisoners. Later, North, Jones and Cohen were acquitted.

GOD SAVE THE SOUTH

LAND AND SEA INVASION BUILD-UP

Ben 'Beast' Butler had prepared for the election in his usual efficient way. He commanded dozens of ferry boats and positioned them in Jersey City's slips. 15,000 seasoned troops were loaded aboard. At a given signal, they would be launched for a massive amphibious assault on New York's shoreline and across the Hudson River. Gunboats flanked the attack route. And infantry had been steadily infiltrated into the city over the previous two weeks to cover the polls and all other locations where the citizens might rise up as they had the previous year.

Horatio Seymour made one last desperate threatening proclamation against Butler's Union Army presence: *"The power of this State is ample to protect all classes in the free exercise of their political duties. Sheriffs and other officials were directed to take care that every voter should have a free ballot and they were required to see that 'no military or other organized force shall be allowed to show themselves in the vicinity of the places where the elections are held, with any view of menacing or intimidating citizens attending thereon.' Against such interference they must exercise the full force of the law."* Butler paid no attention to this threat but the order to send in the water-borne attack never materialized. New York's citizens and militia had been sufficiently broken up or imprisoned and terrorized in the aftermath of 1863 battle. Large-scale resistance did not occur.

CONCLUSION

General Grant sent this telegram to Stanton about the expected and pre-ordained Republican landslide in New York: *"The election has passed quietly; no bloodshed or riot ... it is a victory worth more to the country than a battle won. Rebeldom and Europe will construe it so."* Yet the results, despite all the chicanery and, military terror, were not as overwhelming as Lincoln had hoped for. In fact, so close were the contests, that for several days after the election, the Albany Argus claimed a Democratic victory. But in the end, Lincoln edged McClellan by less than 9,000 votes and Fenton defeated Horatio Seymour by 7,000.

With Fenton at the head and backed by a Radical Republican Assembly, New Yorkers soon learn that political rebellion had a high price. For the remainder of the war and into peace time, the Empire State would have to pay, in the loss of its freedom and rights. Just like any other conquered Confederate territory.

All these events destroy the long-held myth that Abraham Lincoln was a moderate, kind leader, who would have healed the nation's wounds after the war, had he lived. What transpired in New York proves he was actually a

Radical, as dangerous as Thaddeus Stevens or Ben Wade. Lincoln conducted the same kind of reconstruction on this, and other loyal States, during the war, as was forced on the South in the post-war years.

Part 1 & 2 of Abraham Lincoln's Civil War against New York came from the Southern Events/ Vol. 8 of No. 1. Mr. John Chodes is a former Chairman of the League of the South's New York Chapter.

FOOTNOTES FOR—(THE SECOND INVASION.)

1. *Lous Taylor Merrill, 'Ben Butler in the Presidential Campaign of 1864. The Mississippi Historical Review. Vol. xxxiii, No. 4. March 1947. P. 565.*
2. *Merrill, P. 538.*
3. *Ibid. P. 540.*
4. *Benjamin Butler's Book: Autobiography and Personal Reminiscences of Major-General Benjamin Butler (Boston: A.M. Thayer and Company, 1892) P. 754.*
5. *Butler. P. 756.*
6. *Albany Argus. 8th of November of 1864.*
7. *David Croly. 'Seymour and Blair. Their Lives and Services' (New York. Richardson and Company. 1868) P. 124.*
8. *Croly, P. 126.*
9. *Sidney David Brummer. 'Political History of New York: Columbia University and Longman's Green & Company agents. 1911) P. 432.*
10. *Albany Argus, 28th of October of 1864.*
11. *Brummer. P. 437.*
12. *Ibid. P. 771.*

THE JACOBIN YANKEES

Martin Scorcese, in an interview, candidly described his film, "Gangs of New York," as an 'opera.' He had been asked as to whether the events portrayed were true to history. I took his reply to mean that the events of the movie were selected and organized for the dramatic emphasis and was not to be taken as literal factual record.

And, indeed, as an historical record of 19th Century New York, the film has many failings. Nevertheless, it has provoked some useful discussion of the historical context-specifically for the light it sheds on the Lincolnite mythology of the Civil War era. It seems that the accepted idea of the gloriously united North trampling out the wrathful grapes of slavery and treason is not so sound a picture of the real thing after all.

For one thing, the film gives a glimpse of the rather nativism among Northerners, a great many of whom hated Catholics and immigrants as much or more than they hated Southerners. None of the above fit into the Yankee ideal of true Americanism. Nativist gangs burned down convents in Philadelphia and Boston when such things were never dreamed of in the South. This window into the real history of the antebellum North becomes even more significant for three reasons.

1. Nativists of the American Party went en masse into Lincoln's Republican Party and made up a strong element of his support. Though, of course, Lincoln cared nothing about religion and the other leading Republicans were too savvy politicians to embrace overt nativism. Republicans did not generally like immigrants, but they loved the militaristic German centralizers who flooded into the Midwest after the failed (socialist revolutions of 1848.) Confederate General Richard Taylor recorded in his memoirs that when he surrendered at the end of the war, a German Union General lectured him on how Southerners were now to be taught (true Americanism.) Taylor was the grandson of a Revolutionary officer and son of a President. (Does this maybe give you a little hint of where Straussians and Neocons are coming

from?) These Germans made the most solid core of Lincoln's support, with the possible exception of tariff-protected manufacturers and New England 'intellectuals.'

2. The film can open the door on another dirty secret. We have heard a lot about immigrant criminal gangs. The fact that vigilante law prevailed over much of the North during the war has been conveniently forgotten. Besides the thousands of his critics Lincoln had jailed without due process, thousands more were killed, injured, intimidated, and run out of town by proto-fascist gangs of Republican bully boys called "Wade Awakes." They played a major role in making sure Northern elections turned out right, i.e., Republicans won. And you thought the ugly mob violence was something that only happened in the South!

3. Although the film does not give a satisfactory view of the New York City draft riots, it lets us in on at least part of the secret when the draft rioters pointed out the $300.00, as men who bought exemption from conscription. The fact is that no affluent Northerner fought in the war if he didn't want to-certainly not Rockefeller, Morgan, Gould, Swift, Armour, Goodyear and the others who were making fortunes out of government contracts. Nor most of the pratricians-only one of five military age Adamses and Teddy Roosevelt's father bought an exemption. Lincoln's worthless son Robert, spent most of the war at Harvard. Sherman once complained that men of wealth were found in the ranks of the Southern army and lamented that Northerners were not like that.

But that is not the entire story. The 'riots' did not start out as a race pogroms, though they degenerated into that. They started out as organized civic resistance to the draft, encouraged by the Democratic State government. Everyone knew very well that the Lincolnites enforced the draft at a much higher rate in areas that opposed them than they did in friendly areas-according to forthcoming studies by the New York playwright and historian, John Chodes; the draft was imposed in New York City at four times the rate for Massachusetts. And the conscripts were aware that they stood a good chance of being used as cannon fodder by the Republicans who knew it they lost four men for every Southerner killed, they would still end up on top, as long as the immigrant flow kept up.

About a fourth of the total enrollments of Lincoln's Armies were immigrants, many of whom were brought over and paid bounties for enlisting. The situation was so bad that the Pope sent one of his most persuasive priestly orators to Ireland, to warn the people about being used up for Union cannon fodder. Perhaps we can begin to recognize the historical fact that millions of Northern citizens did not willingly go along with Lincoln's war. And the opponents were not limited to the New York City draft rioters. A forth coming book by Misses Fellow H.A. Scott Trask will enlighten us about who opposed the war: free traders who were on to the Republican tariff game;

traditional Jeffersonians and descendants of Revolutionary families (outside of New England) who understood that killing Southerners and overthrowing legitimate State governments, as well as suppressing freedom of speech and press, were not exactly what the Founding Fathers had in mind; Irish and German Catholics, though that history has been suppressed as one of the fruits of Lincoln's victory.

<u>The truth is that Lincoln's party did not save the Union and the Constitution. It was a Jacobin party that seized power and revolutionized the North as well as conquering the South.</u> "Gangs of New York" can perhaps open a window that will encourage further historical discovery along these lines. Alas, the wrong lesson is drawn by the usually fine writers at vdare.com, Steve Sailer, who sees the movie as Scorsese making points for the immigrants against the natives. According to Sailor:

"When the Civil War came, many Irish and other immigrants in New York City refused to fight for the Union that had given them refuge."

Waite a minute! That was a Civil War going on here! Can a newcomer really be faulted for not wanting to take sides in a Civil War? I think it shows real patriotism and good sense. And how about that is 'refuge?' Here is a Dublin paper commenting in 1861: *"We cannot but recollect that in the South our countrymen were safe from insult and persecution, while 'Nativism' and 'Know-Nothingism' assailed them in the North."* How about John Mitchel, the Irish patriot who had been exiled to Van Diemen's Land, from whence he escaped to the land of freedom, where he joined the Confederate cause of liberty, to which he gave the lives of two sons? It is not true, by the way, that the Union General Burnside's sacrifice of the Irish Brigade at Fredericksburg was a great exhibit of Irish devotion to the Union cause.

The so-called enthusiasm was political propaganda drummed up by a Republican promotion of Gen. Meagher as an Irish Leader, which he was not. Irish recruiting fell off sharply after Fredericksburg. Let me recommend to those who want to use conditions in War of Southern Independence as a tool for the otherwise worthy cause, of immigration a recent work: Clear the Confederate Way! The Irish in the Army of Northern Virginia; by; Kelly J. O' Grady. The book covers much more than the title suggests. And while you are at it, take a look also at (The Jewish Confederates) by; Robert N. Rosen.—January 15th 2003

Dr. Wilson is a professor of history at the University of South Carolina and editor of (The Papers of John C. Calhoun. And Dr.Wilson is Author of his new book, (Defending Dixie) Essays in Southern History and Culture-2006.

FEDERAL POW PROPAGANDA

It has been said that history is created by those who write it rather than those who live it. This is hyperbole, of course, but each historian does indeed write from a particular perspective. So Americans, depending on what schools they attend and which historians they rely on, may have differing views of the same event. Also, many Americans rely on public libraries for their knowledge of history. But, contrary to what many think, the purpose of public libraries is not to present balanced views but to make available to their patrons the most sought after books.

Public libraries, unlike libraries affiliated with Universities, stock their shelves with sellers of books receiving favorable reviews in mass market journals. Quite a few people derive their knowledge of history from fictional accounts; novels, plays, films, and TV. This is especially true of depictions of the War Between the States. This unparalleled event in our history has continued to inspire fictional works for 140 years.

Finally, there are versions of history that combine fiction with fact, such as the Public Broadcasting System's Civil War series. With advice from competent historians, Filmmaker Ken Burns accurately portrays the overall story of the Civil War. But in relating to certain events, Burns abandons his hired historians and spins a version that is skewed to cause viewers to empathize with Burn's political agendas. Because this modus operandi is used so frequently by Ken Burns, I refer to it as 'kenitized' history. PBS's videos have profoundly influenced contemporary views of the War Between the States. So if you asked the average American to identify the prisons used during the Civil War, they could probably name only one: the Confederate prison in Andersonville, Georgia. The Kenitized version of Andersonville goes something like this. During the Civil War, the Union discontinued the exchange of prisoners because Confederates refused to exchange Black prisoners. Since the reason Northern men were willing to risk their lives on the battlefield was their overwhelming moral opposition to slave labor, how could they exchange of White prisoners only?

★ GOD SAVE THE SOUTH ★

On this issue the Union commanders, especially Secretary of War Edwin Stanton and General Grant, took a firm ethical stand. Burns states that of all the Civil War prisons, 'The worst was Andersonville.' Burns describes the prison's commander, Major Henry Wirz, as 'a temperish German-Swiss immigrant (who) forbade prisoners to build shelters; most lived in holes scratched in the ground, covered by a blanket. Any man caught closer than 15 feet of the stockade was shot.'

Wirz is depicted as brutalizing his prisoners and denying them adequate food and medical care. Consequently, 13,000 prisoners died during their confinement at Andersonville. This depiction of Andersonville is considered by many to be authentic, but the actual events are more complicated and not easily converted into time-constrained television programming. In fact, it is difficult to understand Andersonville and the other prisons, unless you understand the nature of the Civil War fatalities, as well as the conditions existing at the time-especially the quality of medical care available.

Of the fatalities during the War Between the States, only about 30% were killed in action or mortally wounded. The vast majority died as a result of disease or other debilitating health impairments. With adequate medical care and medications, most of the deaths could have been prevented. But, at the time of the Civil War, the doctors that did exist knew little about disease, used crude surgical techniques and has very limited forms of medication. But ether and chloroform were available so those accounts of soldiers having limbs amputated without an anesthetic are largely fiction.

Nevertheless, the period is described as 'being at the end of the medical Middle Ages.' To illustrate, one of the better medical schools, Harvard University, did not own a single stethoscope or microscope until after the Civil War. Throughout the War, there were an insufficient number of trained medical professionals on both sides, although the Union's medical corps exceeded the Confederate medical corps by a ratio of more than three to one.

In the first year of the War, U.S. President Lincoln would not allow the exchange of prisoners because he refused to acknowledge the existence of the Confederacy. According to Lincoln, what was occurring was only an insurrection and therefore not subject to the rules of war. Pressure from the U.S. Congress as well as members of his administration finally forced the President to relent, and in the summer of 1862, a prisoner exchange agreement was negotiated between the Union and the Confederacy.

In 1863, Secretary of War, Edwin M. Stanton directed Union Army General Henry Halleck to drastically reduce the number of exchanges. Historians disagree on the motive for Secretary Stanton's action. Some claim the rate of exchanges was decreased because Confederates refused to exchange Black prisoners. Other claim that, because Union forces greatly outnumbered Confederate forces, the exchange was forces greatly outnumbered Confederate forces, the exchange was more beneficial to the South than the North.

This school maintains that concern for Black Union prisoners was not authentic but simply an attempt to make a pragmatic military tactic appear humanitarian. Black POWs never were more than a miniscule amount of the total Union prisoners and at the time of Stanton's order. There were practically no Black prisoners. Later, when Ulysses S. Grant became Commander of the Union Army, all exchanges were ceased. Union General Benjamin Butler later stated that:

"He (Grant) said I would agree with him that exchange of prisoners we get, no men are fit to go into our army, and every soldier we give the Confederates went immediately into theirs, so that the exchange was virtually so much aid to them and none to us."

With the end of the exchange system the number of prisoners of war mushroomed and both sides were forced to construct new prisons. Including temporary internment camps, more than 150 prisons were used during the Civil War. Of these, there were a dozen or so that held thousands of prisoners; these facilities were equally divided between North and South. The Confederates hurriedly constructed Andersonville Prison in South Georgia in early 1864. Believing that the exchange system would be reactivated, the prison was designed to accommodate only 10,000 prisoners but, because the Union refused to resume exchanges, the prison population tragically increased to 33,000.

In July of 1864, Major Wirz paroled a group of Union prisoners so they could take a petition to Washington pleading for a resumption of the exchange system. As incredible as it may sound, Union President Lincoln refused to meet with the prisoners. Secretary of War Stanton did meet with the petitioners, but the exchange system was still rejected. One Union prisoner later wrote: *"When the Andersonville emissaries returned from Washington there was not one word about the exchange of Negro soldiers being in the way of our release."*

Another Union prisoner later stated: *"There was not a Negro soldier in Andersonville or in any other prison for a considerable time. When they were captured, they were either sent back to their old masters or put to work on rebel fortifications. The Washington authorities had concluded to stop the exchange before there were any Negro prisoners."* The Confederacy continued to press for resumption of the exchange system, but their dispatches went unanswered.

★ GOD SAVE THE SOUTH ★

The South proposed sending home all sick and wounded Union soldiers without an equivalent exchange of Confederates.

Incredibly, this remarkable gesture went unanswered for five months during which conditions at Andersonville worsened. Diseases could not be adequately treated because an order of the Federal government made 'medicines' (contraband of war.) The Confederate administration offered to buy medicines from the United States payable in gold, cotton, or tobacco. The South even stipulated that Federal doctors could dispense all medicines so purchased solely to Union soldiers in the prison camp.

But still there was no response to this offer and the blockade of medicines remained in effect. Washington was under extreme pressure from Northern families and Northern newspapers to resume the exchanges so that captured, and especially wounded and sick Union soldiers could return home. The pressure became so intense that the Lincoln Administration was forced to publicly explain its reasons for refusing to reactivate the exchange program.

Obviously, whatever justification was given had to be approved by President Lincoln, Secretary of War Stanton, and possibly other cabinet members. General Grant was assigned the unpleasant duty of making the public announcement. Grant informed the press and public that the reason was for 'military necessity.' This threadbare justification was the Federal government's only official explanation to its impassioned citizens-and, not surprisingly, there was no mention of the South's refusal to exchange Black prisoners. On August 18th, 1864, General Grant sent a dispatch to General Butler stating: *"It is hard on our men held in Southern prisons not to exchange them, but it is humanity to those left in the ranks to fight the battles. Every man released on parole or otherwise become an active soldier against us once, either directly or indirectly. If we commence a system of exchange which liberates all prisoners taken, we will have to fight on until the whole South is exterminated."*

Eventually, many of the prisoners at Andersonville were relocated to a less crowded facility but the virulent conditions were not significantly improved. Impure water, lack of adequate sanitation, exposure to the elements and the inability to obtain medicines continued to plague the prison camp. But the drastically insufficient supply of food created the worst crisis, one that was exacerbated by the intentional destruction of crops, livestock, mills and other stocks of foodstuffs by Union General Sherman during his devastating march through Georgia.

When the war had finally ended, there was a general feeling among many Northern politicians as well as newspaper editors that retribution must be made against Confederate leaders, especially 'President Jefferson Davis' and 'General Robert E. Lee.' After Union President Abraham Lincoln's assassination, this sentiment intensified until sacrificial scapegoats had to be found. An attempt was made to connect Jefferson Davis with the conspirators indicted for Lincoln's assassination, but such a charge could not be proven.

In the month following the 'questionable' trail and hanging of the Lincoln conspirators, when the passion for revenge was still burning fiercely, CS Major Henry Wirz was brought to trial for [War Crimes] conspiracy to destroy prisoner's lives in violation of the laws and customs of war. CS President and CS General Robert E. Lee were named as co-conspirators. The trail of CS Major Wirz was pure theater and has been admirably dissected by attorney and former Army Captain Glen W. LaForce in his article: The Trail of Major Henry Wirz; A National Disgrace. LaForce makes it clear that, from the beginning, Wirz's conviction was a foregone conclusion and the sham trail that ensued was only for show. Regarding former prisoners called as witnesses, LaForce says: *"Out of the 160 witnesses called, 145 testified that they had no knowledge of Wirz ever killing anyone or treating a prisoner badly."*

"Much of the evidence favorable to Wirz was rejected, but "The commission did, however, allow the defense to prove that the Confederate guards at Andersonville received the same quality and quantity of rations as the prisoners, and that the death rate of the guards was approximately that the same as the prisoners."

A Catholic priest, Reverend Whelan, testified that he visited the prison daily for several months and found Major Wirz to be sincerely concerned about the welfare of the prisoners. Father Whelan also testified that, although he talked with multitude of prisoners every day, he never heard a single complaint of the prisoner being mistreated by Major Wirz.

After Major Wirz was convicted and sentenced to death, he was visited in his cell by three men who presented themselves as agents of an influential member of Congress. They informed Wirz that he would be pardoned and set free if he would testify that orders from the Confederate States President Jefferson Davis were responsible for the deaths of the prisoners at Andersonville. Wirz adamantly refused. Next the men repeated the offer to Wirz's attorney, Lewis Shade, and his attending priest, Reverend F. E. Boyle. The offer was again refused and Wirz was hanged.

In a letter to Jefferson Davis, Father Boyle wrote: *"I attended the Major to the scaffold, and he died in the peace of God and praying for his enemies. I know he was indeed innocent of all cruel charges on which his life was sworn away, and I was edified by that the Christian spirit in which he submitted to his persecutors."* In his article: Andersonville: A Legacy of Shame ... But Whose? Gary Walt rip states: "Ken Burns, in his companion book to the PBS television series 'The Civil War,' says this of Henry Wirz, the commander of Andersonville: *"On November 10th, 1865,*

★ GOD SAVE THE SOUTH ★

Henry Wirz, commandant of Andersonville Prison in Georgia, was hanged in the yard of the Old Capitol Prison in Washington for [War Crimes.] He pleaded he had only followed orders." Burns subliminal comparison to the well-publicized pleadings of the Nuremburg Trails should not be wasted on the reader, where 'Nazi War Criminals likewise claimed that they 'had only followed orders.' Burns insinuation that Wirz was guilty of Nazi-like 'War Crimes' only gives new life to the myth of Southern infamy at Andersonville.

This is an example of how history can be subtly by kenitized by political types like filmmaker Ken Burns. Unfortunately, via the medium of television, PBS can foist Burn's fraudulent depiction of Andersonville and major Wirz on literally thousands of viewers. Now, even public schools throughout the country use the PBS Civil War Videos to instruct students about that momentous event in American history.

But Burns half-truths are not supported by reputable historians. Regarding Henry Wirz, James M. McPherson, Princeton Professor of American History, said: *"Whether Wirz was actually guilty of anything worse that bad temper and inefficiency remains controversial today. In any case, he served as a scapegoat for the purported sins of the South. The large genre of prisoner memoirs, which lost nothing in melodramatics with passage of time, kept alive the bitterness for decades after the war. On this matter, at least the victors wrote the history, for at least five-sixths of the memoirs were written by Northerners."*

McPherson makes this assessment of the Confederate States prisons: *"Few if any historians would now content that the Confederacy would deliberately mistreated Union prisoners. Rather, they would concur with contemporary opinions-held by some Northerners as well as Southerners-that a deficiency of resources and the deterioration of the Southern economy were mainly responsible for the sufferings of Union prisoners. The South could not feed its own soldiers and civilians; how could they feed enemy prisoners?"*

In the larger Civil War prisons, both North and South, there were outbreaks of scurvy, dropsy, dysentery and diarrhea and photographs show some of the prisoners in emaciated, almost skeletal conditions. Although disease and death at all of the Civil War prisons were tragic, they were not deliberate. And statistics that both sides suffered substantial prison deaths-26,436 Confederate American soldiers died in Northern Prisons and 22,576 Federal American soldiers died in Southern prisons.

Since the South held approximately fifty thousand more prisoners, the death rate in the Northern prisons was about twelve percent whereas the death rate in Southern prisons was roughly eight percent. If this statistic were reversed a higher percentage of death in Southern prisons, Ken Burns would kenitized it by inferring that it indicates the brutal neglect of Southern prison commanders.

James Madison Page, a lieutenant with the Sixth Michigan Cavalry and former Union prisoner held at Andersonville, wanted to testify to Wirz kind treatment of prisoners but was denied the opportunity. Page later wrote a book; The True Story of Andersonville, in which he refers to Wirz's trial as *"The greatest judicial farce enacted since Oliver Cromwell instituted the commission to try and condemn Charles I."* Page portrays Major Wirz as a decent and honorable man who was thrust into an unmanageable situation; a situation that would have defeated the best of men. But Henry Wirz became the fall guy for the pent rage over the war and President Lincoln's assassination. He was martyred at the age of 42, leaving behind a wife and three daughters. September 8th, 2003.

By: Gail Jarvis.

CHAPTER FIVE

★ ★ ★

OUR AMERICAN HOLOCAUST

My name is Jackie Dolby and I have been asked to address you at this solemn yet historic occasion on behalf of Point Lookout POW Descendants Org. Point Lookout was the largest Prison during the 'War to Prevent Southern Independence.' It is in St. Mary's County MD and is situated on a very narrow peninsula, with the Chesapeake Bay on one side and the Potomac River on the other. We are the only Confederate POW descendant's organization currently. We are 13yrs old and have 1,100 members, in 41 States.

We are 1,100 people who have come together with all the records of our ancestors, letters, diaries, journals, and documents. Some members had as many as 100 members of their family imprisoned at Point Lookout. Together, we have incredible amount of documentation of the experiences of our ancestors as prisoners of war.

There were members of our family who were POWs at Point Lookout, two remain there and share a mass grave with 14,000 men, women and children who died as prisoners there. Every year we meet and hold a service in remembrance of those who suffered and died there. My son Mark is proud to be one of Lee's Miserable's, he re-enacts his POW 3rd Great Grandfather, Cpl. G. W. Clary of Coleman's Heavy Artillery, while hanging around the refreshment table, after the service, Mark had found a human bones sticking up and put off the ground. We only hope that they were not the bones of our family members.

You see this Cemetery? It is in stark contrast to that of Point Lookout. These here received a decent burial thanks to (John W. Jones, an escaped slave) and the sexton of the Cemetery. At Point Lookout, the bodies were moved to a mass grave and all the bones that they cared together up were tossed into one big hole. Children walking to school found body part and pieces of clothing along the way.

The skull was the important part as they were paid per skull. This Cemetery by comparison is a beautiful site with their graves, decorated with the flag that honestly and truly belongs to them, for they gave it definition.

They consecrated this emblem by their blood and heroic efforts. Many of the prisoners in Elmira were sent here from Point Lookout as, kind of, overflow housing.

It was so crowded at Point Lookout that one POW said, *"That if you wanted to stand up you couldn't because there was already somebody standing there and if you wanted to sit down you couldn't because there was already somebody sitting there."*

I remember the first night I spent at the re-enactment up on the New Town Battlefield. It made my blood run cold to hear those trains coming and going all night long. It reminded me of the trains full of Confederate POWs that were brought to Elmira Prison, which the inmates duded 'Helmira.'

Our family has quite an extensive background in POWs. My dad, a WWII Veteran who served in the Philippines, had a friend who survived the Baton Death March, he has no fingernails. During WWII, our Confederate POW ancestor, Cpl. George Washington Clary, had two great grandsons proudly serving in the United States Army. One was, Pvt. H. Telton Whitby, who was taken POW by the Germans. He is about 80 years old and he says there is not one day that he does not cry, for the things that he saw and suffered as a POW.

At that same time, the other great grandson, Capt. Clifford Clary in the US Medical corps was one of the first in to liberate Dachau. Uncle Cliff does not talk of his experiences during the war. But deep scars from the brutal things he experienced are a burden that he carries alone.

My mother in-law was a Jewish orphan, her family came from Germany and we may never know what happened to her family in Nazi Germany. Let me tell you it sure sets you back when you find your mother in-law's name on a Holocaust Dachau Victims list … You know it's not her, but who was this? An aunt or some relative? How many more family members ended up on such a list?

As we tell the horrible stories of the Holocaust, we say NEVER AGAIN! Nobody would say that was just the past, get over it! It is too bad that these people don't hold the same consideration for us of Southern ancestry, where 50,000 civilians, Black & White were slain by the invading Union Armies. There are those here today who could tell you of the torture and rape of their elderly family members at the hands of Sherman's Army.

What about the hundreds of thousands who died on the battlefield and the death camps of the North, like Helmira? To this American Holocaust we should also say NEVER AGAIN!

★ GOD SAVE THE SOUTH ★

The problem we have always had is that my kids are told to forget about their Southern Confederate ancestors and to get over it, were the suffering of their Jewish ancestors are to always be remembered so that this kind of thing never happens again. If it is true for one then it is true for the other, if we forget and bury the past, how do we learn from it and prevent these things from happening again?

In 1781 the sovereign States gained their freedom when they defeated lord Cornwallace at the battle of Yorktown. [King George III acknowledges the sovereignty of each State.] The South played a major role in the formation of a new government. C.S. General Robert E. Lee's father, Richard Henry lee, signed the Articles of Confederation for his State of Virginia. He also served with distinction alongside of General George Washington as Light Horse Harry Lee.

Who can forget the great Virginian Thomas Jefferson who wrote the Declaration of Independence? It was Thomas Jefferson who said *"Rebellion against tyranny was obedience to God."* His Grandson, a VMI Cadet served in the Confederate States Army, and died in the battle of New Market. The great Statesman, Patrick Henry, also had a grandson fighting in the Confederate States Army.

Francis Scott Key, who wrote the (Star Spangled Banner,) had a grandson, Frank Key Howard. He was imprisoned, by the Yankees, on the anniversary of his grandfather's writing the (Star Spangled Banner) in the same prison, Ft. McHenry, because he dared to exercise his amendment right to freedom of speech.

Not only were the Confederate soldiers' extraordinary men of valor, but they were led by honorable, religious men of principal, of the highest integrity like Generals Lee & Jackson. Following the admonition of is savor, to love your enemies, bless them that curse you, do good to them that hate you, and pray for them which despitefully use you and persecute you. That ye may be the children of your Father which is in Heaven. General Lee said: *"I have fought against the people of the North because I believed they were seeking to wrest from the South its dearest rights." But I have never seen a day when I did not pray for them."*

He also said: *"Knowing that intercessory prayer is our mightiest weapon and supreme call for Christians today, I pleadingly urge our people everywhere to pray ... Let there be prayer at sun-up, at noonday, at sundown, at midnight, all through the day. Let us pray for our children, our youth, our aged, our pastors, our homes, Let us pray for our churches. Let us pray for ourselves, that we may not lose the word, 'concern' for those who have known Jesus Christ and redeeming love, for moral forces everywhere, for our national leaders. Let prayer be our passion. Let prayer be our practice."*

There are those who would demonize rare men of character like General Lee. I would remind them of the words of Isaiah (5:20) Woe unto them that call evil good and good evil; that put darkness for light, and light for darkness; that put bitter for sweet, and sweet for bitter! During the Spotsylvania Campaign, a Confederate General was very upset with the cavalry for allowing the Union General, Phil Sheridan, to demolish a food depot: *"If I were in command of this army,* says he, *I would notify Gen. Grant that, insomuch as he had sent his cavalry to the real and destroyed our rations. I should not give his prisoners whom we hold a morsel of food, and if he wanted to save them from starvation, he would have to send rations here to them!"*

About that time Gen. Lee came up and the General repeated the whole outburst. Gen. Lee replied, *"The prisoners that we have here, General, are my prisoners; they are not Gen. Grant's prisoners and as long as I have any rations at all, I shall divide them with my prisoners."*

The compassionate Confederate POW Policy was a stark contrast to that of the Federal government. There were some Union soldiers who were held prisoners in South Carolina who were so well treated that they joined the Southern forces. While at the same time Confederate officers are being held as POW's, later called the (immortal 600,) were used as [HUMAN SHIELDS,] and penned in around the Union's artillery during the bombardment of Charleston, SC.

There was one group of Yankees who had surrendered to General Nathan Bedford Forrest, he treated them so well that they didn't feel any compunction about surrendering to him a second time. They knew he would treat them well and fairly. One Point Lookout survivor told his story to a MD newspaper some years after the war.

He was well aware of the dead line, which when crossed he would get shot. Despite the deadline, there was a knot hole in the wall, just about eye level, through which he could get a clear view of what was on the outside. He was so anxious to know what it would have looked like without his prison walls that curiosity got the better of him.

When the guard was not looking he ran and crossed the deadline and took a peek out that knot hole and ran back before the guard could catch him. He said that was the last time he ever desired to see outside the prison, for what he saw outside the walls was all too telling of what his Yankee brethren had in store for them. What he saw was, *"Acres and acres of coffins one stacked on top of the other."* Letters and diaries are full of testimonies of torture, murder and starvation, which all played their part in filling those acres and acres of coffins ... to the tune of 14,000 dead at Point Lookout in only 18 months.

★ GOD SAVE THE SOUTH ★

The Federal bullet that took the lives of many Confederate POW's is the attitude that is reflected in the <u>U.S. House Resolution 97. It proposed taking vengeance on Confederate Prisoners of War into their own hands, and making it legal to systematically starve (exterminate) POW's</u> a major force behind this was Senator Lane of Indiana and in fact it became known as the **[Lane Resolution]** to the 38th Congress. He wanted vengeance on the South, saying on the floor of Congress,

"I would make the war still bloodier, I would make every rocky ravine in Southern Georgia and Alabama run red with the blood of traitors, and drive them into the Gulf Stream, to the last rebel there, before I would recognize their independence."

<u>This was also especially supported by Edwin Stanton, of United States Secretary of War, who was well aware of the Geneva Convention of 1863, international laws and the United States Army's own lieber Code, all of which denounces and condemns the abuse and mistreatment and certainly the starvation of prisoners of war.</u>

Now tell me, where have you heard of such a thing outside of Nazi Germany? What kind of people, what kind of nation would consider making such a law and implement such policies? It truly makes me cringe to think that Jesus said, *"In as much as ye have done it unto the least of these my brethren, ye have done it unto me also."* Evil flourishes when good people do nothing, perhaps like Elmira citizens who paid 15cents, just to go up on a tower to look at the suffering prisoners like in a circus or side show. And how much could they really do consider the Federal POW policy is in effect?

What were these people think about, during that brutal winter, when they saw the prisoners standing in deep snow with only the rags around their frozen and swollen feet to answering the mourning roll calls? Is it any wonder that the number of sick and dead had raised sharply, when these prisoners, fighting diseases, the filth and starvation, could not the weather be any of the bitter or cold of a New York winter, when temperatures dropped to 18 below zero!

I can't tell you how many times last winter I thought about these prisoners as I was shoveling out my driveway. I asked myself how in the world could anybody live out in this weather? How could a human being survive in such cold? I could hardly stand it and I had my winter clothing on.

One Elmira prisoner from Virginia wrote the compound was, *"an excellent summer prison for the Southern soldiers, but an excellent place for them to find their graves in the winter."*

★ JOHN THOMAS NALL ★

Just as people have had great success in rewriting American History, they are trying to re-write history and say the Holocaust didn't happen. What will people believe after another 100 years of the work of Revisionist Historians? We are criticized for trying to preserve our Confederate symbols, our heroes, and our culture. We will not give into our detractors a posthumous victory by having us to forget our past, our people and our heritage.

At the dedication of the United States Holocaust Memorial Museum in Washington, DC, Elie Wiesel said: *"To forget would mean to kill the victims a second time. We could not prevent their first deaths: We must not allow them to be killed again."* Today we are here to remember those who died at Elmira & those who died in route in the Shohola train wreck. In preparing this talk, I asked myself, what would these Confederate soldiers want you to know?

Well? I thought they would want you to know who they were and what they were fighting for and lastly, how they ended up in this Cemetery, so far from home. The Confederate soldier personified the best qualities of America. I could stop right there, but I won't because there seems to be a lot of miss information about the Confederate soldier, whose good name is being viciously attacked. There seems to be an all-out war on the Confederate soldier, his flag, statues, memorials, songs, and Southern Couture and values.

[*"The first step in liquidating a people is to erase its memory. And then a nation that's ignorant of its past is ripe for deception and manipulation."*]

Our education systems are a fine example of this deception & manipulation, as they do not teach the true history of the South, neither does it teach the true history of the Northern States. I think it would be pleasing to these buried here to set the record straight. Each grave here represents the life of an individual that mattered to someone just as much as you or I, with a home and a family and dreams of a better future.

They were fathers, husbands, sons, brothers, uncles, and grandfathers to somebody. They were farmers, merchants, tailors, and teachers, ministers, & students, whose lives were cut short, they were short REBELS, they were not seeking to destroy the government of the United States, and quite on the contrary, they were law abiding citizens who treasured their Constitutional government, which they tried to preserve for their posterity.

They were good people who struggled to defend their families and homes with honor, in the face of overwhelming numbers of marauding savages who raped, torched and murdered the civilian population into submission to gain a victory through inhuman atrocities, a victory that the Yankee thugs could not win on the field of battle. On the battlefield, the Confederate soldier, conducted himself with honor and was unmatched even when vastly our numbered. They were the greatest army to ever shake a Continent. Why even U.S. General Grant had to admit that *"One Confederate soldier was as good as three of his."* That is one of the reasons he stopped the prisoner exchange, it wasn't a good deal for him. It was this action that caused the prison camps, North and South to swell in size.

The Confederate soldier fought, bled, and died, that the Government of the People. By the People and for the People's might be preserved for their posterity, that our future generations might enjoy the blessings of liberty as set forth in the Constitutional government, established by our founding fathers. They were citizens soldiers like their fathers before them, during the American Revolution. Among those in the Confederate forces were, the sons and grandsons of great patriots like Thomas Jefferson, Patrick Henry and the famous, Light Horse Harry Lee.

Those left back at Point Lookout, would spend the winter trying to live on sheets of ice as it was only four feet above sea level and as the water washed up on the shores it would freeze solid. The day after Christmas, President Lincoln & Sec. Of War Stanton, came down to check into the operations of their death camp at Point Lookout, two weeks later our family's Pvt. James Huskey of Coleman's Heavy Arty, would be dead from starvation and exposure. Major Buttler who oversaw the prison wrote in a letter to his wife how (he had saved the Federal government, one million dollars by withholding provisions from the prisoners.)

To be a doctor is considered an honorable profession and they even take a [Hippocratic Oath,] which says, first to do no harm … yet is was the Surgeon at Elmira Prison who boasted that he 'killed more Reb's than any soldier at the front.' There are two forces at work in this life, good and evil. And as we can see, evil has great power because it has no shame. Righteousness has rules and feels shame if those rules are broken. The POW Camps were torn down immediately after the war, to hide their crimes lest their national consciousness be pricked and the nation feels shame for what they have done here.

At Elmira, an eyewitness seen:

"I speak in all reverence when I say that I do not believe such a spectacle was seen before on earth … On they came, a ghastly tide, with skeleton bones and lusterless eyes".

My Uncle Cliff might have said the same thing when they liberated Dachau. For me this is not something that I have just looked up on the internet, I make a point of interviewing all the elderly people I meet in the South. I tape them, and video those telling of the horrendous things their families suffered during [The War to Prevent Southern Independence.]

A ninety-six-year-old Mrs. Clara Hartzel of Emporia, Virginia, told me about her grandfather who came home on his hands and knees, his hair and beard was long, and louse ridden, he was so emaciate that his family did not recognize him when he came crawling into the front door licking the floor for crumbs as he crawled. Time and time again I hear of stories of the unrecognizable skeletons of men returning from the Northern Prisons.

I have over fifty Confederate ancestors and I am very proud of, just as I am proud of those buried here in Woodlawn National Cemetery, every single one of them is a hero. And will be, as long as we remember who they were and for what they fought for. They were true to their oath to the Confederate States, their home and families and God, even under the most desperate and trying of circumstances. People have said to me, *"your ancestors were Confederates; they were a bunch of losers."* To them I would say, *"it isn't over till it is over and that doesn't always happen in this life".* These people might be surprised to see who the real winners are. The real winners will be those who conducted themselves with honor and integrity, regardless of circumstances. Though they did not achieve a temporal victory, theirs is an eternal triumph.

One of the most profound Confederate Symbols is the Great Seal of the Confederacy, with George Washington riding on horseback and with the words, **(Deo Vindice).** Meaning that **(The Lord Vindicates),** and He will, and it will be, in His own time, and His own way.

I want to thank all of you for joining us here today that these soldiers might not die a second time, by being forgotten, but that these gallant soldiers might live in our hearts and minds from this day forward.

By: Jackie Dolby

Due to the constraints of time, this speech was not delivered. Woodlawn National Cemetery, Elmira, NY. USA the First Annual Confederate Memorial Day Service. May 4th 2003. The Dolby's Confederacy 76 Stearns Dr. Churchville NY 14428.

DEMOCRACY VERSUS REPUBLIC: DEFINITION ONE

Democracy:

A government of the masses. Authority derived through mass meeting or any other form of 'direct' expression. Results in mobocracy. Attitude toward property is communistic-negating property rights. Attitude toward law is that the will of the majority shall regulate. Whether it be based upon deliberation or governed by passion, prejudice, and impulse, without restraint or regard to consequences. Results in demagogism license, agitation, discontent, anarchy. Democracy is the 'direct' rule of the people and has been repeatedly tried without success.

A certain Professor Alexander Fraser Tytler, nearly two centuries ago, had said this to say about Democracy: *"A Democracy cannot exist as a permanent form of government. It can only exist until the voters discover they can vote themselves largess out of the public treasury. From that moment on the majority always votes for the candidate promising the most benefits from the public treasury with the results that Democracy always collapses over a loose fiscal policy, always to be followed by a Dictatorship."*

A Democracy is majority rule is destructive of liberty because there is no law to prevent the majority from trampling on individual rights. Whatever the majority says goes! A lynch mob is an example of pure democracy in action. There is only one dissenting vote, and that is cast by the person at the end of the rope.

Republic:

Authority is derived through the election by the people of public officials best fitted to represent them. Attitude toward property is respect for laws and individual rights, and sensible economic procedure. Attitude toward law is the administration of justice in accord with fixed principles and established evidence, with a strict regard to consequences.

A greater number of citizens and extent of territory may be brought within its compass. Avoids the dangerous extreme of either tyranny or mobocracy. Results in statesmanship, liberty, reason, justice, contentment, and progress. Is the 'standard form' of government throughout the world.

A republic is a form of government <u>under a Constitution</u> which provides for the election of:

1. An executive and,
2. A legislative body, who working together in a representative capacity, have all the power of appointment, all power of legislation all power to raise revenue and appropriate expenditures, and are required to create.
3. A judiciary to pass upon the justice and legality of their governmental acts and to recognize.
4. Certain inherent individual rights.

Take away any one or more of those four elements and you are drifting into an autocracy. Add one or more to those four elements and you are drifting into a democracy. Our Constitutional fathers are familiar with the strength and weakness of both autocracy and democracy, with fixed principles definitely in mind, defined a representative Republican form of government.

They 'made a very marked distinction between a republic and a democracy and said repeatedly and emphatically that they had founded a Republic.' A **Republic** is a government of law under a Constitution. The Constitution holds the government in check and prevents the majority (acting through their government) from violating the rights of the individual.

Under this system of government, a lynch mob is illegal. The suspected criminal cannot be denied his right to a fair trial even if much of the citizenry demands otherwise.

Difference between a Democracy and a Republic, in brief:

Democracy:

    A: A government by the people; especially [Rule of the Majority.]
    B: A government in which the supreme power is vested in the people and exercised by them directly or indirectly through a system of representation usually involving periodically held free elections.

Attitude toward the law is that the will of the majority shall regulate, whether it be based upon deliberation or governed by passion, prejudice, and impulse, without restraint or regard to consequences.

Republic:

    A: A government having a Chief of States who is not a Monarch and who in modern times is usually a President. A political unit (as a Nation) having such a form of government.
    B: A government in which supreme power resides in a body of Citizens entitled to vote and is exercised by elected officers and representatives responsible to them and governing to law.

Democracy and Republic are often taken as one of the same thing, but there is a fundamental difference. Whilst in both cases the government is elected by the people, in a Democracy the majority rules according to their whims, whilst in the Republic, the government rules according to the law. This is framed in the Constitution to limit the power of government and ensuring some rights and protection to the minorities and individuals.

The difference between a Republic and a Righteous Republic is that in the Republic, the government rules according to the law that was set by men, in the Righteous Republic, the law is the **'Law of God.'** Only in the Righteous Republic it can truly be said *"One Nation under God"* for it is governed under the Commandments of the only **'One True God'** and there is no pluralism of religions.

[Autocracy] declares the divine right of Kings; its authority cannot be questioned; its powers are arbitrarily or unjustly administered.

[Mobocracy] 1. Political control by a mob. 2. The mass of common peoples as the source of political control. This succinct definition of what is a Democracy and what is a Republic was produced by the U.S. Army in the year of 1928. These definitions have been quietly withdrawn since, soon after.

AN IMPORTANT DISTINCTION: DEMOCRACY VERSES REPUBLIC DEFINITION TWO

It is important to keep in mind the difference between a Democracy and a Republic, as dissimilar forms of government. Understanding the difference is essential to comprehension of the fundamentals involved. It should be noted, in passing, that use of the World Democracy as the meaning merely the popular type of government-that is, featuring genuinely free elections by the people periodically-is not helpful in discussing, as here, the difference between alternative and dissimilar forms of a popular government:

A Democracy verses a Republic, this double meaning of a Democracy-a popular-type of government in general, as well as a specific form of popular government-needs to be made clear in any discussion, or writing. Regarding this subject, for the sake of sound understanding.

These two forms of government: Democracy and Republic are not only dissimilar but antithetical, reflecting the sharp contrast between (A) the majority unlimited, in a Democracy, lacking any legal safeguard of the [Rights of Individual] and the [Minority,] and (B) the [Majority Limited,] in a Republic under a written Constitution safeguarding the [Rights of the

Individual] and the [Minority]; as we shall see.

JOHN THOMAS NALL

A Democracy:

The chief characteristic and distinguishing feature of a Democracy is: Rule by omnipotent majority. In a Democracy, the individual, and any group of individuals composing any minority, have no protection against the unlimited power of the majority. It is a case of [Majority-over-Man.]

This is true whether it be a Direct Democracy, or a Representative Democracy. In the direct type, applicable only to several people as in the little city-States of Greece, or in a New England town-meeting, all of the electorate assembles to debate and decide all government questions, and all decisions are reached by a Majority Vote (of at least half-plus-one.) Decisions of the Majority in New England town-meeting are of course subject to the Constitutions of the States and of the United States which will protect the Individual's Rights; so, in this case, the Majority is not omnipotent and such a town-meeting is, therefore, not an example of a true Direct Democracy.

Under a Representative Democracy is like Britain's Parliamentary form of government, the people will elect Representatives to the National Legislature-the Elective Body there being the House of Commons-and it functions by a similar vote of at least half-plus one in the making of all Legislative Decisions. Under a Representative Democracy like Britain's Parliamentary form of government, the people elect representatives to the National Legislature-the elective body there being the House of Commons-and it functions by a similar vote of at least half-plus-one in making all Legislative Decisions.

In both the direst type and the Representative type of Democracy, the Majority is absolute and unlimited; its decisions are unappealable under the legal system established to give effect to this form of government. This opens the door to unlimited tyranny-by-Majority. This was what the framers of the United States Constitution meant in 1787, in the debates of the Federal (Framing) Convention, when they condemned the 'Excesses of Democracy' and abuses under any Democracy of Unalienable Rights of the individual by the Majority. Examples were provided in the immediate post-1776 years by the Legislatures of some of the States.

In the reaction against an earlier Royal tyranny, this had been exercised through oppressions by Royal Governors and judged of the new States governments, while the Legislatures acted as if they were virtually omnipotent. There were no effective States Constitutions to limit the Legislatures because most State governments were operation under mere acts of their Respective Legislatures which were mislabeled 'Constitutions.' Neither the governors nor the Courts of the offending States were able to exercise any substantial and effective restraining influence upon the Legislatures in defense of the individual's unalienable right, when violated by the Legislative infringements.

(Connecticut and Rhode Island continued under their Old Charters for many of years. It was not until 1780 that the first genuine Republic through Constitutionally limited government was adopted by Massachusetts- next was New Hampshire in 1784 and the other States later. It was in this connection that Jefferson, in his 'notes on the State of Virginia' had written in 1781-1782, protected against such excesses by the Virginia in the years following the Declaration of Independence, saying: *"An elective despotism was not the government we fought for ..."* (Emphasis Jefferson's.) He also denounced the despotic concentration of power in the Virginia Legislature, under the so-called 'Constitution'-in reality a mere act of that body:

"All the powers of government, Legislative, Executive, Judiciary, results to the Legislative body. The concentrating these in the same hands are precisely the definition of 'Despotic Government.' It will be no alleviation that these powers will be exercised by a plurality of hands, and not by a single one. 173 despots would surely be as oppressive as one. Let those who doubt it turn their eyes on the Republic of Venice."

This topic-the danger to the people's liberties due to the turbulence of Democracies and omnipotent, Legislative Majority-is discussed in the Federalist, for example in numbers <u>10</u> and <u>48</u> by Madison (In the latter noting of Jefferson's above quoted comments.) The framing Convention's records prove that by decrying the 'excesses of Democracy' the Framers were, of course, not opposing popular type of government for the United States; Their whole aim and effort was to create a sound system of this type.

To contend to the contrary is to falsify history. Such a falsification not only maligns the high purpose and good character of the framers but belittles the spirit of the truly free man in America. The people at large of that period-who happily accepted and lived with gratification under the Constitution as their own fundamental law and under the Republic which it created, especially because they felt confident for the first time of the security of their Liberties thereby protected against abuse by all possible violators, including the Majority momentarily control of government. The truth is that the Framers, by their protests the 'Excesses of Democracy,' were merely making clear their sound reasons for preferring a Republic as the proper form of government.

They well knew, considering history, that nothing but a (Republic can provide the best safeguards. In truth in the long run the only affective safeguards (if enforced in practice.) For these people's liberties which are inescapably victimized by Democracy's form and system of unlimited government-over-man featuring the majority omnipotent. They also knew that the American people (U.S. Citizens) would not consent to any form of government but that of a Republic.

It is of special interest to note that Jefferson, who had been in Paris as the U.S. Minister for several years, wrote to Madison from there in March of 1789 that:

"The tyranny of the Legislatures is the most formidable dread at present and will be for long years. That of the executive will come its turn, but it will be at a remote period." (Text per original) Somewhat earlier, Madison had written to Jefferson about the violation of the Bill of Rights by the State Legislatures, stating: *"Repeated violations of those parchment barriers have been committed by overbearing Majorities in every State, In Virginia I have seen the Bill of Rights violated in every instance where it has been opposed to a popular current."*

It is correct to say that in any Democracy either a Direct or Representative Type-as a form of government, there can be no legal system protects the individual or the Minority (any or all Minorities) against unlimited tyranny by the Majority. The undependable sense of self-restraint of the persons of making up the Majority at any times offers, of course, no protection whatever. Such a form of government is characterized by the Majority omnipotent and unlimited. This is true, for example, of the Representative Democracy of Great Britain.

Because unlimited government power is possessed by the House of Lords, under the Act of Parliament of 1949-indeed, it has power to abolish anything and everything governmental in Great Britain. For a period of some centuries ago, some English Judges did argue that their decisions could restrain Parliament; but this theory had to be abandoned because it was founded to be untenable in the light of sound political theory and governmental realities in a Representative Democracy. Under this form of government, neither the Courts nor not any other part of the government can effectively challenge, much less block, any action by the Majority in the Legislative Body, no matter how arbitrary, tyrannous, or totalitarian they might become in practice. The Parliamentary system of Great Britain is a perfect example of Representative Democracy and of the potential tyranny inherent in its system of unlimited rule by omnipotent Majority.

This pertains only to the potential, to the theory, involved; government practices there are irrelevant to this discussion. Madison's observations in the Federalist Number <u>10</u> would be noteworthy at this point, because they highlighted a grave error that was made through the centuries in regarding Democracy as a form of government. He commented as follows:

"Theoretic politicians, who have patronized this species of government, have erroneously supposed, that by reducing mankind to a perfect equality in their political rights, they would, at the same time, be perfectly equalized and assimilated in their possessions, their opinions, and their passions." Democracy, as a form of government, is utterly repugnant to-is

the very antithesis of-the traditional American (U.S.) system: That a Republic, and its underlying philosophy, as expressed in essence in the Declaration of Independence with the primary emphasis upon the people's forming their own government so as to permit them to possess only 'just powers' (Limited Powers) in order to make and keep secure the God-Given, Unalienable Rights of each and every individual and therefore of all groups of individuals.

A REPUBLIC:

A Republic, on the other hand, has a very different purpose and an entirely different form, or system, of government. Its purpose is to control the majority strictly, as well as all others among the people, primarily to protect the individual's and therefore for the protection for the rights of the minority, of all minorities, and the liberties of the people in general. The definition of a Republic is: A Constitutionally Limited government of the Representative type, created by a written Constitution-adopted by the people and changeable (from its original meaning) by them only its Amendment-with its powers divided between three separate branches: Executive, Legislative and Judicial.

Here the term 'The People' means, of course, the electorate. The people adopted the Constitution as their fundamental law by utilizing a Constitutional Convention that's especially chosen by them for this express and sole purpose-to frame it for consideration and approval by them either Directly or by their Representatives in a Ratifying Convention, similarly chosen.

Such a Constitutional Convention, for either framing or Ratification, is one of America's (U.S.) greatest contributions, if not her greatest contribution, to the mechanics of government-of-self government through a Constitutionally limited government, comparable in importance to America's (U.S.) greatest contribution to the science of government:

The formation and adoption by the sovereign people, of a written Constitution as the basis for self-government. One of the earliest, if not the first, specific discussions of this new American (U.S.) development (A Constitutional Convention) in the historical records as an entry in June 1775, in John Adams 'Autobiography' commenting on the framing by a Convention and Ratification by the people as follows:

"By Conventions of Representatives, freely, fairly, and proportionately chosen … The Convention may send out their project of a Constitution, to the people in their several towns, Counties, or Districts and the people may make the acceptance of their own act."

★ JOHN THOMAS NALL ★

Yet the first proposal in 1778 of a Constitution for Massachusetts was rejected for the reason, in part, as stated in the 'Essex Result' (the result, or report, of the Convention of towns of Essex County,) that it had been framed and proposed not by a specially chosen Convention but by members of the Legislature who were involved in the General Legislative Duties, including those pertaining to the [Conduct of the War.]

The first genuine and soundly founded Republic in all of history was the one created by the first genuine Constitution, which was adopted by the people of Massachusetts in 1780, after being framed for their Confederation by a specially chosen Constitutional Convention. (As previously noted, the so-called 'Constitutions' adopted by some of the States in 1776 were mere acts of Legislatures not genuine Constitutions.) That Constitutional Convention of Massachusetts was the first successful one ever held in the world; although New Hampshire had an earlier one held unsuccessfully. It took several years and several successive Conventions to produce the New Hampshire Constitution of 1784.

Next, in the years of 1787 to 1788, the United States Constitution was framed by the Federal Convention for the people's Confederation and then ratified by the people of the several States through a Ratifying Convention in each State specially chosen by them for this sole purpose. Thereafter, the other States gradually followed in general of the Massachusetts pattern of in the Constitutional making in adoption for the genuine Constitutions; But there was a delay of a number of years in this regard as to some of them, several decades as to a few.

This system of Constitution-making, for the purpose of establishing a Constitutionally Limited Government, is designed to put into practice the Principle of the Declaration of Independence: That the people forms their governments and grants to them only 'Just Powers,' in order primarily to secure (to make and keep secured their God-Given, Unalienable Rights. The American philosophy and system of government thus bar equally the 'Snob-Rule of a government elite and the 'mob-Rule' of an Omnipotent Majority.

This is designed, above all else, to preclude the existence in the United States of America of any governmental power capable of being misused so as to violate the (Individual's Rights)-to endanger the (People's Liberties.) Regarding the Republican form of Government (that of a Republic), Madison made an observation in Federalist Papers which merits quoting here-As follows:

As there is a degree of depravity in Mankind which requires a certain degree of circumspection and distrust: So, there are other qualities in Human Nature, which justify a certain portion of esteem and confidence. Republican government (that of a Republic) presupposes the existence of these qualities in a higher degree than any other form. Were the pictures which have been drawn by the political jealousy of some among us, faithful likenesses of the Human Character, the inference would be that there is not sufficient virtue among men for self-government:

"And that nothing less than the "Chains of Despotism" can restrain them from destroying and devouring one another." (Emphasis Added.)

It is noteworthy here that the above discussion, though brief, is sufficient to indicate the reasons why the label 'Republic' has been misapplied in other Countries to other and other and different forms of Government throughout history. It has been greatly misunderstood and widely misused-for example as long ago as the time of Plato, when he wrote his celebrated volume' (The Republic); in which he did not discuss anything governmental even remotely resembling-having essential Characteristics of-a genuine Republic.

Frequent references is to be found, in the writings of the period of the Framing of the Constitution for instance, to 'The Ancient Republics,' but in any such connection the term was used loosely-by way of contrast to a Monarchy or to a Direct Democracy-often using the term in the sense merely of a system of Rule-By-Law featuring Representative Government; As indicated, for example, by John Adams in his 'thoughts on government' and by Madison in the Federalist Numbers 10 and 39. But this is an incomplete definition because it can include a Representative Democracy, lacking a written Constitution limiting the Majority.

From: The American ideal of 1776-The Twelve Basic American Principles.

★ ★ ★

A PRINCIPLE OF THE TRADITIONAL AMERICAN PHILOSOPHY

**Unalienable Rights/From God
" ... endowed by their Creator with certain
<u>Unalienable rights</u> ..."
<u>(Declaration of Independence)</u>**

The Principle

(One) The traditional American philosophy teaches that Man, The Individual, is endowed at birth with (rights) which are unalienable because it was and is given by his Creator.

The Only Moral Basis

(Two) This governmental philosophy is uniquely American. The concept of (Man's Rights) being unalienable is based solely upon the belief in their Divine origin. Lacking this belief, there is no moral basis for any claim that they are unalienable or for any claim to the great benefits flowing from this concept. (God-given-Rights) are sometimes called (Natural Rights)-those possessed by Man under the (Laws of Nature), <u>meaning under the laws of God's creation and therefore by the gift of God.</u> *Man has no power to alienate*-to dispose of, by surrender, barter or gift-his (God-given-Rights), according to the American philosophy. This is the meaning of being 'unalienable'.

One underlying consideration is that for every such right there is a correlative, inseparable duty-for every aspect of freedom there is a corresponding responsibility: so that it is always a (Right-Duty) and (Freedom-Responsibility), or (Liberty-Responsibility). **There is a duty, or responsibility, to God as the giver of these unalienable rights:**

A moral duty-to keep secure and use soundly these gifts, with due respect for the (Equal Rights) of others and for the (Rights of Posterity) to <u>their just heritage of liberty.</u> Since the moral duty cannot be surrendered, bartered, given away, abandoned, delegated or otherwise alienated, so is the 'Inseparable Right' likewise unalienable. This concept of rights of being unalienable is thus dependent upon the belief in God as the giver. This indicates the basis and the soundness of 'Jefferson's statement in a (1796 letter to John Adams):

"If ever the morals of a people could be made the basis of their own government, it is our case …"

Right, Reason, and Capacity to be Self-governing

(Three) For the security and enjoyment **by Man of his divinely created rights**, it follows implicitly that Man is endowed by his Creator not only the right to be self-governing but also with the capacity to reason and, therefore, with the capacity to be self-governing. This is implicit in the philosophy proclaimed in the **<u>Declaration of Independence.</u>** Otherwise, Man's unalienable rights would be of little or no use or benefit to him. Faith in Man-in his capacity to be self-governing-is thus related to faith in God as his Creator, as the giver of these unalienable rights and this capacity.

Rights-As Prohibitions against Government

(Four) Certain specific rights of **<u>The Individual</u>** are protected in the original **Constitution,** but this is by way of statements 'in reverse'-by way of express prohibitions against government. The word 'right' does not appear in the original instrument. This is because it was designed to express the grant by the people of specific, limited powers to the central government-created by them through this basic law-as well as certain specific limitations on its powers, and on the preexisting powers of the State governments, expressed as prohibitions of things forbidden. Every provision in it pertains to power.

The Constitution's first eight **(Bill of Rights)** amendments list certain rights of the Individual and prohibit the doing of certain things by the central, or Federal, government which, if done, would violate these rights. These amendments were intended by their Framers and Adopters merely to make express a few of the already-existing, implied prohibitions against the Federal government only supplementing the prohibitions previously specifies expressly in the original Constitution and supplementing and conforming its general, over-all, implied, prohibitions as to all things concerning which it withheld power from this government. Merely conforming expressly some of the already-existing, implied prohibitions, these amendments did not create any new ones.

They are, therefore, more properly referred to as a partial list of limitations-or a partial Bill of Prohibitions-as was indicated by Hamilton in the Federalist Number <u>84.</u> This hinges upon the uniquely American concepts stated in the **Declaration of Independence**: that Men, created of God, in turn create their governments and grant to them only 'just' (Limited Powers)-primarily to make and keep secure their (God-given), unalienable rights, in part, the right to Life, Liberty and the pursuit of Happiness. As Hamilton stated, under the American philosophy and system of constitutionally limited government, *"<u>the people surrender nothing;</u> instead, they merely delegate to government-to public servants as public trustees-limited powers and therefore,* he added, *"they have no need of particular reservations"* (in a Bill of Rights). This is the basic reason why the Framing Convention omitted from the Constitution anything in a separate Bill of Rights, as being unnecessary.

An Endless List of Rights

(Five) To attempt to name all of these rights-starting with 'Life, Liberty and the pursuit of Happiness' mentioned in the **Declaration of Independence**-would be to start an endless list which would add up to the whole of Man's Freedom (Freedom from Government-over-Man). They would add up to the entirety of individual Liberty (Liberty against Government-over-Man). Innumerable rights of The Individual are embraced **<u>in the Ninth Amendment, which states: "The enumeration in the Constitution of certain rights shall not be construed to deny or disparage others retained by the people".</u>**

(Here 'Constitution' includes the amendments.) Some idea how vast the list would be is indicated by just one general freedom which leads into almost all Free Man's activities of daily living throughout life: Freedom of Choice. This term stands for the right to do-and equally not to do-this or that, as conscience, whim or judgment, taste, or desire, of The Individual may prompt from moment to moment, day by day, for as long as life lasts; of course, with due regard for the equal rights of others and for the just laws expressive of the above-mentioned 'just powers' of government design to help safeguard the equal rights of all individuals. Spelled out in detail, this single freedom-freedom of choice-is almost all-embracing.

Right to Be Let Alone

(Six) In one sense, such freedom to choose involves Man's right to be let alone, which is possessed by The Individual in keeping with the **Declaration of Independence** as against government; enjoyment of his unalienable rights, while respecting the equal rights of others and just laws (as defined in Paragraph five above). This right to be let alone is the most comprehensive of rights and the right of most prized by civilized Men. This right is, of course, also possessed as against all other Individuals, all obligated to act strictly within the limits of their own rights. Consequently any infringement of any Individual's right is precluded.

Rights Inviolable by Government or by Others

(Seven) Neither government nor any Individuals-acting singly, or in groups, or in organizations-could possibly possess any 'just powers' (to use again the significant term of the Declaration) to violate any Individual's God-given, unalienable rights or the supporting rights. No government can abolish or destroy-nor can it rightfully, or constitutionally, violate-Man's God given rights. Government cannot justly interfere with Man's deserved enjoyment of any of these rights. No public official, nor all such officials combined, could possibly have any such power morally.

Governments can, to be sure, unjustly, and unconstitutionally interfere by force with the deserved enjoyment of Man's unalienable rights. It is, however, completely powerless to abolish or destroy them. It is in defense of these rights of all Individuals, in last analysis, that the self-governing people-acting in accordance with, and in support of, the Constitution-oppose any and all violators, whether public officials or usurpers, or others (par. Nine below.)

Each Individual Consent to Some Limitations

(Eight) In creating governments as their tools, or instruments, and equally in continuing to maintain them-for the purpose primarily of making and keeping their unalienable rights-all Individuals composing the self-governing people impliedly and in effect consent to some degree of Limitation of their freedom to exercise some of their rights. This does not involve the surrender, or the alienation, of any of these rights but only the partial, conditional and limited relinquishment of freedom to exercise a few of them and solely for the purpose of insuring the greater security and enjoyment of all of them: and, moreover, such relinquishment is always upon condition that public officials, as public servants and trustees, faithfully use the limited powers delegated to government strictly in keeping with their prescribed limits and with this limited purpose at all times. It was in this sense that George Washington, as President of the Framing Convention in September 1787, wrote to the Congress of the Confederation-in transmitting to it, for consideration, the draft of the proposed Constitution: **" … Individuals entering into society must give up a share of liberty to preserve the rest".** Here he meant merely conditional relinquishment of liberty of action in the exercise of certain aspects of unalienable rights-not the surrender of rights, which would be impossible because a nullity, a void act.

An Offender's just Punishment

(Nine) Whenever Man violates either the equal rights of others of the above-mentioned just laws, he thereby forfeits his immunity in this regard; by his misconduct, he destroys the moral and legal basis for his immunity and opens the door to just reprisal against himself, by government. This means that any person, as such offender, may justly be punished by the people's proper instrumentality-the government, including the courts-under a sound system of equal justice under equal laws; that is, under Rule-by-Law (basically the people's fundamental law, the Constitution.) Such punishment is justified morally because of the duty of all individuals-in keeping with Individual Liberty-Responsibility-to cooperate, through their instrumentality, government, for the mutual protection of the unalienable rights of all Individuals.

The offender is also justly answerable to the aggrieved Individual, acting properly through duly established machinery of government, including courts, designed for the protection of equal rights of all Individuals. It is the offender's breach of the duty aspect of Individual Liberty-Responsibility which makes just, proper, and necessary government's punitive action and deprives him of any moral basis for protest. By such breach he forfeits his moral claim to the inviolability of his rights and makes himself vulnerable to reprisal by the people, through government, in defense of their own unalienable rights. By this lack of self-discipline required by that duty, he invites and makes necessary his being disciplined by government.

The Conclusion

(Ten) *Man's unalienable rights are sacred for the same reason that they are unalienable-because of their Divine origin, according to the traditional philosophy.*

Quotes from the American Ideal of 1776 supporting this Principle. For more information visit http://lexrex.com/enlightened/AmericanIdeal/yardstick/pr3.html

SIC SEMPER TYRANNIS

Freedom implies to one's sovereignty, and sovereignty implies to one's Individual Rights. And to bear arms is to maintain your rights as an individual. Including protecting your own life as well as your loved ones. To protect your property and even a possible invasion by an outside foreign nation. Most importantly to defend against tyranny from your government that may become corrupted. Freedom is not being forced on your knees and calling the politicians 'Master'.

Freedom is not allowing the politicians to declare in what way you can defend your home, unless they somehow believe that your land belongs to the Government. Freedom is not learning that the government declares your children in belonging to the State, instead of the parents. Freedom is not learning as what value your life is once they have removed your weapons of defense. Freedom is not allowing anyone to tell you what you should think, and how you should submit to their will.

Freedom is not allowing a tyrant to lead your people to the slaughterhouse. Freedom is not allowing the criminals to look upon you as if you are prey. Freedom does not believe that know body would not dare to rob you of your personal rights. Liberty cannot be given to you by any-known-Man, but, most assuredly those who are dishonorable, with evil hearts will rob and murder you for it! An honorable citizen would obey the law, yet an disobedient citizen will not. So, why should the lawless been given the reign over the just and honorable people? Unless someone desires to rule over the respectful citizens. Thus, freedom is gone and who shall they bow down too and call them 'Master'?

The voice of only one may be faint and yet not heard. But, the voices of the people are like the sound of thunder and power as it pours out fear to their enemies. The sovereignty of only one voice is the sound of the clear water running down a stream. Yet, the sovereignty of a million voices is the sound of a waterfall that's crashing down with such uncontrollable force, and determination. Freedom is the freewill that will not be denied in staying forever free! Putting your trust in any government is like trusting a criminal with your personal finances and giving him the keys to your home and believing in his promises that he would never break into your house. <u>Such a foolish thought, such foolish people</u>!

★ ★ ★

WHAT YOU DIDN'T KNOW ABOUT ISREAL

1. Nationhood and Jerusalem, Israel became a nation in 1312 BCE-BC, Two thousand years before the rise of Islam.
2. Arab refugees in Israel began identifying themselves as part of a Palestinian people in 1967, two decades after the establishment of the modern State of Israel.
3. Since the Jewish conquest in 1272 BCE-BC, the Jews have had dominion over the land for one thousand years with a continuous presence in the land for the past 3,300 years.
4. The only Arab dominion since the conquest in 635 CE-AD lasted no more than 22 years.
5. For over 3,300 years, Jerusalem has been the Capital Jerusalem and has never been the Capital of any Arab or Muslim entity. Even when the Jordanians occupied Jerusalem, they never sought to make it their Capital, and the Arab leaders did not come to visit it.
6. King David founded the city of Jerusalem. Mohammed never came to the City of Jerusalem.
7. Jerusalem is mentioned over 700 times in the Tanach, the Jewish Holy Scriptures. Jerusalem is not mentioned not once in the Koran.
8. Jews pray facing Jerusalem. Muslims pray with their backs toward Jerusalem.
9. Arab and Jewish Refugees: In 1948 the Arab refugees were encourage to leave Israel by Arab leaders promising to purge the land of the Jews. Sixty-eight percent left without ever seeing an Israeli soldier.
10. The Jewish refugees were forced to flee from Arab lands due to the Arabs brutality, persecution and pogroms.
11. The number of Arab refugees who left Israel in 1948 is estimated to be around 630,000. The number of Jewish refugees from Arab lands is estimated to be the same.
12. Arab refugees were intentionally not absorbed or integrated into the Arab lands to which they fled. Despite the vast Arab territory. Out of the 100,000,000 refugees since World War II, theirs is the only refugee grouping in the world that has never been absorbed or integrated into their own people's land. Jewish refugees were completely absorbed into Israel, a country no larger than the State of New Jersey.

13. The Arab-Israeli Conflict: The Arabs are represented by eight separate nations, not including the Palestinians. There is only one Jewish N. The Arab Nations initiated all five wars and lost. Israel has defended itself each time and won.
14. The PLO's Charter still calls for the destruction of the State of Israel. Israel has given the Palestinians most of the West Bank land, autonomy under the Palestinian Authority, and has supplied them.
15. Under Jordanian rule, Jewish Holy sites were desecrated and the Jews were denied access to places of worship. Under Israeli rule, all Muslim and Christian sites have been preserved and made accessible to the people of all faiths.
16. The United Nations Record on Israel and the Arabs: Of the 175 Security Council resolutions passed before 1990, 97 were directed against Israel.
17. Of the 690 General Assembly resolutions voted on before 1990, 429 were directed against Israel.
18. The United Nations was silent while 58 Jerusalem Synagogues were destroyed by the Jordanians.
19. The United Nations was silent while the Jordanians systematically desecrated the ancient Jewish Cemetery on the Mount of Olives.
20. The United Nations was silent while the Jordanians have enforced an apartheid-like a policy of preventing Jews from visiting the Temple Mount and the Western Wall.
21. *These were completed by Christian University professor.-Jewish Believers in Jesus News Letter [Eleventh Month/ February-5769/2009].*

★ ★ ★
THE BIBLE SPEAKS OF THE CONFEDERATE ...

There are two questions that Craig Maus, Chairman of the Confederate Alliance, likes to ask. The first one is, *"Are you a confederate"?* It is here that I would like to expand on the word 'Confederate'. This poor word has been demonized by the forces against us, but I would like to share a little insight and a slightly different perspective that you will find both refreshing yet profound.

Let's start with the obvious: Webster's Third unabridged dictionary definition*: "A person, group, Nation or State united with another or others for some common purpose, an ally, and an accomplice."* The Confederate States of 1861 really was the second Confederacy in American History. In the HBO movie series 'John Adams'. I was surprised to hear an accurate description of the **(New Constitutional Republic of the late 1780's referred to by its rightful name-A Confederacy.) (BTW surprising historical accuracy for a recent movie—I recommend viewing this.)**

Now, let's travel back in time across the centuries and millennia way back to the First Book of the Bible 'Genesis'. In the King James Bible, we see what very well may be the oldest reference to the word 'Confederate'. It starts in Chapter 14, and is the story of Abraham when he rescues Lot with a much smaller military alliance of sorts.

In verse 8) And there went out the King of Sodom, and the King of Gomorrah, and the King of Admah, and the King of Zeboiim, and the King of Bela (the same is Zoar,) and they joined battle with them in the vale of Siddim; Verse 9) With Chedorlaomer the King of Elam, and with Tidal King of nations, and Amraphel King of Shinar, and Arioch King of Ellasar; four Kings with five. Verse 10) And the value of Siddim was full of slimepits; and the kings of Sodom and Gomorrah fled. And fell there; and they that remained fled to the Mountain. In verse 11) And they took all the goods of Sodom and Gomorrah fled, and their victuals, and went their way.

In verse 12) And they took Lot, Abram's brother's son, who dwelt in Sodom, and his goods, and departed. In verse 13) And there came one that had escaped and told Abram the Hebrew; for he dwelt in the plain of Mamre the Amorite, brother of Eshcol, and brother of Aner: and these were *'confederate with Abram.'* In verse 14) And when Abram heard that his brother was taken captive, he armed his trained servants, born in his house, three hundred and eighteen, and pursued them unto Dan.

In verse 15) And he divided himself against them, he and his servants, by night, and smote them, and pursued them unto Hobah, which is on the left hand of Damascus. In verse 16) And he brought back all the goods, and also brought again his brother Lot, and his goods, and the women also, and his people. In verse 17) And the King of Sodom went out to meet him after his return from the slaughter of Chedorlaomer, and of the Kings that were with him, at the valley of Shaveh, which is the King's dale. In verse 18) And Melchizedek King of Salem brought forth bread and wine; and he was the priest of the highest God. In verse 19) And he blessed him, and said, blessed be Abram of the highest God, possessor of heaven and earth. In verse 20) And blessed be the highest God, which hath delivered thine enemies into thy hand. And he gave him tithes of all.

In verse 21) And the King of Sodom said unto Abram, "give me the persons, and take the goods to thyself. In verse 22) And Abram said to the King of Sodom, I have lift up mine hand unto the Lord, the highest God, the possessor of heaven and earth. In verse 23) That I will not take from a thread even to a shoelatchet, and that I will not take anything that is thine, least thou shouldest say, I have made Abram rich. In verse 24) Save that which the young men have eaten, and the portion of the men which went with me, Aner, Eshcol, and Mamre; let them take their portion.

The Hebrew word for **Confederate** if formed by the Hebrew letters: Beit, Resh, Yod, Tav and is pronounced Brit (Breet. Brit in Hebrew means Covenant. Abraham formed a Covenant alliance with Mamre, Aner & Eschol. But they were still sovereigns!!! Notice in verse 23 & 24, when Abraham was successful, he chose not to take of the spoils of his victory, but he only spoke for himself. The others, in alliance with him, were free to take their portion if they chose to do so. They did not lose their sovereignty.

When you say you are a **Confederate**, let no one rob you of a heritage that is as rich, solid & rooted in antiquity as a teaching from Genesis. Let no one demonize you for being a *(Confederate)* or deny your rightful existence as a Citizen of the C.S.A. Deo Vindice!

At your service, Mark Motto/CSAgov

GOD VERSES SCIENCE

A science professor begins his school year with a lecture to the students, "Lets me explain the problem science has with religion." The atheist professor of philosophy pauses before his class and then asks one of his new students to stand.

'You're a Christian, aren't you, son?
'Yes sir,' the student says.
'So you believe in God?
'Absolutely.'
'Is God good?'
'Sure! God's good.'
'Is God all-powerful? Can God do anything?'
'Yes.'
'Are you good or evil?'
'The Bible says I'm evil.'
'The professor grins knowingly. Aha! The Bible! 'He considers for a moment. 'Here's one for you. Let's say there's a sick person over here and you can cure him. You can do it. Would you help him? Would you try?
'Yes sir, I would.'
'So, you're good … !
'I wouldn't say that.'
'But why not say that? You'd help a sick and maimed person if you could. But God doesn't.'
The student does not answer, so the professor continues. 'He doesn't, does he? MY brother was a Christian who died of cancer, even though he prayed to Jesus to hear him. How is this Jesus good? Hmmm? Can you answer that one?
The student remains silent.

'No, you can't, can you? The professor says. He takes a sip of water from a glass on his desk to give the student time to relax.

'Let's start again, young fella. Is God good?'

'Er … yes,' the student says.

'Is Satan good?'

The student doesn't hesitate on this one. 'No.'

'Then where does Satan come from?'

The student falters. 'From God"

'That's right. God made Satan, didn't he? Tell me, son. Is there evil in this world?'

'Yes, sir.'

'Evil's everywhere, isn't it? And God did make everything, correct?'

'Yes.'

'So who created evil?' The professor continued, 'If God created everything, then God created evil, since evil exists, and according to the principle that works define who we are, then God is evil.'

Again, the student has no answer. 'Is there sickness? Immorality? Hatred? Ugliness? All these terrible things, do they exist in this world?'

The student squirms on his feet. 'Yes.'

'So who created them?'

The student does not answer again, so the professor repeats his question.

'Who created them? There is still no answer. Suddenly the lecturer breaks away to pace in front of the classroom. The class is mesmerized. 'Tell me,' he continues onto another student. 'Do you believe in Jesus Christ, son?'

The student's voice betrays him and cracks. 'Yes, professor, I do.'

The old man stops pacing. "Science says you have five senses you use to identify and observe the world around you. Have you ever seen Jesus?'

'No sir. I've never seen Him.'

'Then tell us if you've ever heard your Jesus?'

'No, sir, I have not.'

'Have you ever felt your Jesus, tasted your Jesus or smelt you're Jesus? Have you ever had any sensory perception of Jesus Christ, or God for that matter?'

'No sir, I'm afraid I haven't.'

'Yet you still believe in Him?'

'Yes.'

'According to the rules of empirical, testable, demonstrable protocol, science says your God doesn't exist. What do you have to say to that, son?'

'Nothing,' the student replies. 'I only have faith.'

'Yes, faith,' the professor repeats. 'And that is the problem science has with God. There is no evidence, only faith.'

The student stands quietly for a moment, before asking a question of his own. 'Professor, is there such thing as heat?'

'Yes, the professor replies. 'There's heat.'

'And is there such a thing as cold?'

'Yes, son, there's cold too.'

'No sir, there isn't.'

The professor turns to face the student, obviously interested. The room suddenly becomes much quit. The student begins to explain. "You can have lots of heat, even more heat, super-heat, mega-heat, unlimited heat, white heat, a little heat or no heat, but we don't have anything called 'cold.' We can hit up to 458 degrees below zero, which is no heat, but, we can't go any colder than the lowest-458 degrees.'

'Everybody or object is susceptible to study when it has or transmits energy, and heat is what makes a body or matter have or transmit energy. Absolute zero (-458 F) is the total absence of heat. You see, sir, cold is only a word we use to describe the absence of heat. We cannot measure cold. Heat we can measure in thermal units because heat is energy. Cold is not the opposite of heat, sir, just the absence of it.'

Silence fell across the room. A pen drops somewhere in the classroom, sounding like a hammer.

'What about darkness, professor. Is there such a thing as darkness?'

'Yes,' the professor replies without hesitation. 'What is night if it isn't darkness?'

'You're wrong again, sir. Darkness is not something; it is the absence of something. You can have low light, normal light, bright light, flashing light, but if you have no light constantly, because than you'll have nothing and its called darkness, isn't it? That's the meaning we use to define the word.

'In reality, darkness isn't. If it were, you would be able to make darkness darker, wouldn't you?'

The professor begins to smile at the student in front of him. Thinking that this will be a good semester.' 'So what point are you making, young man?'

'Yes, professor. My point is, your philosophical premise is flawed to start with, and so your conclusion must be flawed.'

The professor's face cannot hide his surprise this time. 'Flawed?' Can you explain how?'

'You are working on the premise of duality,' the student explains. 'You argue that if there is life and then there is also death; a good God and a bad God. You are viewing the concept of God as something finite, something we can measure. Sir, science can't even explain a thought.'

'It uses electricity and magnetism, but has never seen, much less fully understood either one. To view death as the opposite of life is to be ignorant of the fact that death cannot exist as a substantive thing. Death is not the opposite of life. Just the absence of it.'

'Now tell me, professor. Do you teach your students that they evolved from a monkey?'

'If you are referring to the natural evolutionary process, young man, yes, of course I do.'

'Have you ever observed evolution with your own eyes, sir?'

The professor begins to shake his head, still smiling, as he realizes where the argument is going. A very good semester, indeed.

'Since no one has ever observed the process of evolution at work and cannot even prove this process is an ongoing endeavor, are you not teaching your own opinion, sir?' Are you now not a scientist, but a preacher?'

The class is in an uproar. The student remains silent until the commotion has subsided.

'To continue the point, you were making earlier to the other student, let me give you an example of what I mean.' The student looks around the room. "Is there anyone in the class who has ever seen the professor's brain?" The class breaks out into laughter.

'Is there anyone here who has ever heard the professor's brain, felt the professor's brain, touched or smelt the professor's brain?' No one appears to have done so. So, according to the established rules of empirical, stable, demonstrable protocol, science says that you have no brain, with all due respect, sir.'

'So, science says you have no brain, how can we trust your lectures, sir?'

Now the room is silent. This professor just stares at the student, while his face is unreadable.

Finally, after what seems an eternity, the old man answers. 'I guess you'll have to take them on faith.'

'Now, you accept that there is faith, and in fact, faith exists with life.' The student continues. 'Now sir, is there such a thing as evil?

'Now uncertain, the professor responds, 'of course, there is! 'We see it every day. It is in the daily example of man's inhumanity toward man. It is in the multitude of crime and violence everywhere in the world'. These manifestations are nothing else but evil?

To this the student replied, 'Evil does not exist sir, or at least it does not exist unto itself.' 'Evil is simple the absence of God.' It is just like darkness and cold, a word that man uses to describe the absence of God. God did not create evil. 'Evil is the result of what happens when man does not have God's love present in his heart.'

It's like the cold that comes when there is no heat or the darkness that comes when there is no light.'

That was when the professor sat back down, in silence.—

By: An Author Unknown.

THE MAYFLOWER COMPACT

IN THE NAME OF GOD, AMEN.

WE WHOSE NAMES ARE UNDERWRITTEN, THE LOYAL SUBJECTS OF OUR DREAD SOVEREIGN LORD, KING JAMES, BY THE GRACE OF GOD, OF GREAT BRITAIN, FRANCE AND IRELAND KING, DEFENDER OF THE FAITH, ETC., HAVING UNDERTAKEN, FOR THE GLORY OF GOD, AND ADVANCEMENT OF THE CHRISTIAN FAITH, AND HONOR OF OUR KING AND COUNTRY, A VOYAGE TO PLANT THE FIRST COLONY IN THE NORTHERN PARTS OF VIRGINIA, DO BY THESE PRESENTS SOLEMNLY AND MUTUALLY IN THE PRESENCE OF GOD, AND ONE OF ANOTHER, COVENANT AND COMBINE OURSELVES TOGETHER INTO A CIVIL BODY POLITIC.

FOR OUR BETTER ORDERING AND PRESERVATION AND FURTHERANCE OF THE ENDS AFORESAID; AND BY VIRTUE, HEREOF TO ENACT, CONSTITUTE. AND FRAME SUCH JUST AND EQUAL LAWS, ORDINANCES, ACTS, CONSTITUTIONS, AND OFFICES FROM TIME TO TIME, AS SHALL BE THOUGHT MOST MEET AND CONVENIENT FOR THE GENERAL GOOD OF THE COLONY. UNTO WHICH WE PROMISE ALL DUE SUBMISSION AND OBEDIENCE.

IN WITNESS WHERE OF WE HAVE HEREUNDER SUBSCRIBED OUR NAMES AT CAPE-COD THE 11 OF NOVEMBER, IN THE YEAR OF THE REIGN OF OUR SOVEREIGN LORD, KING JAMES OF ENGLAND, FRANCE AND IRELAND THE EIGHTEENTH, AND OF SCOTLAND THE FIFTY-FOURTH. ANNO DOMINE 1620.

SEVEN VERSES OF THE BIBLE

Woe to those who call evil good and good evil'
Who put darkness for light and light for darkness,
Who put bitter for sweet and sweet for bitter.
Woe to those who are wise in their own eyes,
And clever in their own sight.

ISAIAH 5:11 verse 20-21]

I am convinced that neither death nor life,
Neither angels nor demons,
Neither the present nor the future,
Nor any powers,
Neither height nor death,
Nor anything else in all creation,
Will be able to separate us from the love
Of God that is in Christ Jesus our Lord.

ROMANS 8: verse 38-39

God saved us, not because of righteous things we have done,
But because of his mercy.
He saved us through the washing of rebirth and renewal by the Holy Spirit,
Whom he poured out on us generously through Jesus Christ our Savior,
So that,

Having been justified by His grace,
We might become heirs having the hope of eternal life.

TITUS 3: verse 5-7

There is a way that seems right to a man,
But in the end it leads to death.

PROVERBS 14:verse 12

The Lord reigns forever;
He has established His throne for judgment.
He will judge the world in righteousness;
He will govern the peoples with justice.
The Lord is a refuge for the oppressed,
A stronghold in times of trouble.
Those who know your name will trust in you,
For you, Lord, have never forsaken those who seek you.

PSALM 10: verse 7-10

It is by grace you have been saved,
Through faith-and this not from yourselves,
It is the gift-not by works,
So that no one can boast.
For we are God's workmanship,
Created in Christ Jesus to do good works,
Which God prepared in advance for us to do.

EPHESIANS 2: verse 8-10

This is what Isaiah son of Amoz saw concerning Judah and Jerusalem:
In the last days the mountain of the Lord's temple will be established as Chief among the mountains;
I will be raised above the hills,
And all nations will stream to it.
Many people's will come and say,
"Come. Let us go up to the mountain of the Lord,

To the house of the God of Jacob,
He will teach us his ways,
So that we may walk his paths."
The law will go out from Zion,
The Word of the Lord from Jerusalem.
He will judge between the nations and will settle disputes for many peoples.
They will beat their swords into plowshares and their spears into pruning hooks.
Nation will not take up the sword against nation,
Nor will they train for war anymore.
Come, O house of Jacob,
Let us walk in the light of the Lord.

ISAIAH 2: Verse 1-5

<u>HOLY BIBLE-NEW INTERNATIONAL VERSION 1993</u>

A BRIEF HISTORY OF THE LEAGUE OF THE SOUTH GOVERNOR ZEBULON B. VANCE CHAPTER OF ROWAN COUNTY *NORTH CAROLINA* CSA

The Vance Chapter was established before the 13th of August of 1997 and held their meetings at the Rowan Public Library for many of years. The Chapter had held four Presidents during her existence. The first President was Mr. Bill McComb, the Second was John T. Nall, the third was Mr. Perry Miller, and the final was Mr. Thomas Kesler.

On the 25th of March of 2000, Dr. Michael Hill, President and Founder of the League of the South, presented the *(Outstanding Chapter Award)* to the Zebulon B. Vance Chapter of Salisbury, North Carolina at the [N.C. State Conference] held in Salisbury N.C …

The Salisbury Constitutional By-Laws of the Vance Chapter was established on the 29th of June of 1998. The Constitution of the United States and the Confederate States was used as a guideline for this project. The officers and State Chairman also voted on certain issues as to the powers of each officer and so-forth. The purpose for the By-Laws was to remove a dictatorship temptation from the President and to give a balance of power and responsibilities to the leading officers. The other goal was to prevent this Chapter from becoming a [Social Club] and remain focus as a political Chapter. To established goals and vote on issues of importance that could affect our Confederate American people's future. It required six months of my time in completing this Chapter By-Laws Project.

Since the time this Chapter was closed, the By-Laws have not been in effect. And being that the Author of these By-Laws does own the Copy Right, I'm giving my readers permission to use these By-Laws as their own or as a guideline to start up other Chapters. [The reader may do so only so long as it is used to promote the History and defending the heritage of the people of the land. To Restore the Constitutional Republic of the United States of America including the Constitutional Republic of the Confederate States of America. To defend the Constitutional Rights of our Christian Nation. However, I the Author, do not give permission to anyone for any reason that would want to use these By-Laws in such a way that would be in the direct violation of anybody's Constitutional Rights as a Citizen or Human Rights for any reason at any time. Nor do I give permission of any Chapter to use these By-Lays in the desire toward the overthrowing of any State or Federal government that had been established by our Founders].

Since the closing of this Chapter, the League members have learned that it was never the intention of the League to restore our Confederate States government. But only to use the symbols of our Confederate Nation and its people to draw in as many new members as possible. It is the desire of the League to establish some sort of Monarchy (King) with a few States. The League has classified the Confederate States Constitution to be joke and that the military enslavement of the Union over the Confederacy defines the Confederacy to no longer as being a (Sovereign Nation).

Also the provisional government of the Confederate States of America that was residing in Texas considers the actions of the League to be in (High Treason). I for one can say that we don't won't [NO EARTHLY KING] to rule over us! Not unless it is, King Jesus Christ! It would be far simpler and legal to restore our Confederate Nation than to establish some form of enslavement to another earthly King. It kind of reminds me of the History of the Jews who left the enslavement in Egypt. When it got rough for them, they started crying to go back into the oppression of the Egyptians' whip.

We can't start longing for the past. Yet, we must look forward in restoring our Constitutional Republic of the Confederacy and give our support to the Constitutional Citizens of the Union in restoring their Republic also. The League of the South does not have the best interest at heart in concerning of *our Confederate American people. So, I ask all true patriots to* stay away from the League and read the book 'The Grey Book' by the organization before joining them.

By: John Thomas Nall

THE SALISBURY CONSTITUTIONAL BY LAWS OF THE ZEBULON B. VANCE CHAPTER WITHIN THE LEAGUE OF THE SOUTH

It is the duty of the Chapter Members to protect and enforce the Chapter By-Laws

★ ★ ★
OUR CHAPTER'S MAIN GOALS

1. *To educate our Southern People about their history and rights as a free people!*
2. *To restore the understanding of God and Country that our founding and Confederate forefathers had.*
3. *To restore the national identity of our country: "THE CONFEDERATE STATES OF AMERICA"*
4. *To establish the respect and support of Salisbury and Rowan County.*
5. *To always build membership for The League of The South.*
6. *To be the leading and best chapter in North Carolina through friendly competition with the other chapters in our beloved Tarheel State.*
7. *To be politically active.*

★ ★ ★
OUTSTANDING CHAPTER AWARD

An outstanding Chapter Award was presented to the Zebulon B. Vance Chapter of the League of the South. By Dr. Michael Hill, during the North Carolina State Conference in Salisbury. On the 25th of March in 2000.

A NORTHERN VIEW OF THE COUNCIL OF CONSERVATIVE CITIZENS

Occasionally when discussing the CofCC, or handing out literature, I am asked whether it is just a Southern organization, or whether it is relevant to those whose ancestors either fought for the North, or perhaps whose ancestors were not even in America in the 1860's. It is my design to provide an answer to those and other questions.

The CofCC was founded by men and women whose political background was rooted in traditional Conservatism, and a very strong Southern heritage. Traditional Conservatives did not shy away from issues regarding State Sovereignty, race relations, and very strong traditional Christian values. It is no secret that the Southern States have had hotbed issues revolving around the rights reserved to the States from the War of Northern Aggression up to the current day of trying to preserve true history and traditional family values and the right to honor ones ancestry unashamed.

Thus, it is only natural that an organization that fights for these issues would be spearheaded by the Southrons in the beginning. Regardless of wherever else you may live; it cannot be denied that the South has had to go above and beyond when it deals with race relations. Though slavery and segregation were just as recognized in the North, it is the South that must bear the cross of an entire nation from Jamestown to the 1964 Civil Rights Act, and beyond. Michael Grissom, in his book (Southern by the Grace of God), goes into detail regarding this.

When one thinks of segregation, they think of Alabama, or Mississippi but certainly not Michigan, or Ohio. Though segregation was practiced widely, it is the South alone that must atone for America. Though riots were widespread by the 'non-violent' marchers, it is the riots in the South that gathered the major focus of bad press, not Chicago or Detroit. It is because of this, that the CofCC attracts many Southerners to its ranks.

The other States have not had to bear constant ridicule and hatred for past policies. The Confederate Flag is spread widely within the ranks of the CofCC. Let's face it, there is no other American symbol so hated as the Battle Flag. Because it is the last flag to stand up for the rights of the States as declared under the 10th Amendment, it does hold a deeper meaning than the average person would imagine. It is this symbol that rich and poor rallied around to preserve a homeland.

To preserve a way of life an America since it's founding. There is no other symbol in America that speaks so much while waving silently. Though a symbol drawn from Scotland (St, Andrews Cross), it represents the last gasp of Americans in a struggle for the Rights of the States. It is more than a relic; it is a contemporary symbol for the same struggle; State Sovereignty.

The issue of State Sovereignty affects all 50 States. Perhaps one from New York, or Wisconsin may find the Battle Flag a bit 'outdated' rest assured that the struggle that baptized it in fire and blood has not lost its importance as we deal with an out-of-control Federal government that wants nothing more than to totally control not only every State, but every individual as well.

Because of the fact, the flag is just as relevant today weather in California or Alabama. When the Southern guns fell silent in the lost struggle for States Rights, we all lost. What was once referred to as (These United States of America) has been forcibly changed to the (United States of America.) Think about it.

We face the same issues today; A Federal government refusing to be bound by the chains of the Constitution. It is the Southern States that took a stand in 1861, because of the flagrant violation of State Sovereignty. The Federal government is now further expanding its desire for more power at the expense of its citizens by being a part of the United Nations, 'Alphabet Soup' economic policies (NAFTA, CAFTA, etc), trade negotiations (WTO) and a host of other programs to plunge America into the Third World and snuff out the Light of the Glory under the dung heap of failed nations who have had no use for Biblical principles and thereby bear the consequences.

General Washington's words in his Farewell Address seem to have fallen on deaf ears when he warned against getting entangled into the affairs of other nations. Though there is a cultural distinction that remains today between North and South, the CofCC brings together Americans, regardless of State citizenship. Who share a dream of an America that will belong to the founding European stock and unapologetic, unashamed population who will rise out of the ash heap of multiculturalism and White Guilt.

It is the CofCC which now stretches coast to coast and from the Gulf of Mexico through our Northern border and into Canada. Its principles are centuries old and have never truly died. Though blooded from time to time, those principles which represent today are those that are the epitome of a great Republic.

The South fired the shots in 1861 which renewed the historic struggle for independence. The battlefield is no longer isolated to a few States, but now a battle is raging in every State. Yea, it is s national struggle as well. You are a citizen of your State, and all the States must join in reasserting their sovereign power against a regime that now operates far outside the limits of the Federal Constitution.

It is now time for all of us to take a public, unapologetic stand for the traditional values that made America a beacon of hope in the past. Isn't it time for you personally to take the step across the line and join the ranks of those patriots who feel the call and responsibility to provide a future for their children in America?

Mr. Raterink is Chairman of the Michigan Chapter of the CofCC, www.micofcc.org. Published in the Citizens Informer of July-September 2008.

✶✶✶
BLOOD AND WATER

'Blood is thicker than water,' Commodore Josiah Tattnall declared as he ordered as his vessel to the aid of a British warship under attack from Chinese forts on the Hai River in 1859. Tattnall's action violated American neutrality, but the old seahorse did sailed on until he quite the US Navy to join the Confederacy two years later.

Tattnall refused to put aside his Southern bonds for the sake of his career Just as he refused to ignore his racial loyalties for the sake of a Chinese diplomacy. Again, blood is thicker than water.

The blood-over-water adage to Medieval Germany, though the saying conveyed racial values until the late 20th century, when Whites gradually lapsed into egalitarian anemia. That's when blood turned into the common denominator signifying universal equality.

"Everybody bleeds the same color red," or so say the gushy liberal (socialist) poets manqué. Nowadays, "blood is thicker than water" obligates White people to renounce national borders, go color-blind, and neutralize family fidelity in the deranged hope that equality prevails once all complexions are flat brown.

"One blood unites us all" … or so Whites have been duped to believe by reductionist pedagogies and evangelical simpletons. White people have taken a bloodbath in a mud hole as a melancholy rite of passage into the Third World. In this post racial scenario, Tattnall should have let the British sink, then loaded his ship with Chinese and steamed home.

Once government schools displaced family as the main conduit and ideals, then the instinctive pull of blood lost traction against an education system which set about pumping into White children the notion that nature abhors racial divisions.

Along with dissecting frogs, high school biology classes teach that White people are mutants who survive as primeval remnants of the Ice Age. The biometrically correct offspring of Mother Africa's darkling prodigies would be enriching diversity today if not for the medicines, vaccines, and hygiene lessons brought to them by color-blind abominable White man.

Post-doctrinal Christianity became a safe haven for racial nihilism shortly after Martin Luther King died to save White people from their own skins, though the overhaul of the Bible into socially relevant coloring book began years before.

Every American Christian knows the song Jesus loves the Little Children, and as grandparents many churchgoers can still sing it straight through. What most Christians don't know is that the lyrics to the bouncy hymn were put to the tune of (Tramp, Tramp, Tramp, the Boys are Marching), a Yankee war song written by an New Englander George Root, himself a devout follower of the heretic Emanuel Swedenborg.

The tune was not chosen accidentally or at random, but was a deliberate attempt to merge racial equality and evangelical zeal into a March drill "Red and Yellow, Black and White/ they all precious in His sight" … but what about when all the children are earth tone? Is God really delighted to watch sanctimonious finger-painters smear His palette into a muddy smudge?

Has God's word degenerated into the 'dream' of a philandering. Lying, 'Communist,' rapist masquerading as a Black preacher?

In [soul-candy churches], race mixing is a post racial act of baptism to wash away the 'sin' of racism. Despite the Communist etymology of the word [racism], some philistine sermonators like evangelist Ken Ham decry racism as an act of hatred equivalent to murder.

<u>Ham's remedy for this sin that the Bible fails to mention is sexual intercourse between Whites and nonwhites. Ham's contempt for White families is so bilious that he suggests that parents who object to their children marrying 'Christians' of another race cannot themselves be a Children, Indeed, children who are Ham-cured of racism get a free pass on that (Honor thy Mother and Father) technicality.</u>

Ham, a 'new earth creationist,' also believes that Adam and Eve rode around on dinosaurs. (Also not found in the Bible: Fred and Wilma Flintstone.) While Ham rejects evolution, he accepts natural selection as a scientific fact, which makes his race-mixing fervor problematic. <u>If God created the races by design, why would God permit race mixing?</u>

<u>If nature created the races, then natural selection favors racial distinction.</u> So Ham, tangled in a fool's dilemma, must choose whether God made a mistake or nature did. Socially engineered, scripturally false baptisms against racism fail blood is thicker than water.

And who did God choose to build an ark to preserve creatures **'after their own kind'** from as watery grave? Noah, perfect in his generations, saved his bloodline from the flood only to be mocked by his son Ham; who's mongrelized grandson Nimrod celebrated diversity by building the multilingual Tower of Babel. Hams of all ages just don't get it: Blood is thicker than water.

EDITOR ON DUTY: Bill Rolen, Citizen Informer, July-September 2010, Page 4.

/The Citizens Informer contains a wide range of views and opinions. The view expressed in columns, articles, letters, and materials advertised in the Citizens Informer are those of the author or contributor and do not necessarily represent the views of the editor, publisher, or the Council of Conservative Citizens./

[Author's Note: Always use the Holy Bible as reference to any statements or opinions that are believed by individuals. Because there are a lot of Bible Myths that are taught and believed down through the generations that may not be true! But the duty falls on you to research for the truth before taken it to heart. However, World History has proven time and time again that Miscegenation is self-destructive and is in truthfulness (Genocide). According to [DNA] & [the shape and size of the human skull's in biology], we can also recognize every individual race. Inter-breeding of any two races is unnatural, including being a sin & an abomination, in the Holy Bible. Homosexuality & Abortions and sterilizing any people would also fall under the classification of being sinful and of a (Genocidal) trait.] In truth, your race is the very extension of your family! This is something that each race can only claim for themselves. And that is the evidence of God's glory! Racial assimilation is the end results of Miscegenation and self-elimination.

Genocide—[Gr genos, race, kind: First applied to the attempted extermination of the Jews by Nazi Germany] the systematic killing of<u>, or a program of action intended to destroy, a whole national or ethnic group-genocidal.</u> [Webster's New World Dictionary-Third College Edition. 1991.

THE MISSION STATEMENT OF THE BRITISH NATIONAL PARTY

The British National Party exists to secure a future for the indigenous peoples of these islands in the North Atlantic which have been our homeland for millennia. We use the term indigenous to describe the people whose ancestors were the earliest settlers here after the last great Ice Age and which have been complemented by the historic migrations from the mainland Europe.

The migrations of the Celts, Anglo-Saxons, Norse and closely related *'kindred peoples'* have been, over the past few thousand years, instrumental in defining the character of our family and nations. While we recognize the United Kingdom as a political entity, the BNP does not arrogantly seek to impose one set of Westminster dominated decisions across these nations. We embrace and cherish the native cultural diversity within the British Isles and wish to extend the concept of democracy to the lowest possible level, where those that are affected by a decision are the ones who influence and make the decision.

Political Battle

The struggle to secure our future is being waged on many fronts. The need for political power is crucial to bring about our goals. Without affective political representation many Britons, who are deeply concerned about their future have no voice in the chambers where decisions are made. Increasingly numbers of voters are expressing apathy and discontent with the endless incompetence, lies, false promises and sleaze coming from the parties that make up the Old Gang.

The BNP will contest and win elections at council, parliamentary, Assembly or European level in order to achieve political power to bring the changes needed.

Torch Bearers of Culture

The rich legacy of tradition, legend, myth and very the wealth of landscape and man-made structures is one of our island's richest treasures. The men and women of the British National Party are motivated by love and admiration of the outpouring of our culture, art, literature and the pattern of living through the ages that has left its mark on our very own landscape. We value the folkways and customs which have been passed down through the countless generations. We enthuse with pride at the vey marvels of architecture and engineering that we have been completed on these islands since the construction of the great megaliths 7,000years ago.

Liberties

Above and beyond our activities in the political world, we daily work with or people in their homes and communities addressing the fundamental issues of civil liberties and reverse discrimination. Increasingly our people are facing denial of service provision, failure to secure business contracts as well as poor job prospects as each reverse discrimination excludes our people from the room, workplace, and boardroom. A key role of the British National Party is to provide legal advice and support to victims of repression and those denied their fundamental Civil Rights.

For more information search the internet [http://bnp.org, UK].
Membership Enquiries: [Membership Department] Po Box 107 Wigton Cumbria CA7 OYA]

A CHRISTIAN CONFEDERATE SOLDIER'S PRAYER

Brave Christian Confederate warriors,
Should fate find us in battle,
May our cause be just.
May our leaders have clear vision.
May our courage not falter.
May we be triumphant an earn victory,
As we show mercy to our enemies.
May our efforts bring lasting peace.
May our sacrifice be always
Appreciated by those we serve.
May we return to our loved ones unharmed.
Should we be harmed, may our wounds hear.
Should we perish in the struggle,
May God embrace us and find for us a place in His Kingdom.

By: Major Arthur H. Rettig … An original Version slightly changed for this prayer.

✶ ✶ ✶

THE HATED WHITE RACE

'Fifty years from now, there won't even be any White people! Said my pathological Middle Eastern neighbor. He knew I was an American Indian, and he expected me to dance in his vision.

I didn't. I found his attitude, and that of his angry Black wife, repulsive. I don't appreciate being presumed upon or being dictated to in any matter, especially in the matter of race. Nobody tells this Indian how to think. I'm free to like and dislike whomever I please, for whatever reasons I choose.

My two neighbors were racists, obviously. And they were making me a victim of their racism. Because I was non-White, they presumed I was a natural partner in their resentment and animosity toward the White race. I was judged by the color of my skin, so to speak.

This all happened many years ago, but I never forgot it. Today, I see the truth in the words of my Middle Eastern neighbor. White women are leaping in bed with Black men, or other darkies of the world, and popping out strange-looking children. <u>Generally speaking, the male in these incidents could not care less about the children. It's all about sexual aggression against the White race.</u> They're happy to conquer for the moment, and create ghastly, permanent consequences. Marriage and family have nothing to do with these misanthropes, nor the *lusus naturae* they create.

This denigration of race is a cruel mockery of manhood. It is a pathetic testimony of the personal irresponsibility and malignant selfishness of failed men. Indeed, a careless woman is generally such for lack of a caring father.

But I will not dismiss this kind of race destruction as sexual caprice or mindless ego in aimless men. It is not some Umber design of social architects, or the express intent of integrationists. While racial disintegration may be the result, there are other inevitabilities at work in the process.

★ GOD SAVE THE SOUTH ★

Like the universal law of aesthetics. We want beauty. Superior beauty lies in the White race. It is the variety of color, the red hair, the blond hair, the green eyes, the blue eyes. All the races in the world have only one coloring, the same black hair, the dark brown eyes and skin. A bit drab in comparison, can't we say?

The darkies of the world are truly fascinated with the White race, and always have been. However, there is a certain envy that naturally, unavoidably develops. It seems Hitler had a point when he referred to (The hated White race.) (Mein Kampf, p.325.) But the sexual encounter with the Whites makes the Whites dark. And what most people ... especially White people ... forget is the fact that the White race is the minority in the world. It is, and has always been, vastly put-numbered by the dark races. Moreover, the pigmentations of the White race are all genetically recessive. The whiteness is first to fade.

Therefore, integration tends to mean elimination for the White race. That's simply the way of the genetic world. That the White race became the most powerful, dominant, ruling race may be attributed to cultural values more than anything else. It was of course the White race that adopted the Judeo-Christian. The social constructs and psychological hierarchies in this tradition evolved a people more astute and agile in every way.

Whatever 'mental' problems the White race developed because of being more powerful are only recent evolutions. In his day, the White man has created a throne like no other in history. If it is criminal at the foundation, the challenge is chiefly from envy ... always the weakest charge. Besides, what's the point of the dark man accusing the White man of not keeping his morals, if the dark man himself does not believe in those morals? The charge of hypocrisy is moot, made in impotence.

(The White man's self-flagellation is the only hope of the darkies.) I would not look forward to a time when there is no White race. My neighbors were nothing I would want to see more of in this world ... certainly not their attitude. But that there are a growing number of people in the world who think like then is a concern. The Muslim world tends to produce such a disposition.

Disguised though it may be in moral and religious terms, political terms, or even genetic terms, the case is fairly obvious: 'The hated White race' is such for its beauty and power.

By: Dr. David Yeagley.

Dr. David Yeagley is the proprietor of the Bad Eagle website (www.badeagle.com) and is an accomplished writer and composer. Mr. Yeagley is also the great-grandson of the Comanche Leader, Bad Eagle. Please visit his website and give a kind donation for his honest and truthful views. [For American Indian Patriots.]

REMEMBER THE "ALAMO"

I love the Crockett quote and only John Wayne could make is as eloquently as it was made. As a native Texan who attended Texas long before the area of 'Political Correctness' there are some points that need to be mentioned here regarding the Texas War for Independence. My grandmother lost two great-uncles at the Alamo (the Blair brothers from Tennessee) and had a great-grandfather who fought to avenge them at San Jacinto.

The siege of the Alamo began on February 14th 1836. At that time, by definition, the defenders of the Alamo 'were' rebels by exact definition. They were rebelling against the Mexican Federal (Central) Government which had abrogated the Constitution of the Mexican Republic (written in 1824 and was a near-exact copy of the U.S. Constitution as it was at that time.)

San Antonio was surrounded and cut off between February 14th and March 6th of 1836 and the men inside the Alamo had no idea that the Texas Declaration had been signed on March 2nd-four days before the fall of the Alamo. They all died for a restoration of the rightful government of Mexico, not independence. Goliad fell a few days later but the news of the Declaration of Independence had not reached them as of yet either.

Keep n mind that about 1/3 of the defenders of the Alamo and Goliad were Mexican origin (not simply in citizenship as were almost all of the 'Anglo' defenders.) The proportion of outside volunteers at this very early stage on the Texas War for Independence was very small.

Out of a known 187 defenders of the Alamo, Colonel Crocket's half-dozen or so from Tennessee and around thirty men who belonged to the 'New Orleans Grays' were the only real 'outsiders' present. The rest, whether Anglo or Mexican origin were, in fact, long, long term residents by the standards of Texas at the time and were all voluntarily Mexican Citizens.

The massacre at the Alamo and at Goliad did more to solidify the Independence movement in Texas than any other factors. Even though both were still holding at the time the Declaration of Independence was signed, all knew that it was a matter of time and that neither place could be reinforced. In essence they bought time for Sam Houston to organize a real 'Army of the Republic of Texas' and ultimately defeat of Santa Anna and his Mexican Federal regime at San Jacinto about six weeks later.

The first battle fought was under the banner of Texas Independence was at San Jacinto in April of 1836. Only from March the 2nd can the Texas War for Independence be called by that name. Until then, it was literally a rebellion fought between two different sides within a still united but politically divided Mexico.

Now-that is not to say that the independence wasn't the original aim of any, all or some of the men who died both at the Alamo and Goliad. It undoubtedly was. It is simply to point out the difference between a rebellion and an actual War for Independence.

None of this applies to the Confederacy, since all declarations had already been made and the Confederacy was already an existing nation when the Federal invasion of 1861 took place.

This puts the Federal invasion outside both the definition of a rebellion or War for Independence and places it solidly into the category of an aggressive war waged by the **Federal Union** against a peaceful neighboring State. *That my friend, constitutes international war and the way it was done constitutes a* <u>War Crime.</u>

By: Dr. James L. Choron.

★ ★ ★
MY DEAREST YANKEES,

For 143 years you have had your way with the Southern nation of the Confederate States of America, but those days are coming to an end. We are taking back that which you stole from us, our heritage, our culture, our ancestry, and our country. You have spread lies about our ancestors, telling our children that they were nothing more than racist traitors. You have made the flying of our flags and honoring of both our ancestors and heritage an offense, an offense that you created to turn our children and others against us. You have shown us Southerners beyond a shadow of a doubt that mercy is for the weak for you have shown us no mercy. Your actions have been like that of the Nazi's and you know what happened to them, they went down to defeat and ruin.

You praise War Criminals like Lincoln, Grant, Sherman, Sheridan and Butler for 'preserving' the Union and abolishing slavery, all the while demonizing the Dictators who only want to emulate them. You claim that the Nazi's were War Criminals and rightfully so, but why would you condemn them when they did exactly what Lincoln did?

Also, have you wondered why the Socialist Dictators such as Lenin, Stalin, Moa Tse Tung, Ho Chi Min, Castro, Hugo Chavez, even Hitler had portraits of Lincoln? During the Spanish Civil War of the 1930's, did you know that the American Brigade that volunteered to fight for the Socialist Government of Spain was called the 'Lincoln Brigade'? Did you know that Lincoln had an ongoing correspondence with (Karl Marx) and (John Engels), the Father and Founders of Communism?

You rant and rail and demand that we Southerners accept and celebrate your diversity, yet you show no toleration for our differences. You expect and demand that we Southerners celebrate your holidays, yet when we try to celebrate ours, you call us racist or un-American. You demand that we Southerners venerate Lincoln, Grant, Sherman, and Sheridan, names that bring terrible memories for us. But when we honor Davis, Lee, or Jackson, you turn your attack dogs on us Southerners.

★ GOD SAVE THE SOUTH ★

You use the N.A.A.C.P., or the Southern Poverty Law Center, or the A.D.L., or Al Sharpton, or Jesse Jackson to attack any Southerner who does not comply with your mandates.

You have placed your monuments and temples to your God's on our Southern soil, then demand that we Southerners worship them. If we try to worship the true God, the God of Abraham, Isaac, and Jacob we are derided and told we are intolerant of other religions. You force Godless lifestyles on us Southerners then you call us intolerant and other demeaning names meant to make us do your will. If trying to shame us to you won't work, you then use force.

You use the Courts, (that you have stacked in your favor) to compel us Southerners to your will. You have shown this with the States of Georgia and South Carolina, forcing them to remove their State flag. You did this evil act by using both the courts and economic terrorism, and you want to call us Southerners intolerant? In the field of education, you have brainwashed our children. You have told them; their Southern ancestry is fit for derision. You tell them that those who fought for the South, were nothing more than racist traitors. You forbid our children from honoring their heritage. We had taught our children to honor their heritage and elders and to treat others as they wanted to be treated with respect and dignity, you teach them to disrespect everyone. You have taught our children to be criminals, you have taught them very well; indeed, you have turned our once peaceful cities into war zones.

"The first step in liquidating a people is to erase its memory. Destroy its books, its culture, and its history. Then have somebody write new books, manufacture a new culture, invent a new history. Before long the nation will begin to forget what it is and what it was." [This quote was made by Milan Kundera.]

You have taken what he said and used is against us Southerners. You have all but annihilated the Southern culture, forcing us Southerners to adapt to yours instead. You have taken our language, our history and perverted them to your liking. You invaded, conquered, subjugated, murdered, and raped the people of the South. You overthrew the duly and rightfully elected Governments of the Southern States by force of arms, and then replaced them with puppet governments of your choosing.

You took land that you didn't work for or bleed over, just so you could pay for your illegal war. You passed laws that made it a crime for ex-Confederate soldiers to obtain meaningful work thus making and forcing them to a life of crime to feed their families. Even today you make it hard for the true Confederates to show their pride in their heritage and hold a job at the same time, you force them, and you force them to make a choice between their heritage and their family's well-being. You know they will choose their families every time, which is how you operate. There is a saying,

"Threaten a man's life and he will be brave, threaten a man's family and you have a slave."

You have used this technique very well, very well indeed. Cowards, Curs, Yellow bellied. There are not enough words in the English language to curse you, for what you have done to the Southern people. Now you want us to pay for your mistake again, with this bailout of YOUR financial institutions. You now want to take even more of OUR money, to help YOUR Empire to maintain its evil power.

You start wars to control us Southerners, and then you send our Southern young to fight these wars. You have wasted the best of OUR blood in your wars, White and Black, Jew and Gentile, as we are being used as <u>cannon fodder to maintain your Empire.</u> Your empire is crumbling even now; We Southerners can hear the bell tolling for the demise of your empire. In nature when something outlives its usefulness, nature has a way of correcting that problem. Like all empires of the past, you have outlived your usefulness.

We as a new Generation of Confederates, we are the descendants of Robert E. Lee, Thomas 'Stonewall' Jackson, P.G.T. Beauregard and President Jefferson Davis. We stand in the forefront. And carry on the battles they fought those many years ago. We are White and Black, Mexican and Native American. We are Jews and Gentiles, Catholics and Protestants. We are the elderly and young, we live next door and all over the South. We are Proud Citizens of the Confederate States of America, we are here and there is nothing you can do about it.

You Yankees think the war ended in 1865 with the surrender of General Robert E. Lee to Grant, but you are dead wrong. We are fighting back. Soon real soon you will have no place in the South you can hide; we are exposing you and your lies. You think you can continue your lies and the masses will just believe you, well think again. No longer will you be able to tell your lies with impunity, we will fight you at every turn. We will make you put back, what you took down. We will make you restore that which you stole. We will humiliate you, just like you have done to us. The day is coming, and it is coming real soon, when you will have to leave the C.S.A. <u>For we are taking it back, to be restored to the Sovereignty of Independent Nations.</u> The Confederate States of America is coming back, so get used to it.

Sign, the Citizens of the Confederate States of America/
This was written by Charles Goodson/

AN INTRODUCTION INTO THE CONFEDERATE'S PRAYER

As we prepare to knell together, we do not as yet know one another in person, yet are we not brethren in the faith, and as such together of the same spirit. I might be likened unto an old war weary Confederate Soldier having crossed the space of time for to deliver unto this generation a message. My memories were born in the small towns, cities, and plantations of the Old South, while I am in every respect a modern man. Yet does my heart remain captive of the surrender, occupation, subjugation, and cultural cleansing of my nation. Thus, I am a Confederate Soldier born out of season.

"Behold. The Lord's hand is not shortened, that it cannot save; neither His ear heavy, that it cannot hear." (Isaiah 59:1)

A CONFEDERATE SOLDIER'S PRAYER

Our most kind and precious Heavenly Father. We gather before you in humble gratitude, for our life, health and the blessings bestowed upon us. For having granted unto us, those things needful to the body. Hear us O Lord, that our prayer may reach beyond ourselves, and touch those of our people.

A people having found their God fearing, free and independent nation, aggressively invaded, conquered, occupied, subjugated and now culturally cleansed. Many of those who might have once been numbered among us have fallen by the way.

Grant unto us O Lord, the wisdom, and the means to restore that which was taken from us, that we might established upon this Southland, a nation after thine own heart. Give us the leadership, talent, material, and resources. Call back our people 'kindred' and culture from the four winds of heaven and breathe into our nation the breath of life. Make of us a lawful and honorable army, capable of standing before our foe. Give us the victory, for which our forefathers, fought, suffered, bled and died in agony.

Grant us the steadfastness and persistence, that we might fight the good fight, finish our course, and keep the faith. In our fellow compatriots, the just and honorable cause of the South, and in our Savior and Lord. Give unto our weary people, the inspiration and the vision of victory, that we might, not only continue the struggle, but, stand in triumph. And Precious Lord, when that glorious day should arrive, give us of thy wisdom with an understanding heart, that we not display a spirit of revenge upon our enemies in the hour of our glorious vindication.

Allow our political cultural Confederate Armies to be truly your armies, that we might pass onto future generations yet unborn, a society, culture, government and nation, which will be found worthy of thy good graces. Amen and Amen!

-Unknown-

WHY SHOULD "GOD BLESS AMERICA?"

The phrase, **God Bless America**, has become as common as Public fixture in recent days as the ubiquitous U.S. flag. We see it heralded on buttons, bumper stickers, pins, posters, banners and billboards. We hear it from political pundits, commentators, columnists, journalists, and various aspirants to political offices that cover the landscape of America just now. In short, it appears to have called on God to bless her in a **jihad (Holy War)** of her own, to rid the world of **terrorists** and **evil**.

It is worth noting that President Bush, gathered in the Cathedral in Washington D.C., just days after the attack on September 11th, political, social, and religious leaders of every conceivable stripe, praying for divine assistance for the course they would take in the days ahead. Many Presidents before him had called the nation to prayer during times of war or national mourning. This was to my knowledge, however, the first time in America's history that the triune God of our fathers was clearly not the focus of this gathering's prayers.

In his place, America's leaders have embraced a **Universalist** God that people of every religion are supposed to embrace in the name of diversity and multiculturalism. The savior of mankind, who died on the Cross for our sins, was noticeably absent in the invocations uttered. Based on this gathering, I believe Christians can disabuse themselves of any notions that their faith, or America's traditional culture on which it is based, will hold any more importance in the future than Buddhism, Islam, or any other religious faith. America's Christian are is clearly past, so far as our elites are concerned. Serious Christians ought to ponder the language now being used in connection with those being described as **terrorists** today. I keep hearing that the only problem with Islam is its **fundamentalists**, which are routinely described as **extremists**.

Have any of you ever heard the media, or some of our political leaders talk about Christian **fundamentalists** as **problematic**, or **extreme**? What does this portend in terms of how these Christians are treated in the near future? Perhaps they will come under the scrutiny of the new Department of Homeland (fatherland) Security. In the early days of our first War for Independence, George Washington issued the following declaration to the men under his command. *"The Continental Congress having earnestly recommended that Thursday next be observed by the inhabitants of all the English Colonies upon this continent as a day of public humiliation, fasting and prayer, that they may with united hearts and voice unfeignedly (sincerely) confess their sins before God, and supplicate all Wise and merciful Disposer of Events, to avert the desolation and calamities of an unnatural war."* George Bush, as well as the rest of America, seems to have forgotten the part about humbling ourselves and confessing our sins before God could bless us, and presumably the war we have decided to make on anyone in the world we say that supports terrorism. My Bible tells me that under God's conditions can we expect Him to bless us.

Have we, as a nation, no sin that needs of forgiveness? In some circles today, to suggest that we do such a thing is considered to be an UN-American. I think precisely the reverse is true. Any Christian worthy of the name should recoil in horror at the thought of the 4.000 abortions that take place in this country every day. Just this morning I heard a well-respected Christian minister say that over the course of the past 28 years, 43 million babies have been (murdered) with our government's sanction. Even if he was wrong by half, we are talking about a holocaust that makes every other pale in comparison.

In a truly Christian society, much less a civilized one, it shouldn't matter what a majority of nine Justices of the Supreme Court says on such an issue, what should matter is [the sanctity of human life] and attempts to undermine it. Abortion is nothing, more than the deliberate killing of innocent human beings and condemned by Sixth Commandment. For a Biblical justification of this position, you can read Psalms 139: 13-16, Genesis 2:7, and Exodus 21: 22-25 for starters. I have heard it said that because there is no afterlife for nations, they must be judged in this life. Does anyone think this is cause for some concern? II Chronicles 7:14 says. *"If my people, which are called by my name, shall humble themselves and pray, and seek my face, and turn from their wicked ways; then I will hear from heaven and will forgive their sin, and will heal their land."*

History clearly teaches us that people from Christendom established the land that we think of, when we say **America**, they confessed their submission to the God of the Bible seeking His blessing upon them. There is no question that God did indeed bless His people here. It is just as clear that the political, social, and religious liberties we have long enjoyed grew out of Christianity and is part of an inheritance we are rapidly losing. Is there a connection between America's turn away from the God of the Bible and the gradual loss of those liberties? I certainly think so.

★ GOD SAVE THE SOUTH ★

A question all of us should ponder today is whether or not an America that has clearly rejected God's Commandments is deserving of His blessings? America cannot be natural on this question. Our founders knew this and spoke of it. God Himself proclaims that He is a Jealous God. He blessed Israel only so far as they remained faithful to Him, and when they sinned, by seeking after mammon, the flesh, or other God's, judgment always followed.

In Proverbs 8:36, God reminds us that *"All they that hate me, love death."* Abortion, Aids, the high crime rate, our never-ending military adventures around the world, and lately, consideration of Euthanasia as 'an idea whose time has come', leaves me to wonder if indeed we live in a culture of death. Many people today, even well meaning Christiana, act as though we still live under a government guided by Christianity. They deceive themselves, Jeremiah 17:5 says. *"Cursed be the man that trusteth in man and maketh flesh his arm."*

Perhaps Americans are convinced that they no longer need God. After all, they might tell themselves, look at how rich and powerful we are. Is this the American pride we hear so much about? If so, remember Proverbs 16:18. *"Pride goeth before destruction, and an haughty spirit before a fall."* As Paul Proctor wrote in a recent editorial, *"It is not pride in ourselves that will restore God's blessings to America. Pride in self is what destroys men and nations."* No, if we are to be delivered from the enemies we have made as the result of or constant foreign meddling, we must humble ourselves and confess our sin before the One True, Triune God, seek to restore Him to His place of sovereignty over our people. We delay at our own peril.

By: Wayne Carlson
October 22nd 2001.

AMERICA'S PATH OF SELF DESTRUCTION

A Confederate Perspective:

America as a Nation is finished! It's no longer an issue of debate. Memories will tear at your heart and tell you to deny this claim but, in the end, memories will also challenge you to REEMEMBER that which was and is NO more! It is ill refutable. America epitaph, as previously mentioned, was written long ago. In the spring to be exact. It was NEVER, then or now, a [regional] issue.

It was much more! And although the Confederate Government & her Sovereign Republic lost that war to Lincoln's invaders, the metamorphosis for that war remains as Omni-present today as it did in 1861. The dictionary defines metamorphosis as; (a change of character OR circumstances.)

The change of character **AND** circumstances had **EVERYTHING** to do with the ideologue of our Government then, and the manner in which a plurality would use their station to enforce their collective will and ways over another. In other words, a greater majority of a certain grouping of States, utilizing a (Central Government) to enact their will through the passage of their **LAWS**, while being totally contradictory to those conscripts that the Republic of Sovereign States agreed to the conclusion of our Revolutionary War, in order to gain an upper hand.

The motivation for these Actions & Laws-**MONEY & POWER!** (Sound familiar with respect to current events- once again disguised as the people's needs?) NOT any different than today EXCEPT, the one making ALL the rules NOW, is the **CENTRAL GOVERNMENT** & **NOT** a body of plurality States! When the war concluded, America was transformed from a **Constitutional Republic of Sovereign States,** and those conscripts of a Voluntary Union as noted within the U.S. Constitution, into the **Socialist Democracy** of today. **Our** country was **VIOLATED** much in the same manner as a woman is violated during a rape! A number of criminal's have violated this land as one would do to an unsuspecting woman … although it was much larger in dimension and has remained on going, while the law's that were once designed to protect them both, have long since been re-written and compromised away in order to protect the criminal invader of both from accountability.

Thus we have become a Nation of Indentured Servants and, in order to understand the scope & magnitude of this exclaim, everyone needs to understand the very basic connection between these two periods in time. Today's events & circumstances are merely an **EXTENSION** of what was **LOST** when the Confederacy lost. Y'all have to understand that **NO MATTER** what side of the Mason Dixon you come from, for today's dilemma affects everyone alike!

Our Government is corrupt. It has become every bit what Winston Churchill describe the Soviet Union as being— [A Mystery Wrapped in an Enigma.] Our Government does **NOT** represent the interests and welfare of this country or its people any longer. Hasn't for some time as a matter of fact. It is married to an international cartel of bankers and special interests that could give a hoot less about any of us. In fact, they despise and disrespect what little remains of the U.S. Constitution and they hate our Christian Confederacy even more, because they both meant & stood for something that was intended to prevent in design & language all that has evolved since 1865!

SOVEREIGNTY is NOT a (language) that is either practiced or recognized by the Federals. **SOVEREIGNTY** is a language that is, in fact a Stumbling Block for them in that it holds their feet to the fire and demands of them accountability & proper representation of that Design of Government they swore an oath to uphold-a Constitutional Republic consisting of Sovereign Republics. Their actions, programs and laws have been BUT those associated with that a Constitutional Republic since 1865! They have been quite the opposite & have elevated & altered the (profile) of Central Government beginning in 1867 with their bogus 13th, 14th & 15th Amendments that clearly Re-Purposed government in their own image. To this end and with the beginning of the 20th Century, the Federal Government took greater (goose-steps) forward in their (re-definement) of the Central Government …

The Federal Reserve Act, the stripping of State Citizenry of the Individual into that of a Federal Citizen, FDR's policies (much like Lincoln's and both in the name of War & Country) accompanied by the 1960's wherein the Kennedy's & ultimately, LBJ, unleashed their Child of Advanced Entitlement called (The great American Society Program), and ALL that ever was has been totally usurped through their clandestine & covert actions all disguised as either being in national interests or in the interests of (fairness) requiring Federal intervention. It has been straight downhill ever since!

That (child) has grown into THE entity we have today in the form of Obama and his Far-Left **(Socialist)** parasites within Congress. How can **ANY** American remotely understand this exclaim when they have **NEVER** been taught anything but Entitlement in one form or another? How can **ANY** American know better of themselves when what little remains of their ancestor's history has been so vilified & eliminated from the contents of the (Public Classroom)? How could they possibly make any distinction or connection of who and what we once were & should have remained? And how can **ANY** American ever hope to question & demand accountability when the whores of government have stripped them naked from knowing any better?

Metamorphosis-(The change of character and circumstance). Is this NOT what is happening right before our very eyes today, and ONLY because they screwed up? They are in Damage Control-Bog Time, yet they will spin this with the same temerity and attempt to portray themselves as the cavalry who is refusing us … but rescuing us from whom? They CREATED this disaster just as they have created and contributed to EVERYTHING since 1865 because of their meddlesome ways and desire & penchant for domination! Obama tells us we should be angry because AIG dared give bonus's, almost half a billion dollars, to executives with) **(THEIR FEDERAL MONEY)** … once known as our money! WHY! Didn't the Republic Rats Ram Down Our Throats a TRILLION DOLLAR TARP bill that NO one wanted that was full of Ear-Marks? …

Only to be followed by Stimulus one and two and the OmiBus that Obama himself said, (I know I am signing an imperfect Bill), EACH of which were LOADED with Pork Barrel spending? So what **MAKES THEM ANY DIFFERENT?** They do IT because they can pass even further Legislation that will force us into total Subjugation … despite us saying NO. Their design is NOT representation-its **DOMINANCE!** They don't represent us-**THEY CONTROL US.** And just as it was **AFTER** the spring of 1865, their actions, as before & as mentioned above, will take an even uglier turn for the unsuspecting American years from NOW when we are NO longer around to remind our children of the consequences & circumstances that lead up to theses horrific times and dark hands who were involved in their procurement.

Increased taxes, higher fuel cost; hyper-inflation and the final transfer of power unto them will be made **COMPLETE!** In the interim, our children, aunts, uncles, cousins, fathers & mother's will continue to fight their War's, shed our blood and ALL for the purpose that HASE'T existed for 145 years! It's been a shell game of the most of the paramount proportion but not unlike most within our civilization's world history.

Our Founding Fathers were well schooled and learned men. My God, do y'all think it was an accident why those first Ten Amendments were written so distinctly and with such a prowess of Common Sense? It has taken them, the Feds, 145 years and a (so-called Civil War) to undo & rewrite them & their original meaning and damn them for so doing! Obama is NOT a stupid man. He is a well-educated and is, in my humble opinion, MORE than a Socialist. He is every bit a Leninist & quite probably, a Stalinist. He knows full well the consequences of his actions and could care less if he is a term President, for he knows only too well that the damage he is and will continue to inflect upon an unsuspecting American Electorate will have far-reaching effects.

That's the mission for which he has been schooled & is committed to NO MATTER WHAT! What he and the Pelosi's, Franks, Schumer's, Reid's, Dodd's, Biden's, Specter's, Geithner's, Kennedy's, & Clinton's are doing will be insurmountable … just as Lincoln & HIS band of Radical Republic-the Republic Rats! He & they are but a **GREATER** and **WORSE EXTENSON** of that bearded bastard from Illinois! Nothing short of a 3rd American Revolution will alter the Path of America's Destruction! They have sunk their collaborative teeth into America's Republic and the poison they have infected her with, must be cut out.

Elections in, this Confederate's humble opinion, are but a mere and useless exercise at this point. There is NO way in which we could ever expect to change their demeanor from the top down for it is beyond hope & repair. Their actions have made this so.

The Original Laws of this land have been deliberately altered with the introduction of those by them that are clearly vague & ambiguous, but clearly allowing for their mantle of confinement to be perpetuated at our expense. They have openly & blatantly re-defined & re-described the American Republic in THEIR IMAGE. One cannot hope to seriously transform them back when the essence of their collective activities over these last 145 years has been to deceive & harpoon the very fiber of this Republic's being! That would be an impossible mission as their mission is to prevent that from ever happening!

These are NOT the mis-guided assertions of a mis-guided person but simply the net-gross of events & circumstances emanating from collective studies made possible by a rigid evaluation into our country's history. One does NOT need to be a rocket scientist to come to these conclusions but simply who is determined to seek the truth no matter how painful the consequences of that truth may be.

I grew up poor. My family worked hard and never blamed another for their station. They got far less than they ever give. And all they ever wanted was to have a little left over for their kid's and maybe, just a little for themselves is those (golden years) that they were ultimately denied! I've seen the face of the Federal Beast up close and personal.

And, as my parents before me, I ask NO special favor from another, other than to treat another as you yourself would expect to be treated-Fairly and God's direction assisting. Government has NO province within these basics!

I believe in teaching a man how to fish rather than giving him a fish. Everyone will always need a helping hand at some time or another, BUT it must be given freely … and NOT via a Federal Power Broker whose laws will only contaminate the element of natural human responsibility. No Government should ever involve itself within the strata of social engineering, for that will only lead to social re-engineering, that benefits none other than he who claims to hold the solution.

History has proven that this has led to dire consequences & ultimate failure! Our original government was based entirely upon simplicity while asking for the invocation & favor of the Almighty to help us. It required NOT extensive Laws, but only those Laws necessary & as an extension of those from God's wisdom & direction in mind.

Have we always been perfect-hell no but this entire civilization has been anything but perfect. However, we learn from our mistakes and to that end we come a long way until such time when the rug is pulled out from beneath us and man once again attempted to use a vessel to control another and for the same reasons ancient history has shown us-**Money & Power.**

WE were on the road for a short time, 1776-1860, but never got the opportunity to fulfill this country's (contract) as man's weakness again prevailed. As such, we are right back where we started … only this time, and because of the greater ways in which we have discovered to annihilate one another, we are living more precipitously & dangerously than ever before.

Does ANYONE seriously believe **ANY GOOD** can come from any of these actions presently underway & being carried out & enforced by the Federal Government? Does anyone seriously believe that they are in **YOUR BEST INTEREST** and will have a positive impact? I am a Confederate Citizen. I have come to realize that it matters not where you hail from but in whose true measure the (compass) really lay's. The South fought and represented a Cause that I am to this day and Proud to be associated with! <u>I am equally convinced that most within the Northern Army thought that they were doing at the time which was equally right.</u> However, had they truly had known that which was never presented to them, I am also convinced that most not all would never take up arms against their brothers.

They were as equally lied to and duped much in the same manner & impunity as we have been today, with the Feds playing one off against the other. The ONLY ONES benefiting from our blood-letting to date is that the same group of old-that Damn Central Government who has grown fatter & hungrier ever since 1865 and always at our expense.

Remember what Thomas Stonewall Jackson said long ago, *"(I would **NEVER** think I would live to see the day when an American President would send an army to invade it's Sovereign States.)"* Think of how incredible & overwhelming this realization must have been to him, and just how in (violation of God's eternal law's was?) He was a man of incredible God-fearing belief! Those actions that were presenting themselves to him were far beyond inconceivable-they were an assault on the Province of God Himself and the Republic to which we had asked His favor to bestow upon us only 80 years earlier when we fought King George … and for the same tyrannical reasons that is the sad trademark of our Federal Government TODAY! I have said it before, *"(When the South Lost, this Nation Lost, only NO ONE knew it at the Time)"*! For God, Family and the Confederacy!

By: Craig Maus.

President of the Confederate Society of America, and a Proud Member of the Confederate Alliance of Organizations. Please visit our web site (www.deovindice.org) & (www.confederatestatesofamerica.org).

A PRAYER FOR THE SOUTH

O God, our Father,
Our country without place or name;
Forget not, O Father, your covenant with our Fathers,
But renew your mercy to us their children,
And so turn the hearts of our people toward you,
That with repentance and joy they would once again
Love and serve you alone;

And grant that,
Having taught us to govern ourselves
By your spirit and your law,
You would be graciously pleased to grant us,
A name and place among the nations of the earth,
That we might lead them in serving you,
Through our Lord Jesus Christ,
Who lives and reigns
With you and the Holy Ghost,
Ever one true God, world without end, Amen.

-Unknown-
Published in the Magnolia 2007

✯ ✯ ✯

YOUR IMPORTANT COLLECTION OF QUOTATIONS AND STATEMENTS

1. "Every record has been destroyed or falsified, every book has been rewritten, every picture has been repainted, every statue and street and building has been renamed, and every date has been altered. And the process is continuing day-by-day and minute-by-minute. History has stopped. Nothing exists except an endless present in which the Party is always right.—George Orwell.
2. "I believe it is the duty of every Confederate whose opportunities are as to enable his to speak now, with anything like accuracy, to put on record what he knows. He owes this duty not only to himself and his associates, but to the truth."—Johnson Hagood, Brigadier, CSA "Memoirs of the war for secession."
3. "If this cause that is so dear to my heart is doomed to fail. I pray Heaven may let me fail with it. While my face is toward the enemy and my arm battling for that which I know to be right."—CSA General; Patrick Cleburne.
4. "The standards for valor and devotion to duty were set by Confederate soldiers during the Civil War and remain today unsurpassed."—Wesley Pruden.
5. "Every Southerner should be proud of the loyalty and devotion of his fellows throughout Dixie Land. Devotion to our common interest is a guarantee of dignity and the respect with which our people will be possessed as long as we remain united."—Sumner A. Cunningham.
6. "There is a true glory and a true honor, the glory of duty done—the honor of the integrity of principle."—Robert E. Lee.
7. "The cause of the South was the cause of constitutional government, the cause of government regulated by law. And the cause of honesty and fidelity in public servants. No nobler cause did man ever fight for!"—Rep. Benjamin Franklin Grady.

8. "A nation preserved with liberty trampled underfoot is much worse than a nation in fragments, but with the spirit of liberty still alive. Southerners persistently claim that their rebellion is for the purpose of preserving this form of government."—Private John H. Haley 17th Maine Regiment, USA
9. "Like most war leaders, he [Lincoln], grossly distorted and exaggerated the motives of his enemy. He constantly insisted that the South wanted to destroy the Union, when it merely wanted to withdraw from it. He called honorable men like Jefferson Davis and Robert E. Lee traitors, though they never betrayed anyone in their lives. He accused the South of aggression, when it was the South being invaded, and truly destroyed, by the Union armies. Having assured the country that he neither the power nor the inclination to disturb slavery. Lincoln made the destruction of slavery his lofty war aim in the middle of the war."—Joseph Sobran.
10. "If I thought this war was to abolish slavery, I would resign my commission, and offer my sword to the other side."—General Ulysses S. Grant USA
11. "What are you fighting for anyway?" "I'm fighting because you are down here."—Confederate prisoner of war to a Union Soldier.
12. "We may be annihilated, but we cannot be conquered."—General Albert S. Johnston, CSA
13. "The flags of the Confederate States of America were very important and a matter of great pride to those citizens living in the Confederacy. They are also a matter of great pride for their descendants as part of their heritage and history."—The Former Prime Minister of Great Briton, Winston Churchill.
14. "The Southern Confederacy will not employ our ships or buy our goods. What is our shipping without it? Literally nothing ... It is very clear that the South gains by this process, and we lose. No, we MUST NOT LET the South go."—Union Democrat, Manchester, NH, USA—Feb/19/1861.
15. "If I could save the Union without freeing the slaves I would do it ... what I do about slavery and the colored race, I do because it helps to save the Union." U.S President: Abe Lincoln in a letter to Horace Gresley 1852.
16. "Truth crushed to the earth is truth still and like a seed will rise again."—Confederate States President: Jefferson Davis.
17. "There are few, I believe, in this enlightened age, who will not acknowledge that slavery as an institution is a moral and political evil."—Confederate States Gen. Robert E. Lee 1856
18. "We didn't go to war to put down slavery, but to put the flag back. And to ask differently at this moment, would, I have no doubt, not only weaken our cause but smack of bad faith."—U.S. President Abe Lincoln, 1861

19. "I am honest in my belief that it is not fair to my men to count Negroes as equals. Let us capture Negroes, of course, and use them to the best advantage."—Union Army Gen. William T. Sherman, to Gen. Killack—September, 14, 1864 O.R. series 1 Vol. 38
20. [ON GOVERNMENT CONTROL] "The history in liberty is a history of limitations of governmental power, not the increase of it".—Woodrow Wilson
21. "The history of the world has been written in vain if it does not teach us that unrestrained authority can never be safely trusted in human hands."—Andrew Johnson
22. [ON JUDICIAL RESTRAINT] "judicial activism includes doing something that is not the judge's right to do. So when courts actually make the laws. They make the rules that govern society, they become the judicial activists."—Hon. Roy Moore, Chief Justice of Alabama
23. [ON LEE THE SOLDER] "He was the very best soldier I ever saw in the field."—U.S. Army Gen. Winfield Scott
24. [ON LEE THE FATHER] "Every member of the household respected, revered, and loved him …—Robert E. Lee, II
25. [ON LEE AND JACKSON] "I am of Virginia and my entire professional life I have studied Lee and Jackson."—U.S. General of the Army, Douglas Macarthur
26. "Wisdom is not an object that is to be placed upon someone's shelf to be admired as viewers are passing by. For wisdom, can only bare its fruit when it is applied within that someone's personal life."—John T. Nall
27. "A government big enough to give you everything you want, is strong enough to take everything you have."—Thomas Jefferson
28. "No man's life, liberty, or property is safe while the legislature is in session."—Mark Twain, 1866
29. "YANKEE, n. In Europe, an American. In the Northern States of the Union, a New Englander. In the Southern States the word is unknown." (See DAMYANK.)—Ambrose Bierce
30. "Whenever I'm asked why Southern writers particularly have a penchant for writing about freaks, I say it is because we are still able to recognize one. To be able to recognize a freak, you have to have some conception of the whole man, and in the South the general conception of man is still, in the main, theological."—Flannery O' Connor
31. "The first step in liquidating a people is to erase its memory. Destroy its books, its culture. its history, Then have somebody write new books, manufacture a new culture, invent a new history."—Milan Kundera
32. "The government is like a baby's alimentary canal, with a happy appetite at one end and no responsibility at the other."—U.S. President Ronald Reagan"

33. "For two years [the North] wage war against the South without attempting to interfere with slavery. It was only when they found the Negro could be used for killing the white people of the South and serve as breastworks for Northern White troops that they declared him free ... they cared nothing for the unhappy Negro; they preferred his destruction to that of their white troops."—Captain Waddell of the C.S.S. Shenandoah
34. "Why hate Liberals for the color of their skin. When there are better reasons to hate them.—Midge Dexter
35. "If you think health care is expensive now, wait until you see what it costs when it's free"!—P.J. O'Rourke
36. "Of all the enemies to public Liberty war is, perhaps, the most to be dreaded, because it comprises and develops the germ of every other. War is the parent of armies; from these proceeds debts and taxes; and armies, and debts, and taxes are the known instruments for bringing the many under the domination of a few. In war, too, the discretionary power of the Executive is extended; its influence in dealing out of offices, honors, and emoluments is multiplied; and all the means of seducing the minds, are added to those of subduing the force, of the people ... [There is also an) inequality of fortunes, and the opportunities of fraud, growing out of a state of war, and ... degeneracy of manners and of morals ... No nation could preserve its freedom in the midst of continual warfare ... [It should be well understood] that the powers proposed to be surrendered [by the Third Congress] to the Executive were those, which the Constitution has most jealously appropriated to the Legislature ... The Constitution expressly and exclusively vests in the Legislature the power of declaring a state of war ... the power of raising armies ... the power of creating offices ...

    A delegation of such powers [to the President] would have struck, not only at the fabric of our Constitution, but also at the foundation of all well organized and well-checked governments. The separation of the power of declaring war from that of conducting it is wisely contrived to exclude the danger of its being declared for the sake of its being conducted. The separation of the power of raising armies from the power of commanding them, is intended to prevent the raising of armies for the sake of commanding them. The separation of the power of creating offices from that of filling them, is an essential guard against the temptation for the sake of gratifying favorites or multiplying dependents."—The fourth U.S President James Madison

37. "Of every one hundred men, ten shouldn't even be there, eighty are nothing but targets, and nine are real fighters. We are lucky to have them. They make the battle. Ah, but the One, One of them is a Warrior, and he will bring the others back."—Heraclitus (circa 500 BC)
38. "This war is immoral, unjust and intrinsically evil. Iraq is no threat to us. It is not our obligation to stomp about the face of the planet inflicting "good" and "democracy" upon otherwise innocent nations."—Quote & note received from retired Special Forces SFC Steven M. Barry, Editor, the Resister
39. "To control all information is to control the masses."—Charles R. Nall.
40. "The Gospel of Jesus Christ has been transformed into false traditions. Causing the understanding of the Holy Bible itself, to become deluded, confused, and polluted by Manmade fictional theologies."—John T. Nall.
41. "Absolute separation of church and state is not in the U.S. Constitution.

The First Amendment is not intended to separate the federal government from all religion or religious-based morality but merely to insure that the Federal government did not make one religious denomination the state Church of the United States. From the very beginning, our founders recognized that America was a Christian nation and that our laws should be based on Christian Morality. Separation of powers of government between the federal government and the governments of the separate states and between the legislative, executive, and judicial branches within the Federal government, however, is in the U.S. Constitution, but this principle is constantly violated and ignored. Under the Constitution, only Congress can make federal laws, yet Supreme Court decisions, as well as presidential executive orders have been improperly used to create laws. Under the Constitution, only Congress can declare war, yet our presidents have involved us in wars in Korea, Vietnam, Kuwait and Iraq by claiming authority from the UN in spite of no declaration of war from Congress.

A supine Congress, meanwhile, ignores this outrageous usurpation of its proper role in government! Separation of powers in government is a keystone of our liberty. Those officials who violate this underpinning of our nation should be separated from their office."—Lawrence Burke—Roslyn, New York, USA. July-September 2006 Citizens Informer

42. "The American people will never knowingly adopt socialism. But, under the name of 'liberalism' they will adopt every fragment of socialist program, until one day America will be a socialist

nation, without knowing how it happened."—Norman Thomas, six-time Presidential Candidate for The Socialist Party of America.

43. "I believe there are more instance of the abridgment of the freedom of the people by gradual and silent encroachments of those in power than by violent and sudden usurpation's."—James Madison

44. "Snake handling, for instance, didn't originate in the hills somewhere. It started when people came down from the hills to discover they were surrounded by a hostile and spiritually dead culture."—Dennis Covington, 1995.

45. "The South is an ideal whipping boy because no magazine with national circulation is published in the South, and most of her leading newspapers owned by residents of the North—some as far north as Moscow."—R. Carter Pittman, 1956.

46. "The only difference between a tax man and a taxidermist is that the taxidermist leaves the skin".—Mark Twain.

47. "I told the officer who took down my name that I was unwilling to take the oath and asked if there was no escaping it. "None whatever," was his reply. "You have to do it, and there is no getting out of it." His rude tone frightened me into half-crying … If perjury it is, which will God punish: me, who was unwilling to commit the crime, or the man who forced me to do it?—Sarah Morgan of Louisiana, CSA April 22, 1863.

48. "Dependence induces a spiritual and moral disintegration fundamentally destructive to the national fiber. To dole out relief in this way is to administer a narcotic, a subtle destroyer of the human spirit."—U.S. President Franklin D. Roosevelt, 1935.

49. "On account of the waste from the commissary a great many rodents from Elmira ran into the prison. As there were not any holes in which they could hide it was an easy catch or the boys by knocking them over with sticks

… As there was very little currency in prison, tobacco, rats, pickles' pork, and light bread were mediums of exchange. Five chews of tobacco would buy a rat, a rat would buy five chews of tobacco, a loaf of bread would buy a rat, a rat would buy a loaf of bread, and so on" …—Tennessee Prisoner, Marcus B. Toney.

50. "One thing alarms me—the eager pursuit of gain which overspreads the land, and which absorbs every faculty of the mind and every felling of the heart".—John C. Calhoun.

51. [ON STATESMANSHIP] "we had great men once and they gave the tone to Public opinion but now the men in power sound the wild impulses of the populace before they venture to act. In the

days of the Revolution such Charlatans as Seward, and educated asses as Sumner, and uneducated as Lincoln would have had little or no weight."—James A. Bayard, Jr. U.S. Senator from Delaware, August 1, 1862.

52. "Those once proud Southerners who had been victorious in many a battle kicked and cuffed, starving and sick at heart, and in despair with no hope sitting waiting for the scraps from the hospital to be washed to their feet with the garbage and excrement all clumped in the same ditch together."—Milton Asbury Ryan, Captain Company G 8th Mississippi Regiment CSA.

53. "We make great mistake in supposing all people are capable of self-government. Acting under that impression, many are anxious to force free governments on all the peoples of this continent, and over the world … [T]hat it is the mission of this country to spread civil and religious liberty all over the globe … even by force, if necessary … is a sad delusion."—John C. Calhoun.

54. [ON MINICRY] "One of the best ways to get yourself a reputation as a dangerous citizen these days is to go about repeating the very phrases which our Founding Fathers used in the great struggle for independence."—Charles A. Beard.

55. "An old man with snow white hair … also attracted my attention, as he walked restlessly up and down the room. Seeing I was looking at him, he approached and said in an excited tone: "Madam, I hope you have no one you love confined yonder," pointing toward the prison building. "Yes, sir; I have a daughter there, a school girl, hardly in her teens, an only child, and her mother dead. I have been here day after day, trying to see my darling, and every day been refused admittance." The tears rolled down his cheeks, and wiping them off, he added: "Excuse me, madam; I am an old man, with but little of life before me, and my lot is a hard one."—Virginia Lomax, Baltimore, Maryland, From "The Lady Who Enjoyed the Hospitalities of the Government for a Season."—Courtesy of the University of North Carolina at Chapel Hill.

56. "Every dollar that we can prevent from coming into the treasury, or every dollar thrown back into the hands of the people, will tend to strengthen the cause of liberty, and unnerve the arm of power."—John C. Calhoun.

57. [ON GROWTH] "Every time I look at Atlanta I see what a quarter of a million Confederate soldiers died to prevent."—John Shelton Reed.

58. " … I have witnessed [Negro guards] fire their muskets indiscriminately into crowded masses of prisoners, shooting two or three men at a single shot and such outrages were tolerated by their white officers, and they never were punished nor their cases investigated."—Walter D. Addison, Stewart's Horse Artillery, Co. A

59. "He who, in estimating the strength of a people, looks only to their numbers and physical force, leaves out of the reckoning the most material elements of power—union and zeal."—John C. Calhoun.
60. [ON VIOLENT SPINSTERS] "The war Between the States emptied the men from the farmhouses of New England and made the New England spinster a social stereo type while it ruined the South. This is now the topic of a cascade of careful books which cleanse the memory of the grief and suffering, blood, and dirt of a dreadful period."—Otto Scott
61. [Megan's Creed] "I will not be brainwashed by liberal, socialist professors. I will not support gay rights, race mixing & marriage or abortions. I will own my gun, fly my Confederate flag, smoke or not smoke, if I choose. I will pray to the only God, Jesus Christ, at any time, any place, and no silent prayer!"—The European American New Letter, Dec 2007 Volume V Issue V.
62. " … It is significant to note that the prison was hastily constructed, using unseasoned green lumber, and give little or no consideration to the construction of a medical facility for the treatment of wounded and/or ill Confederate prisoners. The results of poor construction can be seen in the few extant photos of the camp, showing buildings with large, gaping holes in the walls. The roofs and floors were similarly ill-constructed, allowing the brutal winter cold and the stifling summer heat to compound the miserable conditions of the men imprisoned there."—"Inside of Rock Island Prison," by J. W. Minnich.
63. "[ON IN-LAWD] "American couples have gone to such lengths to avoid the interference of in-laws that they have to pay marriage counselors to interfere between them."—Florence King
64. "Home of the Statue of Liberty and within shouting distance of Ellis Island, Liberty Island was also used to house Confederate prisoners.

    Known as Fort Wood (also called Star Fort) on what was then known as Bedloe Island, it was used as an infirmary for 100 sick Confederate POWs. The fort that held Confederate prisoners of war became the base to the Statue of Liberty. Ward's Island was also used to house Confederate prisoners throughout the war."—[Prison-Pens of the North], by Michael Dann Hayes.

65. [ON PATRIOTISM] "In politics it is necessary either to betray ones country or the electorate. I prefer to betray the electorate."—Charles de Gaulle.
66. "It was impossible to force the minds of the public officers to the importance of attendance on the public money, because we had too much of it."—John C. Calhoun.

67. "I remember seeing a man kill an old black cat and cook it in a tin can picked up near the hospital kitchen. I was offered a share in the feast, but declined, as I drew the line at rats and cats, though I offered ten cents for a small piece of dog, and was unable to buy it, as the possessor said he had none to spare. During the first three months of our incarceration in Camp Morton, twenty-five percent of our men had died of various prison diseases. Many would be picked up in a faint, or collapse from weakness and bowel disease, which they had no strength to combat from their long fast."—By Dr. Thomas E. Spotswood, Fairford, Alabama CSA. Private in Company F Fifty-Third Alabama Cavalry.
68. "If we do not defend ourselves none will defend us; if we yield we will be more and more pressed as we recede; and if we submit we will be trampled underfoot."—John C. Calhoun.
69. "Those very people who basely submit to a despotism so unrelenting and cruel invade our soil without a shadow of right, and declare it to be their purpose to force us back into a union which they have destroyed, under a Constitution which they have rendered a mockery and made a nullity."—Former U.S. President John Tyler 1790-1862 (This remark made during the summer of 1861, when former U.S. President Tyler was running for a seat in the Confederate House of Representatives.)
70. "Not long after my arrival I heard a cry "Rat call! Rat call!' I went out to see what this meant. A number of prisoners were moving and some running up near the partition, over which a sergeant (sic) was standing and presently he began throwing rats down. The prisoners scrambled for the rats like school boy's foe apples. None but some of the most needy prisoners, and the needy were the large majority, would scramble for these rats. Of course but few were lucky enough to get a rat. The rats were cleaned, put in saltwater a while and fried. Their flesh was tender and not unpleasant to the taste."—John Sterling Swann, Captain of Company A 26th Battalion Virginia Infantry.
71. "The United States is still in a quasi-legal condition of war with the Confederate States of America, even though the war was unconstitutionally declared without Congress through proclamation issued on April 15, 1861 by President Abraham Lincoln for the military invasion of the Confederacy where by the military forces of the Union unlawfully invaded the Confederate States of America. This use of force by the military invasion of the Federal Union was not justified in any way."—Number 3 of paragraph a. of page 6 from the CSA Constitutional Court of October 16, 2006.
72. "The invasion was initiated by President Abraham Lincoln with Yankee troops entering into South Carolina to re-enforce Fort Sumter. This fort in South Carolina had been under construction, but was ordered turned over to the Confederacy by President James Buchanan of the United States. As These invading troops refused a truce to retire to the territory of Union. The Confederate militia

did fire upon the Fort in Confederate territory. The Union attempts to claim these were the first shots of the war, but that has been proven wrong as the first shots were fired from Ft. Pickens in Florida by Yankee troops still illegally in possession of that Fort.

Jan 8, Union forces fired upon Confederate recon scouts in the woods who did not return fire. Most other forts in the South had been peacefully turned over to Confederate forces in obedience to orders to do so from U.S. President James Buchanan. Nevertheless, Union forces had initiated the invasion of South Carolina secretly moving 85 Yankee troops into the essentially deserted Fort Sumter on December 26, 1860, prior to Lincoln's Inauguration on March 4, 1861 and prior to his proclamation of military hostilities (unconstitutional declaration of war) against the Confederacy on April 27, 1861 challenging the rights of the States to secede from the Union.

Neither the national government of the Confederate States of America nor the elected Confederate States governments therein ever surrendered although they were overrun by Union forces. The United States government did attempt but failed to gain surrender from President Jefferson Davis. Furthermore, no Peace Treaty has ever yet been signed between the two nations."—Number 3 of paragraph b. and c. of page 6 from the CSA Constitutional Court of October 16' 2006.

73. "The business of war is a serious one. War created the means of its own continuance. It's called into being a mighty influences which were interested in carrying it on …"—John C. Calhoun.
74. "We are without machinery, without means, and threatened by a powerful opposition; but I do not despond, and will not shrink from the task imposed upon me."—CSA President: Jefferson Davis 1808-1889.
75. "MODEST IN PROSPERITY IN PEACE. BRAVE IN BATTLE AND UNDESPAIRING IN DEFEAT. THEY KNEW NO LAW OF LIFE BUT LOYALTY AND TRUTH AND CIVIC FAITH, AND TO THESE VIRTUES THEY CONSECRATED THEIR STRENGTH."—Transcription from Confederate memorial that stands in front of the old courthouse in Decatur, Georgia.
76. "The Presidential election is no longer a struggle for great principles, but only a great struggle as to who shall have the spoils of office."—John C. Calhoun.
77. "To hate and persecute the South has become a high passport to honor and power in the Union."—Robert Barnwell Rhett/ 1828-1905.

78. "Like every other faithful Confederate, I dwell with delight on the many glorious fields where this dishonored standard has gone down before the stainless battle-flag of the Confederacy."—Mrs. Rose O' Neal Greenhow 1814-1864.
79. "I must say I am at loss to see how a free and independent republic can be established in Mexico under the protection and authority of its conquerors … I had always supposed that such a government must be the spontaneous wish of the people …"—John C. Calhoun.
80. "The political elections has transform itself into a Circus Show, where the politician's eyes are blinded to the words of our founders and their hearts are empty without wisdom. And the voters has become to believe that the next President shall fulfill are the needs and problems. Much like in the movie of The Wizard of Oz, might have been.—John T. Nall
81. [ON "CONSERVATIVE"] "Conservative, n: A statesman who is enamored of existing evils, as distinguished from the Liberal who wishes to replace them with others."—Ambrose Bierce.
82. "The first step, towards any effectual reform, is to put down and disgrace party machinery & management. No devise ever was adopted better calculated to gull the community & keep the people in ignorance.—John C. Calhoun.
83. "When did the South ever lay its hand upon the North?"—John C. Calhoun.
84. "Does a righteous God govern the universe? And for what does he hold the thunders in his right hand, if not to smite the oppressor; and deliver the spoiled out of the hand of the spoiler."—Frederick Douglass. Page 92 of AN AMERICAN SLAVE.
85. [ON FICAL RESPONSIBILITY] "We didn't actually overspend our budget.

    The Health Commission allocation simply fell short of our expenditure."—Frank A Clark.

86. "From my earliest recollection, I date the entertainment of deep conviction that slavery would not always be able to hold me within its foul embrace; and in the darkest hours of my career in slavery, this living word of faith and spirit of hope departed not from me, but remained like ministering Angels to cheer me through the gloom. This good spirit was from God, and to Him I offer thanksgiving and praise.—Frederick Douglass. Page 50 of AN AMERICAN SLAVE.
87. [ON WORLD PEACE] ""I have never advocated war except as a means of peace."—Ulysses S. Grant.
88. "Let us cross over the river and rest under the shade of the trees."—(Last words spoken by CS General Stonewall Jackson.
89. "It is a miracle that curiosity survives formal education."—Albert Einstein.

90. [THE GREATEST SOUTHERN INJUSTICE] "The greatest injustice performed against the South, of which there were many, has not been committed by the enemy of the North. Of all the horrors of war suffered by by our Confederate solders, of all the evils visited upon our ancestors, OUR PEOPLE, during reconstruction, nothing can compare to the injustice inflicted by the descendants of these same valiant warriors and noble people, who for whatever reason, do not care to learn about why they fought, or of the cause they upheld and not even care to hear their side of the story."—Randall J. Hamilton, September 12, 1991 of the Confederate Sentry 1st Quarter Edition.

91. "A nation which does not remember what it was yesterday does not know where it is today."—CS General Robert E. Lee.

92. "Honorable people do not speak only to hear themselves. They speak so that others may know the truth or so the listeners may learn from the speakers experience."—John T. Nall

93. [ON DIRTY LAUNDRY] "Only robbers and gypsies say that one must never return where one has been."—Soren Kierkegaard.

94. "Always mystify, mislead, and surprise the enemy; and when you strike and overcome him, never let up in the pursuit. Never fight against heavy odds if you can hurl your own forces on only a part of your enemy and crush it. A small army may thus destroy a large one and repeated victory will make you invincible."—CS General Stonewall Jackson.

95. "For an enemy so relentless in war for our subjugation, we could not be expected to mourn; yet, in view of its political consequences, it could not be regarded otherwise than as a great misfortune for the South.—CS President Jefferson Davis on the assassination of USA President: Abraham Lincoln.

96. [ON PUBLIC EDUCATION] "I can't give you brains, but I can give you a diploma."—The Wizard of Oz movie.

97. "Go back, go back and do your duty, as I have done mine and our country will be safe. Go back, go back ... I had rather die than be whipped."—CS General J. E. B. Stuart. Exhorting his troops to fight on without him, after he was mortally wounded.

98. [ON FINE PRINT] "The minute that you read something that you can't understand, you can almost be sure it was drawn up by a lawyer.—Will Rogers.

99. "Death, in its silent, sure march is fast gathering those whom I have longest loved, so that when he shall knock at my door, I will more willingly follow."—CS General Robert E. Lee, 1869.

100. [GOVERNMENTAL POWER] "The history of liberty is a history of limitations of governmental power, not the increase of it."—US President Woodrow Wilson.

101. "My religious belief teaches me to feel as safe in battle as in bed. God has fixed the time for my death. I do not concern myself about that, but to always be ready, no matter when it may overtake me."—C.S. General S. Jackson.
102. " ... The history of the world has been written in vain if it does not teach us that unrestrained authority can never be safely trusted in human hands."—Andrew Johnson.
103. "Without doing injustice to the living, it may safely be asserted that our loss is irreparable; and that among the shining hosts of the great and good who now cluster around the banner of the country, were there exists no purer spirit, no more heroic soul, than that of the illustrious man whose death I join you in lamenting."—CS President: Jefferson Davis in grieving the death of CS General Albert Sidney Johnston, 1862.
104. "Before a new ideology and government can be established, the old one must be replaced. Thus the Communist Party and their evil affiliations has been pressing forward for many of generations throughout our American Continent."—John T. Nall
105. "Karl Marx wrote letters to Frederick Engels on the subject of Negro slavery. Marx contended that the freeing of the American slaves would be favorable to the cause of the European proletarians. William Z. Foster as Secretary of the American Communist Party in 1993 wrote a book entitled (Towards Soviet America), which championed the desegregation of the South. Leon Trotsky, former number two man as head of the Bolshevik government in Russia, advocated the use of Negroes as the vanguard of the revolution in America. As a further example, Martin Luther King, Jr., was surrounded by known communists like Stanley Levison and Hunter Pitts O' Dell. It is completely logical that Marxist—bred communists should promote the U.S. civil rights revolution."—(Turning America Upside down), paragraph five second column on page 22 of the July-September 2007 of the Citizens Informer.
106. "The truth is this: The march of Providence is so slow and our desires so impatient; the work of progress is so immense and our means of aiding it so feeble; the life of humanity is so long, that of the individual so brief, that we often see only the ebb of the advancing wave and are thus discouraged. it is history that teaches us to hope."—CS General Robert E. Lee, near the end of his life.
107. [ON JUDICIAL RESTRAINT] "Judicial includes doing something that is not the judge's right to do. So when courts actually make the laws, make make the rules that govern society, they become judicial activists."—Hon. Roy Moore, Chief Justice of Alabama.
108. "Duty is ours: consequences are God's"—CS Gen. Stonewall Jackson's final words.

109. "If the freedom of speech is taken away than dumb and silent we may be led like sheep to the slaughter."—US President George Washington.
110. "When those that represents us in government, starts to believe that they are much wiser than our founding fathers. Than it is clear that they have become foolish and can no longer be in charge of our Country."—John T. Nall.
111. "The Internal Revenue Service, is another legal way to prevent someone from having to come to your house and steal from you at gun point."—John T. Nall.
112. "Our Southern Culture, is a combination of different cultures of European nations, with a touch of non-European races from around the world. With this quality of blending in a natural way, with music, our accents and the ideology of life for our society, Southern Culture was born.—John T. Nall
113. "No free man shall ever be debarred the use of arms."—Thomas Jefferson.
114. [CONCLUSION OF EVOLUTION] "A rock is still a rock, a tree is still a tree, a cat is still a cat and a dog is still a dog. And finally, an ape is still an ape and a man is still a man. And yet! Stupidity, is without boundaries."—John T. Nall
115. [Mutt or Heinz 57] "A little bit of everything and a whole lot of nothing. Much like a mongrel dog. Let this not become the same fate for our own people and race."—John T. Nall
116. "Once, our freedom of speech was guaranteed by our Constitution. Now under political correctness and persecution, we are forced to kneel at the altar of humiliation and to apologize to the false gods of socialism for the Freedom of "THOUGHT."—John T. Nall
117. "In this enlightened age, there are few I believe, but what will acknowledge, that slavery as an institution is a moral and political evil in any Country. It is useless to expatiate on its disadvantages."—Robert E. Lee-December 1856.
118. "God is ought to be our aim: and I am quite contented that His designs should be accomplished and not mine."—CS Gen. Robert E. Lee
119. "The theory of communism may be summed up in one sentence; abolish all private property."—Karl Marx
120. "A communist is like a crocodile; when it opens its mouth you cannot tell whether it is trying to smile or preparing to eat you up."—British Prime Minister, Winston Churchill
121. "Communism is the death of the soul. It is the organization of total Conformity—in short, of tyranny—and it is committed to making tyranny universal."—Adlai E. Stevenson
122. "Communism, possess a language which every people can understand—its elements are hunger, envy, and death."—Heinrich Heine

123. "With equal pleasure I have as often taken notice that Providence has been pleased to give this one connected country to one united people—a people descended from the same ancestors, speaking the same language, professing the same religion, attached to the same principles of government, very similar in their manners and customs, and who, by their joint counsels, arms, and efforts, fighting side by side throughout a long and bloody war, have nobly established general liberty and independence."—John Jay, in the 5th paragraph of Federalist No. 2
124. "When it comes to the heart; we cannot judge a person by race or gender. But only by the good and evil actions of the choices that they have acted upon."—John T. Nall.
125. "Freedom is once accepted, when other people accepts that you are truly a free people."—Michael Arnold Nicholls—{Big Mike}—Born on July 14, 1958 in Hackney, England and died July 2, 2008 in Salisbury, North Carolina CSA. He left a Son and a Daughter, including a step-Daughter behind. {A True Confederate American Patriot.}
126. "Good and honorable intensions, can lead to be betrayal by those with wicked hearts."—John T. Nall.
127. [Politicians] "When the Wizard say's to the scarecrow that he is unable to give him a brain. Yet he is able to give him a Diploma. I ask you! What good is a Diploma without a brain? Does this not sound like a politician to you?"—John T. Nall [The Wizard of Oz Movie]
128. "True science is to remain neutral without prejudice and bias believes.To base all evidence on scientific facts and not theories or probabilities. To search for the answers within the logical reasoning and if necessary to search within the non-logical reasoning. To understand that man's research has its limitations and cannot explain all things in science."—John T. Nall.
129. "Secession belongs to a different class of remedies. It is to be justified upon the basis that the States are sovereign. There was a time when none denied it. I hope the time may come again, when a better comprehension of the theory of our Government, and inalienable rights of the people of the States, will prevent anyone from denying that each State is a sovereign, and thus may reclaim the grants which it has made to any agent whomsoever."—Jefferson Davis Farewell Address to U. S. Senate, 21 January 1861
130. "No one should ever underestimate the desire or the termination the underdog to win to the very end."—John T. Nall.
131. "You must study to be frank with the world: frankness is the child of courage. Say just what you mean to do on every occasion, and take it for granted that you mean to do right."—CS General Robert E. Lee

132. [Despotism of the multitude] "However, democracy is the only tolerable form into which human society can be thrown, that a man is not permitted to hesitate about its merits, without the suspicion of being a friend to tyranny, that is, of being a foe to mankind?"—Edmond Burke
133. "A nation is no better than the individuals that compose it."—Cordell Hunt
134. "The North isn't a place. It's just a direction out of the South."—Roy Blount, Jr.
135. "The South-where roots, place, family, and tradition are the essence of identity."—Social historian Carl N. Degler
136. "Liberty without wisdom, and without virtue is folly, vice, and madness, without tuition or restraint."(Reflections on the Revolution in France, 1790.)—Edmond Burke
137. "The South is America. The South is what we started out with this bizarre, slightly troubling, basically wonderful country—fun, danger, friendliness, energy, enthusiasm, and brave, crazy, tough people."—P.J.O' Rourke
138. "The most unjust and impolitic of all things, unequal taxation."—(1797)—Edmond Burke
139. "Whenever you do a thing, act as if the entire world is watching."—Thomas Jefferson
140. "When full grown, it [vanity] is the worst of vices, and the occasional mimic of them all. It makes the whole man false."—(1791)—Edmond Burke
141. "There is as much dignity in plowing a field as in writing a poem."—Booker T. Washington
142. "Superstition is the religion of feeble minds."—(Reflections on the Revolution in France, 1790.)—Edmond Burke
143. "Whatever I have learned from my long affair with Mississippi is that America's greatest strength, and its greatest weakness, is our belief that we can always start over, that things can be made better, transcended.—Anthony Walton
144. "If you are going to be underestimated by people who speak more rapidly, the temptation is to speak slowly and strategically and outwit them."—Doris Betts, on the Southern drawl
145. "You've got to continue to grow, or you're just like last night's cornbread—stale and dry."—Loretta Lynn
146. "What we have done for ourselves alone dies with us; what we have done for others and the world remains and is immortal."—Albert Pike
147. "We must adjust to changing times and still hold to unchanging principles."—Ex-US President, Jimmy Carter, quoting his high school teacher, Ms. Julia Coleman
148. "The fear of God makes heroes; the fear of man makes cowards."—Native of the Confederate State of Tennessee, and a Medal of Honor Winner.—US Sgt. Alvin York
149. "One can only trust politicians not to be trustworthy."—John T. Nall.

150. "To defend the cause of our nation of the Confederate States and States Rights is to defend the cause and the principles of our founding forefathers that had established the United States from its very birth."—John T. Nall.

151. "In the first place, we should insist that if the immigrant who comes here in good faith becomes as American and assimilates himself to us, he shall be treated on an exact equality with everyone else, for it is an outrage to discriminate against any such man because of creed, or birthplace, or origin ... But this is predicated upon the person's becoming in every facet an American, and nothing but an American ... There can be no divided allegiance here. Any man who says he is an American, but something else also, isn't an American at all. We have room for one flag, the American flag (U.S. Flag) ... We have room for but one language here, and that is the English Language (National Language) ... and we have room for but one sole loyalty and that is a loyalty to the American People (U.S. Citizens).—[1907 Personal views from U.S. President Theodore Roosevelt's as to the identity of the American version of the United States only, and intended to be and to remain as such. This is not directed toward other American Nations of this American Continent.

152. "Loyalty above all else, except that of honor." ; Author Unknown.

153. "The historians uses the term "Civil War', to define the disobedience of the Sovereign Southern States, against the former government to which they were volunteer members. The same former government that was transformed from a Constitutional Republic, to a Centralized Democracy."—John T. Nall.

154. "In war, as in peace," observed Weaver, "people remain civilized by acknowledging bounds beyond which they must not go." Echoing the words of Lee, Weaver understood no necessary contradiction in the term "Christian" as applied to the profession of arms. The Christian soldier must seek the verdict of battle always remembering that there is a higher law by which he and his opponent will be judged, and which enjoins against fighting as the barbarian."—Richard M. Weaver/ Page 17, from [WAR CRIMES AGAINST SOUTHERN CIVILIANS]—by: Walter Brian Cisco

155. "Why does Col. Grigsby refer to me to learn how to deal with mutineers?

He should have them shot where they stand."—CS Gen. Stonewall Jackson's response when asked how to proceed with soldiers who refused orders.

156. "I am careful not to confuse excellence with perfection. Excellence, I can reach for; perfection is God's business."—Michael J. Fox, Actor

157. The late F.B.I. Director J. Edgar Hoover once warned the American people that "Communist influence does exist in the Negro movement and it is this influence which is vitally important." He said the Communist Party "strives only to exploit what are often legitimate Negro complaints and grievances for the advancement of communist objectives ... Racial incidents are magnified and dramatized by communists in an effort to generate racial tensions."—Martin Luther King Jr. (His Dream, our nightmare!) By: Pastor Peter J. Peters. Page. 4

158. "A man's got to do what a man's got to do."—John Wayne, Actor

159. "A man has got to know his limitations."—Clint Eastwood, Actor

160. "Never argue with an idiot; they'll drag you down to their level and beat you with experience."—Anonymous

161. "Those who hammer their guns into plows will plow for those who do not."—Thomas Jefferson

162. "The first step in liquidating a people is to erase its memory, Destroy it's books, its Culture, and its history. Then you have somebody write new books manufacture a new Culture, invent a new history. Before long the nation will begin to forget what it is and what it was."—Milan Kundera, {The Book of Laughter and Forgetting.}

163. "In 1860 the population of the United States was just over 31 million. The combined battle deaths of the Union and Confederate Armies in Civil War one were approximately 215,000. The U.S. Census Bureau projected population for 2050 is 393,000,000. Projecting from these figures gives us 2,678,000 battle dead for Civil War Two. This figure should be regarded as a baseline minimum because Civil War One's casualties were largely reserved for military personnel."—Thomas W. Chittum, {Civil War Two, The Coming Breakup of America} Page. 83

164. "America is like a healthy body and its resistance is threefold: its patriotism, its morality, and its spiritual life. If we can undermine these three areas, America will collapse from within."—Joseph Stalin

165. "Yet, incredibly—even after thorough documentation of King's affiliations with communists, after the revelations about his personal moral flaws, and after proof of his brazen dishonesty in plagiarizing his dissertation and several other published writings—incredibly there is no proposal to rescind the holiday that honors him.—Samuel Francis, {the King Holiday and its Meaning} Speech by Senator Jesse Helms, Foreword by Samuel Francis Published by the Council of Conservative Citizens, Page 11 and 12.

166. "Though it may be questionable as to the moral character of, J. Edgar Hoover. Yet his devotion to duty with the F.B.I. and his patriotism to his country is not questionable. It is typical in knowing that the Socialists Americans would condemn any actions of the United States during war against

a Communist nation. But, to attack the character of Mr. Hoover for being a homosexual, as not being trustworthy is indeed insulting to say the least. Yet was it not the Communist Americans that are promoting homosexuality, atheism, and abortion, and so on?"—John T. Nall

167. "God did not intend for the United States to be a "nation of secular laws" and that the separation of church and state is a lie. We have been told this to keep religious people out of politics."—Florida Republican Rep. Katherine Harris.

168. "We have to have the faithful in government, because that is God's will. separating religion and politics is so wrong because God is the one who chooses our rulers."—Florida Republican Rep. Katherine Harris.

169. "If you've not electing Christians, then in essence you are going to legislate sin."—Florida Republican Rep. Katherine Harris.

170. "If we are the ones not actively involved in electing those godly men and women, then we're going to have a nation of secular laws. That's not what our Founding Fathers intended, and certainly isn't what God intended."—Florida Republican Rep. Katherine Harris.

171. "The federal government is sending each and every one of us a $600.00

Rebate. If we spend that money at Wal-Mart, the money will go to China. If we purchase a good car, it will go to Japan. If we spend it on gasoline,

It will go to the Arabs. If we purchase a computer, it will go to India.

If we purchase fruit and vegetables, it will go to Mexico, Honduras and Guatemala. If we purchase useless crap, it will go to Taiwan and none of it will help the American economy. The only way to keep that money here home, is to buy prostitutes and beer, since these are about the only products still produced in the U.S.".—Grapevine Publications 2008

172. "Any society which suppresses the heritage of its conquered minorities, prevents their history and denies them their symbols, has sewn the seed of its own destruction".—Sir W. Wallace.

173. "Here in America we are descended in blood and in spirit from revolutionist and rebels—men and women who dare to dissent from accepted doctrine. As their heirs, may we never confuse honest dissent with disloyal subversion."—Dwight D. Eisenhower 1890-1969.

174. "Any government big enough to give you everything you want is a government big enough to take away everything you have."—Thomas Jefferson.

175. "The reputation of an individual is of minor importance to the opinion posterity may form of the motives which governed the South in their late struggle for the maintenance of the principles of the Constitution. I hope therefore, a true history will be written, and justice will be done them."—CS General Robert E. Lee.
176. "I have accepted Jesus Christ as my personal Savior when I was young and I have the assurance of salvation. I believe in the Bible and I do not believe the government has any right to interfere with the practice of religion, including Christianity. This includes the right to have prayer in school, observe important religious holidays, to allow students to include references to Jesus Christ in their valedictory and salutatory speeches etc.

    Our Constitution was written by men who believed in God and provides for freedom of religion, not freedom from religion as the politically correct are insisting on enforcing today."—Congressman Ron Paul, a 10-term Republican from Texas. Page 24 of the Citizens Informer Oct-Dec 2007

177. "The first step in reducing the Yankee Empire is to restore the Consitutional Republic, thus eliminate the Golden Goose ("Internal Revenue Service"). Then, the second thing to do would be to release the occupied Nation of the Confederate States of America."—John T. Nall
178. "Get correct views of life, and learn to see the world in its true light. It will enable you to live pleasantly, to do good, and when summoned away, to leave without regret."—CS General. Robert E. Lee
179. "Our Southern homes have been pillaged, sacked, and burned; our mothers, wives and little ones, driven forth amid the brutal insults of your soldiers. Is it any wonder that we fight with such desperation?"—John B. Gordon, 1863.
180. "What passes as standard American history is really Yankee history written by New Englanders or their puppets to glorify Yankee heroes and ideals."—Dr. Grady Mcwhitney
181. "With all of my devotion to the Union and the feeling of loyalty and duty of an American citizen, I have not been able to make up my mind to raise my hand against my relatives, my children, my home. I have therefore resigned my commission in the Army, and save in defense of my native State, with the sincere hope that my poor services may never be needed, I hope I may never be called to draw my sword."—Former US General. Robert E. Lee
182. "The country has decided by the most prolonged and fearful war, by the successful operations of vast armies and navies, by an incalculable sacrifice of precious life, and an enormous expenditure of money, that, whether lawful or unlawful, constitutional or unconstitutional, there shall be no secession of states from the Union. The doctrine of State sovereignty, which was the only plea of

the rebellion, has been judged in the battle-field and overthrown by arms."—Harper's Weekly Journal of Civilization, November 25, 1865

183. "I came here as a friend ... Let us stand together. Although we differ in color, we should not differ in sentiment."—LT. General. Nathan B. Forrest, CSA

184. "The War Between the States established this principle; (That the Federal Government is, through its courts, this final judge of its own powers."—US President. Woodrow Wilson

185. "To me, the campaign by certain groups to remove all the symbols and memorials to our Southern past amounts to the same thing ... a desecration of graves. Every flag or monument that is removed, every plaque taken down, every school or street or bridge that is renamed, is no different from a broken tombstone. It is wanton and hateful violence directed at the dead who can no longer defend themselves?"—John Field Pankow

186. "Political correctness has replaced witch trials and communist hearings as the preferred way to torment our fellow countrymen."—Sharyn McCrumb, 2004

187. "Rebellion to tyrants is obedience to God."—Motto on Thomas Jefferson's seal [c. 1776]

188. "I love the Union and the Constitution, but I would rather leave the Union with the Constitution than remain in the Union without it.—CSA President: Jefferson Davis

189. "The war between the North and the South is a tariff war. The war is further, not for any principle, does not touch the question of slavery, and in fact turns on the Northern lust for sovereignty."—Karl Marx, 1861

190. "Modest in prosperity, gentle in peace, brave in battle and undespairing in defeat, they knew no law of life but loyalty and truth and civic faith, and to these virtues they consecrated their strength."—From a Confederate Monument at Decatur, Georgia CSA

191. "The assertion that the South fought for slavery is Yankee propaganda and a monstrous distortion."—CS President; Jefferson Davis

192. "As a Confederate soldier and as a citizen of Virginia, I deny the charge, and denounce it as a calumny. We were not rebels; we did not fight to perpetuate human slavery, but for our rights and privileges under a government established over us by our fathers and in defense of our homes."—Richard Henry Lee, CS Colonel—During an 1893 speech.

193. "At Mount Rushmore, you have the faces of the presidents of two nations.

The two on the left are of the former Constitutional Republic, while the two on the right are of a new Centralized Democracy, which regulates the Constitution, instead of being bound by it."—John T. Nall

194. "Every evil that has befallen our institution is directly traceable to the perversion of the compact of union and the illegal control by the federal government of un-delegated powers."—CS President: Jefferson Davis—after the war.
195. "Let them teach their children that their patriotic fathers fought for their fatherland; that they were inspired by as patriotic motives as ever fired the hearts or nerved the arms of freemen; and though our cause has gone down in disaster, in ruin, in blood, not one stain of dishonor rests upon it."—CS Gen. Wade Hampton 1895
196. "Our cause was so just, so sacred that had I known all that has come to pass, had I had known all that was to be inflicted upon me, all that my country was to suffer, all that our posterity was to endure, I would do it all over again."—CS President: Jefferson Davis
197. "We must educate our children about the difference of truth and lies, so they can understand the difference between freedom and tyranny. They are taught that their heritage is racist and proud symbols of their fathers are of hate."—Milan Kundera
198. "Southern Youth, you have no reason to be ashamed of your ancestors.

    See to it that they have no reason to be ashamed of you"—Charlie Reese

199. [ON TOLERANCE] "Replacing the mercy of disapproval with tolerance is replacing medicine with poison."—Rev. Robert Hart, Canon Theologian Of the Anglican Diocese of the Chesapeake
200. [ON HISTORY] "To be ignorant of what occurred before you were born is to remain always a child. For what is the worth of human life, unless it is woven into the life of our ancestors by the records of history?"—Marcus Tullius Cicero
201. [ON HUMANITARIANISM] "Foreign aid might be defined as a transfer of money from poor people in rich countries to rich people in poor countries."—Douglas Casey, author of Strategic Investing
202. [ON ATROCITIES] "To speak of atrocious crimes in mild language is treason to virtue."—Edmund Burke
203. [ON BROTHERHOOD] "The South is a vital and long-lasting bond, a corporate identity assumed by those who have contributed to it."—M.E. Bradford
204. [ON MISINFOTNATION] "The real problem in America is not so much what people don't know but rather what they think they know that just ain't so"—Will Rogers
205. [ON TAXATION] "The only difference between a tax man and a taxidermist is that the taxidermist leaves the skin."—Mark Twain

206. [ON SCHOOL] "Education is what remains after one has forgotten what one has learned in school."—Albert Einstein
207. [ON THE PILGRIM FATHERS] "Is it not strange that descendants of those Pilgrim Fathers who crossed the Atlantic to pursue their own freedom of opinion, have always proved themselves intolerant of the spiritual liberty of others?"—CS Gen. Robert E. Lee
208. [ON THE PAST] "History is the memory of time, the life of the dead, the happiness of the living."—Capt. John Smith
209. [ON PUBLIC HEALTH CARE] "If you think health care is expensive now, wait until you see what it costs when it's free."—P.J. O'Rourke
210. "In a world full of people and circumstances that change from one moment to the next, the truth that Jesus is always the same is a wonderful source of security. While the winds of change swirl all around us, we can stand firm in the fact that Jesus is the same yesterday, today, and forever."—Steve Miller [One Minute Promises] last paragraph on page 92.
211. [Septic Truck Sign] "Caution: Vehicle may be Transporting Political Promises!"
212. "My shoes are gone; my clothes are almost gone. I'm weary, I'm sick, I'm hungry. My family has been killed or scattered. And I have suffered all of this for my country. I love my country. But if this war is ever over, I'll be damned if I ever love another country."—A Confederate States Soldier's reply, during his retreat to Appomattox.
213. "The state may not acknowledge the sovereignty of the Judeo-Christian God and attribute to that God our religious freedom."—U.S. District Judge Myron Thompson, ACLU Member.
214. "If the posted copies of the Ten Commandments are to have any effect at all, it will be to induce the school children to read, meditate upon, perhaps to venerate and obey, the Commandments … [This] is not a permissible state objective."—U.S. Supreme Court (1980).
215. "The presence of the cross on federal land conveys a message of endorsement of religion."—U.S. District Judge Robert J. Timlin.
216. "The cross must come down, and no amount of political maneuvering or grandstanding will prevent that."—ACLU Attorney Peter Eliasberg.
217. "It is now time, and perhaps long overdue, for this Court to enforce its initial permanent injunction forbidding the presence of Mount Soledad cross on property."—U.S. District Judge Gordon Thompson, Jr.
218. "In this secular world, evolution is man's religion and the evolution of technology will lead them to a world of paradise. Such a foolish notion for those lost souls."—John T. Nall

219. "The man who doesn't read good books has no advantage over the man who can't read them."—Mark Twain.
220. "Character is what you are; reputation is what you try to make people think you are."—Anonymous.
221. "The South is the only place in the world where nothing has to be explained to me."—U.S. President. Woodrow Wilson
222. "The Southern States did not secede from the Union to preserve or to extend slavery. The Constitution of the Confederate States expressly prohibited the African slave trade; and, while it gave slave-holders the right to carry their slaves into any part of the Confederacy, under its provisions, any Territory might become either a free or a slave-holding State, according to the will of its citizens. The determination of the Northern States to prevent the carrying of slaves into the Territories was in no way shaken by the decision of the Supreme Court against them. When Mr. Lincoln was elected by a party pledged to disregard this decision and advocating various measures opposed to Southern interests, the crises came, and the South left the Union.

It can therefore be said that although the North and South had gradually become hostile to each other on account of various conflicting interests, the immediate cause of secession was the question of the extension of slavery into the Territories. The North opposed the extension of slavery and denied that any State had the constitutional right to leave the Union. As the peaceable secession of the Southern States was neither an extension of slavery nor a violation of the Constitution; we may conclude that the war was caused by the determination of the North to preserve the Union. This determination led to open war when the United States flag was fired upon Fort Sumter. The result of the war, though not proving that the South was wrong, has been for the best interests of both sections."—Number 4, of page 262, in LEE'S New School History of the United States 1907 Edition. Grapevine Publications.

223. "American companies have either shifted output to low wage countries or come to buy parts and assembled products from countries like Japan. The U.S. is abandoning its status as an industrial power."—Akio Morita, Co-founder and chairman of Sony Corp.
224. "Compromise, hell! ... If freedom is right and tyranny is wrong, why should those who believe in freedom treat it as if it were a roll of bologna to be bartered a slice at a time?"—From the 1959 editorial of North Carolina Republican Senator; Jesse Helms.
225. "I had sought election in 1972 to try to derail the freight train of liberalism that was gaining speed toward its destination of government-run everything, paid for with big tax bills and record

debt,"—North Carolina Republican Senator; Jesse Helms, in writing his 2005 memoir, "Here's where I stand".

226. "It would indeed be the ultimate tragedy if the history of the human race proved to be nothing more noble than the story of an ape playing with a box of matches on a petrol dump."—David Ormsby—Gore

227. "Rebel prisoners in our hands are to be subjected to a treatment finding

Its parallels only in the conduct of savage tribes and resulting in the death of multitudes by the slow but designed process of starvation and by mortal diseases occasioned by insufficient and unhealthy food and wanton exposure of their persons to the inclemency of the weather."—(Preamble to the H.R. 97) that was passed by both houses of the United States. It is the official War Crime policy toward the genocide against all Confederate American Prisoners of War.

228. "The more Indians we can kill this year, the less will have to kill next year. For the more I see of these Indians, the more convinced I am that they all have to be killed or be maintained as a species of paupers."—United States General; William T. Sherman.

229. "If it is a crime to love the South, its cause and its President, then I am a criminal. I would rather lie down in this prison and die than leave it owing allegiance to a government such as yours."—Belle Boyd, Secret Agent of the Confederate States government.

230. "Out of these troubled times, our fifth objective—A New World Order, can emerge … We are now in sight of a United Nations that performs as envisioned by its founders (note added: i.e., establish a One-World Government."—United States President; George H.W. Bush, Sr.

231. "The government is a juggling Confederacy of a cheat … and enslave the people."—Edmund Burke

232. "Let men not ask what the law requires, but give whatever freedom demands."—Confederate States President: Jefferson Davis.

233. "We can't be so fixated on our desires to preserve the rights of ordinary Americans."—United States President; William Jefferson Clinton, USA today, 11 of March of 1993.

234. "There are two world histories. One is the official and full of lies, destined to be taught in schools. The other is the secret history, which harbors the true causes and occurrences."—Honoree deBalzac.

235. "It is the sacred principles enshrined in the UN Charter to which we will henceforth pledge our allegiance."—United States President; George W. Bush.

236. "The ranks and file were chiefly farmers and small merchants. Comparatively very few were owners of slaves; but they were all descended from ancestors whose fortunes and blood had been freely spent in the war of the revolution. They volunteered in obedience to the call of their State to resist invasion. They came with a firm determination to do their full duty."—Confederate States Captain; Wm. H.S. Burgwyn, 35th Regiment of the North Carolina Troops.
237. "The real rulers in Washington are invisible, an exercise power from behind the scenes." Felix Frankfurter, Supreme Court Justice 1952.
238. "I believe that we are again engaged in a great Civil War, a Cultural War that's about to hijack your birthright to think and say what resides in your heart. I fear you no longer trust the pulsing life blood of liberty inside you ... The stuff that made the country rise from wilderness into the miracle that it is."—Charleston Heston, Actor and Gun Rights supporter speaking at the Harvard Law School Forum, 16th of February of 1999.
239. "No power over the freedom of religion (is) delegated to the United States by the Constitution."—Thomas Jefferson.
240. "Principles don't have funerals. We are safe while we keep a save grip on our principles."—H.W. Johnston, Georgia and Confederate, and author of—"The truth of the War Conspiracy of 1861."
241. "I do not know what the Union would be worth if saved by the sword."—Senator William H. Seward, speaking out against the idea of war."
242. "Whereas most Northern cities have neighborhoods flavored by Cultural Identities, that is missing in the South. Southern cities have no European Ethnic centers. There is no Greek-town, no little Italy and no German Neighborhood ... For the average Southerner, the old country is neither Poland nor France; it is the Confederacy."—Ronald J. Rychalk; Professor of law at the University of Mississippi School of law in Oxford.
243. [The Lost Cause] "A cause which has at its heart the defense of home and family. The independence of individual conscience from the tyranny of government. And the freedom to choose methods of work and worship, was not and never can be "lost". Indeed, the South need not rise again. For in Spirit and in Truth it has never really fallen. May all our causes be so noble, and our defense of them as courageous. For in this alone lies the preservation of our liberty!—Anonymous.
244. "He alone deserves to be remembered by his children who treasures up and preserves the memory of his fathers."—Edmund Burke.
245. "You will take positions by military force of the printing establishments of the New York World and Journal of Commerce. And prohibit any further publication thereof. You are therefore commanded forthwith to arrest and in prison the editors, proprietors and publishers of those newspapers.—U.S.

President, Abraham Lincoln response to the violation of his Nations Constitution. This General order was given to U.S. General John Dicks.

246. "If you tell a lie big enough and long enough, people will begin to believe it.—Nazi Germany President, Adolph Hitler.

247. "Confederate States; President Jefferson Davis, believed that war should consist solely of combat between organized armies. He was against the killing of civilians and the destruction of private property during hostilities. the President proudly proclaimed after the war. "I am happy to remember that when our army invaded the enemy's Country, their property was safe".—Confederate States Military Officer.

248. "Still, if you will not fight for the right when you can easily win without bloodshed; if you will not fight when your victory will be sure and not too costly; you may come to the moment when you will have to fight with all the odds against you and only precarious chance of survival. There may even be a worse case. You may have to fight when there is no hope of victory, because it is better to perish than live as slaves".—Winston Churchill.

249. " … make them so sick of war that generations would pass away before they would again appeal to it".—Union General. William T. Sherman on conducting the war of aggression against the Confederacy.

250. "We must act with vindictive earnestness against the Sioux, even to their extermination, men, women, and children. Nothing less will reach the root of the cause".—Union General; William T. Sherman, on conducting war aggression against the American Indians.

251. "In one sense the charge that I did not fight fair is true. I fought for success and not for display. There was no man in the Confederate army who had less of the spirit of a knight errantry in him, or who took a more practical view of war than I did."—General; John S. Mosby, as the guerilla leader in the Confederate States Army.

252. "Duty is ours, consequences are God's."—C.S. General; Stonewall Jackson.

253. "War loses a great deal of its romance after a soldier has seen his first battle."—C.S. General; John S. Mosby.

254. "If we must be enemies, let us be men, and fight t out as we propose to do, and not deal in hypocritical appeals to God and humanity".—Union General; William T. Sherman to Confederate General; John B. Hood.

255. "There are no easy answers, but there are simple answers. We must have the courage to do what we know is morally right."—United States President; Ronald Reagan.

256. "One of the sad signs of our times is that we have demonized those who produce, subsidized those who refuse to produce, and canonized those who complain."—Thomas Sowell.
257. "Strange times are these in which we live when old and young are taught falsehood's in school. And the one man that dares to tell the truth is called at once a lunatic and fool."—Plato
258. "Consider that it is not entirely clear that member nations may withdraw from the United Nations. Recall our first civil war. Attempted peaceful secession by the southern states was answered by armed invasion and occupation by armies of the northern states even though there was nothing in the Constitution that explicitly forbade secession by member states. Now we find ourselves in a parallel situation with the United Nations. Because (to the best of my knowledge) nothing in the UN Charter expressly allows a nation to withdraw, any attempt by the United States to quite the United Nations may be used as grounds for an invasion by UN troops.—Author: Thomas W. Chittum, of (CIVIL WAR TWO), the Coming Breakup of America. Page.194
259. "Government does not solve problems; it subsidizes them".—United States President: Ronald Reagan.
260. " … Adventurer's swarmed out of the North, as much the enemies of the one race as of the other, to cozen, beguile, and use the Negroes … In the villages the Negroes were the office holder, men who knew none of the uses of authority, except its insolences." The policy of the Congressional leaders wrought … a veritable overthrow of Civilization in the South … In their determination to "put the white South under the heel of the black South."—US President: Woodrow Wilson.
261. "The white men were roused by a mere instinct of self-preservation … until as last there had spring into existence a great Ku Klux Klan, a veritable empire of the South, to protect the Southern Country."—US President: Woodrow Wilson.
262. "My momma told me, and I trust my momma. And her momma told her and she trust her momma and I trust both of them. But my momma told me back in the 50's and the 60's the only kind of white woman that would take up with a black man back in the 50's and the 60's was a trashy white woman. The only kind of white woman that would take up with a black man in the 50's and the 60's was a floozy, was a floozy! Was a low life snail eaten white woman. That's the kind of woman Obama's momma was.

And that's what's my momma told me. And if you don't like it, you can go tell my momma that you don't like it. But my momma told me and my momma's momma told her and all the momma's in the community are black saw those trashy white women hanging around on the outskirts of town called the black bottom where the black men live. Hanging around and the outside of the skirts of town with their skirts jack up and their breast showing hoping that some of these black men would take an interest."—The Honorable Black Minister: James David Manning.

(This was a partial speech he made during the 2008 Presidents Campaign. His response was toward the Liberal Media that was targeting the 17-year-old daughter of Sarah Palin. Sarah Palin was running for Vice President for the U. S. Presidency campaign on the McCain's Republican's ticket.)

263. [The end of State Sovereignty] the son of Daniel Webster calling to America: "Liberty and Union, one and inseparable, now and forever."
264. "States Sovereignty is true liberty, because it is the people that are free. It was States Sovereignty that created the Union and later the Confederacy! Liberty and government cannot become as one! And the freedom of the Union government that had been bounded and chained to the Federal Constitution requires security and liberty for each State. But, in order for the Union to be free, the people must be enslaved."—John T. Nall
265. "Nothing happens in government or the nation that is not planned without reason and purpose!"—U.S. President: Franklin D. Roosevelt.
266. "If we allowed private banks to control the issuance of money. We would one day wake up homeless on this continent.—Thomas Jefferson.
267. "During the battles with the bankers, Andrew Jackson had referred to them as (A Den of Vipers).
268. "Any people, anywhere, being inclined and having the power, have the right to rise up and shake off the existing government, and form a new one that suits them better. This is a most valuable and most sacred right. A right which we hope and believe is to liberate the world. Nor is this right confined to cases in which the whole people of an existing government may choose to exercise it. Any portion of such people that can may revolutionize, and make their own, of so many of the territory as they inhabit."—Abraham Lincoln, January 12, 1848.
269. "We're going to do for blacks exactly what blacks did for the revolution. By which I mean nothing."—Che' Guevara, a Communist Guerrilla in South America, Cuba and the Congo.
270. "The Negro is indolent and lazy and spends his money on frivolities, where as the Europeans is forward-looking, organized and intelligent."—Che' Guevara.
271. "Mexicans are a band of illiterate Indians."—Che Guevara; A Communist Member.
272. "If ever time should come, when vain and aspiring men shall possess the highest seats in government, our Country will stand in need of its experienced patriots to prevent its ruin."—Samuel Adams.

273. "In this present crisis, government is not the solution to our problem; <u>GOVERNMENT</u> is the problem."—Ronald Reagan.
274. "The contest is not over, the strife is not ended. It has entered upon a new and enlarged arena. The champions of constitutional liberty must spring to the struggle, like armed men from the seminated dragon's teeth, until the government of the United States is brought back to its constitutional limits, and the tyrant's plea of "necessity" is bound in chains strong as adamant: {For freedom's battle once begun, Bequeathed by bleeding sire to son, though baffled oft, is ever won."—Confederate States President: Jefferson Davis.
275. "The Negro situation is being exploited fully and continuously by Communists on a national scale. Current programs include intensified attempts to infiltrate Negro mass organizations. The Communist Party's objectives are not to aid the Negroes—but are designed to take advantage of all controversial issues on the race question so as to create unrest, dissension and confusion in the minds of the American people."—The warning was spoken eloquently on January 16, 1958, when FBI Director J. Edgar Hoover appeared before a committee of U.S. Congress.
276. "Being a racialist, not a racist mind you, but a "racialist," meaning one who is proud of his own race of people and committed to their continuation as a race upon this Earth, I understand their motivation. Your race is your extended family, period. If you do not align yourself with your own race, and want to see their continuation and success as a race and do your part to see this happen, than you are not worth your weight in anything. It's as simple as that."—Gary Bankston is a columnist for the Winona (MS) Times.
277. "The visible order of the universe proclaims a supreme intelligence."—Jean—Jacques Rousseau.
278. "Science brings men nearer to God."—Louis Pasteur.
279. "The visible marks of extraordinary wisdom and power appear so plainly in all the works of the creation that rational creature, who will but seriously reflect on them, cannot miss the discovery of a Deity."—John Locke.
280. "As a house implies a builder, and a garment a weaver, and a door a carpenter, so does the existence of the Universe imply a Creator."—Marquis de Vauvenargues.
281. "It is impossible to account for the creation of the universe without the Agency of a Supreme Being."—George Washington.
282. "From knowledge of His work, we shall know Him."—Robert Boyle.
283. "We cannot fathom the mystery of a single flower. Nor is it intended that we should."—John Locke.
284. "In questions of science, the authority of a thousand is not worth the humble reasoning of a single individual."—Galileo Galilei.

285. "So irresistible are thee evidences of an intelligent and powerful Agent that, of the infinite numbers of men who have exited thro' all the time, they have believed, in the proportion of a million at least to unite, in the hypothesis of an external pre-existence of a creator, rather than in that of a self-existent Universe."—Thomas Jefferson.
286. "Nature is the art of God."—Dante Alighieri.
287. "The more I study nature, the more I stand amazed at the work of the Creator."—Louis Pasteur.
288. "It is the duty of the patriot to protect his country from the government".—Thomas Paine.
289. "Whenever the legislators endeavor to take away and destroy the property of the people, or reduce them to slavery under arbitrary power, they put themselves into a state of war with the people, who are thereupon absolved from any further obedience."—John Locke.
290. "Intelligence, does not imply that a person is not ignorant, or that a person is wise. It only implies that the person is smarter than most others.—John T. Nall.
291. {God's attitude about money} "Money is neither good nor bad, moral nor immoral. It is the use of it that will matter eternally."—Larry Burkett.
292. "It is the duty of the patriot to protect his country from the Government."—Thomas Paine.
293. "One of the greatest perils which threaten us now is the tendency to Centralization, the absorption of the rights of the States, and the concentration of all power in the General Government. When that shall be accomplished, if ever, the days of the Republic are numbered."—Orville browning, U.S. President; Andrew Johnson's secretary of the interior.
294. "When anyone at any time speaks negative remarks about the Southern States, its people and the symbols of honor, does so out of ignorance and hatred. Cause by from being small minded in thought, and not understanding all of the real truthful facts our in history of our people."—John T. Nall.
295. "There is only one thing the government is good at, spending somebody else's money."—Charlie Daniels 24th of October of 2008.
296. Speaker: "According to the Southern Poverty Law Center, Michigan in general, peculiarly the 8th district. There's a home to an anti-government militia and Klan groups. How would you use your position to teach respect for government and teach respect for ethnic racial diversity?"

John Mangopoulos: "Regarding the Southern Poverty Law Center. The Southern Poverty Law Center is a hate group as far as I'm concern. It's run by (Radical Socialist Leftist). People need to know that! I frankly don't care what they have to say, what they have to report. I could care less, alright! Now, when you talked about tolerance and diversity? Those are buzz words. We don't have to tolerate flowers. We don't have to tolerate a sweet aroma. What we are being asked to tolerate is perversions. We're being asked to tolerate baby killings. We're being asked to tolerate sodomy and homo-adoptions. I'm not going to ever tolerate that kind of perversions. And the day I do, Susan why don't you set me an appointment with Dr. K."—1998 Congressional Candidate: John Mangopoulos. (Dr. K, is in reference to Dr. Kevorkian, as the Suicide Doctor.

297. "The majority of guns by their silence, indicate they are in safe and sane hands."—George Washington.

298. "When government is in control by private economic power that is fascism.—1939 Franklin Roosevelt.

299. "An over infatuation with political partisanship would lead untimely to the demise of our country because the interest of the party would take over precedent over the interest of America.—George Washington. Farewell Address.

300. "We, must not lose touch with what we were, with what we had been, nor must we allow the well of our history to dry up. For a child without tradition is a child crippled before the world."—Louis L' Amour.

301. "A government big enough to give you everything you want, is strong enough to take everything you have."—Thomas Jefferson.

302. "When a people shall have become incapable of governing themselves and fit for a master, it is of little consequence from what quarter he comes."—George Washington.

303. "I do not believe that anyone can be a true Christian and yet vote for the Democratic Party. [In reference to the pro-gay rights and abortion rights] William Henry Hall Jr., of China Grove, North Carolina occupied [CSA].

304. "Without freedom of thought there can be no such thing as wisdom; and no such thing as Public Liberty, without Freedom of Speech."—Benjamin Franklin.

305. "Over grown military establishments are under any form of government inauspicious to liberty, and to be regarded as particularly hostile to (Republican Liberty)."—George Washington.

306. "Freedom is never dear at any price; it is the breath of life. What would a man not pay for living?"—Mahatma Gandhi.

307. "When people learn no tools of judgment and merely follow their hopes, the seeds of political manipulation is sown."—Stephen Jay Gould.

308. "That government is best which governs the least, because its people discipline themselves."—Thomas Jefferson.

309. "But a Constitution of Government once changed from Freedom, can never be restored. Liberty, once lost, is lost forever."—John Adams.
310. "The leader of genius must have the ability to make different opponents appear as if they belonged to one category." Nazi President; Adolph Hitler.
311. "Firearms are second only to the Constitution in importance; they are the the people's liberty teeth." First President of the government of the Republic;—George Washington.
312. "But what do we mean by American Revolution? Do we mean the American War? The Revolution was affected before the war commenced. The Revolution was in the minds and hearts of the people; a change in their religious sentiments, of their duties and obligations ... This radical change in the principles, opinions, sentiments, and affections of the people was the real American Revolution."—John Adams.
313. "Live as if you were to die tomorrow. Learn as if you were to live forever."—Mahatma Gandhi.
314. "Our new Constitution is now established, and has an appearance that promises permanency; but in this world nothing can be said to be certain, except death and taxes."—Benjamin Franklin.
315. "The strongest reason for the people to retain the right to keep and bear arms is, as a last resort, to protect themselves against tyranny in government."—Thomas Jefferson.
316. "There is danger from all men. The only maxim of free government ought to be to trust no man living with power to endanger the public liberty."—John Adams.
317. "Logic is founded in truth, and wisdom comes from our Father in Heaven.

    But [Common Sense] is a foundation that we are blessed with by birth".—John T. Nall.

318. "Local patriotism is in fact the only true patriotism."—English Writer; G.K. Chesterton.
319. "It is the opinion of the greatest writers, that a very extensive country cannot be governed on democratical principles, on any other plan than a Confederation of a number of small republics, possessing all the powers of internal government. But united in the management of their foreign and general concerns ... [A]nything short of despotism could not bind so great a country under one government."—Centinel' from the Anti—Federalist Papers.
320. "The Union was formed by the voluntary agreement of the states; and these, in uniting together, have not forfeited their nationality. Nor have they been reduced to the condition of one and the same people. If one of the states chose to withdraw its name from the contract, it would be difficult to disprove its right to do so."—Alexis de Tosqueville.

321. "[Double Standard] "A set of principles that applies differently and usually move rigorously to one group of people or circumstances than to another."—Merriam—Webster.
322. "We must secure the existence of our people and a future for white children."—David Lane.
323. "Our war against Communism, is a war for truth, liberty, and the self-preservation for our distinct people and future generations."—John T. Nall.
324. "[Definition of a Nation]: A people or an agragation of men, existing in the form of organized jural society. Usually inhabiting in a distant portion of the Earth. Speaking the same language, using the same customs, possessing the historic continuity and distinguish from all other like groups by their "Racial Origin". And the characteristics and generally but not necessarily living under the same government and sovereignty."—Black's Law Dictionary Fifth Edition.
325. "The truth is this: If only one man among all of the rest will not break … then all of them, all those who despise men that they believe all men can be broken and all men can be bought, all of them have failed and all of them defeated, because one alone destroys them and one alone can give heart to all other men."—Robert Crienton, from the novel "The secret of Santa Vittoria."
326. "It would be a dangerous delusion were a confidence in the men of our choice to silence our fears for the safety of our rights; that confidence is everywhere the parent of despotism-free government is founded in jealousy, and not in confidence; it is jealousy and not confidence which prescribes limited constitutions, to bind down those whom we are obliged to trust with power.—Thomas Jefferson, Kentucky Resolutions 1798.
327. "How soon we forget history … Government is not reason. Government is not eloquence. It is a dangerous servant and a fearful master."—George Washington.
328. When Benjamin Franklin departed the Constitutional Convention in 1787.

A woman waiting in suspense outside and ask him, "What have you given us, Dr. Franklin? He replied, "Why a Republic, mam. That is if you can keep it."

329. "Most Americans aren't the sort of citizens the Founding Fathers expected; they are contented serfs. For from being active critics of government, they assume that its might make it right."—Joseph Sobran
330. "It is interesting to remember, that when scientist are unable to understand something that they may not know. They will try to explain it with a theory. Yet, when it comes to how life began, scientist would quickly reject the idea of God as the Creator in theory and embrace other theories

first. And theories are only the possibilities of what may be or could be and not based on scientific facts. However, theories are taught to be as facts in the Federal Public Schools.—John T. Nall

331. [Racism] (ra'siz'em) A belief that race is the primary determinant of human traits and capabilities and that racial differences produce an inherent superiority of a particular race."—Merriam-Webster's.
332. "For I could wish that I myself were cursed and cut off from Christ for the sake of my brothers, those of my own race, the people of Israel. Ect,—Romans 9:3-5, Holy Bible.
333. [War] "Defiance, is that our enemies must die in order that we may remain free."—John T. Nall.
334. "Those that make war against us, must be reminded as to why they should never make war against us again."—John T. Nall.
335. "Whoever controls the volume of money in any country is absolute master of all industry and commerce.—United States President; James A. Garfield.
336. "If we run into such dept that we must be tax in our meat, and in our drink, and in our necessities and in our comforts, in our labors, in our callings, in our creeds. Our people must come to labor sixteen hours of the twenty-four. Give our earnings of fifteen of these to the government. Have no time to think. No meanings of calling mess manager's to account. But be glad to obtain substance by hiring ourselves out to ridden their chains on the neck on our fellow suffers. And this is the tendency of all human government, until the bulk of society is reduce to mere automatisms of misery and the four horse of this frightful team its public death. Misery and taxation follow that. And in its train and oppression retched.—Thomas Jefferson, 1816.
337. "I will say, then that I am not, nor ever have been in favor of bringing about in any way the social and political equality of the white and black races."—Abraham Lincoln September-18-1858, in the Lincoln and Douglas debates in Charleston, South Carolina.
338. "I had the honor of spending some time with Mr. Edgerton. And I can tell that he is a good and honorable man. He loves his people and cares for what is best for his race. He also cares and respects the white southern folks also.

He still will not bend to ignorance from the political correctness (Socialism) of history. Mr. Edgerton is a true hero in this white man eyes and a true Confederate American. And until someone has spent time with him, I request that no one should prejudge him. Thank You H.K., for what you have done for your people and mine including every Southerner of race.—John T. Nall.

339. "While we may differ in race, we are bounded and band together in the Heritage and Culture. In the security and defenses, of our homeland, in the South. For in Christ Jesus, who has founded and has blessed our beloved Confederacy. In His truth and His salvation for our people and country.—John T. Nall.—January 11, 2009
340. "It is only necessary to turn to the official documents of Tennessee to show that all Forrest said about the alarm which prevailed during the administration of Governor Brownlow was strictly true. No state was ever reduced to such humiliation and degradation as that unhappy commonwealth during the years Brownlow ruled over her."—Report of the House Congressional Committee that interviewed Forrest in 1871-72, regarding the Ku Klux Klan.
341. "Abolish the Loyal League and the Ku Klux Klan; let us come together and stand together.—Nathan Bedford Forrest, calling for an end to civil unrest.
342. "We were born on the same soil, breathe the same air, live on the same land, and why should we not be brothers and sisters?—Nathan Bedford Forrest, addressing the Southern Negro community of Memphis at the city fairgrounds, July 5, 1875.
343. "Parson, I would keep you here to preach for me if you were not needed so much more by the sinners on the other side."—C.S. Gen. Forrest to a captured chaplain of the U.S. army.
344. "Sleeping with another man's wife is like wearing that man's underwear. It's just something that would be unconscionable."—John T. Nall.
345. "But racism means hating others and/or desiring harm to others because of their race. We hate no one, nor do we desire to oppress anyone, yet somehow (so we are told) only whites can be racist! Every other racial group understands that they are a people, with a history, heritage and culture peculiar to themselves and a desire to preserve their group is normal, natural & healthy.

Whites on the other hand are the only racial group in the world who are expected to hand over their countries to the children of aliens. Indeed, we are expected to welcome this dispossession, nay, we are expected to celebrate our dwindling numbers and influence—nay, we are even compelled by force of law to subsidize our own national suicide!—Joel T. Lefevr / October-December 2008. Citizens Informer. Page 24.

346. "The tree of liberty must be refreshed from time to time with the Blood of Patriots and Tyrants.—Thomas Jefferson.
347. "When injustice becomes law, rebellion becomes duty.—Unknown.

348. "The tyranny of an unbridled majority, the most odious and least responsible form of despotism." Jefferson Davis, during his Inaugural Address.
349. [E Pluribus Unum] "Diversity and Community in the 21st Century' is the title of Putnam's five-year study, which makes hash out of ... the Politically Correct clichés, 'our diversity is our strength.' After 30'000 interviews, Putnam concludes; and reports against his own progressive convictions ... that ethnic and racial diversity can be devastating to communities and destructive of community values. The greater the diversity the greater the e distrust, says Putnam ... In racially and ethnically mixed communities, not only do people not trust strangers, they do not even trust their own kind."—Robert Putnam.
350. "The real menace of our Republic is this invisible government which like a giant Octopus sprawls its slimy length over city, state and nation. Like the octopus of real life it operates under cover of a self-created screen. At the head of this octopus are the Rockefeller standard oil interests and a small group of power banking house generally referred to as international bankers virtually run the United States government for their own selfish purposes. They practically control both political parties."—John F. Hylan (Mayor of New York) 1918-1925.
351. "For a long time I felt that FDR had developed many thoughts and ideas that were his own to benefit this country, the United States. But he didn't, most of his thoughts were carefully manufactured for him in advance by the Council on Foreign Relations—One World Money Group.—Curtis Dall, FDR's Son-in-law.
352. "The United Nations is but a long range international banking apparatus clearly set up for financial and economic profit by a small group of powerful (One World Revolutionaries), hungry for profit and power. The One World Government leaders have now acquired full control of the money and credit machinery of the U.S. via the creation of the privately owned Federal Reserve bank.—Curtis Dall—quote from his book, FDR: My Exploited Father-in-law.
353. "The real truth of the matter is, as you and I know, that a financial element in the large centers has owned the government ever since the day's of Andrew Jackson."—U.S. President—Franklin Delano Roosevelt 1933.
354. "We shall have world government weather or not you like it ... by conquest or consent."—James Warburg (Rothschild Banking Agent) 1950.
355. "The real rulers in Washington are invisible, and exercise power from behind the scenes."—Felix Frankfurter (U.S. Supreme Court Justice) 1952.

Northern propaganda used to try to drive a wedge between black folks and white folks.—H.K Edgerton.

356. "Our history has been lied about so much starting back in 1865 with the heritage who sold them out to slavery. Furthermore it is not uncommon for blacks today to follow the Muslim religion and Muslims practice slavery today. No one wants to talk about that" H.K. Edgerton

357. "He likens such propaganda to the current campaign for Reparations to the descendants of slaves: Reparations is just another lie. I'm not looking for reparations. That's just another way to divide white folks and black folks.—H.K. Edgerton.

358. "If you want to ask me about my ancestral roots, I am a Confederate—American. I was born colored, Negro, then one day somebody decided to make me African-American. Nobody asked me about that. Africa didn't want me then, and she certainly doesn't want me now."—H.K. Edgerton.

359. "Why Texas? Well, for one thing it seems a certain former governor of that State offended Southern heritage by removing memorial plaques from the State Supreme Court building, which had been built with Confederate pension funds"—H.K. Edgerton.

360. "The attack on the Confederacy doesn't get the attention it deserves. Those blacks today have no idea what took place back then. (Blacks) earned a place of dignity in that war. If it weren't for Africans that war would have lasted four days, not four years. We made all of the implements of war, we fought, we participated—not one slave insurrection happened during that period of time.

They did not have whips and guns forcing them to be there. God and His infinite wisdom brought these people here. He brought about a love between master and slave that has never happened before. If you search this empirically then you will know the only one who cared about the African was the white man in the South. But we don't want to face that."—H.K. Edgerton.

361. [March from North Carolina to Texas] "My march is a march of heritage, not one of hate. To bring an awareness of the pride we feel. There are folks who look like me who care a lot about Dixie."—H.K. Edgerton.

362. "Let's take a look at the United States. 33% of the entire economy is consumed by government, and it regulates much of the Western World. by any standard in the past, that is socialism. It is Socialist America. The Union of Soviet Socialist of America.—Pat Buchanan, on RT News.

363. "If this were a dictatorship, it would be a heck of a lot easier. Just as long as I'm the dictator."—George W. Bush, Capitol Hill, Washington DC December 2000.

364. "I am marching for freedom," The battle flag stands for freedom and state rights. This U.S. flag is the flag of slavery. It flew over one hundred years of slavery and Native Americans were annihilated under that flag."—Anthony Hervey. For more information write to: Black Confederate Soldier Foundation, P.O. box 3276 University, MS 38677. A non-profit organization.

365. "I don't see [the Ku Klux Klan] as terrorists. I see them as, I hate to use the word 'vigilante'. But vigilante sometimes ain't as bad as you think, when your government fails you and fails to protect you. You have to turn somewhere."—H.K. Edgerton.

366. "I found it appalling what happened in South Carolina, and I'm afraid this is going to happen in Mississippi. We seek only to correct the errors in history—to right the wrong done to the memories of these brave soldiers."—Anthony Hervey, a black Confederate American. (The Sun Herald) on June-22-2000.

367. "Slaves were given a new pair of pants and a new pair of shoes every day and he thinks this white man is cruel! [Black Slaves] had the same medical facilities that the white man had ... You look at most of the slave pictures ... they are not raggedy and torn ... they lived better than most! Most of them looked better than most of the white folks around and lived better than most of the free world!"—H.K Edgerton.

368. "We currently live under a psychological form of reconstruction. Whites are made to feel guilty for sins of their ancestors and blacks are made to feel down trodden. This keeps all of us from communicating. The Political Correctness of today is killing the pride of the people."—Anthony Hervey.

369. "You're beliefs are the conclusions of what your knowledge and understanding on a subject of whatever it may be. But, personal views without facts and the understanding of all of the evidence in fullness, is like opening a box to find nothing within it. Again, it would be like a deceased body or vessel that known longer contains the Spirit of oneself within. You're personal views becomes wasted energy."—John T. Nall.

370. "Those claiming to be Confederate or Southern and who procrastinate in compromise and complacency, refusing to stand with other patriots and nationalists. When and where will you make a stand, and upon what principle? If the liberty and independence of your own people and nation is not sufficient cause, what will be required to inspire you to action? perhaps you are at ease living in a gilded cage, built by the enemies of our nation, the Confederate States of America.

Maybe there exists no moment in which you will make a stand for family, state and nation. The words Confederate and Southern are not interchangeable in their definitions, but are separate and distinct as to their meaning. While at the same time they are conjoined, so that an individual will be either both or neither. The title of Confederate and Southern are but two sides of a single coin. Those who refuse to stand with us in achieving Victory, should not enjoy its fruits once achieved.—Haylea Greersog

371. "I worked night and day for twelve years to prevent the war, but I could not. The North was mad and blind, would not let us govern ourselves, and so the war came." C.S. President Jefferson Davis.
372. "Victory is for those with the persistence and fortitude to resist the temptation to withdraw of whose resolve has been tempered, when conditions worsen and the cost rises. It is not for the weak hearted, nor those who are softened by the ease and comfort of a gilded cage, provided by the enemy at the cost of liberty. It is for those who continue to fight the good fight, even after others who have gone before, having faced overwhelming numbers and fire power found themselves unable to complete the mission."—Jay Buckner.
373. "The urge to save humanity is almost always a false front for the urge to rule."—H.L. Mencken.
374. "Ten years I labored in the cause of Communism. I was a dedicated 'comrade.' All my talents & efforts were zealously used to bring about triumph of Communism in America. To me, the end of capitalism would mark the beginning of an interminable period of plenty, peace & universal comradeship. All racial & class differences & conflicts would end forever after the liquidation of the capitalists, their government & their supporters. A world UNION OF SOVIET STATES under the hegemony of Russia would free & lead mankind on to utopia.

    Little did I realize until I was deeply enmeshed in the Red Conspiracy, that just & seeming grievances are exploited to transform idealism into a cold & ruthless weapon against the capitalist system-that is the end toward which the Communist efforts among Negroes are directed indeed, I had entered the Red Conspiracy in the vain belief that it was the way to a "new, better & superior" world system of society. Ten years later I abandoned Communism.

    I saw Communism in all its naked cruelty, ruthlessness & utter contempt of CHRISTIAN attributes & passions. I saw the low value placed upon human life, the lack of respect for dignity of man, the terror of Secret Police & the bloody hand of the assassin. Thus, as a participant on the highest level of the Communist Conspiracy in America. I observed the cold, calculating, ruthless nature of Red Politics & warfare.

The Reds have deliberately twisted & warped the thinking of those intellectual pygmies who lead the "Freedom by '63" campaign by sending them after quick solutions of a centuries old problem that has never been solved anywhere in the world.

'Obvious to even the most ignorant is the fact that all people are prejudiced.' No one is free of it. Prejudice, in one form or another, has existed as long as the 'Human Family'. They arise out of the complex differences of race, nationality, religion, economic, social & cultural standing.

The Top White Communists leaders know that racial, as well as other differences between people, have existed over a long span of years & will continue to exits even after centuries of re-education under Communist rule. They also know these differences can be used to play race against race, nationality against nationality, class against class, act, to advance their cause. The Red Propagandists distort the facts concerning racial differences for ulterior motives. All the right is not on the Negro side. Neither is all-wrong. The same holds true with regard to the White Man's side.

It is obvious that placing the blame for all the Negroes ills at the door of the White Leaders in America is to remove all responsibility from the Negro.—Mr. Manning Johnson from his published book [Color, Communism and Common Sense] 1958.

375. William Ewart Gladstone (1809-1898)—was Prime Minister of Great Britain Four Times: 1868-74, 1880-85, 1886 and 1892-94. He called the [Qur'an] an "Accursed Book" and once held it up during a session of Parliament. Declaring, "so long as there is this book, there will be no peace in the world."
376. "Nothing is more certainly written in the book of fate than that these people [black] are to be free. Nor is it less certain that the two races, equally free, cannot live in the same government. Nature, habit, opinion has drawn indelible lines of distinction between them."—Thomas Jefferson: Auto-biography. ME 1:72.
377. "I concur entirely in [the] leading principles of gradual emancipation, of establishment on the Coast of Africa, and the patronage of our nation until the emigrants shall be able to protect themselves ... Personally, I am ready and desirous to make any sacrifice which shall ensure their gradual but complete retirement from the state, and effectually, at the same time, establish them elsewhere in freedom and safety."—Thomas Jefferson to Thomas Humphrey's, 1817 ME 15:102.

378. "It will probably be asked, why not retain and incorporate the blacks into the state [instead of colonizing them]? Deep rooted prejudices entertained by the whites, the thousand recollections by the blacks of the injuries they have sustained, new provocations, the real distinctions which nature has made and many other circumstances will divide us into parties and produce convulsions which will probably never end but in the extermination of the one or the other race."—Thomas Jefferson: Notes on Virginia Q. XIV. ME 2:192.

379. "The weapons of the Socialist Liberal's is to twist the truth, attack their enemies verbally and censor everything that is a contradiction to their own views and goals of domination of our people."—John T. Nall.

380. "Of all the dispositions and habits which lead to political prosperity, Religion and morality are indispensable supports ... And let us with caution indulge the supposition, that morality can be maintained without religion. Whatever may be conceded to the influence of refined education on minds of peculiar structure—reason & experience both forbid us to expect that National morality can prevail in exclusion of religious principle." United States President: George Washington.

381. "Ya'll Might Be A YANKEE: If these words describe you ...

Rude, Obnoxious, Adores Diversity, Pro-Abortion, Politically Correct, Elitist, Multi-Cultural, Pushy, Loud, Secular humanist, know-it-all, Delusions of Superiority, Socialist.

(Comment) This is not directed toward the Rightists Yankees that loves God, Family, Country and respects their neighboring states of self-rule.

382. "How foolish we have become when we start to believe that we are much smarter and wiser than [Our Founding Fathers]."—John T. Nall.

383. [Consider this!] "The Catholic Church was established 300 years after the resurrection of Jesus Christ. Jesus was not a Catholic, nor were his twelve disciples. In fact every Christian up to the time of the birth of the Catholic Church we're not Catholic's. And any Christian who did not accept the Catholic faith was tortured or put to death. In fact, the Catholic Church was the very First Denominational Church in world history."—John T. Nall.

384. Diversity & Multiculturalism is a mythical dream land without Jesus Christ. In truth, it is one sided, un-natural, self-destructive and in all truthfulness, evil.—John T. Nall.

385. Politicians will try to use smoke screens time after time after time again to infringe on the rights and freedoms of the people, by allowing them to believe that it's being done for the best interest

and safety of the people. It is my belief that every tyrant desires to die on the altar of liberty. Otherwise they wouldn't be oppressing the people. I say death to anyone that tries to oppress and denies us our [Constitutional Rights]!—John T. Nall.

386. "Ladies and Gentlemen: The very words of secrecy is repugnant in a free and open society. And we are as a people inherently and historically opposed to secret societies. To secret oaths and secret proceedings. For we are oppose to around the world a monolithic and ruthless conspiracy that relies primarily on covets means. For expanding its influence, on infiltration instead of invasion. On subversion instead of elections. On intimidation instead of free choice. It is a system which has a conscripted vast human and material resources in the building of a tightly knit, highly efficient machine that combines military, diplomatic, intelligence, economic, scientific, and political operations.

Its preparations are concealed not published. Its mistakes are buried not headline. Its dissentients are silence not praised. No expenditure is questioned, no secret is reviled. That is why the Athenian lawmakers saw decreed it a crime for any Citizen to shrink from controversy. I am asking you're helping the tremendous task of informing and alerting the American people. Confident with your help, [Man will be what he was born to be, free and independent].—U.S. President: John F. Kennedy.

387. "Powerful government tends to draw into it people with bloated egos, people who think they know than everyone else and have little hesitance in coercing their fellow man. Or as Nobel Laureate Friedrich Hayek said, 'in government, the scum rises to the top.'"—Walter E. Williams.
388. "Americans should renew their faith in God, if they can, and learn once and for all that America is not that pile of marble and granite monuments on the Potomac occupied by politicians and lobbyists. They should learn that government is the problem, not the solution. It should be viewed as what it is: a government entirely foreign to the American tradition and to the constitutional republic established by our forefathers. It is neither controlled by, nor is it responsive to, the American people."—Charley Reese.
389. "This great republic, founded on the concept of inalienable rights and self—government, was never designed for a population of heel clickers and saluters. It was designed for thinking men and women who could independently assess situations and form their own independent judgments about what is good policy and what is bad policy."—Charley Reese,—In "What's in a Name?"

390. "A democracy cannot exist as a permanent form. It can only exist until the voter's discover that they can vote themselves money from the public treasury. From then on, the majority will vote for the candidate promising the most benefits from the public treasury, with the results that democracy always collapses of loose fiscal policy and is always replaced by a dictatorship."—Professor: Alexander Tyler.

391. "We must hold fast to principle: if we compromise our rights, and act from motives of expediency we trust to a broken anchor, and all that is worth preserving will be irretrievably lost."—Thomas Cooper.

392. "If you do not know who you are, you are maimed. If you hate who you are, you are culturally and spiritually paraplegic and perhaps quadriplegic, which left untreated will regress into brain death."—Jimmy Cantrell.

393. "Here in America we are descended in blood and in spirit from revolutionists and rebels—men and women who dare to dissent from accepted doctrine. As their heirs, we may never confuse honest dissent with disloyal subversion."—Dwight D. Eisenhower.

394. "Should the Northern States continue willfully and deliberately to circumvent federal law, the South would no longer be bound to observe the [Constitutional] compact. A bargain cannot be broken on one side and still bind the other side."—Daniel Webster, Senator from Massachusetts U.S.A.

395. " … I shouted sic simper before I fired … our country owed all her troubles to him … The country is not what it was. This forced union is not what I have loved. I care not what becomes of me. I have no desire to outlive my country … For doing what Brutus was honored for, and what made William Tell a hero … yet I, for striking down a greater tyrant than they ever knew am looked upon as a common cutthroat. My action was purer than either of theirs. One hoped to be great himself. The other had not only his country's but his own wrongs to avenge. I hoped for no gain. I knew no private wrong. I struck for my country and that alone. A country groaned beneath this tyranny and prayed for this end.—John Wilkes Booth, written in his diary prior to his questionable execution.

396. "Awarding bonuses to executives who beg for bailout funds is nothing short of criminal; it's no less a crime than pick-pocketing a wallet and should be no less punishable by law. These "leaders" have the audacity to steal from employees who toiled faithfully for years making a company what it was before being railroaded into financial disarray, and then these same "leaders" march off to ask for government bailouts.

This is a criminal act lacking social consciousness; a dereliction of duty; and a complete failure on countless other fronts. Why haven't these executives been prosecuted for misappropriation of funds or whatever label Washington wants to put on it? Why shouldn't their multi-million—or—billion-dollar bank accounts be frozen, the questionable funds seized and returned to taxpayers where they would do an honest, hard-working American some good?

It's because Americans didn't demand accountability. In our role as the "melting pot" nation, Americans now favor political correctness over social duty to the common good. We fear "of offending someone" so much that we've failed to call on the carpet corporations, executives and politicians who wrong us on a daily basis. Our failure to demand what is right and fair has allowed corporations to worship the almighty dollar over the worker who makes it for them; to treat employees as expendable rather than human.

We failed to make our own welfare a priority, so did we really expect executives making millions at our expense to do it for us? Demand change, people! Demand that such reprehensible actions be dealt with expeditiously in criminal courts. Demand that the line between right and wrong be a hard one, not blurred by financial status. Demand transparency from corporations and politicians regarding what's done with our money. If not, you can be sure they won't do it for you.—Nicole Barnhardt Cline of China Grove N.C., in the Letters to the Editor of the Salisbury Post—February 8, 2009.

397. "Now, it is for you, sir, to say whether the whole nation shall be plunged into bankruptcy, whether grass shall grow in the streets of our commercial cities. than will you yield to the just demands of the South?"—William E. Dodge, spokesman for a New York delegation, to Abraham Lincoln, March 1861.
398. "The separation of Church and State is a very different thing from the separation of religion and the State."—James Henley Thornwell.
399. "I have said, that we shall ere long be compelled to calculate the value of our union; and to inquire of what use to us is this most unequal alliance? by which the South has always been the loser and the North always the gainer?"—Thomas Cooper.
400. "I venture to predict that it [the federal government] will become absolute and irresponsible, precisely in proportion as the rights of the States shall cease to be respected and their authority to interpose for the correction of federal abuses shall be denied and overthrown. It should be the

object of every patriot in the United States to encourage a high respect for the State governments. The people should be taught to regard them as their greatest interest, and as the first objects of their duty and affection. Maintained in their just rights and powers, they form the true balance-wheel, the only effectual check on federal encroachments. The danger is, not that the State will interpose too often, but that they will rather submit to federal usurpations, than incur the risk of embarrassing that government, by any attempts to check and control it."—Abel Upshur, Secretary of the Navy and Secretary of State; Virginia Judge, shortly before his death in 1844.

401. "The arts of power and its minions are the same in all countries and in all ages. It marks its victim; denounces it; and excites the public odium and the public hatred, to conceal its own abuses and encroachments."—Henry Clay, 1834.

402. "There will be found to exist at all times an imperious necessity for restraining all the functionaries of the government within the range of their respective power thereby preserving a just balance between the powers granted to this government and those reserved to the States and to the people."—US President; John Tyler.

403. "The people of this country, if ever they loose their liberties, will do it by sacrificing some great principle of government to temporary passion. there are certain great principles, which if they are not held inviolable, at all seasons, our liberty is gone. If we give them up, it is perfectly immaterial what is the character of our sovereign; whether he be King or President, elective or hereditary—it is perfectly immaterial what is his character—we shall be slaves—it is not elective government which will preserve us."—John Randolph of Roanoke.

404. "The only certain consequence of war, except when it is undertaking for the purpose of repelling invasion, is that whichever side gains the victory, the people on both sides are vanquished."—John Taylor of Caroline.

405. "Americans should select and prefer Christians as their rulers."—John Jay, first U.S. Supreme Court Justice.

406. "It would be an absurdity to be required to accept the judge's view of the law, against their own opinion, judgment, and conscience."—John Adams, in not knowing that American judges, beginning in the 20th century, would come to prevent juries from seeing evidence that would exonerate the accused.

407. "In the Federal U.S Public Schools, the propaganda about the invasion into the Confederate States of America was written in an historical form. And Its purpose for this text was to justify the enslavement of the Confederacy & the destruction of the Constitutional Republic of the United States into a Centralize Block of Democracy. In short, to justify the unconstitutional actions of

the radical Republican Party. And when their actions are questioned, they are quick to bring up slavery in order to avoid any other issues on the subject.

Evidence has proven time and time again that the Civil War history is false and is mixed with half-truths. Including of the fact that the U.S. President Abraham Lincoln was a tyrant not only toward the Confederate American people but also toward his own. This propaganda historical tool, is to deceive their subjects into believing that this new nation empire is the true concept of freedom. And while we Southerners do not approve the assassination and murder of this U.S. President. We also cannot deny that because of his evil actions and his violation of his oath to protect his nation's constitution including the violation of his people's trusts, he brought it upon himself. No matter how many times they tell a lie to be the truth, it will always is a lie.—John T. Nall.

408. "I think the one thing we need to clear up. I think that we all agree that Barack Obama was elected by mostly by black racists and white guilty people. Most black Americans, a large majority of them are racists who are qualified American's. And white folks feel guilty and they are afraid of being called racists. Yes sir, without a doubt. Watch me! As we move on, with Barrack Obama being in there, you're not going to be able to speak out against him at all, without being called a racists. A Large majority of black America voted for this man because he's a far left socialist liberal and he's a Democrat. Had he been a black Republican Conservative, they would not have voted for him. Your right about that, they voted for him because they have a socialist mentality. If you wantto know what socialism looks like, look at the slums and ghettos of the black community!

Out of wedlock, birth, crime is spiraling out of control, a dependency on government. And most of the people that they elect are liberal black Democrats who have done nothing but destroy the black community, by bringing in more government and that's what Barack Obama is all about. It's based on race and Democrats takes care of me mentality. You've had most of the black preachers vote for him. And I say that there is no way that you can believe in God and vote for a person like Barack Obama. There is nothing about this guy that's promotes godliness. Yea, the point is that they know that he's going to cut taxes; he's going to take away from those who are willing to work hard and give to those who are unwilling to work. But we don't need Socialism. Socialism is not good for our country. That's why we are doing this national tour to stop Barama socialist agenda, because America can't afford that.—Reverend Jesse Lee Peterson, A black minister, during a conversation on the Hannity Show on Channel Fox News [2-3-09].

409. "In war, as in peace," observed Weaver, "people remain civilized by acknowledge bounds beyond which they must not go." Echoing the words of Lee, Weaver understood no necessary contradiction in the term "Christian" as applied to the profession of arms. "The Christian soldier must seek the verdict of battle always remembering that there is a higher law by which he and his opponent will be judged, and which enjoins against fighting as the barbarian."—Book Title [War Crimes Against Southern Civilians]. By; Walter Brian Cisco/ Second Paragraph of page 17.

410. "Which passages of scripture should guide our public policy?

Should we go with Leviticus? Which suggest slavery is ok.

Or we could go with Deuteronomy? Which suggest stoning your child, if he strays from the faith.

Or should we just stick to the Sermon on the Mount? A passage that is so radical that it's doubtful that our own Defense Department would survive its applications.

Folk's haven't been reading the Bible!—Senator; Barack Obama, June-28-2006.

411. " … it's not surprising then that they get bitter. They cling to guns or religion or antipathies to people who aren't like them. Or anti-immigrant or anti-trade sentiment as a way to explain their frustrations." Democrat Senator; Barack H. Obama's statement about the Citizens of Pennsylvania U S of A. A Presidential Candidate, CNN News.

412. "Our new government is founded … its foundations are laid, its cornerstone rest, upon the great truth that the Negro is not equal to the white man; that slavery, subordination to the superior race, is his natural and normal condition."—Confederate States Vice-President; Alexander Stephens. "[Authors Comment: The personal views of the CS Vice President: Alexander Stephens does not reflect the views of all Confederate American Citizens. During the War, CS President: Jefferson Davis and his wife had adopted a Negro child. Before the War, Stonewall Jackson was teaching Negro slaves how to read. So, that they would be able to study the Holy Bible.]"

413. "Slavery as it existed in the South, was guided by providence to lift heathen Blacks to Christianity; its end might be "the preparation of that race for Civil liberty and social enjoyment"; and "it is quite within the range of possibility that the masters" would eventually, of their own violation, desire to free the slaves "when their slaves [themselves] will object."—Confederate States President; Jefferson Davis.

414. "The Centralist Republicans and the Socialist Liberal Democrats have repeated this statement of Alexander Stephens, as if all Southerners shared the same views as he. And they do this because not that they truly care anything for the truth, but to avoid their un-justifications of any wrong doings of the past, and what they may gain in the future.—John T. Nall.

415. "If such an art of active mass influence through propaganda is joined with the long-term systematic education of a nation, and if both are conducted in a unified and precise way, the relationship between the leadership and the nation will always remain close."—Joseph Goebbels Nazi Propaganda Minister, on the subject of Hitler's Youth.

416. "There is not a truth which I fear or would wish unknown to the whole world."—Thomas Jefferson. what I told people in Illinois and now everybody realizes it's true. He is going to destroy this country. We've either going to stop him, or the United States of America is going to cease to exist … I don't have any regrets, I went into Illinois, and people told me at the time I didn't stand much of a chance of winning. The idea was to bare a true witness.

The man is an abomination. He is someone who is actually advocated infanticide. That when babies are the targets of abortion, if they happened to escape the abortionist intention, and are born alive! He actually supported the idea that those babies should be set aside to die.

That is a man with such a clear consciences, I cannot understand why anybody in their right mind would consider him worthy of political support? That's a violation of consciences. That is inconceivable, and even some of the most hard-line pro-abortionist people in America, rejected that abomination and he did not … Is he? That's another question. Is he the President of the United States? According to the Constitution, in order to be eligible for President, you have to be a natural born citizen. Uh, he has refused to provide proof that he is in fact, a natural born citizen.

And his Kenya relations say that he was born in Nairobi, at a time when his mother was too young to transmit U.S. Citizenship. So, I'm not even sure if he is President of the United States? No! It's not a laughing matter.

Neither are many of our military people who are now going to court, to ask the question, [Do I have to obey a man, who is not qualify under the Constitution?] We're in the midst of greatest crises, this nation has ever seen. And if we don't stop laughing about it and deal with it. We're going to find ourselves in the mist of chaos, confusion, and Civil War.

It's time we started acting like grownups … Sorry? The person who is called President Obama, and I frankly refused to call him that. At the moment he is somebody who is kind of a ledge disserve, who is a ledge to be someone who is occupying that office without [Constitutional Warrant], to do so. And he's rushing forward with ideas like destroying our borders, and Amnesty Bill, that will actually have the American taxpayers footing the bill, for illegal to come to this country to live, to get housing, and to get everything they won't.

He is also somebody who has just announced a program that will accentually destroy the venality of existing mortgages. And encourage everybody in the country to stop paying their mortgage. Because the government is going to pay it instead. This is insanity! It is as if we have put insane children in adolescence, in charge of our government. And I think we need to ask simple questions. A couple of years ago, we we're auguring over every penny in the United States budget.

And it was quite clear that we didn't have enough money to go around. Will somebody ask me where we came up with two trillion dollars in the course of the last six months? Did we wish for it out of the air? Have people gone mad in this country? You don't have that money! We are claming that a bankrupt government can save a bankrupt banking system.

Explain to me how that happens? Because I think that's impossible. And the fact we have just elected an individual who may or may not be qualified. And presents these silly ideas and says, 'let's move forward now'. And we're acting like the laws of economics have been repelled. And we can actually afford to foot the bill with money nobody's got. This is insane. It got to lead to the collapse of our economy. And it's going too!—An interview with Dr. Alan Keyes—2009.

417. "Suppose you were an idiot. And suppose you were a member of Congress. But then I repeat myself.—Mark Twain.
418. "The Spirit of resistance to government, is so valuable on certain occasions. that I wish it to be always kept alive."—Thomas Jefferson.

419. "Silence in the face of evil is itself evil! God will not hold us guiltless. Not to Speak is to speak. Not to act is to act.—Dietrich Bonhoeffer.
420. "No man's life, liberty or property is safe while the legislature is in session."—Mark Twain.
421. "A government resting on the caprice of the people is too unstable to last … [A]ll must obey. Government, that is, the executive, having no discretion but to execute the law must be to that extent despotic."—US General; William Tecumseh Sherman. [In reference to the Constitutional Republic of the United States and the Confederate States of America.]
422. "We have for years been drifting towards an unadulterated democracy or demagoguism. Therefore our government should become a machine, self-regulating, independent of the man."—US General William T. Sherman.
423. [The Holy Bible] "The Scripture is the standard of truth, the judge of controversies; it is the polestar to direct us to heaven … The Scripture is the compass by which the rudder of our will is to be steered; it is the field in which Christ, the Pearl of price, is hid; it is a rock of diamonds; it is a sacred "eye-salve"; it heals their eyes that look upon it; it is a spiritual optic-glass in which the glory of God is resplendent; it is the panacea or "universal medicine" for the soul.—Thomas Watson.
424. "A human life, I think, should be well rooted in some spot of a native land, where it may get the love of tender kinship for the face of the earth, for the labors men go forth to, for the sounds and accents that haunt it. For whatever will give that early home a familiar unmistakable difference a midst the future widening of knowledge. The best introduction to astronomy homestead.—George Eliot.
425. "If I ever disown, repudiate or apologize for the cause for which Lee fought and Jackson died. Let the lightenings from Heaven rend me and the scorn of all good men and true women by my portion. Sun, moon and stars all fall on me when I cease to love the Confederacy. Tis the cause, not the fate of the cause, that is glorious."—Major R.E. Wilson C.S.A.
426. "But today the largest countries of the world, have agreed the global plan for recovery and reform. This involves the biggest interest rate cuts in history, the biggest physical stimulus we have ever seen. The biggest increase in resources' in the history of our inter-national institutions', with 2 hundred and fifty billions, more money than ever before, for trade finances ax well. For the first time, we have a common approach around the world to cleaning up the bank's balance sheets, and restoring lending. We are engaging in a deep process of reform and restricting of our international financial system for now and for the future. And we have maintain our commitments to help the world's poorest, and have good more money aside for that and also for a green recovery. These are not a single collection of actions.

This is collective action people working together at their best. I think the (New World Order) is emerging, and with it the foundations of a new and progressive era of International Corporation. We have resolved that from today, we will together manage the process of globalization. To secure responsibility for all and fairness to all. And we have agreed that in doing so, we will build most sustainable and more open, and a fairer global society.'—Gordon Brown; On Global Warming. The G20 Live Summit in London, England. 2009 Sky Net News.

427. "If it sounds too good to be true? That's because it is!—Anonymous.
428. "It cannot be emphasized too strongly or too often that this great nation was founded, not by religionists, but by Christians; not religions, but on the Gospel of Jesus Christ! For this very reason peoples of other faith have been afforded asylum, prosperity and freedom to worship here."—Patrick Henry.
429. "No people will tamely surrender their liberties, nor can any be easily subdued, when knowledge is diffused and virtue is preserved. On the contrary, when people are universally ignorant and debauched in their manners, they will sink under their own weight without the aid of foreign invaders."—Samuel Adams (Letter to James Warren, 4 November 1775) Reference: Our Sacred Honor, Bennett. (261).
430. Abraham Lincoln once asked General (Winfield) Scott the question: "Why is it that you were once able to take the City of Mexico in three months with five thousand men, and we have been unable to take Richmond with one hundred thousand men?" I will tell you, said General Scott. "The men who who took us into the City of Mexico, are the same men who are keeping us out of Richmond."
431. "Of all the dispositions and habits which lead to political prosperity, Religion and Morality are indispensable supports … let us with caution indulge the supposition that morality can be maintained without religion … reason and experience both forbid us to expect that national morality can prevail in exclusion of religious principle."—George Washington.
432. "We have no government capable of contending with human passions unbridled by morality and religion. Avarice, ambition, revenge … would break the strongest cords of our Constitution as a whale goes through a net. our Constitution was made for only a moral and religious people. It is wholly inadequate to the government of any other."—John Adams.
433. "I do not know whether all Americans have a sincere faith in their religion—for who can search the human heart—but I am certain that they hold it to be indispensable to the maintenance of republican institutions."—Alexis de Toaqueville.

434. "I believe that when someone claims to be a Christian and yet, for someone to vote for a representative of the people who lack's in character and values, is indeed a hypocrite." And to vote for someone that promises you the world in exchange for our liberty and rights, fall's under the classification of a moron. Furthermore, to elect someone out of guilt, or because of wealth and power, or gender and race, does not deserve to maintain the right and privilege to vote or hold office. The freedom of our people should not remain in the hands of those that had no understanding and meaning to the truth of liberty and self-will for all. Ignorance is self-voluntary enslavement.—John T. Nall.

435. "Some Southerners would claim that the Yankee's are trying to take over the world. While the rest of the Southern people would tell you that they already have!—John T. Nall.

436. "When I hear liberals say that we here in Alabama are 'backwoods' and aren't 'progressive', I know that means that we are Conservative Christians, who are Pro-Life, Pro-Family, Anti-Big Government, Anti-Gay Marriage, Anti-Illegal immigration, Pro-Military and Pro-2nd Amendment. I still believe in God, Family, Country and Honor. I will never apologize for my beliefs, morals or values!"—A commenter said from the Journal Forums Page. In concerning the former Alabama Supreme Court Chief Justice; Roy Moore, in running for governor.

437. "Personal emotion's or feelings cannot override or justified any actions on one's part in the violations of the Laws of Nature (In Creations that God had established), or Spiritual Laws (Laws in prevention of Sin). Emotions can lead to selfishness and the lack of concern of one's consequences of actions that is destructive toward family, people of race."—John T. Nall.

438. "We cannot change that which has been done in the past. For that is beyond approach. We can only strive to do what is right according to the word of God (Holy Bible), and follow the footsteps of our founding forefathers. We can only deny the past wrongs from controlling our futures path's toward a more sounder and brighter destiny."—John T. Nall.

439. "Aye, fight and you may die. Run, and you'll live ... at least a while. And dying in your beds many years from now, would you be willing to trade all the days, from this day to that, for one chance, just one chance, to come back here and tell our enemies that they may take our lives, but they'll never take our FREEDOM!!!—William Wallace.

440. "You and I both anticipated that the cause of the country would be advanced advanced by making the attempt to provision Fort-Sumter [sic], even if it should fail; and it is no small consolation now to feel that our anticipation is justified by the results.'—U.S. President Lincoln writes to Assistant Secretary of the Navy; Gustavus Fox, Commander of the expedition to Fort Sumter, on May 1st of 1861.

441. "The preservation of the Union is the supreme law."—Andrew Jackson, December 25, of 1832.
442. "The contest is really for Empire on the side of the North, and for Independence on that of the South and in this respect we recognize an exact analogy between the North and the Government of George III, and the South and the Thirteen Revolted Provinces, These opinions ... are the general opinions of the English Nation.—London Times—November 7th of 1861.
443. "Since, therefore, the abolition of slavery never appeared in the platform of any great political party, since the only appeal ever made to the electorate on that issue was scornfully repulsed, since the spokesman of the Republicans [Lincoln] emphatically declared that his party never intended to interfere with slavery in the states any shape or form. It seems reasonable to assume that the institution of slavery was not the fundamental issue during the epoch presiding the bombardment of Fort Sumter."—Historians—Charles and Mary Beard, 1927 of "The Rise of American Civilization."
444. "Let me be frank, we Southerners are fighting this thing with our backs to the wall, but what we lack in numbers we make up in our determination and will to protect our Southern our Southern States and the welfare of our people. We know that our form of government cannot exist over the years if states are to be mere provinces of a central government."—Senator Byrd-1957.
445. "The Jews ... are a living and the most striking evidence of the falsity of that pernicious doctrine of modern times, the natural equality of man. The particular equality of a particular race is a matter of municipal arrangement, and depends entirely on political considerations and considerations and circumstances; but the natural equality of man now in vogue, and taking the form of cosmopolitan fraternity, is a principle which, were it possible to act on it, would deteriorate the great races and destroy all the genius of the world. What would be the consequences on the great Anglo-Saxon republic, for example, were its citizens to secede from their sound principle of reserve, and mingle with their Negro and colored populations? In the course of time they would become so deteriorated that their states would probably be reconquered and regained by the aborigines whom they expelled, and who would then be their supcriors."—Prime Minister Benjamin Disraeli, 1852.
446. "Every man should endeavor to understand the meaning of subjugation before it is too late. We can give but a faint idea when we say it means the loss of all we now hold most sacred ... personal property, lands, homesteads, liberty, justice, safety, pride, manhood. It means that the history of this heroic struggle will be written by the enemy, that our youth will be trained by Northern school teachers, will learn from Northern school books their version of the War, will be impressed by all influences of history and education to regard our gallant dead as traitors, our maimed veterans as fit objects for their derision. It means the crushing of Southern manhood ... to establish

sectional superiority and a more centralized form of government and to deprive us of our rights and liberties."—Gen. Pat Cleburne C.S.A.

447. "It is only because men are created in the image and likeness of God that they are entitled to equal treatment and inalienable rights. This is quite different from the French Declaration of rights of Man or the whole secular humanist position."—Jim Lloyd.

448. Prayer: " … bless my family, kindred, friends and country, be our God this day and forever for His sake who lay down in the grave and rose again for us, Jesus Christ our Lord, Amen …"—George Washington.

449. Prayer: "Daily frame me more and more into the likeness of thy son Jesus Christ that living in thy fear and dying in thy favor, I may in thy appointed time attain the resurrection of the just unto eternal life."—George Washington.

450. "True religion affords to government its surest support."—George Washington.

451. "Religion is the basis and foundation of government."—James Madison.

452. "We have staked the whole of all our political institutions … to sustain ourselves according to the Ten Commandments of God."—James Madison.

453. " … For Americans the ideas of Christianity and liberty are so completely mingled that is almost impossible to get them to conceive of the one without the other."—Alexis de Tocqueville.

454. "there is no country in the world where the Christian religion retains a greater influence over the souls of men than in America … Alexis de Tocqueville.

455. " … I am certain that they hold it (Christianity) indispensable to the maintenance of republican institutions."—Alexis de Tocqueville.

456. "Tolerance is the last virtue of a degenerate society" and "that when begin to allow every kind of immorality and degeneracy and perversion imaginable, the one thing you will not allow is to have anybody criticize you for doing these things."—Dr. D.J. Kennedy.

457. "Rebellion to Tyrants is Obedience to God."—Ben Franklin.

458. [Tyrants] "It is for freedom that Christ has set us free. Stand firm, then and do not let yourselves be burdened again by a yoke of slavery." Galatians 5:1, New International Version.

459. [Tyrants] The God of Israel spoke, the Rock of Israel said to me: "When one rules over men in righteousness, when he rules in the fear of God".—2 Samuel 23:3.

460. [Tyrants] "If the prince's authority is not just but usurped, or if he commands what is not just, his subjects are not bound to obey him."—Thomas Aquinas.

461. [Tyrants] "If princes forbid us to serve and honor God, if they command us to sully our conscience with idolatry ... then they are not worthy to be ... recognized as having any sort of authority."—John Calvin.
462. [Tyrants] "It is when a ruler ceases to act under that law and denies his or her subjects their rights, as guaranteed by that law."—By Magna Carta, this established English common law.
463. [Tyrants] "A king ceases to be a king, and degenerates to a tyrant, as he leaves off to rule according to his laws."—By pronouncement of King James I.
464. [Tyrants] "It is when English citizens have measures imposed upon them, such as taxation, without their consent or even representation.—An interpretation by Great Britain's Parliament.
465. [Racism] "A belief that race is the primary determinant of human traits and capabilities and that racial differences produce an inherent superiority of a particular race.—Merriam-Webster.
466. [Racism] "The belief that race accounts for differences in human character or ability and that a particular race is superior to others.—American Heritage Dictionary.
467. Sin, is the very character or personality of Satan. Sin, a spiritual disease that would lead oneself to a spiritual death.—John T. Nall.
468. "It is also in the interest of a tyrant to keep his people poor, so that they may not be able to afford the cost of protecting themselves by arms and be so occupied with their daily tasks that they have no time for rebellion."—Aristotle.
469. "The militia can never be in rebellion for it is the whole people, organized and trained in the art of war."—DJ.
470. "When the Communist Parties and the Socialist Liberals are able to influence mankind into miscegenation ... homosexuality and abandonment of all Christian belief and laws of our society, then this self-destruction will lead toward the beginning of enslavement by the new Socialist World Order."—John T. Nall.
471. "The Gospel of Jesus Christ, prescribes the wisest rules for just conduct in every situation of life. Happy they who are enabled to obey them in all situations."—Benjamin Rush.
472. "The great, vital, and conservative element in our system is the belief of our people in the pure doctrines and the divine truths of the Gospel of Jesus Christ."—United States Congress—1854.
473. "Fate is never determined by any individual. It finds you when the time is proper."—Craig Maus, President of the Confederate Society of America.
474. [The Wright Theology] "Well accentually, liberation theology uh, took root in Africa and Central America. It was often offered up by Marxists regimes. Uh, that knew that they couldn't up root

the Church, so they tried to weaken the doctrine of the Church."—Ken Blackwell of the Family research Council.

475. [Black Liberation Theology] "Black Theology refuses to accept a God who is not identified totally with the goals of the Black Community. If God is not for us and against White People, then He is a murderer. And we had better kill Him. The task of Black Theology is to kill God's who do not belong to the Black Community …

   Black Theology will accept only the love of God which participates in the destruction of the White Enemy. What we need is the divine love as expressed in Black Power. Which is the power of Black People to destroy their oppressors here and now by any means at their disposal … unless God is participating in the Holy Activity, we must reject His love."—James Cone PH. D. on "Black Power and Black Theology".

476. "To the distinguished character of a Patriot, it should be our highest glory to add the more distinguished character of a Christian."—May, 1778 of a General Order issued at Valley Forge, by U.S. General: George Washington.
477. "Resistance to tyranny is obedience to God."—John Bradshaw, President of the high court that had tried King Charles I, for treason in 1649.
478. "Grandparents, is the reward for not killing your kid's."—Unknown.
479. "If I thought that this war was being fought by the South in order to preserve slavery and by the North in order to abolish it. I would readily offer my sword and services to the South."—Gen. William T. Sherman of the USA.
480. "I once said, 'we will bury you.' And I got into trouble with it. Of course we will not bury you with a shovel, your own working class will bury you."—the Soviet Union Leader: Nikita Khrushchev, in his reverence toward the United States of America.
481. "Comrades! We must abolish the cult of individual decisively, once and for all."—Soviet Union Leader: Nikita Khrushchev, also once a secretary—general of the Communist Party of the Soviet Union, September 12, 13, of 1953.
482. "Democracy will soon degenerate into … such an anarchy that every man will do what is right in his own eyes, and no man's life or property or reputation or liberty will be secure … Democracy never lasts long. It soon wastes, exhausts, and murders itself. There never was a democracy yet that did not commit suicide."—John Adams.

483. "Dear Jesus, Help our people to stand against the spin doctors who are the purveyors of evil who are bent on erasing our heritage, and enslave our children for generations to come. Give us the courage like our forefathers, who in 1776 pledged their lives, their fortunes, and their sacred honor to make this land free. Help us not allow these brutal tyrants to disarm us. Amen."—The European American Volume VII Issue II September 2009.

484. "All Roads Lead to 1865!"—Craig Maus—President of the Confederate Society of America.

485. "If I we're the only man on Earth. He (Jesus Christ) would still come to die for me!—Daryl Sylvester Cobb—Lexington, North Carolina.

486. "Regardless of any such genetic variation, it is our moral duty to treat all as equal before God and before the law,"—Perry Clark, a retired doctor in Kansas City—in the New York Times blog. On the subject of (Exploring genetic differences in the new DNA age).

487. "I am for socialism, disarmament, and ultimately for abolishing the state Itself as an instrument of violence and compulsion. I seek social ownership of property, the abolition of the propertied class, and sole control by those who produce wealth. Communism is the goal.—Roger Baldwin—A socialist and founder of the (ACLU) American Civil Liberties Union.

488. "God does not cause or approve of sin, but only limits, restrains, overrules it for good. The mode of God's providential government is altogether unexplained. We only know that it is a fact that God does govern all his creatures and all their actions; that this government is universal (Ps. 103; 17-19), particular (Matt. 10:29-31), efficacious (Ps. 33:11; Job 23:13), embraces events apparently contingent (Prov. 16:9, 33; 19 21; 21:1), is consistent with His own perfection (2 Tim. 2:13), and to His own glory (Rom. 9:17; 11:36)—The Holy Bible.

489. "The budget should be balanced, the treasury should be refilled, public debt should be reduced, the arrogance of officialdom should be tempered and controlled, and the assistance to foreign lands should be curtailed lest Rome become bankrupt. People must again learn to work, instead of living on public assistance."—Cicero, 55 B.C.

490. "Political Correctness, by the Socialist Liberals are in truth lies and is very unnatural, including being evil in every way. It is poison and will lead our people and our race toward self-destruction and enslavement from our liberties and freedom. Let Communism be dammed!"—John T. Nall.

491. "Western man towers over the rest of the world in ways so large as to be the almost inexpressible. Its Western exploration, science, and conquest that have revealed the world to itself. Other races feel like subjects of Western power, long after colonialism, Imperialism and slavery have disappeared. The charge of racism puzzles Whites who feel not hostility, but only baffled good will, because they don't grasp what it really means: humiliation. The White man presents an image of superiority even

when he isn't conscious of it. Superiority excites envy. Designated victims we call "Minorities."—Joseph Sobran, 1997.

492. "The tariff, then nearly synonymous with federal taxes, was a prime cause of the Civil War."—American Heritage, June 1996.

493. "What the people haven't come too realized is that by putting Barak Obama in the Oval office of the U.S. Presidency, is like putting the fox in the Hen House. As Obama is the fox, and the nation as being the hen house."—Charles R. Nall.

494. "Socialism, is a philosophy of failure, the creed of ignorance, and the gospel of envy, its inherent virtue is the equal slaving of misery."—Winston Churchill.

495. "It is to the eternal glory of the American nation, that the more hopeless became their cause, the more desperately the Southerner fought."—Winston Churchill.

496. "Firearms, are second only to the Constitution in importance! They are the people's liberty teeth. A free people ought to be armed. When firearm's goes, all goes. We need them every hour."—US President: George Washington.

497. "Great is an army of Sheep that's led by a Lion, than an army of Lion's that's led by a Sheep."—Defoe.

498. "Tolerance is the virtue of men who no longer believe in anything."—G.K. Chesterton.

499. "Today's blacks clearly benefited from slavery. My wealth is far greater than I have far greater liberties than if my ancestor had remained in Africa."—Walter Williams.

500. "The framers had a deathly fear of federal government abuse. They saw State Sovereignty as a protection. That's why they gave us the Ninth and Tenth Amendments. They saw secession as the ultimate protection against Washington's tyranny."—Walter Williams.

501. "History has well substantiated the fact that under the right conditions, fallen and foolish man has always given up independence and freedom, even for the illusion of peace and security. If society's great international architects can manufacture the precise conditions as in their adventures in Europe, all vestiges of freedom will fall in America."—Samuel C. Webster, 1935.

502. "If the Union was formed by the accession of States then the Union may be dissolved by the secession of States."—Daniel Webster, US Senate, February 15th of 1833.

503. "In the War Between the States, Southerners believed that they were fighting to defend the government as it was laid down at Philadelphia in 1787 and as recognized by various State ordinances of ratification. This was a government of restricted powers, commissioned to do certain things which the States could not do for themselves, but strictly defined as to its authority."

As long as each State was viewed as a sovereign entity, "the maximum amount of self-determination by the States" preserved, and State's rights rigorously upheld, any drift towards despotism was automatically nipped in the bud. That, according to Weaver, was ultimately the issue over which the South went to war since it held that the North "was rebelling against this idea which had been accepted by the members of the Constitutional Convention in 1787.

Or to put it in another way, the North was staging a revolution, the purpose of which was to do away with this older concept of the American government." The South rejected this revolution and sought to defend what it insisted were its God-given rights. When the War Between the States is seen in these terms, the issue of slavery, firmly fixed in the minds of so many Americans as the true cause of the war, is understood rather to be merely the catchword of the War Party in the North, and a shallow excuse to wage war and impose a Social Revolution."—Writing from Richard M. Weaver.

504. "The Constitution is just a Goddamn piece of paper."—United States President: George W. Bush—November of 2005 {an apology to the reader from the Author for this bad language}
505. "Honor their valor, emulate the devotion with which they gave themselves to the service of their country. Let it never be said that their sons in these Southern States have forgotten their noble example."—Dixie Outfitters.
506. "Equality is a disorganizing concept in so far as human relations mean order."—Richard Weaver.
507. "It is impossible to rightly govern a nation without God and the Bible."—US President: George Washington.
508. "I have tried at every point to seek God's wisdom on the decisions I've made. And I made it my business to speak up on behalf of the things God tells us are important to Him."—NC Senator: Jesse Helms.
509. "If we desire to avoid insults, we would be able to repel it; if we desire to secure peace, one of the most powerful instruments of our rising prosperity, it must be ready for War."—US President: George Washington.
510. "Conservatism is a hard choice for a society that has become accustomed to big government and big entitlements promoted by liberals."—NC Senator: Jesse Helms.
511. "America, must be the moral leader. It is not enough to have power. Power, must be used to protect freedom and give all people hope for the opportunity to sees the fruit of their own labor."—NC Senator: Jesse Helms.

512. "The Speaker, former Representative: Tom Tancredo, Republican of Colorado, told about 600 delegates in a Nashville Tennessee ballroom dance that in a 2008 elections, America "put a committed Socialist ideologue in the White House … Barack Hussein Obama.

513. [Communist Goal] an American Communist Party member, Israel Cohen, on the eve of World War One, noted in his radical program for the 20th Century: "We must realize that our Party's most powerful weapon is racial tension. By propounding into the consciousness of the dark races that for centuries they have been oppressed by whites, we can mold them to the program of the Communist Party. In America, we will aim for subtle victory. While inflaming the Negro minority against the Whites, we will endeavor to instill in the Whites a guilt complex for their exploitation of the Negroes." This was from page nine of the Southern Patriot Newsletter of the League of the South. And it was also published in the Letters to the Editor, of the Salisbury Post, in Salisbury, North Carolina on the fourth of March of nineteen ninety-nine.

514. "Liberty is always won where there exists the unconquerable will to be free, and we have reason to know the strength that is given by a conscious sense, not only of the magnitude, but of the righteousness of our cause."—CSA President: Jefferson Davis Nov, 18th 1861.

515. "We were not rebels; we did not fight to perpetuate human slavery, but for our rights and privileges under a government established over us by our fathers and in defense of our homes." CSA Col. Richard Henry Lee.

516. "All that was, or is now, desired is that error and injustice be excluded from the text books of the schools and from the literature brought into our homes; that the truth be told, without exaggeration and without omission, truth for its own sake and for the sake of honest history, and that the generations to come after us not be left to bear the burden of shame and dishonor un-righteously laid upon the name of their noble sires."—James P. Smith.

517. "Let us be certain that our children know that the 'War Between The States' was not a contest for the preservation of slavery, as some would have them believe, but that it was a great struggle for the maintenance of Constitutional rights, and that the men who fought were warriors tried and true, Who bore the flags of a Nation's trust, and fell in a cause, though lost, still just, and died for me and you."—J. Taylor Ellyson.

518. "As for the South, it is enough to say that perhaps 80% of her armies were neither slave-holders, nor had the remotest interest in the institution. No other proof, however, is needed than the undeniable fact that at any period of the war from its beginning to near its close the South could have saved slavery by simply laying down its arms and returning to the Union."—John B. Gordon.

519. "The South's enemies can bury the truth deep in the swamp of current myth, but the truth will always come to the surface and the truth will always remain a real threat to those who maintain their power and stolen wealth at the expense of honor and honesty."—Southern Soldier, CSA.

520. "The reasons for secession are not the reasons for the war. The war was fought because Northerners invaded a free and independent country. Lincoln was determined to bring back the Southern States into the Union to collect the tariffs from the Southern States, force Southerners to buy Northerner's industrial products, re-establish trade for Northern shipping and to close the Freeport at New Orleans among other things. All these losses were killing the economy of the Northern States."—Dixie Outfitters.

521. "I enlisted with the hope and desire of rendering aid to the great and glorious cause of Southern Independence, prompted by principle, religiously believing that the time had arrived when we were justifiable in resisting Northern aggression, and even at the expense of this once unparalleled Republic. As for my part I don't want to survive a subjugation of my country."—Col. J. Goodner, CSA.

522. "What is self-determination? The right of a people to decide upon its own political status or form of government, without outside influence."—Source: [yourdictionary.com].

523. "Propaganda, is a tool that is used for those people that have become ignorant of their truthful history and the real understanding of liberty. And ignorant is the condition of those people that that has been enslaved. Propaganda decides truth to be false, good to be evil, and what you should love or hate. And what you should accept or reject in society as a people and nation. In truth, Propaganda can be used to condition the people to freely take the rope and slide the noose around their own neck's without force action from those tyrants"—John T. Nall.

524. [The First Migration To The American Continent] "We have a dozen and a half samples that we call [Ancient Ones] because they are collectively the oldest samples from Native America. Native Americans have, by orthodoxy, been regarded as [Asiatic] in origin. [Kennewick] opens up the opportunity or the likelihood, the possibility, that this was not the entire picture; that there has been at least one additional migration from Europe."—Dr. David Glenn Smith. A Genetics Researcher of the University of California, Davis.

525. [Creation of the Races] "Remember the days of old; consider the generations long past. Ask your father and he will tell you, your elders, and they will explain to you. When the Most High gave the nations their inheritance, when he (divided all mankind), he set boundaries for the peoples according to the number of the sons of Israel."—Deuteronomy 32: 7-8.

526. "Yes, they [the Washington Empire] fear us because history and timing (this time around) is on our side, not theirs. They know it and we know it. The Constitutional right of secession and Southern independence in a 21st century world filled with secession and independence movements all around the globe puts the fear of God into our enemies in Washington and New York. Our success means the end of their rule, domination, control and gravy train of high federal taxes paid for by each one of us. This is why, 'that Rebel Flag' and our movement are hated so much. This is why so many lies and so much irresponsible reporting goes on about the defenders of Southern heritage. This is why the 'Lebanese' student in Texas was made a scapegoat and object of scorn by school officials and therefore creating the conditions for an unprovoked attack by students for the hate crime of having checked a book out of the school library for a report with a picture of Robert E. Lee and the Confederate Battle Flag in his possession."—Ron Holland.

527. "Ever since the enslavement of the nation of the Confederate States, and the violation of the Principles of the Declaration of Independence, Socialism has been slowly moving on forward and toward a transformation into a Communist USA. Since 1860, the Centralist and the Socialists have been dancing around, over and under the Constitution of the United States. from a Constitutional Republic, to a Centralized Democracy, on into a Socialist Republic of America. The question I have for you is this! A real Civil War is coming to the United States. And the men and women who are now serving in the Armed Forces of the United States will have to make a choice. Who are you going to serve? Will it be the people in restoring you're nations original government, of a Constitutional Republic? Are will it be for something else? It is time to think on these things for that time will come. And you better hope that you choose wisely! I say, restore the Constitutional Republic of the United States and of the Confederate States of America!"—John T. Nall.

528. " ... That the United States form, for many and for most important purposes, a single nation has not yet been denied. In war, we are one people. In making peace, we are one people. In all commercial regulations, we are one and the same people. In many other respects, the American People are one; and the government which is alone capable of controlling and managing their interests in all these respects is the government of the Union. It is their government, and, in that character, they have no other. America has chosen to be, in many respects and to many purposes, a nation; and for all these purposes her government is complete; to all these objects, it is competent. The people have declared that the exercise of all powers given for these objects it is supreme. It can, then, in effecting these objects, legitimately control all individuals or governments within the American territory. The constitution and laws of a state, so far as they are repugnant to the Constitution and laws of the United States, are absolutely void. [These states are constituent parts of the United

States; they are members of one great empire-for some purposes sovereign, for some purposes subordinate …"]—Chief Justice: John Marshall statement on the Cohens v. Virginia in (1821).

529. "It has been taught in the Federal Public Schools, that the United States fought the Confederate States in order to overthrow slavery. If this we're to be true, than how many other countries has the United States invaded to trample out slavery throughout this world? None! That's how many! It is also believed that the Confederacy should not be in existence because of slavery. If this is also to be true, than every nations in this world, including the United States should not be in existence. Why? Because every nation or country has been involved in slavery in one way or another. Every race has enslaved their own race and other races. The Socialist Americans and the Abolitionists Cult, have been using this arguments as hatred against the Confederate People to this very present day."—John T. Nall.

530. " … For when the revolution took place, the people of each state became themselves sovereign; And in that character hold the absolute right to all their navigable waters, and the soils under them, for their own common use, subject only to the rights since surrendered by the constitution to the general government …"—By Justice Taney in (Martin v. Waddell's Lessee.

531. "It is the opinion of the greatest writers, that a very extensive country cannot be governed on democratical principles, on any other plan than a Confederation of a number of small republics, possessing all the powers of internal government, but united in the management of their foreign and general concerns … [A]anything short of despotism could not bind so great a a country under one government."—'Sentinel' from the Anti-Federalist Papers.

532. [A Nation Under Occupation] "Part of the claims of the Confederate Movement is that the Confederacy is a Nation under occupation by the United States Government; in reality it is more than a simple belief, and is actually a legitimate fact. Not only is it a fact that the CSA is a Nation under occupation, but it is a fact that the Current State Governments in Virginia, North Carolina, South Carolina, Georgia, Alabama, Florida, Mississippi, Arkansas, Louisiana, and Texas were illegally put in place."—Curtis Patranella. First Paragraph of page one under Southern History by DixieOutfitters.com.

533. "The American Public overwhelmingly voted for Socialism when the elected President Obama."—Al Sharpton, a Civil Rights Activist, Socialist and a Race Hustler. March of 2010.

534. "He must indeed have a blind soul who cannot see that some great purpose and design is being worked out here below."—Winston Churchill.

535. "You never want a serious crisis to go to waste. What I mean by that, is a opportunity to do the things that you think that you could not do before."—Democrat, Rahm Emanuel as the White House Chief of Staff.

536. "It is believed by some that the [Confederate States of America] shouldn't be a nation of its own, because of the institution of slavery. If this were to be true, than every nation including the United States of America and the African Nations that have enslaved their own people of race, should remain as Sovereign Nations no more. Because the institution of slavery, is a thing of this world that still remains to this very day."—John T. Nall.

537. [In his famous text (Constitutional Problems Under Lincoln) James G. Randall, documented Lincoln's litany of unconstitutional actions.—"He arrested and imprisoned tens of thousands of political opponents, shut down over 300 newspapers, censored all telegraph communications, and rigged or prevented elections, just to name a few. While Lincoln made nice sounding speeches, his actions destroyed the Constitutional Republic, and set us firmly on track to where we are today."

538. [A Southerner Speaks] "I have always been proud of my time spent as an officer in the United States Marine Corps. I served in the Republic of Vietnam in 1969 and, while I was certainly no "John Wayne" type, I tried to do my duty to the best of my ability and I did bring all of my platoon out of Vietnam alive. This past summer, the son of a friend of mine was very 'gung ho' about joining the Marines and asked my opinion, which I tried to give as honestly as possible, warts and all. I don't know if my discussions had any influence on him, but he enlisted, completed all of the pre-enlistment tests and physical exams and went to all of the pre-enlistment meetings. To say the least, he was very excited about serving his country in the Corps. Shortly before he left Nashville for boot camp, he was told he could not serve his country because he had [Confederate Battle Flag] tattooed on his shoulder in an area that would be completely covered by a t-shirt, and certainly by his uniform.

When informed of this, I went to the local recruiting station that had processed this young man to see if I were getting the entire story. The recruiter, a staff sergeant, told me, "Yes, sir. The Marine Corps considers the Confederate Flag a 'hate symbol,' but if the young man in question had a state or U.S. Flag tattoo that would be acceptable." I informed the young sergeant that my Family had defended the State of Tennessee (also his home State) against a sadistic invasion under that flag and to call our sacred flag oh honor a 'hate symbol was an insult to ALL SOUTHERNERS, but especially to those Southerners who had risked or even given their lives in service to the Marine Corps.

Southerners had served at Belleau Woods, at Taraw and Iwo Jima, at Inchon and the Chosen Reservoir, and at Khe Sahn and Hue City, but now we are no longer wanted in the politically—correct don't-offend-any-minorities military? (This was just prior to the Fort Hood massacre). He was polite, even sympathetic, but said the flag policy was a Marine Corps policy from Quarters Marine Corps and not a local decision. After informing the sergeant that it seemed to me that our military was building a mercenary force of illegal aliens while rejecting native-born Americans in order to have a ready force to turn, without question, on American Citizens, I asked the sergeant if he had taken out the trash yet. He replied that he hadn't. I then said, "Please add these to the day's garbage," and returned mu Lieutenant's bars, my gold and silver

Marine Corps emblem from my dress blues, my shooting badges and my Vietnam ribbons. I, like many of you, have always been told, "Once a Marine, always a Marine," and "There are no ex-Marines, only former Marines," but for me that is no longer true.

I was born in the South. I was raised here. I raised my family in the South and someday, God-willing, I hope to be buried in the native soil of our Southern homeland. I have always considered myself a Southerner first, and will remain so, despite any other organization that I may temporarily join. I will never make a critical remark about a veteran, from any branch of the service, but from now on, I will do everything in my power to discourage any Southern young man, or lady, from becoming a future veteran. I am now an ex-Marine.—Gene Andrews Ex-Marine, 1st Lieutenant 3rd Marine division Vietnam. From The Sons of Confederate Veterans—A Missouri Division.

539. "Secession ... is to be justified upon the basis that the States are sovereign. There was a time when none denied it. I hope the time may come again when a better comprehension of the theory of our Government, and the inalienable rights of the people of the States, will prevent anyone from denying that each State is a sovereign, and thus may reclaim the grants which it has made to any agent whomsoever."—Jefferson Davis, Farewell Address to the U.S. Congress on January 21, 1861.
540. "Any act of discrimination or of prejudice against a Negro will become a crime under the revolutionary law. The basis of race prejudice will no longer exist because capitalism will no longer exist ... Then it will no longer be a question of wiping out the basis for such prejudice, but of merely obliterating the remnants ... To the first generation of New Soviet Americans, race prejudice and discrimination will appear like a horrible disease of a past age ..."—From: [Negroes

in Soviet America]. (Workers Library Publishers: New York.) Quoted by The Citizens' Council, November1955.

541. "Why Southerners shouldn't join the Marines ... Among many other reasons I could give, tattoos of Confederate Flags render one unfit for "service." Now if the Marines would just offend Northerners, Easterners, and Westerners there would be no one left to enlist and meddle in the affairs of other Countries on behalf of the U.S. Empire."—Laurence Vance at Lew Rockwell. Com.

542. "According to the laws of God, my sins has condemned me to death. I'm a criminal by flesh, yet I was pardon by the blood of Jesus Christ, and was set free from eternal death."—John T. Nall

543. "No man has a right to hear the gospel twice until every man has heard it once."—T.L. Osborn.

544. "A Union that can only be maintained by swords and bayonets, and in which strife and Civil War are to take the place of brotherly love and kindness, has no charm for me."—A letter that C.S. General Robert E. Lee that was written to his son on January of 1861.

545. "Socialism, in general has a record of failure so blatant that only an intellectual could ignore or evade it."—Thomas Sowell.

546. "Multicultural nations are inherently unstable."—A Negro Professor: Walter Williams.

547. "It cannot be emphasized too strongly or too often that this great nation was founded, not by religionist, but by Christians; not on religions, but on the Gospel of Jesus Christ! For this very reason peoples of other faiths have been afforded asylum, prosperity and freedom to worship here"—Patrick Henry.

548. "It is in my own opinion that we as Human Beings we're made by God and while we are all Human Beings, yet we are not all the same, nor one as a people. To be descendents of Noah's Family, yet in the Infinite Wisdom of God, we we're transform into the verities of Mankind through the boundaries of Language, Race, Cultures. So that we would all feel the need for Him (God). We are all Humans, regardless if some are savages are more highly advance in Civilization. Or if some are morally right with God or highly against Him. Our existence makes us all unique and special in the eyes of our Maker. It is also with these unique blessings and abilities that God has given to each and every race of Man. A blessing and ability does not make anyone superior or inferior to other people of race or individual person. Because this would be a judgment by personal observation without understanding the nature of God's Creation. To respect and to maintain our Creators creation is to maintain the balance of nature of all of Mankind. And to recognize and respect the difference is to give acknowledgements and glory to our Father in heaven. There are three way's to indentify the verities of Man of Race.

- By simple observation of color, not including (miscegenation): To destroy both races by cross breeding them with one another.
- DNA Information of Ethnic origins (by blood).
- By Racial differences in Skull shapes: 1. White Caucasoid Skull 2. East Asian Mongoloid Skull 3. Black Negroid Skull.—John T. Nall.

549. "When Socialism begins to invade a nation, they become much more like the Termites that would invade a house. They will not devour the house all at once. Instead, they will eat slowly at the foundation of the house. The same is true of Socialism; they too will work to destroy anything and anyone to bring a nation and its people to their knees, in order to enslaved them. By promoting good to be evil and evil to be good. By removing Christian Principles from government and society. By supporting miscegenation, homosexual rights, abortions and all open borders. By protecting the criminals and denying justice to the victims. By denying the right to self-defense (owning Guns) and when the crime rate goes up, they won't more Gun Control laws. By replacing the foundation of government with one that they can control. By perverting the history of that nation and of its people with history of half-truths and fiction. By stripping the heritage and culture of any people and replace their true identity with Multicultural and Diversity. By destroying the economy from within. Once again, Socialism; is like a pack of wolfs in sheep's clothing. For they are ready to pounce upon the heard and feast upon their flesh, all the while the sheep would panic in a shock of ignorance."—John T. Nall.

550. [The (Framework) of the New World Order] "Governance is not Government—It is the framework of rules, institutions, and practices that set limits on behavior of individuals, organizations and companies."—United Nations Development Report 1999.

551. [Slaves and Masters] "Slaves, obey your earthly masters with respect and fear, and with sincerity of heart, just as you would obey Christ. Obey them not only to win their favor when their eye is on you, but like slaves of Christ, doing the will of God from your heart. Serve wholeheartedly, as if you were serving the Lord, not men, because you know that the Lord will reward everyone for whatever good he does, whether he is slave or free. And Master's, treat your slaves in the same way. Do not threaten them, since you know that he who is both their Master and yours is in heaven, and there is no favoritism with Him.—Ephesians 6:5-9 New International Version Holy Bible.

552. [A Bankrupt Nation] "Mr. Traficant. Mr. Speaker, we are here now in chapter11. Members of Congress are official trustees presiding over the greatest reorganization of any bankrupt entity in world history, the U.S. Government. We are setting fourth hopefully a blue print for our future.

There are some who say it is a coroner's report that will lead to our demise."—Copy—Second column of third paragraph of the U.S. Congressional Records-House-March 17, 1993 H1303.

553. [U.S. Test or Experiment] "1520. Use of human subjects of chemical or biological agents by Department of Defense; accounting to Congressional committees with respect to experiments and studies; notification of local civilian officials.

(a) No later than thirty days after final approval within the Department of Defense of plans for any experiment or study to be conducted by the Department of Defense, whether directly or under contract, involving the use of human subjects for the testing of chemical or biological agents, the Secretary of Defense shall supply the Committees on Armed Services of the Senate and House of Representatives with full accounting of such plans for such experiment or study, and such experiment or study may then be conducted only after the expiration of the thirty-day period beginning on the date such accounting is received by such committees.

(b) (bxThe Secretary of Defense may not conduct any test or experiment involving the use of any chemical or biological agent on civilian populations unless local civilian officials in the area in which the test or experiment is to conducted are notified in advance of such test or experiment, and such test or experiment may then be conducted only after the expiration of the thirty-day period beginning on the date of such notification.

(c) (Paragraph (1) shall apply to test and experiments conducted by Department of Defense personal and tests and experiments conducted on behalf of the Department of Defense by contractors."—Copy-Title 50 U.S. War and National Defense—1521 Page 1147. (Codification—Section was enacted as part of the Department of Defense Authorization Act. 1984, and not as Part of Pub. L 91-121. Title IV 409, Nov.19. 1969. 83 Stat.—First column Paragraph 3 and 4.

554. "Despite what some may choose to believe! Socialism has integrated the very fabric of our constitutional American freedom since the Eighteen Hundreds. With Abraham Lincoln's affiliations with Carl Marx and with the U.S. President Lincoln's flooding his Federal Army's with the Socialist outcast from Europe. To the Communist Party USA, and with Martin Luther King's affiliations with the Communist Party. Now the State of California, has become A breeding ground for this political Plague. Even with illegal Aliens that may be Socialist who might receive

citizenship and then to vote for more Socialist Politicians into office. Even some of the U.S. President's we're Socialist (Liberal's or Progressives).

When Lincoln and his radical Republican Party transformed the United States into a Centralized Democracy and World Empire, this is in truth was treason against the people of the United States of America. And now by transforming the United States into a Socialist America, this is still treason against our definition of freedom by our founding fathers. In all reality the Southern States that left the Union and created the nation of the Confederate States of America, did not commit treason and are still constitutionally still a separate nation under occupation by the United States. Yet! I have not heard one person to declare Communism or Socialism against the government of the United States to be an act of treason! The question that comes to my mind is why?—John T. Nall.

555. "If there be any among us who would wish to dissolve this Union or to change its Republican form, let them stand undisturbed as monuments of the safety with which error of opinion may be tolerated where reason is left free to combat it."—Thomas Jefferson, in his first inaugural address.
556. "Whether we remain in one confederacy, or form into Atlantic and Mississippi Confederacies, I believe not very important to the happiness of either part. Those of the Western confederacy will be as much our children & descendants as those of the eastern … and did I now foresee a separation [i.e., secession] at some future day, yet I should feel the duty & the desire to promote the western interests as zealously as the eastern …"—A letter written from Thomas Jefferson to Dr. Joseph Priestly in 29th of January of 1804.
557. "Separation" then "God bless them both [North and South] & keep them in the union if it be for their good, but separate them, if it be better."—A letter that Thomas Jefferson wrote to John Breckenridge on the 12th of August of 1803 concerning the New England Federalists, who were at that time threatening to secede from the Union.
558. "Tyranny consists in the wanton and improper use of strength by the stronger, in the use of it to do things which one equal would not attempt against another. A majority is Tyrannical when it forces men to contribute money to objects which they disapprove, and which the common interest does not demand."—James Bryce, the American Commonwealth, II.
559. "You cannot play by the rules of the Devil, and still expect to win his game. Never become the very reflection of evil by repaying the same actions to your enemy."—John T. Nall

560. [The United States President] "The danger to America is not Barack Obama but a citizenry capable of entrusting a man like him with the Presidency. It will be far easier to limit and undo the follies of an Obama presidency than to restore the necessary common sense and good judgment to a depraved electorate willing to have such a man for their president."

The problem is much deeper and far more serious than Mr. Obama, who is a mere symptom of what ails America. Blaming the prince of fools should not blind anyone to the vast confederacy of fools that made him their prince."

"The Republic can survive a Barack Obama, who is, after all, merely a fool."

"It is less likely to survive a multitude of fools such as those who made him their president." This quote was translated into English from an article appearing in the Prager Zeitung on the 28 of April of 2010. The Prager Zeitung is a German newspaper in the Czech Republic, issued Weekly, in Prague. It is the largest non-Czech newspaper published in the Czech Republic.

561. "Life's tough … it's even tougher if you're stupid." Actor—John Wayne.
562. "You don't need (God) anymore, you have us Democrats." Nancy Pelosi (Quoted in 2006).
563. "We just have to pass the Health Bill to see what's in it". Nancy Pelosi (Quoted in 2010)
564. "If you're going to win, do so with some humility. And if you are bound to lose, then remain so in your stances of dignity. For it is in your character that defines your true-self during the good and hard times. Known of us are without sin, nor are we without fault. But striving in our daily lives' can bring forth the very fruit of our inner spirit and mind."—John T. Nall
565. "Here is the difference between the Democrats and the Republicans! The Democrats wants to Sodomize you, while the Republicans will kiss you first.—Curtis Patranella. September of 6th of 2010.
566. [Fall of the Republic] "Your dispatch is received, and … I have to say in reply, that I regard the levy of troops made by the administration for the purpose of subjugating the States of the South, as a gross usurpation of power. I can be no party to this wicked violation of the laws of the country and to this war upon the liberties of a free people. You can get no troops from North Carolina."—Governor Ellis (to Lincoln) 1861.
567. [Bankers] "Don't ever let the Private Bankers get control of the Public Treasure."—Thomas Jefferson.

568. "According to the myth of the Federal American Empire, the Yankee's fought to free the slaves in the Confederacy. [However, in the year of 2001, the office of the United Nations High Commissioner for Human Rights, Geneva, Switzerland has reported that slavery and slavery-like practices are carried on in these countries today. *Bangladesh/Congo/Ivory Coast/Pakistan/ Brazil/Dominican Republic/Mauritania//Philippines/Burkina Fazo/Ghana/Myanmar/Sudan/ China/India/Nigeria/ Togo*.] With their self-righteous attitude, how many other foreign nations has been invaded and liberated from slavery by the Yankee nation?—John T. Nall.
569. "Let me write the songs of a nation-I don't care who writes its laws."—Andrew Fletcher (1653-1716) Scottish Writer, politician and Patriot. He was a commissioner of the old Parliament of Scotland and opposed the 1707 Act of Union between Scotland and England.
570. "You need only reflect that one of the best ways to get yourself a reputation as a dangerous citizen these is to go about repeating the very phrases which our founding fathers used in the struggle for independence."—Charles Austin Beard (1874-1948).
571. "There was a time when the pen was mightier than the sword. That was a time when people believed in truth & regarded truth as an independent power & not as an auxiliary for government, class, racial, ideological, personal or financial interest. Today Americans are ruled by propaganda. Americans have little regard for truth, little access to it, and little ability to recognize it. Truth is an unwelcome entity. It is disturbing. It is off limits. Those who speak it run the risk of being branded "anti-American", "anti-Semite" or "conspiracy theorist." Truth is an inconvenience for government & for special interest groups whose campaign contributions control government. Truth is an inconvenience for prosecutors who want convictions, not the discovery of innocence or guilt. Truth is inconvenient for ideologues."—Paul Craig Roberts.
572. "The spirit of resistance to government is so valuable on certain occasions, that I wish it to be always kept alive."—Thomas Jefferson.
573. "Politics is the second oldest profession, and it bears a striking resemblance to the first."—Ronald Reagan.
574. "If you expect a nation to be ignorant and free, you expect what never was and can never be."—Thomas Jefferson.
575. "There's no left or right. There's only freedom or control."—Dr. Katherine Albrecht.
576. "The only thing government does well is nothing at all."—Lew Rockwell.
577. "If Centralism is ultimately to prevail; if our entire system of free institutions as established by our common ancestors is to be subverted, and an [Empire] is to be established in their stead; if that is to be the last scene of the great tragic drama now being enacted: then, be assured, that we

of the South will be acquitted, not only in our own consciences, but in the judgment of Mankind, of all responsibility for so terrible a catastrophe, and from all guilt of so great a crime against humanity."—Alexander H. Stephens: Vice President of the Confederate States of America.

578. "Times change and Men often change with them, but principles never!"—Alexander H. Stephens, CSA Vice President.

579. "I have destroyed the Republic to save the Union." Abe Lincoln: President of the USA.

580. "As long as there was fairness & a subscription to those laws written by one and all to which we all agreed, we were able to co-exist. But once justice & fairness were shelved & usurpation & miss-use of station evolved, resulting in & subjecting "Our States" to un-fair regulations and taxes negatively impacting us and our Citizens, "we were left no other choice other than to exercise our right to leave under the 10th Amendment of the U.S. Constitution." They, these Federals, were doing to us the exact same thing that King George & his bandits did to us only 65 years earlier ... and 145 years later it and they have gotten worse and just as we predicted they would! ... Again, following that War of Wars. Our President was smart enough "NOT TO SURRENDER OUR COUNTRY" to them. Thus, we are the last remaining door to Constitutional Freedom & Liberty."—Craig Maus: President of the Confederate Society of America.

581. [Reconstructed Southerner] "A reconstructed Southerner is a Confederate American that has been brainwashed in the Federal Public government schools. Regardless of all of the evidence that Southern History has shinnied the light upon the flaws in the Federal Government history books. These Southerners would reject all of the evidence without thoroughly studying it, and later to declare it all to be Southern Propaganda."—John T. Nall.

582. [States Rights] (Amendment 10—Powers of the States and People). "The powers not delegated to the United States by the Constitution, nor prohibited by it to the States, are reserved to the States respectively, or to the People. [Note] Anything not expressly granted to the Federal government is reserved for the States or the people. Although this amendment is very liberally interpreted, it is one of the tenants of the Constitution. This amendment is also known as the [States' Rights Amendment].

583. [States Rights] (ARTICLE IV—Section Six—Powers of the States and People). "The powers not delegated to the Confederate States by the Constitution, nor prohibited by it to the States, are reserved to the States respectively, or to the people."

584. [Fighting to End Slavery] "Throughout the old world, European nation were phasing out slavery. While other non-European and non-Christian nations we're still practicing this system. Including the Confederate States. The United States wanted to end Slavery in the Confederacy however,

the Industrial Revolution could have been shared with the new confederate nation and replace or reduce the amount of Slaves on the plantation. They were not shared with the confederate farmers or any other slave nations in the world.—John T. Nall.

585. "They [South] know that it is their import trade that draws from the people's pockets sixty or seventy millions of dollars per annum, in the shape of duties, to be expended mainly in the North, and in the protection and encouragement of Northern interests … These are the reasons why these people do not wish the South to secede from the Union. They [the North] are enraged at the prospect of being despoiled of the rich feast upon which they have so long fed and fattened, and which they were just getting ready to enjoy with still greater gout and gusto. They are as mad as hornets because the prize slips from them just as they are ready to grasp It."—New Orleans Daily Crescent Paper—explaining the causes of secession 21st of January of 1861.

586. "War and imperialism, so long the most admired oh human activities."—Kenneth Clark. Civilization, 1969.

587. "Before the Representatives of the Southern States were allowed to retake their seats, they were told that because they seceded from the Union, that they were no longer able to hold those seats. Before they could retake those seats they must submit to the reconstruction act or (enslavement) first. Yet the U.S. Congress would not recognize those States being a sovereign nation of the Confederate States of America. But, according to the Declaration of Independence of the United States, all sovereign States or countries are within their rights to do what the South did as it was done during the Colonel War for Independence. Meaning that the Declaration of Independence does recognize the Confederate States as a sovereign and independent nation. Not by name I would say, but by her actions."—John T. Nall.

588. [IN A REFERENCE TO THE PARTIAL BIRTH CONTROL] "If you want to get an abortion, why don't you jump off the highest building? So the baby won't have any pain …—Anonymous-.

589. "The Republicans will skin you from the top to down. And the Democrats will skin you from the bottom up."—Governor: Huey Long, Louisiana.

590. "If the American People ever allow the banks to control the issuance of their currency, first by Inflation, then by deflation, the banks and the corporations that grow up around them will deprive the people of all property, until their children wake up homeless on the Continent their Fathers Conquered. This issuing power of money should be taken from banks and restored to Congress and the People to whom it belongs. I sincerely believe the banking institutions having the issuing power of money, are more dangerous to liberty than standing armies.—Thomas Jefferson.

591. "Fascism, should more appropriately be called corporatism because it is a merger of State and Corporate Power."—Benito Mussolini.
592. "Our political leaders, setting themselves above the law, have forged an unholy alliance with large Corporations and the international (Money Cartel). Those elites have purchased the lawmakers who are sworn to serve the people, enabling them to expropriate our wealth in the greatest act of plunder in human history. ... The burden of confiscatory taxation, combined with runaway federal spending and currency manipulated to benefit the ruling elites, has brought our Country to the brink of bankruptcy and economic collapse, with all the political and social turmoil that must inevitably follow."—Southern National Covenant; September/12th/2009.
593. "We are fast approaching the stage of the ultimate inversion: the stage where government is free to do anything it pleases, while the Citizens may act only by permission; which is the stage of the darkest periods of human history, the stage of rule by brute force."—Ayn Rand (The Nature of Government).
594. "Instead of the land of the free and the home of the brave, we've become a land on our knee's and the home of the slaves."—D.R. "Doc" Smith Sr. Tennessee 2010.
595. "The seeds of our deliverance remain alive within our faith, culture and historic principles of governance of individual liberty, rule of law and impartial justice. Southern Culture is founded on the enduring and permanent: trust in God, family, tradition, manners, property, community, loyalty, courage and honor. We know that free and just government cannot derive from laws, regulations, bureaucracies and ideologies. It springs only from the soil and sacrifice, the harvest of which is liberty, justice, prosperity and peace."—Southern National Covenant; September/12th/2009.
596. "The North likes to flatter itself that they fought the War Between the States to free the slaves. But all they really did, was to expand the plantation."—D.R. "Doc" Smith Sr. Tennessee 2010.
597. [ARTICLE VI SECTIONS FIVE] "The enumeration in the Constitution, of certain rights, shall not be construed to deny or disparage others retained by the people of the several States."—Confederate States Constitution.
598. [AMENDMENT 9] "The enumeration in the Constitution, of certain rights, shall not be construed to deny or disparage others retained by the people."—United States Constitution.
599. [Reparation Proposals for whom?] "If the question was asked, should reparations for slavery be paid? The answer would be automatically YES! When the old form of economy in using slavery in the European nations was replaced with a new one, reparations was given directly to the former slaves. But, the situation in the American Nations was far different. Slavery would have slowly

come to an end in the Confederate nation. A new form of economy with the Industrial Revolution would have taken the place of slaves. The former slaves in the Confederacy would have paid the reparations in full to the former slaves. The masters would have received the difference in cost by the State or national government. The Constitution of the Confederate States, had taken the first step in phasing out the system, a slow process to say the least. But it would have prevent the Confederate People from having the economy from collapsing all around them.

unfortunately, the United States invaded the new nation who had no desire for war and was blasted back into the Stone Age. With the Confederate States government dispersing and the intentional act of extermination against the Confederate people. Reparations to the slaves would never take place. When the Congress of the United States and not the President had withdrew slavery from it's Constitution, which by the way the [Southern States is Constitutionally not members of], reparations should have been paid to any Yankee former slaves, but it never happened. Since that time all of the former slaves haves passed away. We have far more people here on this American Continent than before. We may even have African decedents who sold their own race to the Yankee Slave Ships living in the United States today. We may have decedents of former Negro Slave Masters living in the United States also. We may also have Native Indians and Jews who decedents own Negro slaves. We also may have decedents of White family members that owned White slaves before the introduction of the Negro slave market. It would be impossible to know who should receive such a proposal. In fact, this stunt is more likely to force the Negro Americans to become more co-dependents toward the government than they already are!"—John T. Nall.

600. According to Mr. Charles Adams, in his book [Those Dirty Rotten Taxes]: The North did make an effort to save the Union by offering the South, full and permanent protection over slavery. But, the South had refused the offer in believing that she would have a better future in going her own way. Also, in his view, the United States was fighting over taxes because under the rules of international law, a blockade is an act of war, and not the previous firing on Fort Sumter.
601. "Man is not free, unless government is limited."—U.S. President Ronald Reagan.
602. "All of creation in life and of beyond is the very Testimony of our Creator, (GOD). It does not bring you closer in knowing Him, but in respecting Him and realizing that He must exist in this world of life. He had made us in His image and through us we come to know Him. His words are the words of man so that we may hear and come to learn and understand his will for us. For with out His words, [The Holy Bible], we would be lost in not knowing Him. Then we would fall into our

imaginations of false gods to worship and serve. To argue that the Holy Book of God was written by man and therefore is manmade is to deny that the Creator of all things is unable to control what shall be written in His own Holy Scriptures. In truth, it was the Holy Sprite who is the author through man. Spirit and flesh, we are bound to fulfill the history of man and the Creator and His creation in His image shall come together in full circle. Our spirits are intertwined in this war between good and evil and Jesus Christ is the main prize for us to receive."—John T. Nall.

603. "I've chosen not to live in ignorance, that's why I have spent most of my time in studying and learning the Holy Bible, Confederate American (Southern) History and the principles and writings of our Founding Fathers. It has set me apart from the rest of the sheep, which has chosen ignorance over free will of thought and rejected the natural rights of men that we're given to them by our Creator."—John T. Nall.

604. [Valuing Human Life] "In our land today, we have laws against murder and yet murders continue to escalate throughout America. In the United States, we continue to pass more and more legislation against assault and violence, and yet the violence on our streets becomes worse with each passing day. There are defined punishments on the books for those who commit sexual and/ or physical abuse on a child, and yet we read every day of countless cases of child abuse in neighborhoods from the most exclusive to the ghetto. We continue to hear of the ongoing controversy concerning euthanasia or assisted suicide and about the struggles lawmakers are having with this issue.

There is also the ongoing issue of abortion with which our nation and our legal system continue to struggle and battle. Presently, the law of the land says that abortion is legal. Is this right or wrong? Each of us has our personal convictions concerning this sanctity of life issue as well as the life issues I mentioned in the previous paragraph. I wonder, however, if the Roe v. Wade case was overturned tomorrow, would there be a changed in the number of abortions performed or would women continue to find doctors to do the abortions?

My thinking is that we cannot legislate the value of human beings. No matter what the law says, people are still going to do what they want. The increase in violence, abuse, suicide, and murder shows that the law is not what will bring back the value of human life.

Instead of laws being changed, I believe that attitudes must be changed. Until we are able to help people see the value of each and every human life, we will continue to see the senseless violence and deaths taking place across our nation and throughout the world. Does this mean I think we should forsake our legal system? No, I think it is important and, for the most part, very good. There are areas of the law that we as Christians, under the leadership of the Holy Spirit and through our personal convictions, should strive to change. However, we must always remember as we strive for change that the ways and means of doing something are just as important as the end result. After all, people are watching us and, therefore, what we do "in the name of God" must be godly and righteous. We are to be the "salt of the earth" and the "light of the world."

Do I think that the people's attitudes can be changed overnight? Of course not! Just as it took us a long time to reach to this point where life has such little value and meaning, it will take us quite some time to restore to the people's attitudes that the value of human life and see it as something to be sacred. It must begin with us as Christians. We must show others that we value all human life. We must show forth the attitude that every human being, rich or poor, black or white, tall or short, American or otherwise has been created in the image of God.

If we will mirror this attitude before our children, before our youth, and before other adults, slowly but surely the value and sanctity of human life will rise back to the high status it deserves. It will not come through laws, but through our living the laws of God in our lives."—Reverend Charlie Bryan of Tennessee—January 12th, 1994 (Genesis 1:27; Matthew 5:13-16, 21-22, 27-28, 43-45a.

605. "Secession filled me with hope, not as the destruction but as the redemption of Democracy … (Lord Acton to Robert E. Lee, November 4, 1866).
606. "In my heart, I have always believed it to be our duty and inspiration to be falling the footsteps and ideas of our founding fathers, and to apply those principles to our daily lives, just as it had been done by our Confederate forefathers before us. As Christians, we should also be falling the footsteps and teachings of our Messiah, Jesus Christ. By living by these values and principles, we have done our duty in being patriots and serving our Father in Heaven. We must do this, not just for our own sake, But, for the sake of our people in the near future to come".—John T. Nall.
607. "We should constantly analyze our own opinions for errors, using the lessons of the Bible. And we should see that our nation is drifting away from God and His Son, Jesus Christ. Our nation seems to have the idea that because we are Americans, we will always survive and prevail. A good hard look at biblical and non-biblical history will show many instances of the fall of great nations and empires, and why they fell. If God chooses to bring us down, he can place us under our enemies, to humble or even destroy us. The faith and influence of Christians is under attack, under the

guise of "tolerance". We may reach a point where it will be illegal to proclaim publicly that Jesus Christ is the Son of God, because it may offend someone. Our nation needs revival, and we need Godly men in power who will return our laws to biblically based laws. There are other countries where people can go for governments and laws that are based on atheist or non-Christian ideas. They would rather not go there, but rather stay here and force us to change what our founding fathers created, and re-interpret their intentions. It is our Christianity that has allowed tolerance of non-Christians, of those who do not believe, and that is why God, Jesus Christ, and the Bible must remain our main sources of guidance."—Ted Fuller, Salisbury N.C. February 5, 2011.

608. "God is not a "vending machine!" He is not something that you can use without giving something in return. God is not some kind of "Genie in a bottle!" You can't just use Him when you feel like it, than to return Him back into His bottle."—Ted Fuller, Salisbury N.C. February 5, 2011.

609. [Treason]: Who was it really that has committed treason? Our Confederate people have been accused of treason for not submitting to the United States government and for Constitutionally leaving the Union. Since when, is it treason not to submit to a government that was created by the States? Should we submit to the political leaders that we voted to put in office? Of course not! Is it treason to not just speak about freedom, but to act on it? No! Is it treason to act on the Declaration of Independence and on the ninth and tenth Amendments in the U.S. Constitution? Absolutely not! A free State is able to act on the freedoms of liberty, not people who are enslaved. So. It could only be that since the Southern States refused to submit to the Northern States rule of power [Federal control], they call this to be treason.
But, in truth, it was not just Abraham Lincoln and his radical Republican Party that destroyed the Union of a Constitutional Republic! It wasn't just them that committed treason! It was every State that joined in the war to enslave the nation of the Confederate States of America! Why? Because they trample upon the very documents of freedom and liberty that the United States had been founded on. Regardless of their reasons of justifications. In order to create an empire, the States in the Union had sacrificed their personal sovereign rights of the people; in order to enslaved the Southern States. Yet, everyone accepts Communism in its influence over the American Empire. Communism will destroy what very little freedom that may be left.—John T. Nall. February the 13th of 2011.

610. [To Be Thankful For] "There is so much to be thankful for … as we go through this life … so much, so much, so very much … to dull misery's knife … be we rich or be we poor … God gives to everyone … the means to cope with darkness … until we find the sun … even those afflicted

... with the cruelest grief ... through the power of great faith ... somehow they find relief ... and those who labor hard and long ... are blessed by God above ... to list all of the priceless treasures ... we should be grateful for ... would take a thousand pages ... and a whole lot more ... whatever be our lot in life ... be it taking or giving ... there's so much to be thankful for ... yes, even just for living."—Ben Burroughs of Pensacola, Florida. 1970's. Not sure of date/

611. "That it be born in mind, that the tragedy of life does not lie in not reaching your goals. But, tragedy lies in having no goals to reach for ... It's not a calamity to die with dreams unfulfilled. But, it is a calamity to have no dreams.—Herman Cain, A Black Southern radio talk show host. Atlanta Georgia. 2011.

612. "Some people believe a lie can be the truth, if enough fools believe It."—Johnny Van Zant. A Southern Rock Singer.

613. "The Devil made me do it the first time, the second time I did it on my own."—Billy Joe Shaver.

614. "Politics has been concerned too long with Left or Right, as opposed to right or wrong."—Richard Armour.

615. "Hell, I never vote for anybody ... I always vote against."—WC Fields.

616. "Politicians are all the same. They promise to build a bridge even if there is no river."—Nikita Khrushchev.

617. "A piece of spaghetti or a military unit can only be led from the front."—George Patton.

618. "If everyone is thinking alike, then someone is not thinking."—George Patton.

619. "A 'no' whispered from conviction is better than a 'yes' shouted in order to please."—Gandhi.

620. [THE SOUTHERN CROSS] "It is far better to offend the Socialist and the ignorance of others by flying the Confederate battle Flag than to offend the honor and memory of all Confederates of race and their descendants, by not flying it out of fear and of false guilt. It is far better to fly the Confederate flag in honor of one Black Confederate than in not flying in fear that it may offend thousands in that race. The Socialist, Communist Party, New World supporters and the Main Stream Media has a strong hatred for this symbol. Not because of slavery, for it is they who desire to enslave the whole world! It is because it is a symbol of individual sovereignty of States and the rights of Man. A Constitutional Republic that is founded on a Christian Foundation. So slavery will always be the battle cry for the far left!—John T. Nall.

621. [The West awakens to Islam's intent to dominate, not assimilate]" Europeans are finally awakening from their self-imposed [Rumple stiltskin] deep slumber to discover that multiculturalism is actually cultural rot and is ripping their countries apart. From the United Kingdom to France

to Spain to Germany, leaders or former leaders have decried multiculturalism as a poisonous experiment for their nations. What's next—is Europe going to rediscover that the earth is not flat?

You have to wonder how these leaders ever could have signed on to encouraging Muslims to lead separate lives and not to assimilate in the first place. Pardon me, but even a venison-fueled guitar slayer knows that playing politically correct games always leads to death, destruction and decay. The brain-dead politically correct faced of multiculturalism was primarily for the benefit of Muslims, and you know it. European leaders were scared to be labeled as intolerant religious bigots by Muslims. Their fear was misplaced. They should have been vociferously condemning Muslims who wanted to be treated separately.

Instead of condemning Muslim extremists, Europe instead condemned a Danish cartoonist who poked fun at Muhammad—frees speech be damned. German government censured an author for writing a popular book that Muslim immigrants were lowering the intelligence of Germany. Not to be outdone by the Europeans, the American media implied that those Americans who protested the proposed placement of a Mosque in downtown Manhattan were bigoted and anti-Muslim. And while Europe and America to some extent, were embracing Multiculturalism, Muslims were murdering Christians and burning down their Churches in Muslim countries. Let us not forget Multiculturalism lesson no.1: Islam is the religion of peace

While Europe was imploding because of political correctness and doing it! Best to accommodate Muslims praying in the street and what not, many Muslims were—and still are—working hard to impose their religious/political customs, traditions and values on those European nations and right here in America. Instead of encouraging Muslims to assimilate and embrace European culture, tradition, norms and values, European leaders buried their heads in the sand and ignored the problem.

The bold, unfiltered truth is that some Muslims are not in the least bit interested in assimilating and embracing Western Traditions, values and Democracy. Their goal is taking over and transplanting Islam as the mandatory religion and government. Those Muslims do not believe in universal, basic human rights, such as woman's rights, freedom of speech, the right to practice their faith and the rule of law. The definition of Islam is subjugation. For Muslim extremists and radicals, Islam is about totalitarianism and enslavement, not freedom.—Ted Nugent, in the National Rifle Association.

622. [Slavery verses Technology] "Some small minded and (Socialist people) believes that if the Confederate States of America had won the war, the Southern nation would still have slavery in the 21st Century. But consider this! The tractor had replaced the mule and the plow, and farm machinery would have replace slavery just like the mule. A farmer doesn't have to pay medical bills on his tractor. A farmer doesn't have to buy accidental insurance for his tractor. A farmer doesn't have to buy food or cloths for his tractor. And while a farmers tractor requires a barn to be stored in. He doesn't have to worry about an electrical bill to keep his barn at room temperature. Some may believe that they would still be in slavery today, but they shouldn't be flattering themselves. Machinery has replaced forced labor, and in truth it was for the best for everybody. Just like in every other European country, slavery would have been faded out in our Confederate history. It's just a question of time—John T. Nall.

623. "Courage is what it takes to stand and speak. Courage is also what it takes to sit down and listen."—Winston Churchill.

624. "Justice must not only be done, it must also seem to be done."—Lord Chief Justice Hewark.

625. [The following is the definition of "Genocide" as defined by the United Nations General Assembly.]
" ... Any of the following acts committed with intent to destroy, in whole or in part, a national, ethnic, racial or religious group, as such:

   (a) Killing members of the group;
   (b) Causing serious bodily or mental harm to members of the group; (C) Deliberately inflicting its physical destruction in whole or in part; (D) Imposing measures intended to prevent births within the group; (E) Forcibly transferring children of the group to another group.

[Convention on the prevention and punishment of the crime of genocide, Article II]

(Authors note): The Communist, Socialist, Liberals, Progressives who are one in the same, have violated this Article II throughout the whole world against the Christian people and European race. And yet the United Nations ignores the signs! Why? Could it be that this Article II was meant for non-Christians and non-Whites? Could it be that Christians and Europeans would put up a strong resistance against a New World Order? Could it be that the people of third world countries are more fit for the enslavement into this New Order? Only time will tell! Yet, thanks to the Internet, You Tube, Council of Conservative Citizens web site, have brought most of these inhumane crimes to the public eyes.)

626. The Communist Party are experts at [psychological warfare]. If they can't invade by military force, than infiltration is the answer. Manipulation the structure of society, is used to transform the nations society to except unmoral and unnatural life styles that would bring them down or destroy that nation and people, and to prepare those people for a Communist government. Like a virus in a computer, they will infiltrate every part of society, while being undercover. Everything that is good, is now evil, everything that was once evil is now good. Everything that is unnatural is now accepted to be normal and so forth. Lately, the Communist and the Socialist mainstream media have been harassing the (Sons of Confederate Veterans) and the War Between the States re-reactors, for teaching their side of history which would be a contradiction to the reconstruction public school books from the federal government and the communist professors in college universities. By using hate and fear tactics, the left is claiming that if the South had won the war, slavery would still be alive and well. Please note: The Sons of Confederate Veterans purpose, is to preserve the history and the legacy of our Southern ancestral heroes. So that the future generations of our people can understand the motives that animated the Southern Cause for Independence and for defending this new found freedom that God had bless them with. However, that they are not a political organization or a party that would gain anything by lying to the public.—John T. Nall.

627. "I am a red man. If the Great Spirit had desired me to be a white man he would have made me so in the first place. Now we are poor but we are free. No white man controls our footsteps. If we must die we die defending our rights.—Sitting Bull, Hunkpapa Sioux.

(Authors note): If a white man we're to say such a thing in our times. The Liberals would automatically brand him to be a races!

628. [An Interesting Internet Comment] The media is an entertainment circus. Fortunately for them, Americans have become lazy fact finders. They hear a story on the almighty TV, and they hear it from a "journalist", and think it's true. Or they hear something from a politician, an innuendo, a false charge, and because it's a politician of their political party, they again will believe it without any investigating. You really need to look beyond the smoke and mirrors, and realize all these people are serving themselves—not you.—SirWnity—http:/news.yahoo.com/s/yblog—4/16/2011.

629. "Liberals are in fact "idiotic morons" who blindly ignore all bi-logical evidence about race and gender, to push their socialist will on everyone ells. They totally ignore the evil and crimes that Communism has committed in world history. The United States and the occupation of the Confederacy is becoming more like a Communist/Fascist Empire.—John T. Nall.

630. "Believe this or not! God is not a Socialist or a member of the Communist Party. Nor is He is a Fascist. And more importantly, He is not a passiveness. When Jesus Christ, a Hebrew, died on the cross and later to be resurrected from the dead, God did not re-write the laws of nature. He created the races and meant for them to continual the existence of each race. He never meant for them to destroy themselves by inter-breeding and abortions. He did not change the relationship between a Man and a Woman. The only thing that He did change was in the spiritual realm. And that would be to give full pardon against those who repent of their sins and accept Jesus Christ as their Lord and Savor and if possible, to baptized. We are all human being's' and we're created by God. But, we are not at all, one people!

In Christ, a person of one race is more of a brother to a man of another race. The mixing of two races into a [none-race] does not really make that person an equal. It only makes them a victim of miscegenation. But, the blood of Christ is eternal and will never end! So, the two men of different races will remain brothers in spirit, forever! The blood of all men is bound to this world alone. But, in spirit, they become equal. And this is done without compromising the bloodline or DNA of both parties of race and of their descendants. We are all created perfected in our Fathers eyes! It's our spirits within us that requires redemption and salvation, not physical change.—John T. Nall.

631. [South Carolina Flag] (20th of December of 1860) The Right of Secession is simply government by consent. Without the Right of Secession, freedom evaporates and government rules by force."

632. [Southern Gun Owners] "If guns kill people, then …
-Pencils cause you to miss (spel) your words.

- Vehicles cause people to drive drunk.
- Kitchen Utensils causes people to become fat.
- Matches cause someone to become an arsonist.

633. "Patriot must always be ready to defend his country against his government;"-Edward Abbey.

634. "The spirit of resistance to government is so valuable on certain occasions, that I wish it to be always kept alive."—Thomas Jefferson.

635. "In a time of universal deceit, telling the truth becomes a revolutionary act."—George Orwell.

636. "Teaching Southern History, always results in the counter attack of lies or half-truth by the Federal loyalist and Scalawags. Naturally, they never have any or enough evidence to back up their accusations. That is why it's important that a person with a free will can search for the whole truth without taking just one side as face value. American History in my personal view, is filled with political propaganda in defense of the Federalist, against the Confederate States of America, and against the Native Indians that fought for the Southern Nation against the unconstitutional war by the United States of America.—John T. Nall.

637. "When you eliminate the Black Confederate Soldier, You've eliminated the history of the South."—CSA General Robert Edward Lee 1864.

638. " … No finer Confederates ever rode with me."—CSA General Forrest. [In reference to the Confederate Negroes that served with him.]

639. "Christians are compromising their Biblical beliefs in order to be politically Correct. Being that (Secular Humanism) is the religion of the Communist, Christians will no longer be able to straddle the fence between Conservatism and Socialism.—John T. Nall.

640. "The Islamic belief is not based on the spiritual convection by the Holy Ghost, but it is based on the persecution and submission upon the victim. This is a direct violation of free will. Just as Catholicism used to have the same violations against the Christians (Non-Catholics) and Muslims in our past world history."—John T. Nall.

641. "Ever since the 1860's the Federalist has had a love and hate relationship with Marxism. Yet they do not support hard core Communism at best.—John T. Nall.

642. "No matter how tight of a grip the hands of life has on you, you can always find a light at the end of the tunnel. For some, it's harder to see, but always remember, that the light you see will only get bigger if you follow it."—Mark Alexander Smith.

643. [November 6, 1860] Republican Abraham Lincoln is elected as the Sixteenth President of the United States with Hannibal Hamlin of Maine as his Vice-President. Historian David M. Potter in Lincoln and His Party in the Secession Crisis (New Haven CT: Yale University Press, 1942; reprint, New Haven, CT: Yale University Press, 1979), 189, Writes that Lincoln was elected by a Northern Sectional Minority, representing the smallest plurality of popular votes in American history.

The loser in the next five Presidential Elections got more popular votes than Lincoln received 1,866,452, which is 39.9%. The eighteen States voting for him were all above the Mason/Dixon line. He received no electoral votes in fifteen of the thirty-three States. His name was not even on the ballots in ten of the Southern States. Lincoln's opponents together totaled 2,815,617. Which was almost a million votes more then he got.

644. [I HAD A DREAM] "I had a dream last night, that I woke up this morning and White People realized it's time to live out the true meaning of the CREED that was given to them: "WE HOLD THESE TRUTHS TO BE SELF-EVIDENT. THAT ALL MEN ARE CREATED EQUAL."

I had a dream last night, that all White Children woke up this morning in a nation where they are no longer judged guilty because of the color of their skin.

I had a dream last night, that all White Americans from sea to shining sea, joined hands in unity to sit down together at the table of brotherhood and work for our common good instead of fighting against each other.

I had a dream last night, that not one White Person will be satisfied until our rightful place in the world is regained and are not any longer treated like second class citizens in our own lands.

This is our hope, That we have faith that our people, all White People, will work together in unity, pray together with strength, struggle together with courage and stand up for our freedom together, knowing that one day, we will be free of our enemies together.

Now is the time to lift our people from the quicksand of injustice that is forced on us by the enemies of our people.

Now is the time to make justice for all White People a reality. For too long our rights have been subverted, abused and trampled upon in the name of (EQUALITY). The goal of Life, Liberty and the pursuit of happiness, no longer counts for our people in the White Man's Land.

I had a dream last night, that a new and marvelous non-violent militancy had engulfed the White Community and they realized that their destiny is tied up with their own people and so they joined together in unity to take back what is rightfully ours.

I had a dream last night, a marvelous, hopeful dream of a wonderful future for my children—and yours."—By. L.R. OLSEN.

645. "Men go abroad to wonder at the height of mountains, the huge waves of the sea, the long course of rivers, the vast compass of the ocean, the circular motion of the stars … but they pass by themselves and don't even notice.—Augustine.
646. "Governments is like a baby: an alimentary canal with a big appetite at one end and no sense of responsibility at the other." United States President: Ronald Reagan.
647. "To compel a man to subsidize with his taxes the propagation of ideas which he disbelieves and abhors is sinful and tyrannical."—Thomas Jefferson.
648. "When they, the United States invaded the Confederate States unconstitutionally, and then to invade the sovereign States in the Union to overthrow their governments in-order to prevent them from voting on the issue of secession, that was when the Union of the Constitutional Republic was destroyed. That was when an American Empire was formed and that was when the Confederate States became the first victim of their Socialistic Centralized Democracy!—John T. Nall.
649. [To bear Arms] "Crime is a great deterrent against individual sovereignty and liberty of the people. By limiting the kind of weapons of defense to a sporting weapon, prevents the people from withstanding an invasion by NATO, United Nations, or New World Order. At one time in history, the people from the United States was self-sufficient and could create everything they need for war. Now the people are at the mercy against any invader and the self will of the political vipers that hold office over them.—John T. Nall.
650. " … When did liberty ever exist when the sword and the purse were given up from the people? Unless a miracle shall interpose, no nation ever did, nor ever can retain its liberty after the loss of the sword & the purse."—Patrick Henry.
651. "To avoid being mistaken for a sellout, I chose my friends carefully. The more politically active Black Students, the Foreign Student, the Chicano, the Marxist Professors, the structural Feminists & Punk Rock—rock performance poets."—Barack Hussein Obama. [A Story of Race & Inheritance. From the book—(Dreams From My Father.)

652. "Christians cannot ignore this fundamental problem of heredity. We try to reform the adult, or punish the criminal, but we never ask would-be parents to consider whether something in their descent may harm the unborn.)—Pastor Richard Wurmbrand.

653. "A democracy is always temporary in nature; it simply cannot exist as a permanent form of government. A democracy will continue to exist up until the time that voters discover that they can vote themselves generous gifts from the public treasury.

From that moment on, the majority always votes for the candidates who promise the most benefits from the public treasury, with the results that every democracy will finally collapse over loose fiscal policy, (which is) always followed by a dictatorship."—In 1887, Alexander Tyler, a Scottish Professor at the University of Edinborough, had to say about the fall of the Athenian Republic, some 2,000 years prior.

654. "The famous "Stars and Bars" flag of the CSA had 13 stars, because both Missouri and Kentucky had a "government in exile" in Richmond, Virginia and were considered by the CSA government to be Member States."—Answers.Com

655. "The greatest enemies of Jesus are the doctrines and creeds of the Church."—Thomas Jefferson.

656. "The Weather Channel, says today's east coast earthquake was caused by an unknown fault-line running under D.C. And through Virginia. It is now being called Obama's Fault, though Obama will say it's really Bush's Fault. Other theories are that it was the founding fathers rolling over in their graves. Or that what we all believed to be an earthquake was actually the effects of a 14.6 trillion dollar checks bouncing in Washington."—e-mail August 25, 2011. Authors note: All jokes aside! It could just be God's way of getting our attention, in order for the U.S. And the occupied C.S. to repent of our sins and turn back to Him!

657. "Even after the Super Bowl victory of the New Orleans Saints, I have noticed a large number of people implying with bad jokes that Cajuns aren't smart. I would like to state, for the record, that I disagree with that assessment. Anybody who would build a city 5 feet below sea level in a hurricane zone and fill it with Democrats who can't swim is a damn genius"—Direct Quote from "Larry the Cable Guy"-August 31, 2011 e-mail.

658. [BACK ON UNCLE SAM'S PLATATION] "Six years ago I wrote a book called (Uncle Sam's Plantation. I wrote the book to tell my own story of what I saw living inside the welfare state and my own transformation out of it. I said in that book that indeed there are two Americans—a poor American on socialism and a wealthy American on capitalism. I talked about government

programs like Temporary Assistance for Needy Families (TANF), Job Opportunities and Basic Skills Training (JOBS), Emergency Assistance to Needy Families with Children (EANF), Section 8 Housing, and Food Stamps.

A vast sea of perhaps well-intentioned government programs, all initially set into motion in the 1960's by the Democrat's that were going to lift the nation's poor out of poverty. A benevolent Uncle Sam welcomed mostly poor black Americans into the government plantation. Those who accepted the invitation switched mindsets from "How do I take care of myself?" to "What do I have to do to stay on the plantation?"

Instead of solving economic problems, government welfare socialism created monstrous moral and spiritual problems—the kind of problems that are inevitable when individuals turn responsibility for their lives over to others. The legacy of American socialism is our blighted inner cities, dysfunctional inner city schools, and broken black families. Through God's grace, I found my way out. It was then that I understood what freedom meant and how great this country is.

I had the privilege of working on the welfare reform in 1996 which was passed by a Republican controlled Congress. I thought we were on the road to moving socialism out of our poor black communities and replacing it with wealth-producing American capitalism. But, incredibly, we are now going in the opposite direction. Instead of poor America on socialism becoming more like rich American on capitalism, rich America on capitalism is becoming more like poor America on socialism."—Star Parker/ A African American Syndicated Columnist.

659. "Every officer and man should live and act, as becomes a Christian Soldier defending the dearest rights and liberties of his country."—U.S. President George Washington.

WHEN GRANDMA GOES TO COURT

[Lawyers should never ask a Mississippi Grandma a question if they aren't prepared for the answer].

In a trial, a Southern small-town prosecuting attorney called his first witness, a grandmotherly, elderly woman to the stand. He approached her and asked, "Mrs. Jones, do you know me?" She responded, "Why, yes, I do know you, Mr. Williams. I've known you since you were a boy, and frankly, you've been a big disappointment to me. You lie, you cheat on your wife, and you manipulate people and talk about them behind their backs. You think you're a big shot when you haven't the brains to realize you'll never amount to anything more than a two-bit paper pusher, Yes, I know you."

The lawyer was stunned. Not knowing what else to do, he pointed across the room and asked, "Mrs. Jones, do you know the defense attorney?"

She again replied, "Why yes, I do. I've known Mr. Bradley since he was a youngster, too. He's lazy, bigoted, and he has a drinking problem. He can't build a normal relationship with anyone, and his law practice is one of the worst in the entire State. Not to mention he cheated on his wife with three different women. One of them was your wife! Yes, I know him."

The defense attorney nearly died!

The judge asked both counselors to approach the bench and, in a very quiet voice, said, "If either of you idiots asks her if she knows me, I'll send you both to the electric chair."

[Internet e-mail/unknown/2011

FREE ADVERTISEMENTS

★ JOHN THOMAS NALL ★

SOUTHERN NATIONAL CONGRESS
A voice For the Southern Peoples!
For more information write to: **Southern National Congress**
P.O. Box 71 Floyd, Virginia CSA 24091
Website: http://southernnationalcongress.org

CONFEDERATE STATES OF AMERICA

C.S.A. Confederate Creed

- Confederates are <u>not</u> Politically Correct and are damned proud of it.
- Confederates do not accept the <u>Dictatorship of the "Supposedly Offended."</u>
- Confederates believe that everyone <u>has the right to be offended</u> at times because of other's freedoms.
- Confederates know that the government of the Confederate States of America never surrendered.
- Confederates know that Lincoln declared War on the South because it was anti-Federalist.
- Confederates are anti-Federalist in favor of State's Rights and Home rule.
- Confederates know that only 3-6% of the Southerns owned slaves and Yankees owned thousands also.
- Confederates know that the C.S.A. freed the slaves in the South during the war of Northern aggression.
- Confederates know the Rebel Flag never flew over a slave ship and is not a flag of slavery, nor anti-Black.
- Confederates know that 160,000 Blacks fought for the C.S.A … As did Whites, Hispanics & Native Americans.
- Confederates are against involuntary servitude of any type including the personal income tax.
- Confederates are vehemently against invasion of our States be illegal immigrants.
- Confederates believe in Freedom of Religion, prayer and the Ten Commandments in our schools.
- Confederates know that the C.S.A … is a nation and will fight to keep it that way.
- Confederates revere their Southern Heritage, Culture and respect Dixie's glorious C.S.A. History.
- Confederates do not believe in legalized abortion, euthanasia or homosexual marriage.
- Confederates do not believe in the U.S. Department of Education or the United Nations.
- Confederates do not accept the IRS, the Federal Reserve Bank nor most foreign treaties.
- Confederates do not like Yankee managers running industry in Dixie or Scalawags controlling our States.

- Confederates want an end to U.S. Federal Courts and Yankee occupation of our Southern Nation.
- Confederates believe in strong State and Private Militias and the personal rights to bear arms.
- Confederates "Wave Their Rebel Flags Where They Want to and Will not let anyone tell them not to."
- Confederates are now working to RESTORE THE CONFEDERATE STATES OF AMERICA.

Become a Registered Citizen and help re-staff your State Confederate Gov. now! Visit the web site www.CSA.org for more information. Citizenship is free!

★ ★ ★

SO, YOU WANT TO SECEDE?

I don't blame you! The fact is we don't have to. Been there, done that and got the "T" shirt! We are already seceded! The people were never allowed to vote on returning to the Union after the last unpleasantness. The loss of a war, by an Army, does not give license to annexing a nation with an un-surrendered, sitting government but, that's what happened.

The South was forced back into the union and, when we didn't vote as we we're told, we we're expelled and put under martial law. Over all State governments were disbanded and new governments appointed and we're forced to rewrite our constitutions. We were then 'readmitted', at the point of bayonets.

What wasn't stolen or destroyed during the war was stolen after the war by union's 'War Tax' which destroyed most Southern farmers and businessmen. There is a remedy for our current situation. A movement is afoot to restore the government of the CSA, because the government structure is there. A constitution is in place and there are laws on the books, none of which are intrusive upon the individual, the family or business.

This government is operating in a limited provisional role at present. It has called for the restoration of the Militia in its constitutional role. Once fully formed, it is the intent to sue for peace and recognition as a sovereign nation.

The Militia **is not** anti-government. It is the citizen's direct participation in government, contrary to what you have been told by the propaganda spinners. It is the only entity charged with law enforcement in the nation, state or local jurisdiction. It is **not** the National Guard!

For additional information, visit http://www.CSAgov.org or www.FederationofStates.org.

Point of contact; Chairman: Dennis Joyce
Federation of States 972-218-9338

★ ★ ★

OFFICIAL CONFEDEERATE STATES OF AMERICA GOVERNMENT WEBSITE

Are you interested in becoming a Confederate Citizen? Requirements: To be 18 years of age. No race & gender requirements. And you have to live in the South. You will remain a U.S. Citizen until the peaceful withdrawal of all U.S. forces. Registration is required for voting rights. Registration fee is no longer a requirement.

Due to the unexpected circumstances during the writing of this book. The CSA Government Web-Page was removed due to internal issues and of the cost to maintain the web-page. Rest assures that the C.S. Government is still active on a small scale. Please be advised that if the Confederate Alliance dose not recognizes any CSA Government or its web page, than it's not the real deal. A new web-site for the C.S Government is up and running at this time. (www.confederatestatesofamerica.org/), and replaced the old site (//csagov.org). Thank You// [Warning: The Socialist/Communist/Liberals will use hate & fear propaganda tactics to dismantle any efforts in restoring our founded liberties!

★ ★ ★
LEE'S NEW SCHOOL HISTORY OF THE UNITED STATES

It is often stated that American history has been modified, distorted, and ignored by many of today's history text book writers. Claims are heard that students are ill informed in the area of history, and the blame is placed on out-dated text books. I wish to offer an exception to that charge with the presentation of this book.

The NEW SCHOOL HISTORY of the UNITED STATES validates the assertions by many historians that public school educators recognized the Christian faith as a intricate part of America's moral fiber. This fine book is evidence of America's spiritual heritage in it's history, and it presents, to the student, this fact.

It appears that this book was printed on three different occasions. Once in 1899, again in 1900, and this 1907 edition. It is also important to note that setting type for this book was a laborious process at that time. For this book to have been printed on three different occasions suggest to me that it must have been a popular book There may have been subsequent printings that I am not aware of.

First—it will make the perfect history text book for educating your children, both as a primary reader and as a comparison to present day "history."

Second—use it to validate claims that Christianity was part of America's heritage and that it was taught as such.

Third—use this book as a tool to prove just how much history has been revised and distorted or completely ignored.

★ JOHN THOMAS NALL ★

Presently this book is available in ebook format (pdf file) either on CDRom or downloadable file. A "print on demand" book is also available. The book contains 424 pages with illustrations, index, the Constitution, vocabulary chart, and questions at the end of each chapter.

Check the website: www.grapevinepublications.com/lees.htm for current prices.

If you are interested in the **{Copperhead Chronicle}** Subscription, then write to: The Copperhead Chronicle P.O. Box 55 Sterlington, Louisiana 71280. Or visit the web site: http://albensonjr.com & http://www.cakewalkblogs.com/antiedtablishmenthistory/.

★ ★ ★

FOR CHRIST AND COUNTRY

Understanding the foundation of a Nation
By: John Thomas Nall

History and the understanding of what true liberty is, I could not bring to light of its real meaning without the wisdom of our God. I shall share with you as I see the world from my perspective, with philosophies and poetry and political views. You will also read other statements from other people that are worth reading. So, let's begin our journey!

/This book is Pro-Christian, Pro-Constitutional Republic, & Pro-Confederate/

Visit our website: (www.authorHouse.com) or (www.amazon.com) (www.litprime.com)

A CONVERSATION ABOUT RACE

A FILM BY Craig Bodeker,

"Very, Very Good … I think you will find it instructive … and you'll enjoy it! Mike Rosen.

"This is certainly a conversation that America needs to have but has yet to engage in and Bodeker's film is a good first step."-Warner Todd Houston.

"Savvy, Funny, Scary, Brilliant."—Bill Rolen, Citizens Informer.

Everybody talks about talking about race, but few have the courage to do so …

"A conversation about race" probes attitudes about race at the level. If you didn't know the interviews were real, you'd think this was a satire.

For more information, visit the website (www.aconversationaboutrace.com).

★ ★ ★
WEBSITES AND MAILING ADDRESSES

Interested in requesting for an application of C.S. Citizenship? Official CSA Government Webpage: (www.confederatestatesofamerica.org/)

Or write to Confederate States of America 3708 East 29th Street. #102, Bryan, Texas CSA 77802

Looking for Honorable Organizations?
Confederate Society of America Webpage: (www.deovindice.org/)
Or write to: CSA Post Office Box 55 Sterlington, Louisiana CSA 71280

Counsel of Conservative Citizens Webpage: (www.cofcc.org/)
Or write to: CofCC P.O. Box 221683 St. Louis Mo, CSA 63122

Gun Owners of America Webpage: (www.gunowners.org/)
Or write to: Gun Owners of America 8001 Forbes Place, Suite 102 Springfield, Virginia CSA 22151

Are you a Motorcyclist?
Motorcycle Riders Club of America Webpage: (www.motorcycleridersclubofamerica.com).
Or write to: Motorcycle Riders Club of America PO Box 3527 Minnetonka, MN USA 55343
Motorcyclist Rights in North Carolina-
Concerned Bikers Association Webpage: (www.cba-abatenc.org/).
Or write to: CBA/ABATE of North Carolina P.O. Box 1189 Fuquay-Varina, NC CSA 27526-1189
Notice: All Websites and Addresses can change without notice.

★ ★ ★
TRUTHFUL READING FOR YOU'RE LIBRARY

- The Holy Bible.
- FOR CHRIST AND COUNTRY-By: John Thomas Nall.
- THE CONFEDERATE HANDBOOK-By: Curtis Patranella. [A must have in your library! Buy it or find it free on the internet.]
- LEE's NEW SCHOOL HISTORY OF THE UNITED STATES-[www.grapevinepublications.com/lees.htm].
- A SOUTHERN VIEW OF THE INVASION OF THE SOUTHERN STATES AND WAR OF 1861-65/ By: CSS Captain S.A. Ashe, of Raleigh, N.C. CSA.
- WHOM HAS GOD JOIND TOGETHER?-A Biblical examination of Miscegenation-By: Dallas Jackson.
- THE UNITED STATES AND GREAT BRITAIN IN PROPHECY-By: Hebert W. Armstrong.
- AMERICA AND BRITIAN IN PROPHECY-By: David C. Pack.
- 1492 & 1793-By: Peter Marshall and David Manual. Part one.
- 1787 & 1837-By: Peter Marshall and David Manual. Part two.
- 1737 & 1860-By: Peter Marshall and David Manual. Part three.
- DEFENDING DIXIE/ ESSAYS IN SOUTHERN HISTORY AND CULTURE-By: Clyde N. Wilson.
- WAR CRIMES AGAINST SOUTHERN CIVILIANS-By: Walter Brain Cisco.
- POLITICALLY INCORRECT GUIDE TO THE SOUTH (AND WHY IT WILL RISE AGAIN)-By: Clint Johnson.
- THE POLITICALLY INCORECT GUIDE TO THE CVIL WAR-By: H.W. Crocker III.
- THE SOUTHERN NATION/THE NEW RISE OF THE OLD SOUTH-By: R. Gordon Thornton.

- THOSE DIRTY ROTTEN TAXES/THE TAX REVOLTS THAT BUILT AMERICA-By: Charles Adams.
- THE GREAT BETRAYAL—By: Patrick J. Buchanan.
- WAS JEFFERSON DAVIS RIGHT?-By: James Ronald Kennedy & Walter Donald Kennedy.
- RED REPUBLICANS AND LINCOLN'S MARXISTS! /MARXISM IN THE CIVIL WAR-By: Walter D. Kennedy & Al. Benson.
- THE CHRISTIAN LIFE AND CHARACTER/OF THE INSTITUTIONS OF THE UNITED STATES-By: Benjamin F. Morris.
- THE ANTI/FEDERALIST PAPERS.
- THE FEDERALIST PAPERS.
- AMERICAN'S CEASAR/THE DECLINE AND FALL OF REPUBLICAN GOVERNMENT IN UNITED STATES OF MERICA/VOLUME 1 & 2 By: Thomas J. Dilorenzo.
- The Real Lincoln-By: Thomas J Dilorenzo.
- THE POLITICALLY INCORRECT GUIDE TO THE TO THE CONSTITUTION-By: Keven R.C. Gutzman.
- THE POLITICALLY INCORRECT GUIDE TO THE FOUNDING FATHERS-By: Brion McClananhan.
- STATE SOVEREIGNTY BEING THE CONSTITUTION/PART II OF THE RISE AND FALL OF THE CONFEDERATE GOVERNMENT-By: Jefferson Davis.
- THE CONSERVATIVE MIND/FROM BURK TO ELIOT-By: Russell Kirk.
- GEORGE WASHINGTON'S SACRED FIRE-By: Peter A. Lillback.
- STONEWALL JACKSON/THE MAN, THE SOLDIER, THE LEDGEND-By: James I. Robertson, Jr.
- FIRST PEOPLES IN A NEW WORLD: COLONIZING ICE AGE AMERICA-By: David J. Meltzer.
- ACROSS ATLANTIC ICE: THE ORIGIN OF AMERICA'S CLOVIS CULTURE-By: Dennis J. Stanford.

MY BOOK PROJECT

From the time I was 18, I have written short opinions to the letters of the editor in the Salisbury Post in North Carolina. After becoming the Chapter first Vice-President I had received a lot of complements from my viewers. So, I started writing materials or flyers of my personal views about the issues we were facing during around that time. We would have our meetings once a month and I would make multiple copies of my work and lay them out on the table for our welcoming guest. Therefore, in my first book {For Christ & Country}; you will find some dates and my name underneath some of the material.

The Foundation of a Nation was an idea of mine that I had shared with my father, (Charles Ray Nall). He took the idea to work with him and drew it up on his office computer. The original was printed on Dec 17th 1996. This version of mine was modified by my original proofreader, (Marie Howell of Marie's Print Shop), in Salisbury. And she had also created the second improved version, while using the same date of Dec 17th 1996 and gave me the credit for it. My third improved version once again came from a Comrade of mine at that time. And he created his version my work which was printed by him in 1997, (Thomas E. Guinn) of Florida.

MY CLOSING STATEMENTS

The views or opinions of this author or other writings are not necessarily the views of this publishing company. This author would like to thank everyone that has bought and read this book and hope that it could be useful in some way to his readers. May our Father in heaven and our Lord Jesus Christ keep you and bless you all as you take life day, by day. J.T.N

{DEO VINDICE}

www.ingramcontent.com/pod-product-compliance
Lightning Source LLC
Chambersburg PA
CBHW080014090526
44578CB00013B/692